The Presidency: CRISIS AND REGENERATION

The Presidency

CRISIS AND REGENERATION

An Essay in Possibilities

HERMAN FINER

 THE UNIVERSITY OF CHICAGO PRESS

Methinks I see in my mind a noble and puissant nation rousing herself like a strong man after sleep, and shaking her invincible locks. Methinks I see her as an eagle mewing her mighty youth, and kindling her undazzled eyes at the full midday beam.

JOHN MILTON, *Areopagitica*

The University of Chicago Press, Chicago 60637

The University of Chicago Press, Ltd., London

Second Impression 1974

Printed in the United States of America

International Standard Book Number: 0-226-24969-7 (clothbound)

Library of Congress Catalog Card Number: 60-14230

Contents

Preface

The quality of the government of the American nation is staked almost entirely on a gamble — the gamble of the sufficiency of one man's personal qualities of mind and character and physique, pitted against the appalling tasks that history has thrust on the office of the President of the United States. It is an intolerable hazard by every criterion, decision-efficiency or democratic responsibility. So it will remain as long as the President is unassisted by colleagues who bear equal elective responsibility with collective executive leadership, as long as he is chosen by a hit-and-miss plebiscitary process. To such a predicament has the mighty and inexorable surge of history brought us.

This book, therefore, proposes substantial changes in the office of the Presidency. It is a study in the possibilities of making the institutions of American political leadership more adequate — not perfect! — to the needs and purposes of our times, so full of promise, so pregnant with danger. As such, it is bound to focus on the Presidency of the United States and touch the heart of the living Constitution. The strings of that heart are tied into the being of every citizen. He who has the temerity to pluck those strings awakens the response of every man and woman in America and thereby runs the risk of arousing passion and some resentment.

To suggest that the office of the Presidency needs to be modernized requires a sober, critical weighing of its past as well as its contemporary effectiveness. Yet such a venture is certain to evoke hostile emotions in some quarters. The work will face attack. Yet it is essential that from time to time the nation's apparatus of supreme statesmanship be re-examined to discover, in a reasonable and solicitous spirit, whether it is still able to fulfil its trust. I "accentuate the positive," and have certainly not aimed at being roasted alive. But if that be my fate, it is still necessary that someone dare conduct such a reconsideration of the nation's leadership.

What do I say? This — that the office of the Presidency needs regeneration. The United States needs leadership in the executive branch, a President and (say) eleven Vice-Presidents, elected on the same ticket for four years, elected by the nation as a whole after the candidates have been chosen by party conventions. For no one man alone can handle the job with efficiency and democratic responsibility.

I do not say this in order to curb tyranny; presidential tyranny can hardly arise in the United States, for reasons both spiritual and social; it is rather a question of a more talented discharge of the highest temporal office on earth and the election of men clearly accountable to the people they represent. The candidates must have served in Congress on their way to this expanded White House team. For the presidential electoral system is a haphazard gamble of smoke-filled rooms and demagogic tumult, so risky as to make it entirely unsure that the best of the few men available reach that high and solitary office. And on their way, as matters now stand, the contenders are not encouraged to tell us what they believe, what they hope, what they intend to do with our lives and labor; it is rather like a masked ball — only the voters are required to unmask and declare themselves.

Yet the President has far more personal power to commit the nation than has the British prime minister, and he is less tethered by responsibility. His personal power almost equals Khrushchev's, often with fewer independent checks to guide or restrain him. By failure to decide, by errors of command and commitment, he can endanger the nation.

The burdens of the presidential office today are necessarily so multifarious that to avoid a fatal collapse of efficiency and responsibility the President would have to be a titan and a genius. A collective Presidency might have these qualities, but not a solitary man. A solitary President is a gamble this nation cannot afford.

There is no higher concern of man — after the dictates of his conscience and the prayers of his faith — than the proper government of his nation. Yet critical appraisal may give pain to those who believe that the nation is, after all, perfect. The reforms I propose may offend those who disagree with my implied or outspoken standards. The constructive suggestions may upset the ingrained habits of many. Hence I have followed Edmund Burke's admonition that whereas the Constitution may have its deficiencies it must be tended as reverently as one would the wounds of a father.

The possibilities presented here for consideration are supported by due attention to the historic and contemporary operation of the Presidency. The essay turns to the founders of the Republic for the inspiration they afford, for their experience, their theories, and it brings the discussion as close to the present as possible.

In the course of argument I refer occasionally to the experience of other political systems. This is to copy the sagacious behavior of the founders of the Republic at the Federal Convention in Philadelphia in 1788 and the papers they wrote to commend to the people's will the new Constitution. Again and again they adduced the lessons of ancient Greece and Rome, the German confederation, Venice, and, of course, Britain, their mother-country and their recent foe. Was this not a prudent attitude, to avoid repeating the mistakes of others, to benefit from their successes? It is in this utilitarian spirit that I refer to the political systems of comparable nations.

I have lived and taught in the Midwest for the last sixteen years and have here taken a steady part in local public affairs and in the affairs of our nation. Since 1924, when I came to the United States as a Rockefeller Fellow, I have visited this country many times and for protracted periods, perhaps living in more places, north, south, east, and west, than many of my fellow Americans. Travel has enabled me to contemplate America's domestic and foreign anxieties from many angles, not simply from Washington or from New York or Boston, and I have conferred with literally thousands of colleagues, officials, and citizens in every part of the nation. Many scholars and practical politicans support me in my evaluation, even if not to the full extent of my constructive proposals. But the question is, What ought we to do? To propound and justify improvement is surely the first step.

May I make one disclaimer? It is not to be inferred because I argue that no one man can perform the miracles asked of him in the White House, therefore it does not matter who is nominated and elected as President. The citizens of the United States have the whole world in their hands when they choose their delegates and make their choice. For there is still the better and the worse man, if not the perfect President.

I have kept footnotes and scholarly apparatus to a minimum; the documentation otherwise would have resulted in one or more referents for almost every sentence.

This work was in page proof when the U-2 spy plane episode shocked the nation. Consequently, only two terse references to it appear. I both love and hate to say, "I told you so!" But validly to be able to say it is to verify my analysis of the presidential office and to claim attested foresight; and, again validly, to say it is also to hate the evil consequences to our nation and the world of avoidable bungling. Almost every paragraph of the present text foretells: "This kind of disaster is inevitable, it not today, then tomorrow, as a logical consequence of our system of government." The blunder lies in the system, as well as the men. There is inevitably worse to come; we must pray, without national and international catastrophe.

Our fears might be calmed a little if the best statesman available reached the top. Yet the electoral gamble, and all the "ghosts" who manipulate and ventriloquize our Presidents and candidates, makes it impossible to tell who has ever been responsible for what policy. Are we not obliged to modernize Beaumarchais' caustic comment on the government of France's *ancien régime*? "A mathematician was needed, but they appointed a dancer instead." Are we now to record, "In the twentieth century, America needed an eagle for President, but they elected a cockatoo!"

I warmly thank my old friend, Professor J. M. Gaus of Harvard, and my young friend, Professor W. H. Riker of Lawrence College, for their most valuable, sagacious, and sinewy comments on my manuscript. They saved me from many an error in the comprehension of America. The specific constructive proposals, of course, are mine.

U.S. News and World Report kindly permits me to quote its reporting of the President's timetable for March 8, 1957, of course, applicable to that day alone, as also some excerpts from another issue, duly specified in the notes. I also acknowledge the generosity of *Time, Life, Inc.*, for permission to quote some excerpts from Truman's *Memoirs*, also duly specified.

The Presidency: CRISIS AND REGENERATION

"A More Perfect Union"

In the days when its people felt they had a virile and exacting purpose, the founders of the American Republic pursued a noble object — "a more perfect Union."

Today, throughout the Republic, after all these magnificent and creative years, noteworthy and responsible voices cry out that our nation needs a revived sense of purpose if it is to lift itself from the moral slump which weakens constructive vitality and undermines its capacity to survive in the extremely dangerous politics of power-laden and hostile nations. I would like to forward the classic venture of the founders of the Republic and add one more voice to those of my fellow-citizens who see us dangerously addicted to paltry comforts and amenities at a time when the nation's way of life is marred by hideous blemishes. This is not said in a grudging spirit by one who lacks appetite for fun and conviviality. Who would wish to be a Savonarola in America?

Not long ago a very cheerful professor admonished an audience of American undergraduates with the slogan: "Relax. Sit back and enjoy the inevitable!" Relax! — in the United States of America, whose life and meaning in the world have been the product of vigor of thought and inventive achievement. Those who are concerned that our way of life shall be toward a good society

3

must be equally concerned that our political leadership rise to its challenge. It allows little time for relaxation. Is this not a more honorable course than to permit the Republic to be enfeebled and demoralized by the weakness and pettiness of its statesmen?

The most powerful force for raising the moral vitality of a nation is its government. Many people regret that the evolution of nations over the last three hundred years has accorded this immensity of power and responsibility to the state, but it is urgent to remind ourselves that it is true, and that it is, as far as we can foresee, an irreversible truth. The churches, business, labor, the professions, the academic world, the family, and the arts are precious to us all, yet for good or ill they are unlikely to approach government in influence or plastic effectiveness until they achieve some measure of spontaneous harmony in their social aims and agree upon life's significance and the comparative worth of their rival gifts.

The men and women among us who are not interested in promoting a good society in order to avert the degeneration of our national character will not be interested in its political leadership except as it promises personal gain, cash, office, legal and administrative favors, "pork," the "gravy train." Profiteers are absolved from reading this study. Those who believe that a Constitution grows without earnest inventiveness and are content to clothe themselves in reach-me-downs, in slovenliness and complacency, also may be spared, but a word of reminder to them is not out of place.

There was a time when the Constitution of the United States did not exist. It had to be invented.

There was a time when large numbers of Americans, perhaps a majority, declared that it was not possible to establish a Constitution. They had time to be shown that it could be devised and built.

There was a time when many people, perhaps a majority, thought that "a more perfect Union" was not to be desired. At length they were persuaded that they were witnessing a rising and not a setting sun.

There was a time when Congress and the courts and the President were compelled to open the way of the American future by revising and reinterpreting the Constitution, even in order that it might be said to live. When they took this initiative they were often reviled, but the nation prospered.

Today, many who are in a position to know better demonstrate by their behavior that they believe the nation is perfect in every respect. They will be irritated by what I have to say and will turn away or scoff. They will be joined, if only passively, by millions of good companions who are glad to enjoy the daily benefits of America and who surrender to others the onerous burden of democratic social and political renewal. There are historians who glow with praise of our past conquests but are inspired only to remain beside the pool and worship Narcissus when he was young.

Yet we live in a harsh and menacing world. Other nations are fast gaining physical power, increasing their demands upon the United States and its allies, and seeking historic eminence. They challenge our standards, question our attainments (which are many and glorious), and flauntingly threaten our way of life. Is our leadership adequate to meet the challenge of the Soviet Union and its satellites, of China, the turmoil that grips the Arab nations, Africa, the Far East, the Pacific, and Old Europe? Can we say that America today, reminded by day and by night to "count its blessings," approaches the perfect society? Let us glance at some of the social and political evils revealed in the last few decades.

The nation's crime rate in every category — murder, manslaughter, assault with deadly weapons, theft, robbery, rape — is one of the highest in the world and increases year by year. There are far too many districts in American cities where an individual, man, woman, or child, cannot venture upon a fairly-lighted street without fear of attack. A good society should be able to assure its people personal security and the due administration of justice. If they appeal for justice, can they be sure that they will get it? Far too frequently, juries are chosen for their prejudices, elected or appointed judges are found to be incompetent, witnesses are suborned or intimidated, prosecutors are corrupted, the police are shown to be dishonest, lawyers prove to be cheats, and justice is not done or is long-delayed.

Fifty years after the publication of Lincoln Steffens' *The Shame of the Cities* our civic administrations are no less riddled by graft and inefficiency, no less lurid than Steffens described them, hardly diminished in effrontery, as damaging, as audacious, as costly, as disgraceful. Police, civil servants, public contractors connive in fraud and guile. Scores of citizens have exposed malpractice and have sought the reform of the governments of states and cities. But no vigorous conscience insures that their recommendations are fulfilled. There is no center of government to gather up the spontaneous forces of the nation and lift them to effectiveness.

Corrupt and damaging practices have been exposed. Racketeers acting on the flanks of labor unions have found confederates at the heart of our economy, connivers as malign as themselves among businessmen, government officials, and police. In the interest of profit, men have beaten and murdered their competitors. If you kill conscience for profit, why flinch at homicide? If business efficiency and the wealth of the nation depend on rivalry between individuals and between corporations, who will put a limit to fraud and violence in pursuit of gain?

If the health of the nation depends on the morality of the family, the schools, and the churches, then a moral legislator must have the power to guide them. At once the question of the quality of America's political leadership is raised. If the principle of laissez-faire insists that competition be limited only by criminal law, then we are in need of a government prepared to define these crimes and to punish those criminals. Sometimes we are ready to tolerate the exposed evils of the economic war in America in the optimistic belief that today's ugly behavior is the unfortunate exception — that, exceptional or not, lurid exposure and public indignation will guarantee that it does not happen again. But, alas, it happens again, and it happens worse.

Many of our prisons and mental institutions are in a disgraceful condition, some little more than medieval, in a land where the study of criminology and psychology is more intelligent than anywhere else in the world. The textbooks are superb, their illustrations brilliant, the blueprints of reform easy to follow; but the actual conditions in our institutions are disgusting. Instances of shocking cruelty, lamentable neglect, brutal inhumanity, are exposed day after day in by far the richest nation in the world, so rich indeed that millions of Americans can be expected to go insane under the ever-increasing burden of their dissatisfactions and their failure to find outlets for their leisure time.

The criminality and misdemeanors of the young threaten to outstrip public control. Our record is by far the worst in the world. There were times in 1957 and 1958 when the school authorities of New York City were on the point of surrender, helpless beneath the wave of juvenile crime in and around the public schools. It is not simply that juvenile delinquency is a national disgrace; score after score of young people are lost to their best selves, to a decent share in the collective activities of a community in which they should have been nurtured to take pride. But where is the adult example that might lift youngsters on the margin of doubt? It is at least arguable, is it not, that the political process in the United States does not set a good example? A sixteen-year-old becomes cynical at the rumor and innuendo about the morals in office of congressmen, senators, yes, even the President, and when he sees for himself the tactics of men who covet public office and their deeds (and the reasoning behind them) when, sometimes, they succeed. The oppressive nature of some congressional committees, the procedures employed to "get results," televised refusals to listen to reason, the astute and ultimately self-damning evasion of responsible behavior, cannot be an elevating example to young people beset by problems of conflict and insecurity.

Consider the demoralizing effect of learning how many planks of hypocrisy constitute a party platform. Bad political examples seep down more surely than prosperity is reputed to do in a free economy. It is easier to subvert moral integrity than to create it. Temptations are easier to enjoy than are the aspirations that gird a man to undertake sacrifice, effort, and self-control in the attempt to fulfil his better self.

Our thoughts inevitably lead to education. America should be outraged by the quality of its education, yet all we hear is the dying away of the anguished outcry of wounded pride that rose with the Soviet launching of its first satellite, one of those famous events that shake the world. But American education has been debated by an anxious few for at least half a century. The needs of education in America, as in other countries, are both personal to the individual and of concern to the nation. In America, the national aspect has been obscured and frustrated by certain professional organizations in the name of the individual and in the name of the sovereign right of the locality, of each village and township, to decide for itself how the schools are to be financed and what, if anything, is to be taught in them. They have ignored or perhaps forgotten their responsibility to the nation. Even as they raise Old Glory each morning and intone the pledge to the Republic, "one and indivisible," they divide it at its roots. Too large a contingent of the products of these schools are physically unfit, prepared for nothing, and so empty-minded as to be easy prey to brainwashing.

This state of affairs has come about, in large part, because our leaders have neglected their own responsibility to present — continuously, zealously, and prophetically — the national vision and national necessities to the local monopolists of education, who thus might be inspired to modify their narrow-mindedness. And they have not come to the aid of communities which lack sufficient resources to satisfy a national minimum standard.

Why does our system of education, necessarily the political salvation of a nation made up of many diverse elements, remain at a low level? Because it has lost its purpose and its spirit. It no longer serves the individual, for it does not bring him to the excellence of which he is capable; it does not discover and develop needed talents; and it makes little or no provision for the exceptional child. It no longer serves the nation, for the subjects taught have slim correspondence to our needs for survival. The conceivable purposes of the nation are not conveyed to school authorities. Emphasis remains on consumption, not production. Social justice is neglected because our leaders do not care intensely enough that justice be done. Democracy is not avowed because our leaders do not know how it can be maintained and do not seem to care when it is not.

Had the general standard been democracy, what would this have entailed? What responsibilities would it have required of our political leaders? It would have required them to define, to clarify and make vividly present, to themselves as well as to others, all the basic aspirations and qualities of human salvation involved in the democratic ideal. It would have demanded of them that they apply these truths to all the problems of the community and see that, in fact, they inspire the curriculum of every school. It would have required them to throw down many economic, social, and institutional barriers. It would have required the establishment of standards of excellence in every field of life. It would have required them to know thoroughly, excellently, the ethos and processes of their own revered Constitution, to give to it at least as much of their hearts and minds as of their tongues. This, surely, at the very least?

America possesses more than sufficient brains for the solution of its problems, and it has the necessary spiritual qualities, though lulled by governmental hush-hush. The mobilizing spirit, the gathering spirit, is absent. The knowledge provided by scholars has been plentifully available, thrust upon Congress and upon the President's desk (in the report on American manpower resources), but it has been passed by, out of sheer fecklessness, mindlessness.

Two important results (among others) have been observed. In the first place, in Korea, captured American soldiers could not defend the principles for which they fought. When there is nothing in the brain, brainwashing is not difficult; the water in a washing machine swishes through most rapidly when there is nothing to engage it. It is no help to the schools when the President of the United States confesses he would not know what arguments to use to persuade Soviet Marshal Zhukov of the superiority of democracy.[1] Second, the Soviet Union has forged far ahead in ways dangerous to the survival of the democratic system. It is a harsh fate to be compelled to compete with other nations for survival and honor. It is much pleasanter, no doubt, to live lackadaisically; it is possible to shuffle away freedom for slavery. The question is whether so many who may be "slaves by nature" shall prevail to hinder the efforts of those who seek freedom, justice, and a less ignoble life.

Every nation needs a hero, I mean a figure believed worthy of emulation, as some through the centuries have sought to follow the teachings of Christ, and as some have followed Lenin. Who is the American hero today? Who can say? Or has the nation several heroes, if it is, as it is flattered to be, a "pluralistic" civilization? I search for an American exemplar and find to name Washington, Jefferson, and Lincoln, Woodrow Wilson, and

Franklin Roosevelt. But are there others I have missed? And are
the magnificent qualities of each emulated by the generations?
Since the days of the founders of the Republic (say to the time of
Andrew Jackson) who have been the nation's heroes? What virtues did they possess? What virtues have our leaders now? It
must be admitted, or it must be allowed for debate, that we seem
to praise only the feeblest of virtues — hardly virtues; call them
facilities.

(I am aware that I am asking the questions which annoy the
man who stands having a peaceful drink at a bar.)

The Pursuit of Happiness

The essential gospel of the American nation is, I think, to be
found in the Declaration of Independence and in the Constitution
of the United States. Life, liberty, and the pursuit of happiness.
Just as Plato's *Republic* does not contain a single word about
freedom, so the Declaration of Independence does not contain a
single word about virtue or duty or the obligations of man to man
or man to society. It is possible that the founders of the Republic
believed so implicitly in the natural goodness of man that they
presumed, free to govern himself, he would accept spontaneously
all the unstated responsibilities of those who would live in union.

In a nation dedicated to self-government everything depends
upon where the emphasis is placed — on "self" or on "self-government." It cannot be denied that in America there has been
a heavy preference for self. The Constitution, by its wide and
noble donation of rights and civil liberties, by its deliberate en-
feeblement of government split into three separate branches, the
executive, the legislative, and the judicial, has helped to per-
petuate the supremacy of self. All that is asked in return is civic
virtue, even as the only means of sustaining life, liberty and the
pursuit of happiness. It is a kind of chemical prescription whereby
life — liberty — happiness consumes itself, making less certain
each year the possibility of its continuation. For the weakness of
America is not what it has been bruited to be, namely, that its
people have become "other-directed." This is what one may call
a typically conventional unconventionality of view. America's
weakness lies in excessive self-direction, a gyroscope of tradition
set by years of good living in a land where most material wants

are satisfied in the moment a wish is formulated. This makes for satiety, discontent, and failure.

If one were to investigate the creation of the American character, it might be possible to decide at what moment in time a sense of public purpose vanished and to describe how this has infected the character and quality of once-great manifestations of culture among all segments of the populace whose forebears were the offspring of the Reformation and the Renaissance.

The United States has inherited a dire responsibility, leadership of the free world in the conflicts among nations and the struggle with the Soviet Union. This responsibility has been thrust upon the United States, against the will of millions of its citizens and a substantial number of its politicians, by the decline of Great Britain, France, Germany, and Japan, and by the colossal increase in Soviet strength, the multiplication of the number of its allies and satellites, and, above all, by its ideological conquest of China. American world leadership has been accepted by Americans, willingly or not, in recognition of the dangerous possibility of the loss of the freedom it prevents. America's leadership must continue for the sake of America itself, and it seems that it must continue for many decades, for the nations friendly to America are weak in comparison with the mighty Soviet Union and never out of danger of total and swift destruction by Soviet missiles. The United States is equally vulnerable unless it remains unconquerably equipped in spirit and in arms, for the Soviet Union, its leaders boast, is intent on expansion and has the strength and the tenacity to accomplish it. Can we doubt that the rulers of Russia intend to assume control of other territories and peoples, to neutralize by intimidation, as has been done in the case of Finland and others, to subvert native governments and support Communist rule, as in Poland and Hungary, and to win other peoples to neutrality by calculated generosity, all in the name of "peaceful co-existence" and peaceful competition? Soviet strategy is to seek to undermine every element of strength in the Western world, to threaten the oil supplies of the Middle East on which the United States and its allies depend, and to damage allied economy by competitive exports and the massive dumping of goods. This they, the Soviet leaders, will do as long as they are not restrained by us or by their own powerless, obedient, and victimized people.

Russian Power

The swift growth of Soviet economic output and scientific advancement constitutes a major threat to the free world, and that threat is planned to increase. The facts are these:

Soviet economic growth moves steadily toward equality with, and perhaps eventual superiority to, the economic might of the United States. Major efforts are set on heavy industry and, within that classification, on the materials of war. The heart of this advance has been the conquest of science and technology at a rate and with a quality in some instances surpassing that of the United States, by the endowment of scientists, the purposeful organization of all phases of the economy, and the discovery of able students to enter the fields of science and engineering supported by scholarships, on a scale far beyond similar provisions in the United States.[2] The proficiency of Soviet development has disheartened us and cost us much foreign respect, for a large part of American prestige abroad was the result only of the many decades in which our nation led the world by bold, ingenious, and useful invention. Years late, the U.S. Information Agency has made public acknowledgment of our drastic loss of prestige.[3]

What prodigies the Soviet Union has performed since the twenties, in spite of the horrible devastation of World War II! To me the Soviet regime for its atrocities against human dignity is hateful, but I must not blind myself to the fact that its scientific advance has been the more remarkable for the conditions under which it came about. In 1917 Russia had an industrial force numbering about three million; in 1926 it was not much greater; today, it is nearly sixty million. The population of the Soviet Union has grown by natural increase and annexation; an illiterate population has been educated and employed, transformed from a predominantly inert, rural people into a manufacturing force of remarkable potential. Forty years is a short time for so mighty an accomplishment. How was the advance achieved? Of course: In a dictatorial economy. What is it devoted to? The raising of total production and the productivity of each person as rapidly as possible, especially in heavy industry and allied processing industries. By what means? The purposeful redirection of a considerable portion of the annual product to further development. It is reported that current gross investment in the USSR is 30 per cent, compared to about 17 per cent in the United States. (This is the widest disparity among many diverse calculations made by American economists.) And in consequence? The Russian total industrial production has increased six times since 1913 (only four times in the United States), and for the same period to 1955 the productivity of each worker has multiplied 3.6 times (2.64 times in the United States).[4] Russia was far behind us in both these respects before World War I. Today, the total of Russian industrial production is somewhere between one-third and one-half that of the United States; but the rate of increase in recent years is alarming. Between 1950 and 1958 (that is, after partial recovery from the destruction of factories and the loss of manpower during World War II), the Gross National Product of the USSR has risen year by year at the rate of about 7 per cent each year; the United States shows no more than a 3 per cent annual growth. A fair calculation on the principle of compound interest shows that in a very few years Russia will match the United States in total production. If the Soviet rate of industrial growth is 9 per cent (the forecast of the Seven-Year Plan of 1958), and the industrial growth of the United States remains at 3 per cent, which seems likely, Soviet industry will equal that of the United States in fourteen years (about 1974).[5] Khrushchev claims it will be by 1970. This is not so distant a time that our Secretary of State and our President can afford to ignore its implications.

So far, the Soviet peasants and workers alone have suffered as the result of this wrenching from their daily labor of the means of investment their government needs for its imperial purposes. Would American farmers and workers make the same sacrifice? Though the Gross National Product of the Soviet is between one-third and one-half that of the United States, Soviet families are compelled to live on about one-sixth of the real income of goods and services that Americans consume. But, as has been observed by wiser men before me, "It is surprising what you can do without." Food, housing, clothes, necessities as well as amenities, are kept at a miserable level in the Soviet Union, though Khrushchev has promised there will be better civilian supplies. Steel, other metals, cement, machines, electric power, gasoline, transport, cotton, rubber, tools, coals, new plant — all these have first priority, and always with a calculation of the Soviet total compared to that of the United States and its allies. Consider Soviet ambitions, according to the current Seven-Year Plan:

	Soviet in 1970	U.S. Today
	(millions of tons)	
Steel	104	91.5
Pig Iron	74	52
Coal	700	415
Cement	91	53

Nor is that all. From its growing wealth the Soviet Union has sent economic aid to other countries and works to develop foreign trade. In 1938 the Soviet Union imported goods valued at $268 million and exported goods worth $251 million. In the three years 1954–57 (and the trend continues), Russia's imports averaged $3.5 billion, exports about $4 billion. To this must be added the planned and associated efforts of the satellite countries. Of course the totals are small beside the world total in 1957 of over $100 billion, but it is the rate of growth that is of prime significance.

In the period from mid-1954 to mid-1959, the Sino-Soviet bloc granted assistance to twenty countries, to the value of rather less than $3 billion; in the same period the United States gave economic assistance amounting to about $5.3 billion, and to the same twenty nations. The United States was, to her everlasting credit, giving aid long before the Soviet, until the Soviet learned the tremendous political value of challenging the subsidy program of the United States. They followed the lesson with their usual astuteness, attaching fewer strings but offering credits rather than gifts, loans repayable in local products, lower rates of interest, longer periods for repayment, and putting emphasis on productive plant of a basic (and conspicuous) kind. The number of Soviet technicians sent abroad roughly equals the number sent by the United States to assist undeveloped countries.

The fact which should most alarm us is that we were the

first to produce an atomic bomb and a hydrogen bomb, but it was the Soviet Union that was first to produce an intercontinental ballistic missile, the first to send up earth satellites, to shoot beyond the moon, and to send up a solar planet bearing the Soviet crest. Missiles and satellites are military weapons, or they can be made so, and are capable of destroying any city in the world by direct attack.

I could cite in aid of my plea the admissions of government officials of our failure to plan for the future with adventurous foresight in an age of missiles and atomic weapons. I prefer to append a concise statement which appeared in *Life*, a source that cannot be said to have been hostile to those who have directed our government during the past seven years:

> In the race to catch up with Russia, the U.S. has the tools and the know-how. It lacks decisiveness and a compelling sense of urgency to put the tools and skills to immediate and imaginative use. One big stumbling block is the U.S. administration of space projects. They are still parceled out between competing civilian and military agencies. There is no central ruling authority — except the White House — and no pressing timetable for what the U.S. would do in space even if it had the thrust to get there.[6]

And in the same issue a diagram shows the maximum Soviet rocket thrust to be 700,000 pounds, the best American effort to be 175,000 pounds, the Soviet payload to be 796 pounds, compared to the American payload of 13.4 pounds.

To this some official statement must surely be added, since there is a universal disinclination to hear bad news, even when that knowledge is essential to one's efforts toward self-rescue. On leaving the Defense Department in November, 1959, Neil McElroy, who had served for two years as Secretary of Defense, was quoted as saying that if the Russians built what they were capable of building, the intercontinental ballistic missile, and if we built what we are able to build, the Soviet Union was likely to have more "missile capability for the period 1961 through 1962 and maybe into 1963" than we would have. It is an officially accepted fact that the Russian capability is a three-to-one superiority in ICBMs — or perhaps even greater.[7]

In a report from the London Institute of Strategic Studies (December 1, 1959) it was stated that the Soviet Union has about one hundred principal missile bases, served by some 200,000 men, the chief weapons having a range of more than five thousand miles, and others with a range of from one thousand to sixteen hundred miles. The bases are deployed on the west, the south, and the Baltic frontiers.[8]

From the report of the House of Representatives' committee on appropriations concerning defense expenditures for 1960:

> . . . at this critical period in world history, [the committee] is not happy over the prospect of being in second place to the USSR in the highly significant ICBM field. The committee feels that a missile gap exists and does not wish to see it widened.[9]

And, again:

> The growing Soviet submarine fleet is an unprecedented threat to our control of the seas. It can not be minimized. It must be contained if there is to be assurance that the sealines of communication are to be available, in the event of war, to the oceanic confederation which is the free world. Of even greater concern is the threat of surprise attack from missile firing submarines lying hidden off our coasts. . . .
>
> Admiral Burke, the Chief of Naval Operations, . . . stated to the committee: The Russian Navy is second only to ours in size. Most of their ships have been built since World War II. Of greatest concern to the Navy is their submarine force numbering about 450. The Russians are capable of building nuclear powered submarines.
>
> Progress has been made in the anti-submarine warfare capability of the Navy, but the submarine has progressed faster than the anti-submarine warfare capability to combat it.
>
> This last factor together with the number of Soviet submarines constitutes a shocking and dangerous situation.

The committee observed that the German submarine force of only forty-eight submarines at the beginning of World War II ". . . almost swept Allied shipping from the seas and threatened to become a decisive factor in the war."

Russia has been able to become a military colossus because it has devoted a far larger proportion of its total national production to military strength than has any other country in the world. If American defense expenditure had kept pace with the increase in national product since 1953 and the same proportion had been maintained, we would be spending $66 billion, not $46 billion, on defense in 1959.

It is a pity to have to put on armor. It happens that we are menaced by a mortal foe and that each of us cannot, for self-defense, make an intercontinental ballistic missile in his own backyard. And no single individual can assure his own survival if attacked by the Soviet Union. Defense demands the organization of many skills, the provision of vast resources, and the co-ordination of all of these if it is to be successful.

The most vital part of a nation's armor is its political leadership — that is, its government. The Soviet Union has provided itself formidably. It has a large and prolific population; it is technically equipped and economically powerful; it has immensely strategic frontiers; it has allies, some of them brutally acquired but all overawed, seduously cultivated, cunningly seduced; it has a stark and fanatical purpose, not entirely communistic, but patriotic — as in centuries of tsarist command; it is tautly governed — that is to say, purposefully, ideologically; and it has tenacious and dynamic leaders. Soviet leaders boast that where once they were encircled by capitalist enemies, today it is the Soviet Union that encircles. They have constructed a vast and intricate, tightly planned economy and an administration which comes close to being, in principle and very largely in practice, one single organized and directed machine for the achievement of the collective will. It is this tautness, this integration, this coherence, the responsiveness of all the parts to the central intent, that alarms us. And it is missing, even in moderate form, in the United States and in our leaders; while in *moderate* form, it is necessary.

America's Strength Assayed

What strengths have we with which to oppose the force of the Soviet Union?

In the first place, our native strength, nourished by our population and our natural and technological resources, is enormous.

But it is not sufficient to allow us the luxury of isolation in a private fortress. This means that America has need of its allies. The creation and the sustaining of alliance is fraught with enormous difficulties. Our allies are more vulnerable and anxious than we; they are nearer the threat and may be more easily coerced. American leaders must contrive steady, friendly, and understanding relations between the United States and its allies. (How to fail in this respect was demonstrated by Secretary of State John Foster Dulles in his relationship with the British government between 1954 and 1957, especially upon the issue of Suez.) [10] In addition, we have the problem of ascertaining that those who will not be our allies at least will not be our enemies.

The basis of American strength, apart from government leadership and the skill of our military leaders, is a stable economy. Our system of free enterprise enables us to maintain a high level of production, but it does have its weaknesses. It is an economy geared to consumption; much of our productive genius is squandered on trivialities. The significance is this, that though Soviet total production today is much inferior in total to that of the United States, in military strength the Soviet Union is at least as strong as we are because it has made the choice implied in Adam Smith's classic phrase, "Defense is more than opulence." Our judgment does not stem from distaste for the department store dictum "Give the lady what she wants!" but from a determination to put first things first, when bitter circumstance has dictated what does indeed come first from a hostile sky.

Our present economy is committed to two weaknesses — tariffs against the free entry of foreign goods and, more heinously, the heavy subsidization of farmers. The former stimulates foreign rancor, the latter demands the expenditure of resources of manpower and materials that might better be used in industrial production. The only good thing that can be said of the continued subsidization of agriculture is that some portion of the surplus can be used in foreign aid. This mis-economy is allowed to continue because of the disproportionate representation of the farm vote on controlling committees of Congress, a representation which cannot be justified under any of the principles of democracy.

Until 1910 the chief budgetary anxiety of the President and

Congress was to discover means of spending the surplus of high tariff customs duties and excise taxes — there were as yet no income taxes to speak of — at a time when the total national budget was only $600 million, or about 2 per cent of the national product. Today, public funds are heavily pressed by swollen appropriations for defense, for multifarious social services, and for the expansion of our economy. The yearly budget is now $80 billion or over 16 per cent of the national product.

The demands of the nation will not decrease; every penny counts, but to make it really ring requires a government that plans economically and efficiently and has the brains and energy to secure the fulfilment of a rational policy.

The "peaceful competition" to which we are challenged by the Soviet Union is military, economic, scientific, political, cultural, and moral. Yes, the American economy is a consumer's paradise. Missiles may keep it so, character may keep it so, but hardly the bright and cheap magazines, the new design for a prettier mudguard on next year's automobile.[11]

American strength in military matters is mighty, especially since rearmament and the mobilization of the economy during and since the conflict in Korea. I do not in any way underestimate it. The financial provision for military defense is the chief inroad made by American political leadership on free enterprise; it is America's chief venture into a planned economy. The nation's Gross National Product could allow for a far greater percentage to be used for scientific advancement, education, military equipment, and foreign aid.

America's power has been enhanced by its democratic form of government. Its foundation on the creed of freedom, and its organization according to that principle, has allowed the population over many scores of years to use its own varied ingenuity and energies to pursue the path of invention, innovation, construction, and skilled management and enterprise in economy, law, moral endeavor, and in the life of culture and art. Is not this a sublime spectacle? So vast a population, no less than 180,000,000 people of all ethnic strains, a multinational community, dwelling in concert in so vast an area, governing themselves and making safe the endurance of civil liberties. What potentialities have been released — free speech, free assembly, a free press; the unhindered right to go and come as the heart yearns and the mind suggests; freedom of worship, since men and women need the strength of Providence; independent courts and humane procedures, offering to the pitiable accused many Cities of Refuge and the right to appeal the judgments of authority; where force is the last, reluctant remedy, the marginal safeguard of a society's peace and not a grim hourly certainty; where every man has an equal right to a voice in what government shall do; where he is at liberty to create or ignore representative political parties at his own sweet will; and where there prevails a spirit to render to a troubled individual the benefit of the doubt, the individual who, "in this dark world and wide," needs mercy and is most apt to find it in a democracy. It is far from fulsome to repeat that the United States offers "the last, best hope on earth." A resilient, self-reliant people has been nurtured, self-confident and able to learn from its own mistakes as well as its successes, of whom almost any magnificent work, individual or collective, may be expected when the occasion calls for drastic, self-sacrificing improvisation.

Improvisation? Is it not true that Americans have given that devotion to business which more fruitfully might have been expended on government? Are they less provident then than the English, who have given devotion to government that might more profitably have been invested in business?

A serious, but *not* the most serious, fault of American government, forced to accomplish the tasks dictated by the twentieth century, is its fundamental principle of organization, the separation of powers, and this, chiefly, between the legislature and the President. The separation of powers was intended to weaken the force of government, to throw a monkey wrench into the machinery of politics and administration. It has succeeded, gloriously. In the spacious days of American history, the vast and glowing breadth before that black day in 1914 when World War I began, a do-nothing, know-nothing, hear-nothing government was viable. Economic and scientific advances and involvement in foreign affairs abruptly swept away the happy-go-lucky program of laissez faire. . . .

The division of American political leadership between Congress and the President makes for inadequate laws — or no laws where they are needed. American executive, domestic, and foreign policies have nothing in keeping with Lenin's zigzag policy, only possible to a mind as rigorous and logical as that of a champion chessplayer. Nor is this all, as we shall show, as we are forced to show — for Congress itself is riven in leadership, torn between North and South, between 435 districts; torn by the different terms for which congressmen and senators are elected, each appealing to a different electorate; torn between the two houses; torn, in the Senate, by one hundred senators, each endowed with the right of filibuster. This is not twentieth-century leadership. It is not the kind of leadership to guide our economy and insure the nation's survival in the world.[12]

However, my chief concern is not the inefficiency and irresponsibility of American political leadership produced by the separation of powers. The far more serious concern is with the inefficiencies of each branch of the government in its own assigned sphere. Congress has many deficiencies to appall us, in deciding policy, providing funds, making laws, and controlling the millions of public officials. But the gravest problem of America's government is the inadequacy of the President, any President; all the more so because the office itself is not remedied and is not to be remedied by its auxiliary, Congress, which itself is debilitated and scarcely able to maintain a fumbling grasp on its own concerns. Both institutions are so ill-equipped for the tasks history has thrust upon them that neither can help the other, except perhaps into further stumbling. In a dilemma one must try to grasp both the horns. We are mainly concerned with the more powerful one, the Presidency.

Many nations with human and physical resources vastly inferior to those of America have contrived to secure a far more productive and just management of them. They have better achieved firm political leadership, that is, have sought and found for government office men with broad social goals and the clearly envisaged purposes that follow from them. These nations have established policies and plans marked by diligent and energetic attention to set dates of achievement, always utilizing the brains, devotion, and courage which make possible their fulfilment.

The United States suffers because its people are split into three separate electorates. There is one national state of mind reflected in its 435 parts every two years when the House is elected. There is another, and different, national response when a third of its senators are elected every two years in its states fractions. There is a very different nation, a different national state of mind, every fourth year when the President and the Vice-President are elected. The ostensible gathering of leadership from the popular source is, in fact, trisected, and its parts prove to be mutually antagonistic or at cross-purposes. So, also, the descent of ideas and policies, of appeals and command, is trifurcated and confounded. How are government officials to know to what they should be loyal? This was General MacArthur's dilemma. Was he responsible to the President? Or to Congress? Or to the people? Or was it to none of these, but to his own reading of the Constitution? His testimony was a heartfelt appeal to his friends in Congress, and yet his fellow generals, many congressmen, the Secretary of State, and his President disagreed with him.

This confusion of loyalty, command, and responsibility will continue as long as there is no single-minded national recognition that in choosing the men who are to govern the people of the United States have pledged acceptance of their wisdom as one of the necessities of government. Until that day the tie between pople and government remains almost hopelessly sundered.

The founders of the Republic knew that they could not install Montesquieu's principle of the separation of powers without qualification. As it was, what they did with it tended to destroy governmental leadership and authority. To have separated the powers absolutely would have been to have stopped government absolutely. They left bits of the legislative sticking to the Presidency, and bits of the body executive sticking to Congress, and both bled and still bleed. This enables co-operation, but it also contributes to mutual frustration. Rousseau said of the separation of powers that it reminded him of the fakir's trick of dismembering a boy, throwing the pieces into the air, and restoring the living body before it descended. Nobody believes the Indian tale: The body politic, cut into three, does not descend as articulated political leadership but as disarticulate and numb fragments.

The founders of the Republic did not provide for the contradictions in varying rates of growth; they could not predict how mightily the legislative powers of the President might develop, so that the Presidency has become a legislative body in fact, able at times to have its own way over the will of all but two-thirds of Congress. But such a development shifts the center of gravity of statesmanship to the one-man Presidency, and this, surely, has provoked a crisis in the office and in American government in general. The whole potency of the Presidency is founded on a gamble: The leadership of the United States, agonizingly assailed as never before, is based on the hazards of the nerves, brains, and character of a single man — one man alone, chosen by the most ramshackle, the flimsiest method ever used to select the supreme leader of a nation.

Prowess and Struggle of the American People

It is necessary to offer a brief sketch of the strengths of the American political heritage and achievement in order to avoid the suggestion of bias and, more importantly, to appreciate the virtues of our present nation and to learn what resources must be further mobilized.

What broad features of American tradition and environment have been most influential — and which still are?

First, this nation is of vast size and tremendous economic and cultural diversity. It is a subcontinent with enormous natural resources. As de Tocqueville somewhere said, "Fortune has offered an immense booty to Americans. It is sometimes confused with virtue." It is remarkable that so large an area has not fallen prey to fragmentation. On two occasions this eventuality seemed likely, just before the Constitution was established and in 1812, at the time when New England revolted against the policy of the rest of the country; and on a third occasion, the Civil War, it came about. Size and diversity are dreadful strains on a united government, as is shown by the obstacles to world government in the UN for ninety sovereign nations. When a nation fights against its tremendous size, its leadership is subject to enormous stress; political leaders cannot be aware of all the difficulties that occur in every part of the land, cannot know the problems of every part, and they are defeated in their efforts unless guided by vivid insight into the relationship between all the localities and the nation as a whole. When they contest the flight from the center, or ignorance of the center, of which every locality is the victim (often the willing victim), they are subject to all the recalcitrant strains of the local point of view.

To a mighty and laudable extent in the years since the establishment of the Union, solutions have been found for these problems. But when the federal-state-local relationship is considered, there is evidence of an enormous amount of waste and friction, an incomprehension of an American national vision. Only a person unfamiliar with the labors of government would look upon this herculean effort, so largely successful, with any sourness. The sense of wonder and admiration is heightened as one scans the statutes and ordinances, the decisions and opinions, of thousands of learned judges, the records of the debates of representatives in the legislative and executive bodies; each word felt, meditated, each word scrutinized for its evidence of passion, fact, and will. One recognizes and applauds the labor of the intellect, the work of the heart, the burden of conscience that these records present. It was not created out of nothing, of course. America inherited the philosophy and culture and jurisprudence of the Old World, and the people who brought it were cultivated and skilled with their tools, their books, offering an incalculable contribution to an infant economy.

Nevertheless, law and authority are not as settled in the United States as they are in older countries. They are not, as it were, maturely established. Again and again the development of American civilization has been arrested by abrupt, violent, and bloody struggles, to a point where disruption by systems of separate governments and laws seemed imminent. Disputes between the several colonies among themselves occurred before the War of Independence. They recurred during the period of the Articles of Confederation. Threats of fratricide caused tribulation at the time the Constitution was written and when it was submitted for popular ratification. A fresh shock came in 1828, when a new social class, led by Andrew Jackson, overcame government by a generation of natural aristocrats. In 1861 the Civil War produced a division in the nation, the causes and consequences of which are far from cured or forgotten even now, a century later. Since that time, and steadily, the United States has been subject to successive waves — and very substantial ones at that

— of peoples of varying background, varying ideals, varying concepts of government, who arrive as immigrants. Each brings a change in social consensus which makes extremely difficult the development of a stable set of laws. The United States today is a country which enacts the greatest number of laws, goes most to law over most laws, and defies most laws: It is the most law-making, the most litigating, the most lawless. . . .

The political system in the United States is probably more "partisan" than in any other democratic country, with the possible exceptions of France and Italy, whose political systems are often denounced by American observers as dominated by an excess of party spirit. When an American uses the word "politics," he does so with an air of amusement, contempt, and despair; it signifies little more to him than the machinations of vote-getting and "party-first" electioneering. A well-known book on politics is entitled *Politics: Who Gets What, When and How*.[13] As the accepted definition, this is a fair demonstration of the peculiar relationship between the American citizen and his government. The classic definition of politics covers all phases of the relationship between man and his society and regards government as an assistant to the purposes of civilization. It is used in this sense by some few scholars in our midst, but it is remarkable to what extent the vulgar definition refers only to the maneuvering of individuals and groups to dominate their opponents. This will explain the frequent outcries, "Keep politics out of the farm program!" "Keep politics out of labor!" and "Keep politics out of foreign policy!"

America is the home of a quality for which the French are more usually reproached — *incivisme*, a lack of civic-minded-ness. One cannot live long in any big city in the United States without realizing that when another person's property, life, or physical security is in danger the rest of the population is extraor-dinarily calm about these hazards. In essence, the political question is whether the total body of citizens is prepared to pay taxes, be law-abiding, and preserve a constant demeanor of law-abidingness so that those fellow citizens who might suffer mis-fortune may be protected by established institutions of law, police, welfare agencies, and the rest. Law-abidingness means permanent and taxpaying sympathy with the potential public troubles of our fellow citizens. What we have seen is within the ken of everyone, in cities, towns, and villages — the more general weaknesses of American government from which the country as a whole suffers, whether in each state or in the nation or in the relationship between them. Of course, one of the major elements that produces a sense of community, of law-abidingness, in other countries is missing in (and we may say, in our compassion for human tribulations, has not been suffered by) the United States. We have not starved through a blockade of our frontiers; we have not been bombed; we have never suffered invasion and occupation and subsequent humiliation and hardship; the war casualties of our brave have been slight in comparison with those of other countries; we have never suffered under tyranny. For any of these conditions would have taught us the necessity of more government in self-government, would have impressed on us a loyal sense of community. The cruelties of man to man have had no occasion to stir our patriotic sense of the solidarity, the oneness, of all.

The American people are immensely competent; they are kindly; they are inventive; they are self-reliant; and, unfortunately, they are politics-despising. The problem is not to supply what nature and history have not provided, for this cannot be done, but to invent workable substitutes. For example, if the area of the United States is three million square miles, it cannot in itself be contracted; but distance can be minimized by inventive attention to our network of communications. So also with the diversities of economic outlook, the diversities of climate, the diversities of local cultural development — these cannot be swept away, but they can be governed, the values of each preserved and saved from abuse.

One could not, one would not wish, to simulate war and division and tyranny within the nation. But what is wanting is an established leadership so sensitive and so talented as to act as though the nation did have bitter knowledge of conquest and occupation; better still, leadership able to carry the people with it in the conviction that democracy must be renewed each day, its faults corrected, its abuse avoided — a system that is not perfect but perfectible.

The foregoing observations will have begun to indicate the

part that government leadership can play in meeting domestic and foreign problems. Leadership is needed to supply conviction, insight, and the means to repair the deficiencies of the government itself for the sake of Americans and, I believe, for the sake of the entire world.

An Essay in Possibilities

The observations that follow have a constructive purpose. I believe that there is no one prescription in all political science or philosophy offering the system, procedure, or line of behavior that will make certain of genius in the high places of leadership. I attempt to discover only a more reliable way of securing talent and character adequate (in steady and dependable continuity) to the problems of our time and place. If genius rises to the top, the nation will be especially blessed. A system should not foreclose this happy result, genius in a democracy. Certainly a democratic form of government should be so contrived that it will tend to exclude the ignoramus, those without interest in government, the fainthearted, the knave, and the scoundrel. Indeed, the constituents of democratic leadership will be suggested in later pages; and it is the attainment of these in American politics, in a measure more satisfactory than now, that concerns us here.

The welfare and survival of the people of the United States and those in the world to whom they have obligations have become subject to a gamble every four years — that is, the gamble of the election of a President. The vital interests of America are intrusted to the character of one man alone and made almost exclusively dependent on his intelligence, nerves, conscience, and beliefs. It is essential to realize that, more and more, the institutions of government, especially Congress, are congested with business, most of it of a highly detailed, localized, and exacting kind, with the consequence that leadership in the gravest issues, particularly foreign affairs, has been thrust solely on the shoulders of the President. If the tasks of leadership are not shouldered by the political parties and by Congress, then their concentration falls to one man. The parties, the House of Representatives, and the Senate are, as the founders of the Republic called them, "numerous bodies." Here personal idiosyncrasies, while never obliterated, are balanced and moderated; various personalities check and balance the expression of ideas and repair the presence of personal weakness by the remedial power of criticism and assistance. But the President, at the summit of commitment and often forced to make irreversible decisions, is never more than one man made officially "unitary" in his responsibility by the Constitution. The word "solitary" more truly expresses the situation.

In the past half-century scholars and critics have well-nigh surrendered their hope of improving the political parties and Congress. This is not to say that no improvement has been or can be achieved; but in the main it has been recognized that certain basic components of Congress are so obstinately rooted that Congress itself, after plenty of prodding, has refused to consider any basic change. Bereft of hope in congressional reform, the reformers have concentrated on the Presidency. Their ideas in this respect have taken two directions — to add to the responsibilities of the President, both in the functions to be undertaken by him and in the severity of his responsibilities; and, second, to give him the assistance he needs — virtually, to overcome his solitary role, as established by the Constitution.

In consequence of historical development and theoretical urging, the President of the United States, within the functions alloted to him and as further acquired by custom, has a power on his own initiative to make decisions, to indulge choices, and to order action surpassing anything granted the British prime minister, a Stalin, or a Khrushchev. The British prime minister must carry both the cabinet and the House of Commons if he wishes to exert as much power as that given the President of the United States. Stalin, as first secretary of the Communist Party, had to carry — carry or kill — a majority of the eleven members of the Presidium; since the death of Stalin, probably a majority of the central committee, of some 130 members, must be carried before action can be taken. And yet for many fatal decisions the President of the United States is not compelled to seek the assent of anyone. This is why I say we gamble with the Presidency — offering independent power, without restraint, in many choices of the gravest consequence; allowing the man we choose to make irreparable mistakes or to set in motion acts of the wisest beneficence. If the dangers of this hazardous one-man system cannot be met by Congress, then we must look for our salvation in the reform of the Presidency itself. In any system of government there are hazards, and usually more hazardous than the chance involved in the throw of an honest dice. Now, by constitutional arrangement, we must find some way to load the dice so that our chances are better than one in six.

The Constitution of the United States designates Congress as the legislative branch of the government; yet Congress is not simply a legislative factory. Some clearly administrative and executive functions are allotted to it — the appointment of officials and, for treaties, the advice and consent of the Senate. Secondly, Congress has assumed certain important powers through two of its functions. It has sole power to appropriate money for use by the executive branch, and gradually it has taken upon itself the power to direct the administrative activities of the officials in the executive branch. Its power to declare war has enabled Congress to influence our foreign policy. In other words, its share in political leadership is not merely the making of laws, an enormous power it maintains jointly with the President, but authority in the general conduct of government.

The founders of the Republic intended Congress to be the collective expression of the nation's aspirations and needs, not a collection of parts or, as Woodrow Wilson called it, "a jarring conflict of local interests." In foreign trade, taxation, federal legislation, Congress was to be the focus of national clarification in which the national vision was to be defined and through which it was to be transmitted to the people in the form of policies and laws. The motto of the United States has been "the Republic, one and indivisible," but the present incoherence of Congress makes this motto hard to believe. The larger the country, the greater the need for a carefully woven and steadily fostered national policy. It is curious that there seems so little permanent, so little persistent substance in American patriotism, the visible sign of a nation's indivisibility.

However, my intention in this essay in possibilities is not to appraise the role of Congress; it has been done by several generations of American scholars. And it might be well to add that American political parties are not to be given direct and extended treatment *per se*. My views of party behavior and the prospects of change are clear. But one important idea might be stated: Political parties determine the operation of Congress and the Presidency. A change in political institutions cannot fail to have an effect on the parties, making them more or less adequate as links in the active network that binds a people's will, conscience, and character to the men elected to public office. I think that the reforms I propose will give the parties a firmer structure and a more definite responsibility than they now possess.

The deficiencies of Congress and how Congress can be made to participate more fully in national political leadership are sketched in a brief appendix to this volume.

If the inefficiencies of Congress were to be remedied, less responsibility for leadership would be heaped upon the President. To date, congressional reforms of an appropriate character and consequence have been neglected. Is it any wonder that reformers have turned their backs on Congress and have allowed, have encouraged, the President to move toward a monopoly of leadership and command over a mighty nation? It is a trust which, as I shall show, is far too much for a solitary man.

Now the essence of my proposals for the reform of the Presidency is to elect a collective executive, a body of persons, a President and eleven Vice-Presidents, elected on the same ticket and nominated from among men who have had experience in Congress and have learned how the executive branch may be conducted collectively. The reasonableness — indeed, the necessity — of this proposal is founded on an analysis of the burdens of the Presidency in this century and the last, and the clearly demonstrated impossibility of achieving efficiency and responsibility in the present system of a one-man executive branch.

Against my proposals several objections will be directed; among them are these:

1. The institution of a collective executive is counter to American tradition.

2. The United States is a composite of ethnic, economic, and regional groups, diverse, unmelded; a one-man Presidency serves as a unifier of the nation.

3. The President can be granted sufficient advisory and executive assistants to ease his burden under the present system.

4. Finally, it is not the Presidency itself that is at fault but the

caliber of the men who have been elected to the office; if the right man is chosen no one need worry about the formal apparatus of authority, for he will find appropriate answers to the nation's anxieties and see that an appropriate plan of action is carried out.

I recognize the force of these objections. The ensuing discussion will show that they have neither sufficient relevance nor adequate substance to stand against the evidence of strain and stress under which every President staggers; nor do they make one whit less urgent the need for the regeneration of the Presidency.

I

The Solitary Master Builder

The transfixture of one man, one mortal, with the titanic authority and torturing responsibilities of the President constitutes the vital flaw in the government of the United States in the twentieth century. No matter that the sophisticate tries to close his eyes to its challenge, the stark fact is inescapable. The founders of the Republic believed the essential, indeed the cardinal, merit of their system to be that one man alone, not a collective body, should wield the power and bear the load of the Chief Executive. But any reasonable person who reads the notes of their discussions must be persuaded that those very ingenious and prudent men would not have vested a solitary mortal with the duties, towering as they are today, of that highest of offices. The founders of the Republic might be reluctant to institute the bold remedies our times demand, but they would do their duty in their solemn concern to enable Americans to thrive in a more perfect Union.

The powers of the President are colossal, they are increasing, and they ought to be de-unitarized. Or, to put it another way, they ought to be truly shared with equal colleagues elected by the people. No President can exercise, alone, the authority with which the Constitution and subsequent accretions of law and custom have burdened him. No auxiliary agencies established to help him fulfil his responsibilities can assist him in any way significant to the authority the Constitution vests in him alone; they can only clear away a little of the debris in his path and provide him, the architect, with some blueprints, some mortar, and some bricks. He remains the master builder.

The President needs help; indeed, he needs far more than that, he needs rescue. But reliance, in whatever form, on advisory and executive assistants cannot solve the major problems that confront him. These instruments, committees, agencies — arms, eyes, ears, as they have been called — will not meld with him; and he cannot meld with them. These grafts will not take, for they are alien to his brains, conscience, and volition — and it is the exertion of the unique qualities of the man himself that the Constitution ordains. Some of the agencies now surrounding the President are last-moment attempts to escape the terrible realities of autocratic office, made by men who comprehend the impasse occasioned by the descent of vast and awesome functions on one man alone. Some of these ineffectual agencies are praised by men who have never had political responsibility in government. Some who know the office at first hand have said that the President is in danger of suffocation by the very auxiliaries intended to give him opportunity to breathe and think.

There is, I fear, no way to solid improvement of the government except by the apportionment of the President's responsibilities, allowing them to be shared among a twelve-man Presidency; that is to say, to have what the founders of the Republic eschewed in eighteenth-century America, a multiple or plural executive. We have learned well that oneness of political mind and will is more likely to be the product of the collaboration of several true colleagues than of the attempts of a single man to master ten thousand duties. The attempt to remain one, in a formidable situation requiring the exertions of many, is to end in being none. The question is, Can a multitude of homunculi ("the institutions of the President") equal a living man, a many-talented statesman?

The upshot of the ensuing discussion will show, I think, these truths: There ought to be a collective Presidency, with collective responsibility and authority. Failing this, every four years, or every eight years, the American voters who elect, and the behind-the-scenes manipulators who select, the candidates must find a

genius capable of doing what twelve good men can do if conscientious and able. If the second alternative is not accepted
because it is seen to be an impossibility, then we must learn what
means will achieve the first alternative.

These, as was said of the creative achievement of the founders
of the Republic, are "the grinding necessities of a reluctant nation."

Above all, for the sake of the public weal, we ought not to
permit ourselves to be entrapped by the specious frame of mind
which holds that whatever is, is good; that all is for the best in
the best of all possible Americas; that whoever happens to be
elected President is, *ipso facto*, talented and the man for whom
we have been seeking; that office will indeed make the man. Is
there not at least a strong presumption that the nation ought to
be as businesslike about the choice of a President as the President
is expected to be in the fulfilment of the duties of his office? It
will be a sad day for America when the Presidency is envisaged
as an office of retirement, of popular reward, one more bouquet
for the politician, one more medal for the general who has captured the public sentimentality; it could be an irredeemably catastrophic day.

The Weight of Presidential Office

The founders of the Republic did not contemplate the present
weight of decisions faced by the Chief Executive or the vital
significance these affairs would have for the welfare of the nation. Their minds, indeed, were intent on making America one
economic region, on developing the subcontinent, on preserving
it from foreign dangers. They had no inkling of what would be
needed today, the scope and quantity of governmental action, the
intricacy and tentacular depth, the severity of the consequences,
the resultant misery and subjugation if the government should
fail. The founders of the Republic, although Benjamin Franklin,
the experimentalist, was of their company, did not seek to proph-
esy in the manner of a Jules Verne or H. G. Wells, the pioneers of
science fiction. The language of the Philadelphia Convention and
of the *Federalist Papers* is as Arcadian as can be, the vocabulary
of a land of hardly more than a few scattered villages living by

domestic arts and crafts on the edge of the forest primeval. (There were, of course, the mercantile and shipping interests.)

Yet, from the very beginning, every President has groaned at the severity of the burden imposed on him by his oath of office. Let us mention only a few of these:

In midsummer, 1789, Washington complained that he had no leisure to read or answer the dispatches that were pouring in upon him from all quarters.[1] A year later he confided to his friend, David Stuart, "The public meetings . . . with the references *to* and from the different Departments of State . . . is as much, if not more, than I am able to undergo. . . ."[2] Yet Washington presided over only six executive departments, employing only about 2,000 public officials, and he had Alexander Hamilton to do his work for him.

John Adams wrote his wife, "The business of all kinds, and writing particularly, out of the habit of which I have been so long, press upon me very severely. . . ."[3] Jefferson took on himself more than did Washington — the leadership of Congress by all the arts of party management. He did his duty as his predecessors had done, but in 1809 he wrote to James Monroe:

> Five weeks more will relieve me from a drudgery to which I am no longer equal, and restore me to a scene of tranquility, amidst my family and friends, more congenial to my age and natural inclinations.[4]

And, later, to James Madison:

> I sincerely congratulate you on your release from incessant labors, corroding anxieties, active enemies & interested friends, & on your return to your books & farm, to tranquility & independence. A day of these is worth ages of the former. But all this you know. . . .[5]

As Monroe was about to leave the White House, he sent Congress "a few remarks . . . founded on my own experience, in this office."[6] Beyond a certain limit, he wrote, no one can go. If unimportant details are forced upon the attention of the President he loses the time he ought to devote to matters of greater importance. The higher duties of his office, said Monroe, "are sufficient to employ the whole mind, and unceasing labors, of any individual. . . ." Among these duties he cited the message to Congress, the replies to calls for information, personal contact with members of Congress, and "the supervision and control of the several departments so as to preserve efficiency in each, and order and consistency in the general movement of the Government." [7] Monroe was one of the first to suggest the desirability of aid to the President. At the end of his tenure in office, James Madison wrote:

> I know well the uncertainty incident to our hopes and calculations; but I have the consolation, that if the enjoyments I anticipate should not be fully realized, they will be at least a welcome exchange for the arduous and anxious responsibilities, from which I shall be released.

In December, 1848, Polk, who immersed himself deliberately in detail as well as in main policy, made this entry in his diary:

> The public have no idea of the constant accumulation of business requiring the President's attention. No President who performs his duty faithfully and conscientiously can have any leisure. If he entrusts the details and smaller matters to subordinates constant errors will occur. I prefer to supervise the whole operations of the Government myself rather than entrust the public business to subordinates, and this makes my duties very great. [8]

The task undermined Polk's health, and he died shortly after leaving the White House. President Buchanan declared that in the brief period of four years Polk had assumed the appearance of an old man. [9]

Grant declared that he was weary of office: "I never wanted to get out of a place as much as I did to get out of the Presidency." [10] Hayes wrote in his diary in 1879 that Mrs. Hayes agreed with him in saying, "Well, I am heartily tired of this life of bondage, responsibility, and toil. I wish it was at an end." [11] After four years in the White House, Cleveland wrote: "You cannot imagine the relief which has come to me with the termination of my official term." [12]

Finally, in our own time, President Wilson found that he had to breakfast at five or six and work well into the night to fulfil the responsibilities of the office as he felt them, commenting also that the burden would kill him.[13]

President Truman, incessantly at work and an extraordinarily industrious man, reflected on "the weight of its unbelievable burdens," referred to the Presidency as a "man-killer," and concluded that "the pressures and complexities of the Presidency have grown to a state where they are almost too much for one man to endure."[14] He decided against seeking re-election on the ground that he did not want to be carried out of the White House in a casket.

The more sensitive the conscience of the President, the more capacious his mind, the heavier his groans or the efforts to subdue them. Yet it must not be thought that when a President does not complain of the burden it does not exist; he may diminish the office to accommodate a smaller brain, a pettier conscience.

When the President seeks a second term, what then? Can we assume that the complaint of burden is not always justified, that it may be a way of venting annoyance or gaining sympathy and admiration? And yet . . . I have not yet come across the suggestion that the Presidency was established to help the man keep his health. Indeed, when it is said that a President is leaving office in better health than the day he entered it, it is right to suspect that the state of the nation has degenerated.

In a moment, we shall assess the dimensions of the President's problems. But let us dwell briefly on the office the founders of the Republic intended — and established.

The President in 1788

It is not to be denied that Congress was intended to be the primary engine of will and decision; it was made the prime repository of the power to legislate, to raise taxes, to vote appropriations, to summon military forces, and to declare war and peace. It had other functions than these, and yet these alone, especially in a liberal interpretation of specific legislative powers, were enough to give it primacy in statesmanship — if its members were able and willing to exercise it. It is true that most of the members of the Philadelphia Convention distrusted the man in the street (and the fields) and were alarmed at the headstrong, usurping tendencies of the state legislators and an interfering, ambitious Congress. But it was far from their intention to remedy an undue lust for power by its denial, complete or in considerable part. There is no evidence to indicate that the founders of the Republic intended leadership to pass to the President. Definitely not. It was a democracy they sought, even if a restrained one. They would not allow the political heads of departments, or cabinet members, to sit in Congress; they were convinced that Congress ought to remain an independent body. With the exception of Hamilton and perhaps one or two other members, they were ready to see the President assume a general kind of government leadership, such as a prime minister at that time might have had under the king of England (a leadership then exercised by George III himself), if, in the course of time, American circumstances made this necessary, or simply opportune. But the initiating force, at least in domestic affairs, was to be centered in Congress.

Yet, the founders wanted an executive branch with authority to do those things which Congress (small as it was in those days) would not be able to do with the same success. They felt the need of an executive, remembering the woeful, almost fatal, debility of the Confederation they had assembled to cure. They did not want the President swamped by congressional interference in the day-by-day execution of the laws, the command of the army and the navy, and the conduct of diplomatic negotiations.[15] They were intent on establishing the independent strength of the Presidency, and to achieve this they rejected the proposal, made no less than five times, that the President be elected by Congress itself.

They had before them as a model the strong governor of New York State, contrasted with the ineffective governors of other states, and they remembered the detested, foreign-appointed governors of the original colonies. The Chief Executive's assigned functions must be free from invasion by the legislators. He must be able to defend himself by the exercise of the veto vested in him. He was to assist in plans of congressional legislation by his periodic messages on the state of the Union, for this would tend to focus and make consistent the business of the legislature, coming as it would from one man, one mind.

Some saw that a body governing a large area must have the power to pervade every part of it with vigor; governing the original thirteen states called for such energy. The attribution of the power to negotiate with other countries, to make treaties, to see to the disposition of the armed forces — these were the traditional responsibilities of the Chief Executive in almost all civilized countries during the eighteenth century and in almost all of the governments the founders of the Republic had so anxiously observed and studiously pondered.

It must be admitted that the role of the President, as delineated in the course of involved debates and as expressed in the Constitution, remained uncertain. It was argued by Pierce Butler that great powers had been intrusted to the President because the founders of the Republic had deep faith in the civic virtues of George Washington, the man who would first take office.[16] Moreover, the courts, with the Supreme Court at the summit, gave the President great latitude and immunity in his personal judgments and commands. In 1867, in *Mississippi* v. *Johnson*, the Supreme Court ruled that the President could not be forced to carry out his duties or prevented from going beyond his powers; that the law may command what he shall do, yet he is not in the position of one who must do what is commanded. The President's duty is *political*, that is (in our words), he has a moral duty to uphold the law; the remedy for his failure to act so is not in the courts but in "political" punishment. This immunity is extended to cover the confidential relations between the President and his subordinates. Furthermore, the principle of the separation of powers gives to the President the right to deny information to the law courts if he sees fit, and the courts will respect his defensive silence. The same immunity is applicable to his assistants, who are protected by the President's cloak of authority. The same immunity applies to the President's relationship with Congress. Again and again the Attorney General has vindicated the traditional aloofness of the President, and repeatedly the President has, at his will, defied congressional attempts to force disclosures which he felt it inexpedient to make.[17]

In the power to withhold information from Congress the President is in a rather stronger position than is the prime minister of Great Britain. The prime minister does possess the right, formerly held by the Crown, to deny information to Parliament on the grounds that its disclosure would endanger the public interest. Yet the fact that the prime minister and his cabinet are members of the House of Commons, at almost every moment under the face-to-face scrutiny of other members, and subject to formal question periods, makes for the readier, if rueful, supply of information.

In order that it may not seem that I entertain the thought that the President of the United States is empowered to exercise the tyranny of a Stalin, a Charles I, or even a Charles II, let me say that I am well aware of the restraints practiced by other branches of the government, the judiciary and Congress, not to mention the press. Moreover, the distribution of federal power puts much political authority beyond the President's reach. Even so, the gigantic powers available, the enormous share of those powers now vested in the President alone, the generous, almost unlimited powers accorded to the President by the courts, make possible the perpetration of catastrophic errors of judgment, and the more chronic, and likely, failure that comes of innumerable acts of omission. The President's power is formidable, indeed, to the fate of the nation and in its significance to the world.

The President Today

Surely there can be no doubt that the founders of the Republic would be amazed to see what has become of their pristine creation. They would be amazed and fascinated, and frequently alarmed, by what was made of the office by Andrew Jackson and Abraham Lincoln, and by its autocratic evolution since the days of Theodore Roosevelt. A committee which considered in 1936 the problem of the swollen authority of the President, at the direction of President Franklin D. Roosevelt, summarized the office of the President in these words:

> Our Presidency unites at least three important functions. From one point of view the President is a political leader — leader of a party, leader of the Congress, leader of a people. From another point of view he is head of the Nation in the ceremonial sense of the term, the symbol of our American national solidarity. From still another point of view the

President is the Chief Executive and administrator within the Federal system and service.[18]

Twenty-five years have passed — tense and anxious years, in which modern warfare and the "balance of terror," a precarious economy, a swifter tempo, a series of crises, and both lethal and creative advances in science have engorged the responsibilities of government, and, more especially, of the President. We must appraise the authority the often abysmally illiterate public has come to expect the President to exercise as well as the responsibility which much learned opinion assigns to the office, apparently without foreseeing and being prepared to accept the potentially dire consequences of such concentration of power.

It has become the habit of political scientists to dignify with capital letters the multiplicity of presidential roles, not merely, I think, for the benefit of undergraduates whose reading habits may need the stimulation of emphasis. Let us, likewise, pay court to a court before we assess whether one man ought to be throned so autocratically. Without granting him a change of costume, this is what we ask the man to be: In the twentieth century the President of the United States is Chief Executive and Chief Legislator and Chief of Foreign Policy and Commander in Chief and Party Leader and Chief of State — the state's unifying symbol.

II

Power and Responsibility of the President

Chief Executive of the Laws

The role of Chief Executive has two aspects. The first, as simple and pure as human nature in government allows it, is the execution of the laws made by Congress and assented to by the President, as provided by the Constitution, Article II, section 3 (saying, "He shall take care that the Laws be faithfully executed."). This is the only example of vested authority on which there has been unanimity — at least this! But what began as a minimum authority has become vast in scope and gravity. The second aspect is embodied in the general grant of power to the President, Article II, section 1 ("The executive Power shall be vested in a President of the United States of America."). It has been suggested that the committee of five (Johnson, Hamilton, Gouverneur Morris, Madison, and King — but especially Morris) who polished the style of the drafts of the Constitution for the Convention deliberately evaded an enumeration of the powers of an "executive nature," the kind of list supplied for legislative action by Congress and restricted by the words *herein granted*, that is, granted specifically in the Constitution. It is now the general consensus, and it can be persuasively argued among contemporary justices of the Supreme Court, that there is *no limit* to the Chief Executive's power.[1]

It is generally held that the power to act at the national level is not defined in the Constitution, that is, it is not limited. It is argued that the power is similar to the "prerogative" held by English kings before Parliament attained sovereignty — a full power to act for the public good. For example, in the absence of congressional action, the President may, at his discretion, have all aliens interned, seize for public use all property containing steel, or suspend, as Lincoln did, the procedure of habeas corpus.

To see that the laws are executed faithfully. Let us note this phrase and the word "faithfully". There are thousands of laws on the statute books, living laws, all those unrepealed as well as those that have not fallen into desuetude. When Congress passes a law, with what responsibilities does it saddle the President? Does it present him with a blueprint of authority to demand specified behavior from some people, to keep certain records for the government, to give pensions and packets of free seeds? Are the statutes on lobbyists, labor unions, and monopolies self-explanatory? The answer is decidedly no; quite apart from Congress' ofttimes faulty procedures, it is next to impossible to draft a statute to express all of the standards of administrative conduct necessary for its implementation. How a law is interpreted decides its character. It may be carried out in full, in part, or not at all. It may be carried out competently or incompetently. The Constitution requires that laws be carried out "faithfully". How shall we seek to define this term? The President must do it.

The number of federal officials since 1801 has increased almost a thousand times, from 2,120 to nearly 2,500,000. They are organized — to see that laws are executed faithfully — in some sixty agencies and some hundreds of bureaus, commissions, services, and government corporations.[2] These agencies and bureaus are engaged in interpreting the laws and adapting them to circumstances that continually and swiftly change.

What is considered the "faithful" execution of a law? In part, it is an interpretation that will satisfy Congress. Who in Congress? certainly a majority? But the majority is a shifting one, hard to identify. Nor is the congressional minority of today to be ignored. Is it the chairman of the congressional committee having jurisdiction over the department or bureau concerned? But this allows for enormous latitude. The President's interpretation may be capricious, or it may be sound but contrary to congressional intention; even so, it may be a long time before Congress discovers the discrepancy. And the President — for example, Eisenhower in 1958, in regard to certain military appropriations — may refuse to administer in advance of their passage certain laws or certain parts of a law, declaring them unwise. And the President — Truman, for example — may order the air force to spend only as much as he had earlier requested from Congress, though Congress itself has appropriated much more. In retaliation, Congress may pass a new law retracting the appropriations already passed in the budget. Or, if warranted, Congress may threaten the President with impeachment for his refusal to carry out congressional decisions.

But it must be admitted that impeachment or retraction of appropriations is an impractical recourse against a President's personal interpretation of what is meant by "faithfully." He is not obstructed or constrained (or assisted!) by any such force as the need to face Congress and answer questions in the way that the British prime minister and his cabinet must answer to the House of Commons. The day of reckoning for the President is far off, so far off that the influence of it may be altogether forgotten in the onrush of events, the pitfalls of party politics, and the legislative spasms of Congress. He may be far from adequately energizing, as Truman was, in seeing that the income tax administration is efficient and lawful; he may, like Eisenhower, be lax in impelling the FTC and the FCC to intervene in the scandalous practices of radio and television networks, or the sale of contaminated foods. In each case we are brought back to ponder the meaning of the word "faithfully."

Sometimes Congress makes its will and its wishes manifest by appropriations that directly challenge the President's program. If it gives the President less than he asks for, the will of Congress prevails. In the summer of 1959 an interesting variation of this difference of opinion was seen. The Senate asked for information on the use of funds for foreign economic aid and made its grant of money dependent on the furnishing of this information; the President's spokesman declared that the information would not be given. Such authority puts an enormous power in the hands of the President. The establishment of the Bureau of the Budget in 1921 and the burgeoning of its power did not bring this result; it is a simple corollary of the principle of the separation of powers. There are ways whereby the President can divert moneys appropriated by Congress to purposes not authorized by Congress, and the machinery does not exist to bring him to account.[3]

Connected with the power of solely deciding the meaning of laws, and with what vigor, wisdom, and, yes, policy, these laws are to be translated into effective action, is the power to appoint and to remove officials. The Constitution gives the President almost complete authority over the appointment of many and removal of almost all public officials, and even the power to remove members of independent regulatory commissions, under certain conditions.[4] In 1796, President Washington submitted to the Senate 85 nominations of military and civil officials; in 1834, the comparable number was 785; in 1914, 3,418; in 1935, 14,998; in 1945, 40,557; in 1955, 40,686; in 1958, 59,079. How formidable a weapon of Presidential will this power can become!

Let us, once again, envisage the role of the President as an agent who sees that the laws are carried out faithfully. He must impart the correct tempo to the operation of public officials; if he does not, the nation suffers waste whenever equipment and personnel are idle. He must see that emergency requirements are met in time of drought and flood, economic crises, and so on. He must select efficient, honest, and public spirited officials to fill technical and administrative posts; for, if he does so, each department will carry out its responsibilities without an excessive demand on his position as supervisor. He must use discretion in implementing chosen policy — to accomplish the legal purpose this way rather than that, by devising rules and procedures to meet stated objectives. Finally, all this must be done with the most careful regard for the cost to the nation's economy.

The President has the responsibility of integrating and coordinating the operation of many departments. The total work of government is chopped up into departments, and the departments into agencies and sub-sub-sections, for convenience in accomplishing specialized and skilled operations. If it were humanly possible it would be most efficient and economical to keep the naturally unified tasks of government one massive complex, interwoven and undepartmentalized. Departmentalization tends to become *compartment*alization, nourishes jealousy, and encourages alienation and obstructionism among rival departments. There is apt to be undue identification of officials with the responsibilities of their own departments, an identification valuable when it fosters morale and industrious service but detrimental when rivalry results and employees forget that government is one functioning whole.

Congress is able to encourage the departments to march along in mutual helpfulness; and pressure groups also exert an influence — but only when it is to their interest to do so. Only the President is clearly intrusted with this responsibility by the Constitution. Interdepartmental committees, less formal arrangements for cooperation, and an enormous personal staff help the President to unify government operations, the "simplest" of his responsibilities.

The Constitution provides for aid to the President. Of the nearly two and a half million federal officials, the majority are in civil service, but at the top are some 1,600 civil officials, who have not been chosen by congressional statute but are nominated by the President with the consent of the Senate. Among these are the ten cabinet members, the heads of important departments, assistant secretaries, and those who fill many hundreds of positions concerned with "policy" and "confidential affairs," at the top of the administrative pyramid. The "inner core" of political executives is estimated at around seven hundred.[5]

For his administrative-executive job the President has desperate need of the help of these officials. Let us look at the need as reflected in the bland statement made by the Hoover Commission in 1949:

> At the present time there are 65 departments, administrations, agencies, boards and commissions engaged in executive work, all of which report directly to the President — if they report to anyone. This number does not include "independent" regulatory agencies in their quasi-judicial or quasi-legislative functions. It is manifestly impossible for the President to give adequate supervision to so many agencies. . . . Even one hour a week devoted to each of them would require a 65-hour work week for the President, to say nothing of the time he must devote to his great duties in

developing and directing major policies as his constitutional obligations require.[6]

The reader is invited to imagine the qualities necessary if the President is to begin to exercise these responsibilities, especially if the word *devoted* has any intensity of appeal. He may consider whether even a remote inkling of this demand, itself but a minor part of the President's duties, is known to the millions of voters who every four years choose a man for the job. Is the Constitution serious or has it put the President in an incredible role?

Another question of a serious nature arises. As I shall show, the President is far from being the sole master of highest-level management and, through it, or the vast proliferation of officials. Formally, he appoints to office with the Senate's concurrence. Now so insistent were the founders of the Republic on executive management that, having endowed the President with certain functions and responsibilities, they gave him a qualified power of appointment and absolute power of removal of officials. For efficiency and, above all (as the debates in the Convention and the First Congress show), to make his responsibility to the nation plain, they intrusted these powers to him alone. The Supreme Court has since confirmed this executive power for reasons of efficiency.[7]

The political responsibilities of the Senate, and the putative electoral responsibilities of the President as a party leader, have limited his freedom to appoint cabinet members and department heads. The Senate has comported itself with sober responsibility in confirming the highest appointments. Only seven times before 1959 had Congress refused to confirm a cabinet nominee. In July, 1959, it refused, by a vote of 48 to 47, to confirm L. L. Strauss as Secretary of Commerce. Strauss, a most efficient man, was unable to win the votes of the majority, even though most southern Democrats abandoned their colleagues in order to vote for Eisenhower's nominee.

A far more serious defect is the inability of the President, for politico-electoral reasons, to achieve the support of cabinet members. The President is handicapped greatly if he lacks a top staff entirely of his state of mind, or even men who might be his other self because they belong to his political party and share his concerns and intent. But even if this need is met, cabinet members do not bear a responsibility equal to that of the President. The Constitution has given to one man not simply the primacy of responsibility but the only responsibility. The heads of the departments have their functions defined by statute, which implies a departmental responsibility; but the responsibility over all responsibilities is not statutory but constitutional, and it belongs solely to the President. Moreover, though the President himself is vested with a multitude of specific administrative-executive functions (for example, departmental reorganization), his responsibility for such matters already exists in the Constitution, should he care so to interpret it. Even so, the President has no certain way of compelling co-operation between the various departments.

Paradoxically, the President can have the strength he needs only if he does not have total responsibility — if his constitutional reach does not exceed his personal grasp; that is, if the functions of the Presidency were vested in, say, eleven men who would share with the President all responsibility for seeing that laws are executed faithfully.

The most heinous contemporary example of the failure of the capabilities of one man to do what the combined capacities of twelve might accomplish was a recent attempt to combine the three defense departments to provide strategic readiness and administrative economy. Why was a military hero, renowned for his skill in logistics (having the men and supplies at the right place at the critical time), unable to "knock the heads of the defense services together," as the popular expectation phrased it? Perhaps because he was too kind to the men of his own profession. More surely, however, for the simple reason that one man alone cannot afford the expense of spirit needed to dominate three political chiefs and literally thousands of top military, naval, and air force leaders. The President and the Secretary of Defense are alone among the multitudes. When they turn their backs, as they must, the power of their presence is withdrawn, and the same old feuds and stalemates rise to block co-operation. In the British cabinet some eighteen or twenty ministers, collectively responsible, stand firm before the military and naval chiefs of staff. The Minister of Defense is obeyed in the three service departments, which since 1945 have had no other representatives in the cabinet.

But in the United States, Secretary Forrestal's death was hastened by his vain attempts to unify the service departments under the direction of the President.

The British cabinet starts with the clear principle that the body is one in policy and will remain one, and that each cabinet member, even the prime minister, is subordinate to that oneness without sacrifice of the energetic right to internal persuasion. The American system begins with the principle that the President alone is responsible and that his convictions are to dominate the administration; but if he lacks the personal qualities, and has not the kind of assistance such a man would need, he will surely fail. For he is impotent then to secure steady and unfailing loyalty by the very assumption of one-man, solitary responsibility, and his departmental chiefs will not be recognized to be his true self projected. Not that nothing is accomplished; much is done that is right and beneficial; but not enough by far, dangerously not enough, is done to preserve economic well-being and insure survival. How grave a matter is the inability to weld the defense services into one can be surmised by reflection upon our time-lag in applying all of the resources of science and technology to the production of missiles of intermediate and (more important) intercontinental range.[8]

Let the reader scan the vast ocean of indispensable scientific minutiae presented in 1958 in the two volumes, some 2,300 pages, of the Hearings on Satellite and Missile Programs before the Senate Committee on the Armed Services. The onlooker might ask, How can you expect the President, alone in the White House, to know the composition of even one of those billions of molecules? Yes; how can he know? yet if he does not, how can he govern to the satisfaction and safety of the nation by making the choices the facts reveal as open to him?

It was the intention of the founders of the Republic that the President should be alone responsible for the executive function. The view of the large majority in the First Congress is best summed up by Fisher Ames, one of the most astute of the Federalists:

> The Constitution places all executive power in the hands of the President, and could he personally execute all the laws, there would be no occasion for auxiliaries; but the

circumscribed powers of human nature in one man, demand the aid of others. When the objects are widely stretched, or greatly diversified, meandering through an extent of territory as that the United States possesses, a minister cannot see with his own eyes every transaction, or feel with his hands the minutiae that pass through his department. He must therefore have assistants. But in order that he may be responsible to his country, he must have a choice in selecting his assistants, a control over them, with power to remove them when he finds the qualifications which induced their appointment to cease.[9]

Let the theme of the President's responsibility *to the country* be noted; his responsibility is not to Congress. This is a very solemn, indeed, a sacred, principle. Ames continues:

The executive powers are delegated to the President, with a view to have a responsible officer to superintend, control, inspect, and check the officers necessarily employed in administering the laws. The only bond between him and those he employs, is the confidence he has in their integrity and talents; when that confidence ceases, the principal ought to have the power to remove those whom he can no longer trust with safety.

The theme of the *bond* is most important, both administratively and politically. It ought to be as an artery in a living body, not simply a knot of twine, a length of chewed string. We shall see that present bonds are inadequate for twentieth-century America. It is possible to stretch executive responsibility until it loses its elastic force and cannot be restored.

And the dire truth is that the great public departments float about like monstrous monopolistic elephants, for good or ill, tended by thousands of public-spirited and conscientious career officials, untended by a single prick from the President's will. One day or another day, a scandal breaks out. Are we not due for one soon in an investigation of the administration of the Highway Act of 1956, involving a total expenditure of some $45 *billion* by Washington and the states on the interstate and defense highway system?

The President as Chief Executive of Policy

If the difficulties of securing the responsibility of the President and, more, his efficiency in contriving that the laws are faithfully executed were all, we would be quick to appreciate the weight of the President's office and, indeed, the impossibility of his fulfilling it in any but a formal sense. But we now reach a phase of the President's role of far more momentous gravity to the destiny of the nation — that undefined range of responsibility summed up in the Constitution as "The Executive power shall be vested in a President of the United States." What is "executive power"? There is no definition; it is a most unguarded phrase. Some, like Alexander Hamilton, have wanted it to mean almost all government powers conceivable save the judicial (always excepting this) and the clearly stated powers of Congress. The power of the President as Chief Executive has grown to the proportions of a comprehensive government of itself, comprising the establishment of law by executive fiat in any domestic or foreign emergency that, in the judgment of the President, ordain obedience. This would include the extremes of foreign policy, the disposition of the armed forces, and the conduct of war without the express declaration of Congress, the only body authorized to declare war. In the power to lead the nation into war, the Chief Executive is now paramount in every political system.

This mighty and awesome growth of presidential authority is the result of three forces: the President's own convictions of political purpose and constitutional rights; the incessant danger of foreign affairs which call for executive concentration; and the growing dependency of most social groups and individuals on government support. Every demand for rights is, in effect, a demand for government, a transfer of individual responsibility to the Chief Executive.

The first force, presidential conviction of political purpose and constitutional rights, is dependent upon the personal character of each President. Its consideration is postponed until I discuss the President's view of his responsibility, from the so-called stewardship theory pronounced by Theodore Roosevelt to the recessive theories of lesser men — bold responsibility or submissive responsibility, all the difference between Franklin Roosevelt, Andrew Jackson, a Harding, an Eisenhower.

The second force, foreign relations, must wait to be discussed.

The third force (which has given rise to the role of the President as Chief Legislator) may be seen in two pronouncements made in our own generation. In the first, Franklin Roosevelt, being faced in September, 1942, with the problem of the adjustment of wartime prices and wages, and finding that Congress was prepared to balk, demanded that Congress act at once — "failing which," he said, inaction "will leave me an inescapable responsibility to the people of the country to see to it that the war effort is no longer imperiled by the threat of economic chaos." Roosevelt warned Congress that he would take the responsibility and would act. In any case, he claimed, he had the powers he sought, "under the Constitution and under congressional acts, to take measures necessary to avert a disaster which would interfere with the winning of the war."

The justificatory passage is of some importance. Roosevelt was no innocent in matters of government; he had served as governor of New York, as a member of the New York Assembly, as Assistant Secretary of the Navy, and was now in his third term as President of the United States.

> The American people can be sure that I will use my powers with a full sense of responsibility to the Constitution and to my country. The American people can also be sure that I shall not hesitate to use every power vested in me to accomplish the defeat of our enemies in any part of the world where our own safety demands such defeat.
>
> When the war is won, the powers under which I act automatically revert to the people — to whom they belong.[10]

Long before this, President Roosevelt had established more than forty executive agencies (for example, the Board of Economic Warfare and the War Production Board, with extremely important functions) without previous authorization from Congress. Woodrow Wilson had done much the same at the beginning of World War I. (The power to decide the disposition of the armed forces is justified under the authority of the President as Commander in Chief, a separate source of presidential authority. We may grant that someone in a government must be able to undertake emergency measures of this kind when the nation's safety demands it.) [11] But we must immediately ask, Should it be permitted to one man, no matter how intensely he may feel his responsibility, to make such decisions? And the question that follows immediately is, Has any one man the conviction, the ability, the courage, and the sensitivity to be able in such emergencies to make the right decision at the right time? Is it safe to rely on the mind and character of a single man? Ought not the President be a *body* of men, not one man in one body? Would that not be a safer bet for a modern nation subject to sudden attack, or the presage of one, by nuclear weapons? The nature of the danger dictates the nature of the responsibility needed to cope with it: is it prudent to leave it to one man?

The second instance of portentous presidential action occurred in April, 1952. It represented a clash between President Truman's intervention in labor disputes and an equally important need to make certain that military supplies for our troops in Korea would not be jeopardized by a threatened steel strike. The Taft-Hartley Act, vetoed by President Truman but passed by Congress over his objections, enabled the Attorney General to ask the courts to enjoin strikes or lockouts that were deemed to "imperil the national health and safety." The Secretary of Commerce was ready to seize the steel mills under presidential order. President Truman justified the order by citing the requirements of national security, the aid due America's allies, and "the authority vested in me by the Constitution and the laws of the United States." The steel mill owners took the issue to the Supreme Court. The chief justices could not agree on the measure of presidential authority; three seemed to favor a wide power to deal with emergencies, even in opposition to congressional action. The reasoning of other justices was involved and unclear. The President himself claimed, rather brashly, that in a national emergency he could do "anything." Justice Felix Frankfurter, one of the dissentients, called attention to many examples of presidential seizure of industrial property in both world wars, each time without congressional authorization.

All governments grant emergency powers, usually to the executive branch. The executive is a much smaller body than the legislative, less apt to become involved in prolonged debate, is in immediate touch with events, and is in continuous session. In many countries the power to act in emergencies is concerned with domestic disorders and economic crises capable of leading to violence. The President of the United States has abundant power and funds available to take salvaging and remedial action in times of natural disorder, flood, fire, earthquake, and drought. It is most unlikely that the people of the United States, and Congress itself, would criticize the President if he took such action in the absence of specific authorization when Congress was not in session; indeed, he would be blamed if he did not.

In the course of the decision which ruled on government seizure of the steel plants, the three justices in the minority quoted with approval an argument advanced in 1915 when the Supreme Court sustained the power of the President (Wilson) to withdraw land from the public domain, contrary to congressional statute:

> The function of making laws is peculiar to Congress, and the Executive cannot exercise that function to any degree. But this is not to say that all of the subjects concerning which laws might be made are perforce removed from the possibility of Executive influence. The Executive may act upon things and upon men in many relations which have not, though they might have, been actually regulated by Congress. In other words, just as there are fields which are peculiar to Congress and fields which are peculiar to the Executive, so there are fields which are common to both, in the sense that the Executive may move within them until they shall have been occupied by legislation. . . .
>
> This situation results from the fact that the President is the active agent, not of Congress, but of the Nation. . . . He is the agent of the people of the United States, deriving all his power from them and responsible directly to them. In no sense is he the agent of Congress. . . . Therefore it follows that in ways short of making laws and disobeying them, the Executive may be under a grave constitutional duty for the national protection in situations not covered by the acts of Congress, and in which, even, it may not be said that his action is the direct expression of any particular one of the independent powers which are granted to him specifically by the Constitution. Instances wherein the President has felt and fulfilled such a duty have not been rare in our history

though, being for the public benefit and approval of all, his acts have seldom been challenged in the courts.[12]

Two observations must be made on these episodes. Even if the Supreme Court is not today in the decided majority in a positive assertion of the presidential power so used and so claimed, it has been so in the past and is not now unanimously against it. And when the emergency that comes is of such nature that the court approves in substance the President's action, it is most likely to find some element of the Constitution that will justify it.

The Rescue-facient Function

Government cannot bear a vacuum of leadership-power when it is necessary that it be filled. Some federal institutions will rush to the rescue, or attempt to do so. Indeed, let us raise this idea to the dignity of a law of political science: In every form of government, whenever one of its institutions vested with certain responsibilities of significance fails to exercise them, a contiguous institution will interpret its powers or invent new ones in a "leadership-rescue" operation. This can be called the rescue-facient function. It does not follow that it will do so in time, or with minimum expense, or cleverly; for success depends upon the relationship of the institutions as established and their working habits and degree of co-operation as well as upon the men in office at the moment.

It is important to realize that the Constitution is singularly weak in provision for the rescue-facient function. The reasons why are involved in the separation of powers, in spite of such arrangements as the veto, senatorial confirmations, and so on, for there the founders of the Republic dug a chasm. Although the President is equipped to undertake the rescue of the nation if Congress fails in leadership, Congress and the political parties are far too poorly organized and too loosely motivated to rescue an inept President, above all — above all — from his sins of omission. The nation, alas, has been taught by Congress itself to distrust, if not to despise, Congress; the nation has learned to look for salvation to the President. But if he proves to be inept, where then shall they turn?

One final point on emergency action by the Chief Executive: It has been observed by Lucius Wilmerding, in a brilliant article on the steel seizure case, that it is imprudent to attempt to find in the Constitution itself such undefined power as President Truman claimed to have. It is more prudent, Wilmerding claims, to admit that the Constitution does not give such power and acknowledge that in an emergency the President, according to his judgment, will take what action seems necessary. According to the classic interpretation of English constitutional law, the puissant ancestor of American public law, after the event the President's action will (or will not) be validated by an act of indemnity passed by Congress.[13] Whether this is the more prudent course, the growing recognition of the enormous potential power of the President is worthy of note, even when, as in James Burnham's *Congress and the American Tradition*, it is lamented in a dirge of sonorous conservatism.[14]

If the lament has any validity it derives from a source which I respect, though perhaps Professor Burnham would make light of it: the foreboding that to allow such a potential in the hands of one man cannot be justified either by a principle of efficiency or by one of popular responsibility. The solitary President is all-too-possibly an instrument of future disaster — by what he does not do in time, because he does not sense an emergency in time, because he acts hastily when no emergency exists, or by fumbling the act itself. We are, unfairly, demanding too much of one mortal; and so did the founders of the Republic.

The President as Chief Legislator

Is not "Chief Legislator" an extraordinary designation for the President, even as merely one among others, when the most striking merit attributed to the American system of government, the one that most proudly distinguishes it from other democracies, is the separation of powers?[15] The reflection is particularly pertinent since there are many scholars and politicians who extol Congress as the chief vehicle of American government — and plead that it ought to continue to be so. There is no mistaking the founders' intention: Congress must be the one and only agency for the making of law. It was hardly necessary to argue the justification of this; their arguments were addressed, rather, to the contingency that Congress might exceed its province than that others might attempt to usurp its authority. The justification lay in all the centuries of the rise and ultimate assertion of triumph, indeed, the sovereignty, of Parliament in the English government, of which that generation was so recently a part. The President was to be allowed a role in the legislative process through three instruments. One was the duty to "give to the Congress Information of the State of the Union, and recommend to their Consideration such Measures as he shall judge necessary and expedient. . . ." The word "measures" does not mean, necessarily, drafts of legislation or even ideas for such; it may mean simply proposals of any kind of policy; it could mean, or be taken to mean, legislative proposals. (In the first year of President Washington's term of office, he drafted a bill for a national militia. The bill was to be used by the Secretary of War as the basis of a draft to be presented to Congress.) We shall see what an opportunity for power this provision becomes in the hands of a President who is a man of conviction and courage or falls into the hands of experienced and astute politicians.

To this power let me add two specific variations of such recommendatory power, both instituted by statute of Congress: The President, by law, must send Congress a budget message and an economic report at the beginning of each congressional session. For the President these opportunities become fertile conveyors of projects for legislation. Is it not striking that Congress itself should have required the President to take the lead in two vast domains of legislation by the Budget and Accounting Act of 1921 and the Employment Act of 1946? Is it not equally remarkable that both of these acts were recommended by the President in office at the time, the first by Taft (adopted by Woodrow Wilson, and passed during Harding's term), the second by Franklin Roosevelt (and passed in Truman's first year in office)? The voice was the voice of the President, but the votes were the votes of Congress. (The Employment Act was the brain child of Senator Wagner and his friends, but they conceded the initiative to the President.) The power of recommendation is an open, stimulating, and generative power of presidential leadership.

The second instrument the President is given to influence legislation is the power to veto laws passed by Congress. To override the President's veto, Congress must obtain a two-thirds majority. The veto well-serves the purpose for which it seems to have been intended — to defend the President in the independent use of his constitutional powers. It has become mightier still when it is used to enforce the President's legislative policy, to strike down what he does not like in congressional answers to national problems, and to maneuver into law the solutions he prefers — a power enabling him to dominate his opponents in Congress and to sustain the proposals of his friends. He can make congressmen tremble by his use of the veto, as Eisenhower subdued a Democratic Congress in 1958–59, a Congress elected by the voters against the President's own wishes, policies, or understanding.[16] More, the President can force them to their knees, though, under the authority of the Constitution, they were sent to Congress to be the legislators of the will of the people.

Third, the President may call Congress into special session; he can "put it on the spot," as Franklin Roosevelt did in September, 1939, in an attempt to revise the Neutrality Act, or as Truman did in July, 1948, to try to force Congress to legislate the platform of the Republican party recently adopted.

What impelled the founders of the Republic to give these powers to the President? The power to recommend measures seems an imitation of the only quasi-democratic system they knew, the royal power of the British Crown to address Parliament on the state of the nation, a power of recommendation manipulated, at least in part, by the king's ministers. Second, it was believed by one or more of the members of the Constitutional Convention that the central position of the President in the conduct of everyday affairs would enable him to "bring into focus" a consistent plan based on the deliberations of Congress. This is surely one of the reasons why the President's power of recommendation has become so powerful. He is at the point of focus, whereas the legislators have no constant bonds with the multidepartmental process of everyday administration or with the set supradepartmental principles common to all.

I have referred to the political principle, *rescue-facient* — when one agency of government abdicates in principle or in fact, another tends to assume its functions. It is clear that Congress has most serious deficiencies as a legislative body; the members of Congress are representatives of districts and states rather than of the nation; nor have congressmen established bonds of policy among themselves, giving them coherence in the making of law. Furthermore, Congress is riven by committees, each with its own concerns and hardly amenable to unified deliberation, making it most unlikely that Congress will act as a single whole. We have witnessed the frenzied, paroxysmal attention given to far more business than the legislators can assimilate and master. Congress has become a scuffle of local interests, dominated by conservatives, not of responsibile philosophy but of local appetites, often unable to attain a majority to enact urgently needed laws, each member hopeful of being returned again and again to a seat. Congress ought to be our supreme legislative body, but it has given up this responsibility because it has failed to establish integrated leadership, an agenda-enacting body, an agenda-enforcing body, with foresight, a reasonable response to the exigencies of time and the priority of measures, and a system of considered and open debate. It is being relegated, by its own fecklessness, to the position of a chamber of revision, a second chamber, to act upon or delay presidential legislation, when it is not agitating for those hundreds of small (often private) bills which confer benefits on individuals and pork-barrel tidbits on cities, counties, and states, and bills which cater to pressure groups, of which no congressman need be proud.

The President's power to legislate — it can be put in those terms — has come about because the President is the one man, call him the one institution, elected by the entire nation. Because he appeals for office to the electorate, he is obliged to promise the voters something. His promises cannot be inordinately vague, for his rivals inside and outside his own party force him to make some fairly definite commitments. If he desires a second term he must be able to show that he attempted to keep his promises. (Every able President desires a second term — if only, in the words of Woodrow Wilson, because "There is still so much that remains to be done.")

The President does not fight an election alone; he is the nominee of a political party, and that party is the vote-catching apparatus that insures his victory. The party has a past and it hopes to have a future as well as a happy present in Congress and a share in the "spoils." Much as it might like to, a political party cannot hedge on every plank of its platform. Nor can a

President-to-be move toward the office without a modicum of expressed convictions, though some have arrived with precious little, whether through sheer lack of character, like President Warren G. Harding, or from careers that leave them political illiterates if national heroes, like President Ulysses S. Grant.

Among American Presidents have been men with intense convictions regarding social, economic, and moral right and wrong. I do not mean a collection of common prejudices, which, to my disgust, is sometimes labeled "the President's philosophy of government." I mean well-considered, well-cogitated ideals of national progress such as those cherished by Washington, Jefferson, Jackson, Lincoln, Cleveland, Theodore Roosevelt, Woodrow Wilson, Franklin Roosevelt (to a surprising degree), and his successor, Harry Truman, or, on the conservative side, the Adamses, McKinley, Taft, and Hoover. They were statesmen and leaders; the terms are not always apposite. They had convictions for the national welfare, the nation's survival, and a policy of civil rights. In the American system of government it is as likely for one man to have such a cogent and comprehensive national policy as for Congress to have it; indeed, it is easier and much more likely. It is also possible that a man may be elected President who possesses no such policy and does not seek to acquire it on his own responsibility.

As legislative leader the President has a decided advantage over Congress. His status places him at the center; if he has the inclination and the conscientiousness to hear and see what is going on, what is in store for his millions of fellow citizens and his country, he has plenty of counselors at his beck and call, indeed thousands harassing him for a chance to report, warn, advise, and encourage. At every moment he can expect a telegram from a constituent in a distant state, some weeping or exultant egoist who begs this or demands that. Or there will be a cable from a foreign embassy where the security of the United States is being pondered for destruction, subversion, or preservation. Only a dead President would fail to respond (and some have had no heartbeat); and only a feeble President, with all the technical, scientific, and administrative experts at his call, would find it impossible to present a pattern of recommendations to Congress. In fact, the nation has come to expect of the President not only proposals for law and financing but a veritable program, an integrated, well-concerted set of blueprints for the nation's progress and security. It has come to expect so much from him (as it does not from Congress) because he has more political power, the power to get things done, than all the members of Congress. When important issues are at stake, congressmen look to the President for a program of legislation; and they blame him vociferously if he does not act in this wise. I asked a congressman if this were true, and the answer was yes; I asked him whether he and his colleagues minded it, and his answer was, Not at all; they preferred it. I suspected that it did not matter to him if the President took the initiative. "It takes me off the hook, after all; and I can always vote against the President's proposals; for that matter, no one need know what I decide if the decision is unpopular because I can be in at the kill without a direct vote by using some trick of procedure." Other congressmen would answer in much the same way. Most concern themselves with legislation involving the districts they represent and in most other matters expect the President to formulate and promote national policy.

Students of American government will acknowledge that the one, single legislative program that gives unity, direction, and coherence to the timetable of Congress is the program of work put before it by the President — often in the form of carefully drafted bills.

The leadership of the House and Senate is a ramshackle affair. Members are restive under the authority of the speaker and the majority and minority leaders. Party allegiance (or subordination) is very weak. Caucus decisions do not bind, and least of all those who have decided to be absent. They have their obligations to district or state; they are badgered by pressure groups at home and in Washington. When a majority leader tries to lead firmly he is assailed from all sides.

However inadequate may be this method of regulating the agenda of Congress — speaker, majority leaders, policy committees, the Rules Committee, and so on — the members of the ruling group are entitled to the nation's gratitude. Their work must be more grueling, wearing, and exasperating than that of the leaders of any other government — and I include in the comparison the burden borne by Khrushchev, who has in compensation the near-absolute power to command.

Yet the disadvantages leap to the eye. First, leadership of Congress is fragmented; there is a serious incoherence in what should be a single legislative mind. Second, to the press and to the public the tightly closed doors of the committee rooms make a mystery of congressional action. Third, the placing of bills on the statute book depends largely on the order in which the committees complete their work. If proposed legislation is not put on the calendar, the next step, the tollgate function of the Rules Committee, cannot function — nor can the House discharge rule. Hence, whatever the Rules Committee may wish to present as a steady, systematic program is disrupted by the uncoordinated pace of the several committees.

Who calls in the committee chairmen and asks what progress is being made and when there is likely to be a report? Who presses the committees to proceed or delays committee reports in accordance with a pattern set by Congress, with the interests of the nation in mind? Are the chairmen ever called to act in common council for a review of priority?

The answers to these questions allow the judgment that there is scarcely an attempt at co-ordination, though from time to time in the unrhythmic course of the session the majority leaders may undertake a census of intentions among committee chairmen.

The committee and their chairmen aggravate the fragmentation of party principle which otherwise might be a guide to legislative order and a means of assisting the public in making decisions about leaders and current measures. The opinions of these senior and prepotent leaders, the committee chairmen, *may* constitute a party policy, but they do not depend on one and they do not stem from one. They obscure the process of and reasons for the making of decisions by executive, i.e., secret, sessions, the number of committees involved in each piece of legislation, and by discouraging open debate and attendant public interest.

It is rare, indeed, when the majority leaders are successful. Alben Barkley was such a man, and so is Lyndon Johnson; but the majority leader is always on sufferance and must secure his program by personal clearance from all and sundry. The tactics used by the majority leader to achieve successful leadership remain a personal mystery in spite of many attempts at analysis. It is put down to "force of personality." If this is true, surely the implications are very serious. The best that can be said in summary of the hold a majority leader has over the rank and file of his party is this: He has a personal policy which is represented to be that of the party he represents. No party has imposed it on him; no party has adopted it, except by indirection. Whatever he believes to be possible of achievement he "sells" to those he can persuade among his colleagues and among other amenable senators, not excepting the minority leader, who may ask a concession in return. What he regards as possible is made up of his judgment of the sentiment of others, carefully polled, buttonholed, and assessed as to ultimate reliability; of his estimate of the President's influence and prestige; after examination of counterproposals, and after taking into consideration the arguments, clamor, and threats of lobbyists; and, lastly, the "mood of the people" as it is likely to affect the re-election of his friends and himself.

Is not "force of personality" a most inferior substitute for a pattern of policy and action arrived at by a sober collective process among the members of the party? If members of Congress reject party identification and loyalty, what reliability for efficient and responsible leadership can the nation ascribe to them?

Those who establish legislative programs are not amenable to public responsibility. The senators cannot call the majority leader to account once the caucus elects him, for he will regard it as an insult if the convening of another caucus is demanded. The American public has no way to call to account the majority leader, a Senator Taft, a Knowland, a Lyndon Johnson. Only elections in Texas can call the representative from Texas to account; and the electorate in that state, as is true of other states, is more concerned with how well he represents *local* interests, not the interests of the nation. This is true as well for Senator Dirksen of Illinois and was earlier true of Knowland, his predecessor as the Republican leader of the Senate. And to have it so casts a grave blemish on democracy's first principle, the answerability of the government to the governed.

It is not enough to found the legislative primacy of the President on the shortcomings of Congress and the President's own convictions of proper national policy. Economic and social conditions make it necessary for both to intervene in the affairs of the national community. These pressing responsibilities are often too much for Congress, and its members turn away from tasks which torment them. Consider how fumblingly Congress handled the labor union bills between January and August, 1959. No wonder we have scorn for that body's indecisive character.

The Nature of the Present Economy

We live in an economy that thrives upon the division of labor and the specialization of skills yet cannot survive except it learn the unification of economic objectives and processes. What do the American people want above all? A high standard of living? meaning less and less disagreeable work and more and more wealth, meaning goods and services — this is the one, majestic good.[17] America has other standards of values as well, but at this stage economic welfare is the most intense, the most overriding. A higher standard of living depends upon the government's unifying command of the division of labor, the interval between production and consumption, and the special-interest groups which are born of a system of free enterprise, as in any other form of economy, but act mare robustly in a free system. Let us consider the burden placed on government by these factors, the governmental structures that are their inevitable offspring.

Each of the millions of articles for consumption on the American market is grown, manufactured, or processed by many different skills. Self-interest demands the co-operation of many different workers in many sections of the nation. The minimum task of government is to see that the economy is not interrupted. The labor market is a single labor market; it is a national one, since the basis of American economy is the promotion of one common, unified, producing and marketing area. Problems of employment, unemployment, crisis, strikes, lockouts, the mobility of industry, the productivity of farms, the prices that farmers shall receive, the wages paid workers in commerce and industry — all these are of nationwide concern, as are the mobility of labor and capital and relief to poverty-stricken areas.[18]

The government is called upon to act as regulator of the

nation's production so that the component parts, in consumable form, may reach their destined market. In a nation so unified, Congress, by its localized representation and always homeward-looking angelicism, finds it more difficult to envisage and determine what is required than does the President. (But there is some question if even a President does, if he permits a steel strike to continue on a plea that "the free forces of collective bargaining" must be allowed to settle the terms of production in their own time.)

Second, today's economy operates by making long-term plans of production. For the processing of many important commodities it is necessary to bring together such factors as plant, ships, warehouses, machinery, machine tools, power resources and conveyors, pipelines, road, railroads, planes, and the requisite skills, a work-force, material, and credit, until the goods to be manufactured or the services to be rendered are created. From the conception of new goods and services to their final appearance on the market may take, literally, years. All elements in this process, labor, capital, banking, insurance, technical advisers, legal counsel, even the composers of curricula in training schools which produce skilled workers, require the stability of all the conditions they assume when making their production plans. They want serenity; they need calculability; they abhor uncertainty. Interruption (or long delay) leads to ruin.

Among these many elements is the value assigned money. Whether it is to rise or fall is a momentous issue of the highest policy and may enrich or impoverish all of the producers and consumers. The value of money may be made to rise or to fall — but whatever the decision, it must be the result of studied purposes and concerted means. This implies that credit facilities and currency provisions of the nation must be directed by the government for the benefit of all, and this further implies government direction of public and private institutions of banking, savings, tax-raising, federal expenditure, and so forth. This economic-credit-fiscal operation has become one of the most important functions of modern government; and to fulfil it specific statutes have imposed duties on government departments and on the President himself. To the general public it appears in the guise of a series of problems concerned with inflation, prices, rates of interest, mortgage

rates, insurance, pensions, and so on. In this respect, every in-
terest-group in the nation makes its own demands. The problem
is to establish a government policy that will satisfy each interest-
group without threatening the general social and economic welfare of the nation, a policy that will safeguard each group against
its rivals and its own shortsightedness.

Third, millions of people have identified their personal interests
with some larger entity. The public talks of "big business," "big
labor," "big agriculture." There are other vast and potent associ-
ations of interests and within them multitudes of lesser associa-
tions of crucial importance to the nation's economy. Their
immediately envisioned interests are not always harmonious. Labor and capital have their discords; agriculture is in conflict with
manufacture over prices, and the tariff protection of industry
imposes a burden on the farmers. Financiers have interests that
may cause them to invest abroad or to keep their money at home
when foreign policy would be benefited by private investment
abroad. Oil producers are at odds with coal producers, and both
with the producers of hydroelectric power. The split is vertical by
industries, horizontal by social and economic class. Each sees its
own interest, and each is blind to or minimizes the harm it may
do the rest of the nation if it persists in the demands it believes to
be justified. It may not see how these demands undermine the
total welfare of the nation. It may not see that, in the long run,
it injures itself; reprisals are sure to be taken by the victims of
these demands. A strike may bring the steelworkers more pay, but
in turn prices will rise, and once again the workers will have to
use their power to strike for higher pay to offset the rising cost
of living. And so on.

Who is expected to look at the nation as a single economic
producer and market? Who is expected to keep constantly in
mind that an egoistic economic policy results in unemployment,
a falling-off in purchases, and other links in the chain of events
that leads to a depression? Who is to make sure that the economy
expands, that its productivity rises to supply the instruments of
national defense and a constant increase in the standard of living?

Tasks like these — suggested only in the broadest outline here
— are innumerable. They have been imposed on the federal government, which has come to be focused in the President; they are

of the utmost intricacy and have about them a technical myste-
riousness that surpasses the intestinal mazes of Univac. Surrounded by scientists and technicians, the President must intervene
in time and with the necessary sensitivity to a swarm of insistent
factors crowding for consideration. He must have the boldness to
ordain what science and technology suggest to him. The consequences of error are dire; it can be, as it was in 1957–58, five
million people unemployed, inordinate inflation, and, in 1959, a
jolting strike.[19]

Democracy, acting spontaneously, is by nature inflationist.
Each group, each individual, is free to exert political power to
secure more from the economy than it can bear. Having an equal
vote, each is at liberty to overrate his contribution to the national
product. A control must be at hand to save democracy from its
most typical disease. But Congress, because it is a congeries of
local interests, is less able to serve as a control than is the President.

Special Interests and the Public Interest

This raises a very important issue in political theory and practice.
Most, if not all, of the works of the past thirty years on political
science and American government (excluding those of Merriam
and V. O. Key) have followed A. F. Bentley and his so-called
group theory of political process.[20] Broadly speaking, Bentley and
his epigoni declare that the making and administration of law
in the United States are nothing but the peace terms arrived at
by groups in conflict; that the national or public interest in this
respect consists (and ought to consist) of nothing but the com-
mon-denominator policy of the warring groups, arrived at according to the associated power and cunning of the population
which these groups represent.[21] Of course this is a gross error
of both science and morality, even if special-interest groups in
the United States do enjoy more power over policy than groups
in other nations, democratic or otherwise. The Bentleyists have
allowed their insight to be dimmed by their discovery of the facts
of life inside pressure groups, and they have not penetrated far
enough inside to arrive at an understanding of motivation.

Yet, almost in the same breath, groupists will laud the President for entering the conflict — as the sole representative of the

"nation as a whole," as the indicator of the "nation's interest," of the "public interest" opposed to that of special-interest groups, whether they operate through Congress or, more directly, by exerting pressure on the departments or even on the White House itself. But if the special-interest groups are decisive in the making of policy, if all politics is but conflict and peace negotiations among rival groups, then what function are they ascribing to the President? They do not exploit the fact that he receives his authority from another distinct group with a different mentality, a different purpose, a different loyalty; it is the nation itself, a corporate body *unlike* any of its parts, separable — and separated in the mind of the voter — from the myriad private interests that form it.

Millions do not belong to an organized group; millions belong only formally; some hate their own groups; millions maintain a concept of national interest that automatically subordinates their own group; and millions are prepared to listen to a concept of national community as a present and continuing entity.

Once in office the President is in a fairly independent frame of mind. Each situation requires that he listen to the demands of special groups; but it also gives him a chance to sound his own convictions, come to terms with the technical considerations put before him by his advisers, most of whom are not, I repeat, are not, pleading for special-interest groups. The President's advisers take a long view of the economy, of the moral problems of society, of health needs, of conservation needs, and of the problem of poverty, a view that is also expected of an able President. The long view is not the common denominator of contending groups, which generally make only minimum concessions to each other. Of course, how effective the presidential impress is depends on whether he has the attributes of leadership, the convictions, and the conscientiousness. He himself, or his advisers, may be the witting or unwitting champion of a special-interest group. Some Presidents have had convictions, that is, principles of statesmanship and a vision of what the government should do for the progress, welfare, and defense of the nation, of what is to be upheld and what is to be subordinate or suppressed — for example, the New Deal, the New Freedom, the Fair Deal, or even the laissez-faire convictions which inspired Hoover's vetoing of the TVA bills. Other Presidents have been empty-headed, empty-hearted, and utterly lacking in the attributes necessary for the office.

It is the President, as I shall demonstrate, who assists significantly in setting standards of right and wrong by legislation or policy decisions conceived in the nation's name and pressed on the nation, in his capacity as Chief of State, or, as the French would say, the "moral magistracy" of the nation.

The Legislative Program and the Veto

The President, as I have said, leads the process of legislation and dominates the timetable of Congress by his recommendations. These are made in his annual message on the state of the Union, in the budget message, and in the economic report. The first is a general program of lawmaking and is backed up by drafts of proposed laws. The second is financial legislation, appropriating money to each of the many activities of government. The third is a comprehensive account of the nation's economy, with proposals for dealing with its problems, backed by legislative proposals or a statement of intention to use already existing agencies to carry out the proper policies. The statute, the (full) Employment Act of 1946, which imposed this duty on the President and his council of economic advisers, requires that Congress form a joint committee on the economic report. And there are, when necessary, many special presidential messages.

In 1950, during the Eighty-first Congress, a lean year for President Truman, he proposed eighty-six laws; Congress passed thirty-eight, rejected ten, and took partial action on thirty. Some administrative proposals were ignored (for example, mandatory price supports, the Brannan farm plan, unemployment insurance improvements, scholarships for higher education, extension of the authority of the Federal Reserve Board, creation of a Columbia Valley Administration, and extension of time limits on RFC loans). Other proposals were passed (expansion of school construction aid, establishment of the National Science Foundation, expansion of social security benefits and coverage, housing for middle-income groups, continuation of the European Recovery Program, the extension of Selective Service, restoration of the Federal Reserve Board's consumer credit controls).

Let us pass to 1958, a good year for President Eisenhower, a year of depression, international tension, and November elections. He specifically asked for 234 bills. In 109 cases (46.6 per cent), Congress enacted legislation, and he signed the bills. Forty-one requests received no action at all, and fifty-nine were treated unfavorably. The rest received some support but did not result in decisive action. Among the laws asked for and passed were several concerning farm supports, several bringing financial aid to higher education and strengthening the teaching of science, others increasing loan funds for housing, extending the number of weeks in which the unemployed could draw compensation, providing measures for state civil defense, extending the Reciprocal Trade Agreements acts, several statutes concerning the improvement of the organization of the Department of Defense, the establishment of a Federal Aviation Agency to incorporate the CAA and the Airways Modernization Board, and a bill granting statehood to Hawaii. Besides these weighty initiatives from the White House, there were the policies embodied in the appropriations bills and foreign treaties, and foreign and civil and military aid, almost all of which emanated from the President and were passed *in toto*, if not always in the form demanded.[22]

The years we have given are recent. But the legislative leadership of the President goes back many years, and took on most substantial significance in the 1880's. Lawrence Chamberlain has shown that of the ninety most important federal laws passed between 1870 and 1945, 20 per cent were originated and carried through at presidential insistence, 30 per cent by joint presidential-congressional initiation and effectuation, 40 per cent were mainly congressional products, and 10 per cent were fashioned chiefly by pressure groups.[23] Presidential legislation of this magnitude is a most impressive index of the President's responsibility, authority, and effectiveness. It is noteworthy that half of the laws initiated by the President alone were of Franklin Roosevelt's making and more than a third of the twenty-nine statutes initiated jointly by the President and Congress were enacted during Roosevelt's tenure. Of the thirty-five statutes initiated by Congress, only two were passed during Roosevelt's terms in office. The laws passed under the influence of American Presidents include one or more in the categories of agriculture, banking, business, credit, labor, national defense, natural resources, and tariffs.

With most Presidents, the fulfillment of the self-assumed task of Chief Legislator does not stop with the proposal of bills but involves protracted and sometimes agonizing political battles. We return to this responsibility of the President after consideration of his power to veto congressional bills.

The veto was established to enable the Chief Executive to protect his own sphere of authority from invasion by Congress. It was thus conducive to his defense of the constitutional distribution of powers. But, far less specifically, in terms as ill-defined as those governing "executive power," it provided for the participation of the President in congressional formation of policy on the grounds of legislative prudence. It did not elaborate, nor did subsequent debates, on how the President was to use the power of the veto in his attempts to influence Congress, his authority to say *No!* as the tool of power, the *ultima ratio regnum*, a phrase Alexander Hamilton might have relished. Indeed, Hamilton's defense of the qualified negative includes the (politically cautious) argument that it furnishes an "additional security against the enaction of improper laws," and is "calculated to guard the community against the effects of faction, precipitancy, or of any impulse unfriendly to the public good, which may happen to influence a majority of that body." How well President Eisenhower used these objurgations when he claimed the veto to thwart the "spenders" and those who voted expenditures on housing that would allegedly result in inflation![24]

Some of the founders of the Republic proposed that the veto should not be applicable to revenue bills; others did not want the veto to apply to private bills, which were deemed insignificant; but no limitations to the veto were set. Of course, the force of the veto is limited by the fact that Congress may override the veto by a two-thirds vote of both houses. Only in this sense is it a qualified veto.

President Washington once used the veto on constitutional grounds and once on the prudence of a bill. The veto was not exercised by Adams or by Jefferson. Madison applied the veto six times, four on constitutional grounds and two on grounds of policy. From Washington's assumption of the Presidency through Lincoln's time in office, only forty-eight vetoes were exercised. The vetoes were generally on constitutional or technical grounds. Jackson was the first President to veto bills because he disagreed with the policy they embodied. He was a man of considered convictions and took a creative view of presidential responsibility. His first veto message (May, 1830) was of the Maysville Road bill, which asked federal appropriations to help build a road entirely within the boundaries of the state of Kentucky. Jackson reasoned that the proposed road was not to serve the "general welfare," nor could it even be considered a statewide utility; if such a use of federal moneys was to be sanctioned, an amendment to the Constitution ought to say so clearly. His veto (July, 1832) of the Bank of the United States Renewal bill was of even more moment from a standpoint of economic and social policy, and here Congress attempted unsuccessfully to override the presidential veto. In his eight years in office, Jackson vetoed twelve bills.

Thereafter, the use of the veto increased in number and significance. Grover Cleveland vetoed, as did other Presidents, a number of private bills. Ordinarily, they did not represent presidential intervention in major policy, though Cleveland did veto pensions for Civil War veterans in order to stop raids on the Treasury.

With Theodore Roosevelt's term in office the veto became a major instrument of policy in the hands of the President. Only President Harding seemed reluctant to use it. Of 2,264 bills of "public significance," Theodore Roosevelt vetoed one in 98; of 1,148, Taft vetoed one in 328 (i.e., only two vetoes while in office); of 2,764, Calvin Coolidge vetoed one in 84; of 2,827, Franklin Roosevelt vetoed one in every 12; of 1,553 bills, Hoover vetoed one in 55. Truman and Eisenhower have continued to make major use of the veto as an act of high legislative policy. Truman, for example, vetoed the Taft-Hartley bill, but his veto was overridden by Congress.[25]

How does the President apply the veto? The crudest exercise of power is a plain refusal to sign a bill, with the expectation that Congress will not be able to muster a two-thirds majority or will not try to do so. (Here we do not consider the pocket veto that causes a bill to die when Congress is not in session.) Generally, the President's veto is successful in more than nine cases out of ten. The President can express his objections in this way against his own party when it has less than a two-thirds majority in Congress. He can have his own way even where there is a substantial majority of the party opposed to him, provided they do not obtain a two-thirds majority (which is extremely rare), and provided that, as in the tenure of President Eisenhower, the Democrats lose their southern contingent to the Republicans. Nothing illustrates the case so well as the plight of the Democrats from January, 1959, to August, 1960. In spite of a majority victory — 258 to 153 in the House, and 62 to 34 in the Senate — in the November, 1958, elections, the President could not explain to himself why, having won a ten million plurality in 1956, he had been given such an electoral setback. He need not have complained. He was able to defeat Congress time and again by using the veto. He was not overridden, because his policies were pleasing to southern Democrats as well as to the main body of Republicans. The Democratic party lacked unity — indeed, was not truly one party. And without an aggressive opposition, Eisenhower's veto could not be challenged and broken.

The exploitation of the power of veto is either crude or subtle, as the President decides. If he is served by astute minority or majority leaders, for example, Halleck in the House, Dirksen in the Senate, men of much guile, tactical astuteness, and extreme obstinacy, the President can have his own way on some legislation. Imagine the glee of such men, formerly minor entities in Congress, suddenly raised to dizzying heights above the majority party by their use of the President's power to veto. The President can let it be known, and he does, brusquely or subtly, that there are bills or sections of bills he will not tolerate; in turn, congressional leaders may suggest acceptable alternates. The President is able to whittle down the original intentions of Congress. The leaders agree to concessions, not wishing to have nothing at all. But even so, the President may veto the compromise they have arrived at; or veto the original bill if there is no compromise. It depends on the talking strength he has with the public and his ability to present general policies as a crusade. This was a part of the strength of President Eisenhower in 1959. His announced mission was to fight inflation. It was a most popular "crusade," as politically powerful as is the offer of jobs in a time of mass unemployment. Of pervading influence is the President's threat to veto public works and rivers and harbors bills (Eisenhower used it three times, 1959), for these are political plums a district expects its congressmen and senators to bring home.[26]

The President's counterpolicy, his positive alternative to congressional leadership, is embodied in his veto message, instituted by the Constitution that requires him to explain his objections if he withholds his approval of a bill passed by Congress. The President's rejoinder can become an instrument of policy. Sometimes Congress amends its original proposal in order to satisfy him. In any case, his objections can be stated in a form useful in arousing public opinion against specific legislation. President Franklin Roosevelt made of this a fine art; President Truman practiced it; and the militant and vituperative tone that a President gives to such objections can be seen in Eisenhower's veto of the housing bill of July, 1959. To that bill, vetoed twice after congressional concessions, a counterpolicy was proposed; in the vetoes of the farm acreage and price-support bills for wheat and tobacco of June, 1959, again counterpolicies were proposed. The *New York Times* called attention to Eisenhower's "blistering attacks" on congressional legislation.

Sometimes the President agrees to approve a bill he might otherwise veto on a promise from congressional leaders that they will amend the bill to answer his objections. Thus, in August, 1959, Eisenhower signed a bill giving the TVA right to finance itself by the further issue of bonds (some $750 million), thus avoiding federal appropriations. But, as drafted, the bill appeared to be giving the TVA freedom from congressional and executive control, and the President let it be known that unless the bill was amended he would exercise his veto. In his message to Congress, Eisenhower described the financial devices the bill contained as

> a clear invasion of the prerogatives of the Chief Executive. It attempts to divorce TVA's construction program of new power-producing projects from effective executive review and allows Congress to modify the authority's program without regard to the views of the President and without opportunity for the President to exercise his constitutional role in the legislative project.

Eisenhower was assured by the leaders of both parties in both Houses that "legislation will be passed swiftly . . . deleting this objectionable feature." And the bill was signed, said the President, "in accordance with that understanding."

As a rule, the Chief Executive is far from unaware of the constructive power of his veto, and many have taken advantage of it, with occasional expressions of regret at assailing the power of Congress. In his second annual message, Jackson apologized for

> exercising the undoubted right of the Executive to withhold his assent from bills on other than constitutional grounds. It is only in matters of deep interest, when the principle involved may be justly regarded as next in importance to infractions of the Constitution itself, that such a step can be expected to meet with the approbation of the people.

Jackson's awareness of his responsibility to, and the need for, a mandate from "the people" is of the highest political importance, and we shall return to it.

In his *Memoirs*, President Truman explains his use of the veto. He speaks of it apropos of his veto of the 1952 bill transferring rights to offshore oil resources to Texas, Louisiana, and California. Earlier, he had vetoed such legislative measures as the Taft-Hartley Bill, the Kerr Bill, which exempted independent gas producers from price-fixing by the FPC, an internal security bill he thought unjust to public officials, the McCarran-Walter Bill restricting immigration and several tax bills.

> I have never hesitated to veto any bill presented to me when I was convinced that it failed to serve the best interests of the majority of the people in all parts of the country. I found it necessary to veto more major bills than any other President, with the possible exception of Grover Cleveland. . . .
>
> The veto power of the President is one of the most important instruments of his authority, even though the legislation he rejects may later be passed over his veto. In the veto message the Chief Executive has an opportunity to set forth clearly and in detail before the nation the policies of his administration. I always gave more studied attention to the messages which accompanied my disapproval of

congressional legislation than to any other White House pronouncements.[27]

When President Eisenhower was twitted by press correspondents in July, 1959, for his use of the veto, and the phrase "government by veto" was used against him, he claimed that he was thinking of the public good, not the image the public might form of him; since he planned to retire in 1961, and could not be elected again, he had no need to consult political ambition. "So the veto is used by me not lightly. I don't enjoy having to say that these things are bad and to explain the reasons why I think they are bad. What I am trying to do is to get legislation passed that will benefit the United States and keep us solvent at the same time." No doubt parts of his statement were either disingenuous or very innocent. To obtain re-election is not the only reason a man may exercise the veto in a manner so uncharacteristically savage. There is an intoxication in being possessed of power for which one need not answer to the electorate, and one may yearn for the favorable judgment of history. And, as with Eisenhower in 1959, a President may crave credit for having rendered his party a service.

The President has a most potent instrument of legislative leadership and domination in the right to veto. If the President uses it entirely in accordance with his own personal choices and without the advice and moderation of others, it is an inordinate, scarcely justifiable, concentration of power. If it is used on the advice of others, the President's cabinet, say, or the private "kitchen cabinet," it is no more justifiable, less perhaps, for the President's advisers are not subject to electoral influence and are not held accountable if they should offer incompetent counsel.

The President and Congress

Although the legislative role of the President is a powerful one, he is very much at Congress' mercy. He cannot pass a law. He may propose, but it alone disposes. The President has available some effective means of pressing a reluctant Congress to dispose in a fashion not entirely displeasing to him, and he must use those means to gain what he has set his heart on. Congress is a potent and restive body, each house is proud, sometimes arrogant and interfering, especially when, as has happened frequently, the majority is opposed to the President, or when his own party is split in its support of him. Yes, Congress is the President's major torment, and with Congress the President must contend. If poets are the unacknowledged legislators of mankind, Presidents have immortal longings to be the acknowledged legislators. Congress offers them little help.

It could hardly have been a moment of keen pleasure when Senator Borah assured President Franklin Roosevelt that "All this hysteria is manufactured and artificial," and at a time when, with Hitler on the march, Roosevelt was anxious to repeal or amend the embargo clauses of the Neutrality Act in the summer of 1939. Then the President had to hear from Garner the sad result of a census of opinion taken in Congress: "Well, Captain, we may as well face the facts. You haven't got the votes; and that's all there is to it!" For the President knew, and was in a better position than Congress to know, America's peril.

Truman put much of his spirit and a great deal of his time into farm legislation, the Brannan plan, only to have it rejected by a Congress manned in both houses by his own party. The same Congress included in appropriations bills riders which gave heads of departments the power to discharge public officials on grounds of security and without right of appeal. Truman attempted to settle the issue by further legislation, but Congress repudiated his reasonable measure for the far more extreme Internal Security Act. Truman vetoed the bill, and within twenty-four hours Congress had overriden his veto. Republican congressmen continued their assault upon the Secretary of State, Dean Acheson, without offering a temperate, just, and concerted alternative to his policies or his person. Truman's *Memoirs* are a long record of his harrowing experiences with Congress.

As President Eisenhower ruefully confessed, when asked whether he found time for occasional visits with Rayburn and Johnson, the two leaders in a Democratic Congress:

> Now, so far as I know, there has been no damage to the personal relations between the three of us, and therefore there is no reason why we shouldn't have personal meetings. Now, when it comes down to the relations of any President

with a Congress controlled by the opposite party, I just say this — it is no bed of roses.

At which there was much laughter.

This was, perhaps, Eisenhower's only truly personal observation in seven years of office, for once pungent and with a smarting sense of experienced reality. And other Presidents would subscribe to Eisenhower's statement. So bitter were the relations between Franklin Roosevelt and Congress that he declared on one occasion that he wished he could turn loose sixteen lions on Congress (this at a time when his *own* party was in control). When someone asked whether the lions might make a mistake, Roosevelt replied, "Not if they stayed there long enough."

If the President can influence Congress by threatening the veto, the mood of Congress can influence the President's messages. Nothing is gained by proposing laws in a form Congress will not pass, unless the President is prepared for a wearing battle which may well be unsuccessful. When the President confronts Congress he is apt to regard himself as the champion of the nation against representatives of special-interest groups, a habit of mind which will not make him popular with Congress, no matter how it may be expressed. President Truman's viewpoint may be summed up in these words:

> The vast majority of the people have no such organized voice speaking for them. It is only the President who is responsible to all the people. He alone has no sectional, no occupational, no economic ties. If anyone is to speak for the people, it has to be the President.[28]

It is hard to estimate the amount of time the President gives to this wearing relationship with Congress. Woodrow Wilson was estimated to have spent at least three hours a week talking with congressmen, but this does not begin to measure the continuing, nagging preoccupation with tactics, the weight upon the President's conscience, the necessity of persisting in his own intentions while calculating congressional reaction, the planning of legislation in terms most apt to gain congressional approval, and sensing when he must "crack the whip" and when devise stratagems or offer inducements.

To emphasize the intellectual, physical, and spiritual travail of a leader with convictions about the public good, I can adduce Franklin Roosevelt's fight for the reform of the Supreme Court; his struggle to assist anti-Franco forces during the Spanish Civil War; his failure to convince Congress in 1938 to lift the embargo on arms to Spain because Democratic congressmen declared that to do so would lose the Catholic vote in the fall elections. And there are other examples. Roosevelt had to face the opposition of younger New Deal congressmen after 1936 when his policies were supported only by the older generation of Democrats. Above all, considering the drain on time and energies, Roosevelt's efforts on behalf of the Wages and Hours Bill of 1938 (the Fair Labor Standards Act). To this he devoted twelve months of hard labor, only to have it mutilated and emasculated by Congress at a time when both houses were 80 per cent Democrat — surely this illustrates the thanklessness of the President's task.[29] Roosevelt had hoped that such a bill would unite his party by healing the wounds caused by his court reform bill; instead, the earlier squabble made the passing of the labor bill more difficult. Congress and the White House were beset as never before by business and labor lobbies. Congressional committees poked holes in the bill. In the Senate the bill was saved from recommittal by a slim margin, 48 to 36. Certain industries claimed legal exemption from the minima and the maxima. The House played ducks and drakes with the President's proposal; the southern Democrats who controlled the Rules Committee were especially obstructive. Liberal congressmen could not get the committee to act; the supporters necessary to hold a caucus "skulked," in the words of John L. Lewis, "in hallways and closets." The bill failed. The President called a special session of Congress, mobilized the public by "fireside chats," and devised new strategy with the House majority leader John McCormack and the chairman of the Rules Committee. Because of the stubbornness of southern Democrats it was necessary to gather 218 signatures before the bill could be discharged from the committee. The President had to use every trick he knew to procure the signatures. Agricultural legislation was traded for the votes of the farm bloc. About eight months after the bill had been introduced, and many months after it had been drafted, the 218 signatures were at hand.

At this point a rival bill, inspired by the AF of L, was introduced. Procedural maneuvers were attempted to give one precedence over the other on the floor. One bill was defeated, the other was gutted before it reached a vote. The lobbies were utterly selfish and venomous and wielded all their tools of crafty obstruction, including a well-financed campaign to make the farmers believe that such a bill would increase their labor costs and the prices of manufactured goods. Together the southern Democrats and friends of the AF of L disemboweled the proposed legislation.

The President would not give up his fight. He negotiated at a distance and sometimes at close quarters with the farm bloc and the AF of L and the obstructionists in Congress. The bill was redrafted by the Department of Labor. Another subcommittee in the House undertook to find a fresh compromise bill. In April, 1938, the bill was drafted, with the President's approval. Dilatory action by the House Labor Committee forced the President to accept the AF of L draft and to introduce into it as many of his own ideas as possible. Now the Rules Committee balked. Tom Corcoran, an aid to the President, found $10,000 of private money to assist the primary election of Senator Pepper of Florida, in return for which Pepper agreed to speak in favor of the bill to head off southern opposition. In May, 1938, the House bill passed. It took another three weeks before the conference committee was able to reconcile the Senate and the House bills.

The success, limited as it was, was an immense relief to the President. Why? He had a policy, he had commitments, he had convictions of social progress; perhaps even a wish for a third term. He undertook a most grueling experience with amazing valor and tenacity, and conceded a certain measure of defeat because Congress so disposed. The President conceded that it could take two years for the forty-cent minimum and the forty-hour-week maximum to be reached. Exemptions would be sought for many industries, and to satisfy the southern states the administrators of the statute had been given the discretion to allow differential minima to meet regional standards. The demand of the AF of L that wage rates not be set below those already prevailing was also allowed.

I undertook this short and, alas, imperfect sketch of long

months of travail to suggest what a President must go through if he is a creative legislative leader. Yes, the office is no bed of roses, but a man is not forced to seek it.

In drafting and implementing his legislative policy, the Presidents have relied on suggestions from some members of the cabinet, their "kitchen cabinet," and certain trusted public officials. For example, in questions of labor legislation President Wilson depended upon the experience of Louis D. Brandeis, afterwards a justice of the Supreme Court. The "brains trust" around Franklin Roosevelt, expert draftsmen some of them, had the help of the heads of departments and their staffs.

A central clearance of administration proposals for legislation began rather tentatively in late 1921, a function of the powers of the Bureau of the Budget established by the Budget and Accounting Act of that year.[30] Proposals demanding financial appropriations were to be cleared through the bureau, and officials called to testify before Congress were to clear with the bureau. Under Harding, the department chiefs, especially the cabinet members, sabotaged the operation. Under Coolidge, the focusing function of the bureau was resumed with some energy, for Coolidge was a small-minded President whose creed was "economy and more economy." There are small-minded Presidents, and this is their approach. There are no-minded Presidents, as Harding, and they have no approach at all. There are great-minded Presidents, as Franklin Roosevelt, who in his first term introduced a new and creative role for the bureau. Roosevelt created an emergency council to make recommendations for lawmaking in accordance with legislative policy. In addition, the bureau's legislative reference office assembled the comments on proposed legislation of all departments concerned to facilitate study of such measures as they reached the President's desk. In 1937–38, many functions, including information on legislation of all kinds, financial and otherwise, came to be concentrated in the bureau, and the head of the legislative reference section became one of the most important of government officials, with entree to the White House. Under President Truman and President Eisenhower the procedure and routing of proposed legislation the President is to present to Congress became more tautly organized and a greater number of authorities consulted for suggestions. Still, let it not be forgotten, it is the President on whom these processes focus, it is the President who bears sole responsibility for choosing legislation.

Present procedures are of comparatively recent innovation:

> The elaborate paraphernalia of a comprehensive and specific inventory, contents settled and defined as regards substance no less than finance, *presented in detailed fashion and packaged form at the opening of each session of Congress* — this was a "custom" scarcely nine years old, a postwar phenomenon evolving under Truman and now carried further under Eisenhower.[31]

The Bureau of the Budget, vested with responsibility for the formation of the federal budget, asks each department to describe its legislative program at the beginning of each calendar year. The bureau is in touch with the President when he is preparing his state of the Union message, and the White House staff sees that contacts with the bureau, the cabinet, and department heads are made at the right time.

Indeed, months before the beginning of the calendar year the assistants at the White House have begun to investigate proposals of the various departments. There are at least two streams of information reaching the President, one from the bureau and the other directly from the departments. Under Sherman Adams (not the President, but the assistant to the President), his deputy, and several of their staff, and with the assistance of such aids to the President as the cabinet secretary, the chief economic adviser, liaison officers of the National Security Council, and others, a careful review was made of the assembled proposals, charted by the head of the legislative reference section, a career guide through the maze of hundreds of important proposals, able to inform the reviewing body of the significance of each.

The legislative reference section determines which measures are to be brought to the attention of the President. A few measures are selected (the rest are dropped or postponed), "a number of complex and controversial measures, high in policy and partisan significance — among them social security, taxation, agricultural assistance, foreign aid," and sent to the President for presentation to the cabinet or to the National Security Council. After these proposals are examined, they come before the cabinet, at which time the President raises questions, makes suggestions, and offers advice.

Thus, for example, the presidential program of 1954 was developed. Eisenhower presented proposed legislation to the Republican congressional leaders in three days of briefing, the sponsors speaking and the President acting as chairman. Congressional committee chairmen were present, as were various department heads, the White House staff, and some executive officials below cabinet rank. During the proceedings the President offered a running commentary. There is no public record of how informed or how intelligent this commentary was; the perusal of scores of President Eisenhower's press conferences gives us reason to doubt its value. Some proposed measures were stricken from the list when congressional leaders demurred at the possibility of making progress or attempting such legislation at the coming session. The White House did not ask that the congressional leaders approve; it was the President's program. In 1955 the procedure was less elaborate, in part because Congress was under Democratic control.

President Truman instituted this system in a slightly different form; his first act after his election in 1948 was to review his campaign speeches and prepare legislation on the pledges they contained.

Professor R. E. Neustadt has pointed out the value of this legislative clearance process to Congress and to the President. It enables Congress and its committees to obtain solid ground by which to gauge the pleadings of the departments. Second,

> the President becomes agenda-setter for the Congress, the chief continuing initiator of subject-matter to reach actionable stages in committee and on the floor, whether or not passed ultimately. Of course, as Lawrence Chamberlain and others have made plain, most major measures are the product of long germination, much cross-fertilizing. Quite so; the service of contemporary Presidents has been less creativity than crystallization; a matter less of seeding new terrain than of tracing new lines in old ground, thereby to mark the field for current cultivation.[32]

However, we must not lose ourselves in the jungle, as any President, even a bold, initiating President may. Professor Neustadt seems to feel that without a sieving process (a Sherman Adams to assist the President) it would be hard "to shield Presidents from suffocation by the Presidency." Further, the "comprehensive and co-ordinated inventory of the nation's current legislative needs," reflects "the President's own judgments, choices, and priorities in every major area of federal action." But how dangerously tantalizing is the word "reflects." It implies enormous knowledge and conviction on the part of the President. A capacity for reflection is the product of the President's knowledge and convictions. If he lacks it he reveals his ignorance and his prejudices; it depends on the President. Whatever the case, the program appears to the public as the President's program; in some cases it is, but in other cases to talk of the President's "judgments, choices, and priorities" is to mistake their true source. One man cannot make all decisions, even if he is intelligent and quick-witted. In this respect the Presidency is inefficient and irresponsible. All major policy decisions are the President's responsibility, but the decisions themselves are likely to have been made by the President's advisers, who in most cases cannot be held responsible, cannot be replaced, and cannot be dismissed by the electorate.

One conclusion is irresistible: When Congress passed the Budget and Accounting Act of 1921, it endowed the President with a practical power over the finances of the nation and with decisive power for the enactment of laws and the conduct of administration involved in fiscal decisions. Control of the budget becomes the most important single tool of the Chief Executive in his domination of American domestic policy.

If Congress has a penchant for contriving at its own eclipse, all it need do is surrender to the President the "item" veto, the veto that will enable him to pick and choose which articles of the congressional will are to survive and which must die. At the moment, the veto power is unwieldy. The President must either accept a bill in its entirety or reject it in its entirety. If the President were given the power to veto items at his own discretion, Congress would be helpless and the President's dominion virtually unlimited. Congress ought to resist such a surrender in a last-ditch fight, for with the item veto in his hands the vaunted flexibility of the President's personal discretion would add to the inflexibility of the President's contentious will.

As the President's power to mold Congress increases with the use of the veto, the public grows to think the President more important than Congress. Congress is more and more likely to become a registrar of the split personality of the electorate, a place for hedging, a second bet, all of which would reduce its share of responsibility for the nation's welfare. Congress would be no longer a legislative body with initiative and the final decision but a feeble kind of second chamber. If this comes about, then the least for which we must work is an improvement in the quality of presidential candidates. The more the President assumes the authority of Congress, the more essential it is that the quality of leadership be the best available.

The President's Use of Patronage

The President soon finds that men are swayed by considerations other than the good of the nation, that some few are inclined to believe that the good of the nation is not endangered when they trade votes and influence in exchange for the gratification of personal ambition. The founders of the Republic resolutely excluded officeholders from Congress so that congressmen might act without executive influence, especially through patronage, and that congressmen might not subvert the independence of the executive branch.

Yet, subject to presidential influence are two large classes of federal jobs, those that the President nominates and places before the Senate for its advice and consent, and those that are not classified as part of the civil service but where the sponsor's political qualification is as important as personal merit in deciding the appointment of the candidate.

The first category, demanding senatorial consent, resulted in some 59,000 nominations in the year 1958. Of these, all but 4,244 were army, navy, air force, and marine officers; the remainder included 1,394 postmasters and 2,484 other civilian jobs.[33] Suppose we divide 4,200 jobs among half the representatives in the Senate and Congress. Each legislator so inclined would have some fifteen jobs subject to patronage in his domain, the grist for potential dickering. It is not an overpowering number, and the practice in the Senate of supporting announced preferences ("senatorial courtesy") limits considerably the influence of the White House. It may be added that in the sober judgment of those who have studied the advice and consent of the Senate, most contests over nominations have stemmed from political considerations rather than the qualifications or integrity of the nominees. The appointment and confirmation of the great bulk of these positions is a formality. Omitting 98,000 military officers, in all there are about 25,000 positions filled by joint presidential-senatorial appointment. This includes many subordinate positions.[34]

The second category consists of no less than 70,000 posts of interest to politicians and subject to various types of political "clearance." They are in the sole gift of the President and the departmental chiefs, although generally some test of merit is required. But they are not classified as civil service; the incumbents may be turned out by the next administration. They comprise some 30,000 rural letter carriers and over 20,000 first-, second-, and third-class postmasters; 1,000 or so top "political executive" posts; nearly 10,000 moderately important positions, attorneys, U.S. marshals, collectors of customs, collectors of internal revenue; and perhaps another 5,000 to 25,000 miscellaneous positions — the precise figure is unknown — mostly at lower levels. Some of these fall into the first category mentioned, so there is some duplication.[35] When the number of positions available each year is reckoned, the power exercisable, considerable though it is, is insufficient by itself to give anywhere near the dominance the President has attained. Yet the power is useful; and on at least one occasion it has been truly decisive — when President Cleveland obtained the repeal of the Silver Purchase Act in 1893. The President must exercise a strategy of clever delay in making nominations, as did Franklin Roosevelt, so that Congress is kept in a state of expectancy. It would seem to require of the President enormous self-control, artfulness, and great luck to be substantially effective as a device for barter.

The ascendancy of the President over Congress can be gauged in part by the extent to which he shows public scorn for the body of legislators. Franklin Roosevelt and Truman did not spare their opponents; and a statement by President Eisenhower at the close of the congressional session in September, 1959, abounds with terms of excoriation: Congressional proposals were lavish; he condemned "extravagance and legislative excesses"; its actions made "most difficult the maintenance of confidence both at home and abroad in our determination to manage our financial affairs soundly"; "shortsightedness that this unfortunate action reveals"; "my disappointment that the majority in Congress seems to find itself difficult to wean itself from the pork barrel"; "a return to programs discredited long ago"; "Congress distorted the shape of the budget in many respects"; and so on. We have no idea who drafted these fulminations, though of course we know over whose signature they appeared. The statement does no less than thank the public for supporting the President in his campaign against the congressional majority and, by thanking the members of the majority who defected, sustains the wedge within Congress. Thus the President pretends he is the people and that the people are the President. It is a powerful stance.

The Conduct of Foreign Affairs

Power in foreign affairs connotes the conduct of America's relationship with other nations in such a way as to secure the survival of political independence, preserve the integrity of its territories, enhance its voice in the councils of the world, and, further, expend wisely its men and its wealth to support the principles which the nation considers humane and just.

In an age like the present, when all growing things can be destroyed by the lethal power wielded by the Soviet Union, a nation with a spiritual outlook bitterly hostile to that of the United States, leadership in foreign affairs is by far the primary function of the federal government. It is of far greater importance to the nation than a high standard of living, except as the management of the economy is part and parcel of the maintenance of the strength needed to overawe, deter, and, if necessary, defeat an enemy and its satellites and allies.

This power to defend and preserve the Union and to disseminate its public philosophy and donate or lend a share of its wealth to poorer nations has come to be exercised almost exclusively by the President of the United States. The founders of the Republic divided the conduct of foreign relations between Congress and the President. The power to declare war is vested in Congress alone, and in this the founders broke away from the absolutism of the eighteenth century. They espoused the principles of popular sovereignty *and* the attendant principles of Locke, Montesquieu, and Blackstone, which lodged the diplomatic power in the executive alone. The Constitution allowed the President to negotiate treaties, but to be valid such treaties would need the advice and consent of the Senate by a two-thirds majority. It gave the President power to receive foreign representatives, consuls, ministers, and ambassadors; that authority allows the President to determine just which faction is to be considered the official representative of a foreign power. The President may appoint American ambassadors and ministers with the advice and consent of the Senate.

In addition to this distribution of powers, the President benefits from two other elements of authority assigned to him: He is Commander in Chief of the armed forces, and so disposes the militia for domestic purposes and the service of the armed forces abroad — a power which is not limited by the Constitution. Further, he is the possessor of "executive power," and other nations as well as the judicial authorities of the United States consider him alone to be the enforcer of national sovereignty in establishing the rights and obligations of the nation. He alone must carry out America's duties and enforce its rights.

The President is in a position to conduct himself in such a way as to bring the nation under attack or to act in a way that will forfend enmity; or, if an attack comes, empowered to repel its mischief and defeat the aggressor. The two main powers given to Congress to make or mar the President's policy consist of a clear right to reject a treaty he has negotiated and signed (such as the Treaty of Versailles of 1919, embodying the League of Nations). And it can use its legislative powers of taxation and appropriation, to set limits on immigration, to pass laws varying or enfeebling the executive obligations of the President, to debate his measures in such wise as to shake the confidence of allies and other nations in America's reliability, and to arouse the distrust and/or aggressiveness of enemies by the exhibition of a divided and confused national will.

The founders of the Republic seemed intent on establishing the President as the leader in foreign affairs. They recognized, and some said, that his characteristics would enable him to ride the storm. His unity, in contrast to congressional numerousness, provided for swiftness and energy. The immediate, detailed, and fresh information available to him made him more alert and expert. He embodied the possibility of secrecy, as contrasted with the high probability of impolitic disclosures in a body numbering scores of men, and this made him the more formidable. Being in "continuous sessions" at all times, the President was prepared to act at all times. But when they sang *Te Deum* (those who were not rationalists) for the mercy of a harsh war victoriously concluded, the founders might well have pondered Edmund Burke's admonition in a pamphlet closely touching on the tribulations of the colonists:

> Public life is a situation of power and energy; he trespasses against his duty who sleeps upon his watch, as well as he that goes over to the enemy.

The President has come to take upon himself a continuous and recognized initiative, to the point of substantial commitment. Although Congress can dispose, when the President proposes a serious matter of international concern his power of initiative is very nearly the power of absolute commitment. Consequently, it makes the President most careful; and being alone responsible for such a charge, it may make him overcareful, timid, in an age of swift decisions, in the inception of a plan of defense that may take as long as five or ten years to develop.

The American people may suffer, already may have suffered, in Edward Teller's phrase, a "technological Pearl Harbor." For the United States has failed, signally, to shorten its "lead time" in the production of long-range missiles. In 1959, Admiral Rickover, chief of the naval reactors branch of the navy, who developed the atomic-powered submarine, said:

> It is my contention that lead time — the time which elapses between conception of a new idea, its development, and finally its fruition in the completed new article rolling from the production lines — is the factor which more than any

other is likely to win the next war for the nation which succeeds in reducing it significantly below that of its competitor.[36]

We must survey the distribution of powers in order to gauge the President's responsibility. Let us offer this hypothesis: All those men who have been acclaimed as great Presidents have served as their own Secretary of State in foreign affairs. They permitted the Secretary of State to handle (on the whole) only minor executory matters ancillary to the high decisions which they themselves determined to be their own responsibility. And this must be so in the American system, for the President alone is vested with sufficient authority.

When President Eisenhower lauded Secretary John Foster Dulles as "the greatest Secretary of State in my memory" (in the New York *Times*, May 6, 1954), it was a most unhistoric judgment. If the President intended his comparison to reflect his opinion of the men who held that office under Franklin Roosevelt and Harry Truman (not Dean Acheson), then he was making a singularly revealing error. He exposed his failure to understand that a great President serves as his own Secretary of State — surely the clearest and most striking lesson to be learned from American diplomatic history. Only a weak President allows his Secretary of State to make foreign policy.

Executive Power

The President enforces America's commitments to other nations and as representative of the nation is expected to see that foreign nations fulfil their obligations to the United States. None of the several states may interfere, but all must bow to its consequences. A classic example: the President takes action when representatives of foreign nations board American ships to search for wanted men and contraband goods. By so doing, the President vindicates the right of neutrals to the freedom of the seas. The Presidents exerted this obligation against British power in the period 1789 to 1820. Woodrow Wilson fulfilled a similar obligation in World War I when German submarines attacked American vessels. The treaties regarding fisheries are guarded by the President; the treaty obligations of the Soviet Union to respect

Atlantic cables were enforced by a naval boarding party under the authority of President Eisenhower in January, 1959, when a Russian trawler blundered on a cable in Newfoundland waters. In March, 1917, President Wilson posted a guard on American vessels to safeguard them against German attack; it could not but have been considered a provocation, however well justified. And the provocation, if not intended, was as stinging when Franklin Roosevelt ordered American destroyers to fire on German submarines before the nations were at war. Back in 1900 an expeditionary force was thrown against the Boxer rebels who were besieging European and American citizens who had taken refuge in the British legation to escape the massacre in Peking.

Recognition

To "recognize" the sovereignty of another state, that is, of a government installed upon the collapse or overthrow of an old regime, is an act of political approval. It is exerted by the President alone and can have far-reaching effects. It was used to acknowledge the leaders of the French Revolution when Citizen Genêt was accepted as consul; it was used to approve declarations of statehood by five South American countries in 1822, preparatory to the establishment of the Monroe Doctrine. Recognition of the Soviet Union was withheld from 1917 until 1933, at which time President Roosevelt attached political conditions to recognition. The problem of the recognition of General Victoriano Huerta, the dictator of Mexico in 1913–14, was answered by Woodrow Wilson in such a way that a fracas occurred among American sailors and Mexican cadets at Vera Cruz and full-scale war only narrowly averted. Whether the regime in Cuba, close to American shores, should be recognized (in 1898, on severance from Spain, and again in 1959, on Fidel Castro's overthrow of Batista) was a matter of major presidential policy. And, above all, the continued recognition of Chiang Kai-shek and Nationalist China on Formosa as the legitimate government of China and the refusal to recognize the Peiping regime of Mao Tse-tung have been acts of the gravest moment in the balance of power and in the influence and strength of the United States. Congressmen of various persuasions have called for action with militant insistence and have brought pressure on the President and the Secretary of

State in the decade which has seen Communist China attack American soldiers in Korea in 1951 and prepare for attacks on Quemoy, Matsu, and perhaps even Formosa.

Foreign Agents

Ambassadors and ministers are nominated by the President, with senatorial approval. The United States has learned to its cost how valuable are the men and women who represent abroad the nation's interests, power, and dignity. How valuable was W. H. Page in Britain during World War I and Ambassador Dodd in Berlin before World War II, and how feeble Joseph P. Kennedy during World War II! The personal character and ability of these men and women matter very much in the diplomatic process; therefore, the presidential choice is of importance. In this context, other nations seek to avert political embarrassment and failure abroad by making foreign service almost entirely a career affair, with publicly stated standards, strict examinations, and demonstrated ability as the only criteria for advancement.

Congress, so well paid itself, will not pay ambassadors and ministers sufficient to meet American diplomatic obligations, for it prefers to keep these posts as political plums which may one day come the way of personal friends or election campaign donors.[37] The President uses diplomatic posts abroad as rewards for political party favorites and for personal cronies. The Senate almost always extends to the President freedom of appointment. It is the right, indeed, the duty, of the Senate to make inquiry of the fitness of proposed representatives. It has usually neglected its responsibility in this matter, but in a recent case, Clare Booth Luce, formerly Eisenhower's nominee to our embassy in Rome, was nominated as ambassador to Brazil. Both nominations must have been intended as rewards for her support of the Republican party, especially during the President's own election campaigns, and the steady and vigorous fidelity, unshaken by public events, she has rendered the party. At length her appointment was ratified by a small majority; and then some senators so waspishly attacked her waspishness that she withdrew.

Under Senator Fulbright's chairmanship of the Foreign Relations Committee, candidates for our embassies, like Ogden Reid who was nominated as ambassador to Israel, are being required to explain their positive qualifications for the appointment. Yet, generally speaking, the ambassador the President gets is the one he personally wants.

Since such ambassadors are not necessarily gifted to assist the President in the making of foreign policy, and the Senate does not interfere in a function which the President prefers to conduct independently, from the beginning the Chief Executives have appointed special agents, virtually assistants to themselves, to represent them abroad. Omitting visits made by the Vice-President in such a capacity, some recent examples include Colonel House, in the service of Wilson; Harry Hopkins and Henry Wallace, in the service of Franklin Roosevelt; and General Marshall's mission to China for President Truman. The President employs agents to undertake negotiations and to obtain first-hand information unobtainable, for various reasons, through the embassies. This is a special strength of the President, for thus he is possessed, or hopes to be, of knowledge superior to that available to Congress and even to the State Department. Through these agents he may make (and has made) commitments. An example may be recalled: James Polk's appointment of John Slidell in 1845 to undertake a secret mission to buy upper California and New Mexico from Mexico, and the subsequent appointment of Nicholas Trist to negotiate the peace treaty with Mexico.

The principal formal vehicle of American obligations and rights in relationship to other countries is (excepting for international law) the treaty. It is fully subject to the advice and consent of the Senate. But in the first year of the Republic, Washington refused to accept the attempt of the Senate to constitute itself a continuous council to mull over the treaty in a process of joint drafting. Washington instituted the precedent, followed ever since, of presidential negotiation and drafting, only then submitting the proposed treaty to the Senate. However, this does not mean that the Senate is not permanently restive under such procedure. It is allayed somewhat by continuous communication between the two branches on matters of foreign policy; and the machinery of presidential-senatorial relationship, formal and informal, is in operation early in the preparation of any important treaty.

The Senate was not taken unaware by the Treaty of Versailles in 1919. The views of what shape it ought to take had been ventilated in the press, at public meetings, and in discussions conducted by Congress and the President. The Senate can overturn a treaty, and in the case of the Treaty of Versailles it made one of the most disastrous and perhaps the most catastrophic political decisions of the twentieth century. The Senate reversed Canning's famous policy (the Monroe Doctrine's conscience) to "bring in the New World to redress the balance of the Old," for it withdrew the New World and destroyed the balance of the Old in favor of Hitler and Lenin. When the treaty for the United Nations was contemplated in 1945, as at the time of other treaties of grave international interest, the lesson had been learned. The incumbent, President Roosevelt, and his follower, Truman, sought maximum bipartisan support from the Senate. This was successful, of course, largely because American isolationism ended with the attack on Pearl Harbor. America's obligations were acknowledged by a majority of the people and their political leaders, present dangers were better understood, and senatorial susceptibilities were appeased before the treaty went to the Senate. In this way Senator Vandenberg was won over by Franklin Roosevelt and Truman with an appointment as a member of the U.S. delegation to draft the UN Charter; thereafter, he co-operated vigorously in the establishment of the Truman Doctrine, the Marshall Plan (exacting here a quid pro quo in aid for China), and plans for NATO.

The President is able to make valid and binding agreements with other nations by a means independent of the Senate, by so-called executive agreement. It passes my understanding that, given the specific language of the Constitution, the President can use with impunity the instrument of executive agreement, for it has all the validity of a treaty. Executive agreements have regulated the relationship between the United States and Canada on the Great Lakes since 1817; settled the immigration rights of the Japanese, as arranged in 1907 by Theodore Roosevelt, with tremendous political effect; and have been used to determine tariff rates for various goods from various countries. The Yalta and Potsdam agreements were executive agreements, so important that on the election of President Eisenhower the "old guard" leaders of the Republican party urged him to repudiate the Yalta agreement. They were refused because Secretary of State Dulles realized how much would be lost by the United States if the engagements made with Russia at Yalta were reciprocally repudiated; it is a testimony to the political gravity of the agreements and to their binding character.

In a seven-year period, 1939–45, executive agreements almost swamped treaty making; treaties to executive agreements were in this ratio: 1939, 10 to 26; 1940, 12 to 20; 1941, 15 to 39; 1942, 6 to 52; 1943, 4 to 71; 1944, 1 to 74; 1945, 6 to 54. Of course, where a treaty or executive agreement requires implementation by act of Congress, or where its substance lies within the congressional field, Congress can affect its significance by superseding its terms in any way it likes.

Commander in Chief

As Commander in Chief of the armed forces, the President may use American troops to intervene in civil disorders. In 1894, Cleveland sent troops to Chicago to restore order during the Pullman strike, and Hayes did much the same thing under similar circumstances in 1877. Troops are often called out in times of natural emergency, such as floods, tornadoes, explosions, and fires. These are important powers, but they are as nothing compared to the powers of the President when he is in a position, during "a time of emergency" (which is up to him to define), to declare on his sole authority a place to be a theater of war.[38] When Lincoln was confronted with the outbreak of the Civil War, he called some state militias to active duty and raised volunteers for three years' service, added regulars, disbursed from the Treasury $2 million not specifically appropriated by Congress for war purposes (expenditures by the federal government for 1860 totaled $63 million), amended the passport regulations, blockaded the South, had suspected enemies arrested, and suspended the operation of habeas corpus — all without advice and consent of Congress or benefit of statutes. Later he established an army draft, made general the suspension of habeas corpus, and proclaimed the emancipation of the slaves. These emergency measures introduced to the American nation a force of presidential leadership in domestic affairs in time of war not to be surpassed until 1917. These measures involved the total mobilization of almost every citizen and harnessed the whole economy to the manufacture of armaments and the objectives of war. Whether in pursuance of the power of Commander in Chief, or that of "executive power" in a time of emergency, many government departments were established and given duties not provided for in statutes passed by Congress.

In turn, by virtue of his power as Commander in Chief, Wilson armed American merchantmen. And Franklin Roosevelt was to sell surplus guns and warships to Great Britain by a useful re-interpretation of a statute of 1939; the right to "dispose the forces" of the United States became the right to "dispose *of*" some old destroyers in return for British bases. Further, Roosevelt claimed wide areas of the Atlantic as a security zone and sent armed ships to harry the German submarine pack — in short, all measures this side of a formal declaration of war.

The power to dispose the forces of the United States enabled the President to help Texas territory acquire its independence from Mexico, in the end by a war, "Operation Texas-ectomy," and earlier by a disposition of American forces to exert pressure on the Mexican government.

More recently, the President as Commander in Chief governed the policy of the Seventh Fleet in the China seas and the relationship between Formosa and Peiping; he sent the Sixth Fleet to the Middle East during the Lebanon crisis in June, 1958, and sanctioned the landing of American troops in Lebanon in pursuance of an earlier presidential declaration (the Eisenhower, or Middle East, Doctrine) to safeguard "vital" American interests.[39]

What, in essence, do these diverse and disparate actions mean in our own time? The declaration of a "vital interest" in other parts of the world judged to impinge presently and immediately on American security concerns areas very far from the United States, areas not considered to be "theaters of war" in the late eighteenth century or until very recent times, indeed, not even in the first days of the airplane and the submarine. The swifter and more deadly the modern missile, the more certain it is that America's security embraces the great globe itself. What else could have taken American troops to Greece in 1947 — or

American economic aid? What else could have placed the American fleet off the coast of China? What else could have taken our troops to the Middle East and to the defense of Korea, sent our special agents to Vietnam, our military officers to train the armies of Laos?

This raises an attendant question concerning American obligations under certain international pacts, the UNO and the NATO. In both of these, especially as it concerns the use of the atomic bomb and the H-bomb, the sole decision has been left to the President, who will give orders to our military forces — in the first case, as a sanctioning force when the United Nations has made a resolution for economic or war sanctions (as in Korea); in the other, when the governing body of NATO, of which the United States is the most important power, resolves on action. It is held that even if the law arising out of these pacts were not clear on the President's authority for action, he could and should take action in view of his responsibility for the security of the United States. Where such actions have been taken — when authority was as yet unclear or undefined — the Supreme Court has given post facto approval, recognizing the critical necessities of speed and appropriate action in war. (On such grounds, during World War II, the Supreme Court sanctioned the evacuation and incarceration of about 100,000 Nisei from the West Coast and a part of Arizona.) [40]

The idea seems to be growing that if an attack from a foreign country were expected, the Chief Executive, upon military advice, and even in certain cases without it, would be expected to declare a "preventive war." And, in spite of all the congressional fuss it has aroused, an executive commission may be studying the circumstances when the President would be justified in surrendering the nation to a foreign power — that is to say, on his *sole authority*. Such is the swiftness and terror of modern weapons!

Only twice has Congress declared war on its own initiative and without pressure from the President (indeed, against the President's desire), war with England in 1812 and war with Spain in 1898. In World War I and again in World War II, the President took various actions against other powers in the interest of American security, defending American rights under international law as acknowledged by all nations or, by extension, the right of self-defense. Then, in a long and complicated train of events, both Wilson and Franklin Roosevelt were forced to ask Congress to declare war.

The President is at the center of diplomatic foreign relations, watching over the shifting and delicate balance of power, and the "balance of terror," and must be prepared to decide precisely when one-third of the Strategic Air Command must take to the air to prevent the annihilation of the United States. His mood, his demeanor, certainly his policy, steadily commit the nation. The unyielding attitude of President Eisenhower (or rather Dulles) toward Communist China, and the steady conduct of the "cold war" with Russia through armed pressure, through NATO, through the Truman and Marshall plans; in the Middle East; above all, regarding Suez in 1956–57; in Indochina; in West and East Germany; the sudden decision to invite Khrushchev to the United States — all these acts commit the nation.

What is the position of Congress in all this? Congress holds the purse, but it gives the President almost everything he asks, according to his policy, not its own. It gives him the men and arms he asks for, and often betters his policy by additional amounts, accepting the objectives he outlines and providing him with more ample means. It questions the Secretary of State in its own halls, and it accepts his arguments, even if sometimes reluctantly, as Dean Acheson learned at the horny hands of Republican diehards in the Senate. But it rarely offers the nation the smallest alternative to the President's purposes; it forbears to seek additional information when the President declares that to do so would not be in the public interest. The President makes a show, and perhaps it is sincere, of consulting congressional leaders (in committee or informally), and he makes obeisance to the power and status of Congress as a lawmaking representative body. The President will explain his actions at length, through his Secretary of State, when a Pearl Harbor is investigated, or as in the case of the dismissal of General MacArthur for seeking to make a foreign policy of his own. But this is all the President is prepared to do.

It is rare indeed when Congress has a concerted foreign policy. It is rare when there is concerted opposition in Congress to the policy of the President. For the speed of events and the possession of vital facts by an executive in "continuous sessions" have accrued, as the founders of the Republic foresaw, to the advantage of the President — indeed, today, in an age of necessarily entangling alliances, the nation's sole maker of peace and of war.

Congress is faced with a *fait accompli*. The President and his Secretary of State, the combined brains of the State Department's experts, and representatives of all the other departments of government have acquired dominion in deciding the economic and military policies bearing on foreign policy. Against these massed experts, Congress has only the staff of certain congressional committees, some thirty-five persons in all, eight for the Senate Committee on Foreign Relations, five for the House Committee on Foreign Affairs, sixteen in the legislative reference service, and six in the two armed services committees. As Senator Hubert Humphrey pointed out, on these staff experts falls much of the burden of examining the complex budgets for defense, international affairs, and mutual security, budgets totaling $48 billion a year. No wonder the President has the edge over Congress. Yes, he is powerful; can one man be appropriately wise and sensitive?

I do not forget (who can?) that the President moves only within the ambit of the prevailing climate of opinion. It should not be forgotten that Franklin Roosevelt's "quarantine speech" of 1937 found no response in the hearts of the people. It cannot be forgotten that it was not possible for President Roosevelt in 1940 to send help to a dying France, however much he foresaw what that event might eventually mean in American lives. But the President is himself a creator of public opinion, the invoker of men's hearts, the awakener of their minds. To a dreadful extent, war and peace are in the hands of one man, for that is what the Constitution established, believing it good. Is it good now? Those who voted for the Bricker amendment in 1956–57 (and President Eisenhower was shaky on its justification) were trying to limit the President's power to make treaties and executive agreements if to do so would affect the rights of the states to make laws within their own jurisdiction, but had no intention of encroaching on the diplomatic powers of the President.

Presidential power over war and peace is enormous, it is growing, and it ought to be shared by others co-equal with the President in a collective body. So grave a power in the hands of one man almost equals that of the First Secretary of the Presidium of the Soviet Union, and yet even he is expected to consult with ten others, his equals in formal authority, of which at least three or four participate in decisions of serious concern.

Chief of a Party

The function, indeed, the responsibility of the President as leader of a political party is of a different kind from the responsibilities hitherto considered, for these are based fairly directly on permissions and commands in the Constitution itself. Leadership of a party is a vital auxiliary need of the President if he is to fulfil the functions the Constitution has assigned to him, especially as they are interpreted today. He needs a majority in Congress, sometimes a two-thirds majority, and it is only logical to say that he would be assured of this if his party were united behind him, if the party shared with him some unity of philosophy and policy. The President's leadership — or attempt to obtain the leadership — of his party is a direct consequence of the majority vote needed in a system of government founded on popular sovereignty and representative institutions, and of the electoral system by which the President is voted into office (virtually a direct popular vote, a plebiscite).

Let us examine the President's party connections. He needs his party in order to obtain the nomination. Yet as we have seen this process can split the party, viz., the bitter contest between the Eisenhower faction and the Taft faction, each publicly accusing the other of stealing votes. So rancorous was this contest that Taft was later asked what his terms would be to assist the new President by leading the Senate in his support. Concessions of policy and patronage were made — and kept indifferently. On the whole, the cracks in the party wall are papered over with decorative wallpaper during each election campaign. Each party vows that its candidate has all the godly attributes (as well as the concrete advantage of being here on earth), with rich blessings to bestow on each member of the credulous public. This process puts the candidate in debt, debts which must be paid later in office by policy concessions, like the surrender of tidelands oil to Texas, California, and Louisiana.

The candidate's business is to find the maximum number of supporters who can bring to his aid the maximum number of voting groups and individual votes in exchange for the least number of promises. He may be in a very strong position, as was Franklin Roosevelt in 1932, when economic disaster was so crushing, and in 1936, when memory of the depression was strong but fear was fading, when farmers, workers, the poor and the needy were mobilized. Or he may have the appeal of Eisenhower in 1952, when after nearly twenty years of Democratic leadership, the turmoil of World War II and reconstruction, and growing criticism of the pettiness that had tarnished the presidential office enabled him to gain a free hand and bend (poorly) a party to his person.

But is this *party* leadership? Hardly: Congressional rapprochement has to be made later, and it is not easy. When it comes to being leader of his party in Congress the situation differs, radically, from the relationship sustained while party and leader are both looking for the same thing — his election victory. Yet that common victory — dubiously common, divided even at that stage when the appeals are to different electorates — gives to each his own separate share of power in a divided system. The behavior of Congress in enacting laws and voting appropriations makes manifest that the President is not the master of his party in Congress, for its members have other loyalties. They are loyal to their districts, to their own electoral prospects, and, as they always roar in those vast, reverberating halls, "to their consciences alone." The House has its electorate; the Senate another; the President his very own; it is hard for the three to meet.

It is well at this point to introduce Woodrow Wilson's views of the President as party leader, as he thought the President should be. (Once he became President he did not find this relationship to be as happy as he had forecast.) The President "must be the leader of his party. He is the party's choice and is responsible for carrying out the party platform. He therefore should have a large influence in determining legislation." [41] The President, Wilson said, "cannot escape being the leader of his party except by his incapacity and lack of personal force, because he is at once the choice of the party and the nation." [42] Wilson further maintained that the President's party must represent the majority of the nation in order to have elected him; this constituted the mandate to lead in its name. The nation depended upon the personal character of the President and his position as leader of the victorious party.

Wilson had in mind the office of prime minister in the British system of government; but, as we shall shortly see, the leadership of the party is not the only way in which the offices of the British prime minister and the American President are in sharp contrast.

Party Strength of the President

What is the strength of the President as party leader? It comes from four sources. He is elected in the name of the party; no matter how inchoate the party is, its name is one. In the zeal of the campaign the party's name and the standard-bearer's name are one. The successful candidate carries in a few congressmen on his coattails.[43] For the moment they are grateful; as La Rouchefoucauld said, "Gratitude is a lively expectation of favors to come." The public, especially the profoundly unsophisticated public, which is by far the greater part of the contemporary electorate, will continue to associate the two, party and standard-bearer. This association gives the President a lever to use upon refractory congressmen when he wishes to appeal to the nation; and congressmen recognize the President's advantage in this regard and know that sooner or later his assistance will be important and welcome to them. In addition, at least *something* of a party platform is in evidence during an election campaign; *some* promises are made. The President may feel more loyal to this platform than most members of his party do, and he has national prestige to maintain.

It follows that when the prestige of the President has been established during the campaign he is slow to lose it. He may, as some Republicans said of Eisenhower in the first weeks of his campaign in 1952, "run like a dry creek" (and any witness of the Abilene open-air speech must acknowledge the aptness of the simile). Yet the election campaign choreographers have the know-how to make Simple Simon look like Alexander the Great. The President's prestige is his most powerful asset. If it is reduced by steady opposition from Congress, the prestige of other party officeholders, even that of city officials of the same party, is reduced. The President has that hold over Congress. It transcends his own term of office, for it has often enabled him to have a most powerful voice in recommending his successor. And if he himself wants to be the successor, according to a firm custom, it will not be denied him, though many of his party colleagues, as in 1948, may dissent and rebel.

Since the President is not only the political leader of the nation but the Chief of State, the symbol of America's majesty and might, he has an influence rather like that of George III among members of the peerage and among commoners who wished to be peers. The right to attend court was denied to those who disagreed with the king's policy, so much so that the House of Commons was obliged to remonstrate against the royal tactics.[44] And even in this democratic nation the President does not mind holding court. It is doubtful, for example, whether the Democratic senator Clinton Anderson will ever again be invited to play poker with President Eisenhower after his part in the rejection of the President's nomination of Admiral L. L. Strauss for Secretary of Commerce. Or, another instance, one of the unkindest cuts ever given Senator Joseph MacCarthy was the denial of an invitation to attend a White House party. The glamor of kingship has descended on the President, and it will sway a congressman, even of the opposite party, against giving serious affront. When the President is attacked in office it is as if the nation itself had been attacked. Insofar as there is a "fountain of honor" in America, it is the President. When the wives of Jackson's cabinet members expressed disapproval of Peggy O'Neale Eaton, it was not Peggy who was discountenanced but the cabinet, a cabinet undermined by Van Buren, the then Secretary of State, to help Jackson and, trickily, himself.

Other sources of the President's strength as leader of his party in Congress we have mentioned: the right by veto to control legislation; the right to control the patronage at his disposal which his followers can use to pay for local support in their own elections and swap for political leadership in their own communities.

There is also the possibility that the President may intervene in the elections of congressmen and senators in the hope of using their prestige, their own, that of a policy, or of the party itself, to overthrow men who oppose or may oppose them. Only one

President believed himself sufficiently strong in this respect to try. In the off-year election of 1938, Franklin Roosevelt decided to defeat the return of men in his own party who since 1936 had opposed his legislative program. He declared that "not as a President but as head of the Democratic party, charged with the responsibility of carrying out the definitely liberal declaration of principles set forth in the 1936 Democratic platform, I feel that I have every right to speak in those few instances where there may be a clear issue between candidates for a Democratic nomination involving principles or involving a clear misuse of my own name." The last phrase, "a clear misuse of my own name," deserves notice. In local campaigns the candidate often uses a photograph of himself taken with the President to confirm or to suggest that his candidacy has the President's indorsement. President Roosevelt was clearly successful in only one instance: He secured the ouster of the outgoing Democratic chairman of the House Rules Committee. He indorsed a number of Democratic senators (e.g., Senator Alben Barkley, whose leadership of the Senate was an enormous asset to him), but they might have been renominated even without his efforts on their behalf. He failed abjectly to defeat Guy Gillette of Iowa, Senator Walter George of Georgia, a first-class southern Democratic party elder as saturated with antiliberalism as a baba is with rum, and could not defeat another of the same type, Cotton Ed Smith of South Carolina, or Senator Millard Tydings of Maryland; they all won handsomely against opponents supported by the President. As James Farley, chairman of the party, said: "It's a bust!" The President was unable to rally the off-year electorate to the party; the nation had reverted to its 435 districts and its forty-eight states. And this is usually true of the President's leadership of his party, and rather worse for those Presidents who lack Roosevelt's political genius.

Professor James M. Burns recounts a story which has point:

> Not long ago a London editor was trying to guide his readers through the wilderness of the American party system. There are four parties, he explained — liberal Republicans, conservative Republicans, conservative Democrats and liberal Democrats. The first three parties, he went on, combined to

elect Mr. Eisenhower President, and the last three combine to oppose him in Congress.[45]

In attempting to assay the importance of the role of the President as chief of a political party, have we not let the cat out of the bag? How can the President be a leader of something that does not exist?

The founders of the Republic did not constitute the President a party leader; indeed, they insisted he be elected independently of Congress, "by the nation," or "by the people." They were afraid of "faction," by which they meant "party." Washington, in his farewell address, warned against the "spirit of party." And, until Jefferson's term, party connections with the Presidency were scouted. The prevailing wish was that the President should be nothing less than "the father of his country." Of course, for many people, the President, like all symbols of political and ecclesiastical authority, is a substitute for the parent, representing something like the mixture of kindness, protection, love, judgment, and duty that emanates from a father. Hence, many sociologists, following Freud and his interpreters, use the father-image to explain the President's role. There is much truth in the theory, yet if it is to be used, it should be replaced by the parent-image, since, surely, a very large percentage of the world's men and women are guided as much by the image of the mother as the father, taking her to be their model of behavior, guide to morality, the object of their love, reverence, and fear. At any rate, the President obtains the benefit of this attachment, which may give him some immunity from uncompromising criticism.

The President is caught in the toils of the propaganda used in his behalf to gain a majority. He must gather a majority, which means he must make his own adjustment of values and the various notions which comprise his speeches and pledges. Very often these are far from the same as the demands made of him by each of the groups, economic, social, religious, ethnic, which he gathers into the fold. The respective appeals and promises are hot at the time of the campaign; they cool. They remain longest with the President; and they can never be as soon obscured as the promises and evasions of congressmen. What the President promises, he alone promises, and it remains on his personal record. To the people he seems to have the power to carry out his commitments — yet they are so often vapid, so deserving of the epithet, "weasel words."

The President is not subordinate to a well-integrated, traditional party program devised years before he becomes a candidate; there is no organ of authority to establish such a program in either of the parties. Moreover, what platform there is, is composed only in the heat of pre-election bargaining, and the presidential candidate himself makes no pledge to carry it out. Each President, indeed, has his own platform, differing substantially in direction and emphasis from that of his party in Congress, the nominating convention, and national party headquarters. One classic contradiction is the Democratic party's attitude on silver in 1904 and the nomination of a defiant gold-standard candidate, Alton Parker. Another is the Democratic party's gingerliness on the subject of the repeal of Prohibition in 1928 and Al Smith's out-and-out pledge to repeal it. Both Franklin Roosevelt and Harry Truman dictated the platforms they would support; no established platform was imposed on them by the existing party organization. The candidate and his supporters were rather like traveling companions brought together for a safari of six weeks, only to part on their several, related missions (sometimes ending in hostility) when destinations, White House and Capitol, were reached.

The President, particularly in times when Congress thwarts his will, is rather more the leader of the nation than of the party. He is in the dignified position of representing the nation and can appeal to "independents," and even to representatives of the other party, for votes. When he faces Congress, the President often must depend on rival party members to offset the dissident members of his own party. Franklin Roosevelt sometimes found himself in a weak position and then courted Republican support.

So little are political parties united, joined in fellowship by commonly shared political principle, that men in both parties — Truman himself, it is alleged, in the Democratic party — were ready to support Eisenhower as their candidate. Imagine the situation in England if the Conservative party knew so little of a man's convictions that they were willing to have a Labour leader as prime minister (except possibly a senile Ramsay Macdonald they would find it easy to overwhelm), or where the Conservative leader so closely resembled a Labourite, or was so colorless, so lacking in conviction, that the Labour party thought he might well serve them as a leader.

The significant point, the superiority of President to party, cannot be stressed enough. Consider how often Woodrow Wilson was thwarted by the Democratic party between 1913 and 1919 in spite of the readiness of the nation to follow him. His contempt for Congress, even members of his own party, is a marked feature of Wilson's political life. Consider the dissidence of Republican congressmen when asked to provide foreign aid for the Eisenhower policy; the differences on China policy, on Yalta, and so on. Consider the cleft in 1958–60 between the Democratic advisory committee and the chairman of the Democratic national committee and Democratic leaders in Congress — at loggerheads. And yet included among them are aspirants for the Presidency, and all will have some say in the party platform for 1960, for 1964, and so on, happily ever after. All are actually *afraid* to call annual conferences to establish party policies and elect officers, as is done in other democratic nations. Consider Eisenhower's unsuccessful attempts to transform his own party into something he called "modern Republicanism," that is, to move away from an oppositionist conservatism toward a more positive "progressive conservatism." Exactly what this would imply was hardly known to the President himself when he began his term and became scarcely clearer when Arthur Larson, a youngish Republican, a political tyro, produced a book called *A Republican Looks at His Party*. Soon after, Larson became director of the USIA (his reward) and gave it up to become the President's assistant on "psychological warfare," and then was released for a professorial appointment.

The fact that, once in office, the President can appoint the party's campaign manager, and so influence the propaganda machine and party organizations throughout the nation by using his patronage, is not a sure weapon in securing the President as party leader. (There is not so much pliable patronage as is sometimes assumed, though on one remarkable occasion, the advent of the New Deal, an enormous number of offices, one hundred thousand, it is said, were created.) The role of party leader cannot be called negligible; it is not negligible in Congress; but it is not possible to be a powerful leader if the party lacks unity and policy and at times seems scarcely to exist.

The President is left with remarkable freedom of initiative and is apt to overburden himself with fearful responsibilities, far more so than would the leaders of other democratic systems. It does not follow that what he initiates or takes upon himself will be accomplished; Congress has still the power to determine the degree. In the Supreme Court fight, Roosevelt did not consult Congress before publicizing his proposals; it was not a mandate from the electors or a party platform; and his own party congressmen repudiated him so vehemently that he failed to find support. He was forced to look to other groupings of the members of Congress, not simply to members of his own party.

The less Congress and the political parties exercise the functions they could, the heavier the responsibility of the President and the more difficult the task of discovering a man able alone to foster the welfare of the economy and the safety of the nation. We can well understand why the founders of the Republic distrusted the spirit of party and bequeathed a party doctrine inappropriate for later generations. Other nations were still struggling to overcome appalling internal feuds. In 1745 — yesterday to the men of 1776! — England suffered an armed rising in support of the Pretender. France was so divided by the Revolution of 1789 that the nation has never since attained a serene and convivial unity. All the same, it is necessary to question the wisdom of Washington's warnings against the "spirit of party" in his farewell address. A similar utopian complacency is in danger of overwhelming some of us today. It is pleasant to dream that America is (or may be) one and indivisible, without parties; but in the absence of parties the nation would be at the mercy of the naked power of pressure groups, regional interests, and personal ambition bursting with egoism and devoid of a sense of responsibility. Washington asserted that the spirit of party "serves always to distract the public councils." But this is no eternal truth. Some parties unite men in public council and assist in the development of the principles of public good. Washington said that parties "enfeeble the public administration," but some parties at some times do exactly the opposite; they collect and co-ordinate diverse interests and wills, mobilize loyalty and support for legislation, and unite men in collective deliberation. They serve — or can serve — as a link between the public and elected and career officials and hold these officials to their responsibilities as the nation's representatives.

Washington warned that the spirit of party "agitates the community with ill-founded jealousies and false alarms; kindles the animosity of one part against another; foments occasional riot and insurrection." But it may be said with equal justice that the spirit of party, seeking the settlement of conflicts, moderates and appeases the impulses of the nation.

The President as National Symbol

The most insistent yearning of man is the wish to be right and to be thought by others to be right. This unquenchable craving may appear in other guises; often it is not articulate; it is more apt to be expressed in poetry than in prose. Where are the masses to look for guidance in this, their inmost need, in "this dark world, and wide"? As children they looked to their mothers and fathers, their teachers, their church. When they cease to be children, and no longer see through a glass darkly, where do they look for direction? Only a very small proportion of mankind attains to an independent policy in human relations by reading and reflection, as did such men as Tom Paine, Washington, Jefferson, and Lincoln. The rest lead lives of quiet desperation. The masses, the natural masses, with the chaacter described by Émile Faguet as that of the "average, sensual man," seek edification, not necessarily in words, upon the nature of virtue, the respect they owe to their statesmen, and the duties they should render to their fellow citizens. They ask how their anxieties should be posed within the context and as the problems of the state — the services it demands of them and the benefits they can rightly solicit from it. The national community, the Great Society of representative men and women, has become, to all intents and purposes, the supreme standard of morality ("My country, right or wrong!"), the universal protector, the mentor, the Father, the Mother. Men and women are not born free, they are born national; to be free altogether means to be lonely in one's fight for freedom, and even so the course one believes freedom to be is affected by the shaping one has undergone in childhood and early adolescence. The transcendent symbol of the nation is the man who, whether king or elected President, incarnates and personifies the nation. It is personification that makes concrete responses to the questions, What is right, proper, just? given by the leader, answers which, otherwise, for the common man and his wife, might be abstract, doctrinaire, theoretical, and not so easily comprehensible, not so easily grasped.

There are many selves in every self — good and bad, spiritual and coarse; and these are at constant war, with fluctuating fortune. No single self wins the victory. The masses would like the best of all worlds, the noble, the majestic, the dignified, without sacrifice of plenty to eat and drink, and with least effort. Their warring selves are clearly represented in one aspect of present political institutions, the wills engaged in fierce contention. Their better selves are represented in another — reverence for the nation, its future, its survival, its oneness as a foundation for all else, incarnate in its symbols of dignity and its symbols of might, the flag, the anthems and the hymns, national shrines and days of commemoration, and in one aspect of government that focuses all — the Chief of State, sole representative of the nation. Unworthy as they sometimes are, congressmen, addressed as "honorable," share the same aura of reverence, if with less intensity. But it is the President, like a king in other times and in other places, who has come to signify the majesty and the aspirations of the nation.

It is not the purpose of this essay to trace the attribution of majesty to George Washington, when men in the First Congress proposed variously that the President be called "His Elective Majesty," "His Excellency," "His Highness the President of the United States of America and Protector of the Rights of the Same." A puritanical, or rationalist, rejection of the moderate trappings of ceremony was instituted by Jefferson, who remembered the corruption of French and English kings and a degenerate aristocracy. Once the first generation of the descendants of English gentlemen (I refer to Washington, his friends, and their younger contemporaries) were gone, dead, retired, or swept from the political scene, Andrew Jackson himself led his own inaugural procession on a white charger, thus re-establishing for the people a sense of the might, the sovereignty, the majesty of their nation. And just as the people of England in the past seventy-five years have given new dignity to the idea of national sovereignty — a kind of worship of their better selves, what they would be if only it did not cost so much in self-control and effort — so in the United States the President has become the incarnation of the American people in a sacrament resembling that in which the wafer and the wine are seen to be the body and blood of Christ. In secular transubstantiation, the personality of each President, however trumpery, becomes a distillation of the glorious and triumphant past, and forgotten are occasions of defeat, past crimes, trivial vices, and wholesale corruption. In that oceanic flood of "good feeling," the people do not think of the petty men who become President but only of the great men who inspired the nation to heroic deeds. But when he lacks magnanimity, the President is incapable of rallying the nation and inspiring the elevation of its intellectual and moral level.

What the nation as an enduring consensus, as what Hobbes called "an artificial man," would do in its social and cultural life, it does through its vicar, the President. A modest list will tell the story. He lights the national Christmas tree on the White House lawn in the season of good will to men; he issues the Thanksgiving Day message in the season of thankfulness and bicarbonated repletion; his office sends greetings to societies and persons on their birthdays, offering national recognition and a reason for gratitude; he throws out the first baseball of the season and attends the army-navy football game in a spirit of good-fellowship and as a votary of sport; he is host at brilliant banquets for kings and queens and potentates, representing America in its dignity in the comity of nations; he sponsors movements for health and wealth and happiness; gigantic dams and electric works pound into operation as his finger touches the proper button, enhancing America's pride; and he is suitably in mourning on Memorial Day, his hat over his heart, one with the heroes of the past, one with those who mourn the men who died so that the nation might live; at military parades on the Fourth of July he embodies the vigor of American independence; and he is at home, for handshaking, to scores of thousands of worthy and ordinary citizens throughout the year. And with him is the First Lady of the land, presiding, the smartly dressed descendant of Dolly Madison and the rest, over the social life of the capital, the epitome of grace for the women of the nation.[46]

The brightest images in the hymn "America, the Beautiful" sing what the masses feel the President represents, even when his specific decisions have done them harm. America's spacious skies, amber waves of grain, purple mountains' majesty above the fruited plain — a brotherhood from sea to shining sea. American heroes are lauded because they loved their country more than self and mercy more than life, and the wish is that all success shall be by nobleness and every gain divine; and who does not join in the patient dreams that see beyond the years — at that, undimmed by human tears? From sea to shining sea! Heaven spare the President from the fury vented on Grover Cleveland by patriotic groups (including the G.A.R.) when he went fishing on Memorial Day!

The image of the might and glory of the nation, crystallized and humanized in the person of the President, emanating from the office itself, not simply from his own personal qualities, is enormously fortified by his immense power to make mighty and binding decisions, the power we have assessed. And here a dangerous dilemma confronts the American people. It can be summarized in two quotations. William Seward, Abraham Lincoln's Secretary of State, said: "We elect a king for four years and give him absolute power within certain limits, which after all he can interpret for himself." The second quotation is taken from one of the most gifted studies we have of the American political system, Henry J. Ford's *The Rise and Growth of American Politics*: "In the Presidential office as it has been constituted since Jackson's time, American democracy has revived the oldest political institution of the race, the elective kingship." [47]

The confusion of a national symbol and the political role (and even party leadership) tends to make extravagant the part which personal charm plays in the nomination and election of a President. Under the glowing cloak that signifies that "all success be nobleness and all gain be divine," scoundrels may hide; they may make the President they choose a Trojan horse as a way of gaining entrance to the citadel. To the common man, the President is the highest authority in the United States; and for many of them he is the wise man of the world. He is the composite of all the Presidents, as the Pope is the eternal Pope, all Popes gone and to come. The appearances that go with that dignity may be superior to the talent for government that lies beneath. As G. K. Chesterton said of Thomas à Beckett, the saint is conscious of the hairshirt tormenting his flesh, but the onlooker sees only the golden robes of office.

The golden robes may blind the people, especially when politicians do what they can to increase the dazzlement, to the feebleness of the man who wears the hairshirt. A man's physical appearance, his gestures, his speech, may demean the presidential office when they seem most to exalt it. There is no doubt whatever that the electorate, encouraged by a hostile press, believed Truman lacked presidential dignity in 1952; and, in contrast, a war hero, hitherto seen in handsome uniform, represented that majesty the people of America believed themselves entitled to, the majesty the country had won during the war and lost again in the "mess" of Washington politics. It has happened again and again: instead of John Quincy Adams, a General Andrew Jackson; instead of Van Buren, a General W. H. Harrison; instead of (perhaps) Henry Clay or Daniel Webster, a Zachary Taylor, respectable soldier and feeble President; instead of Governor Horatio Seymour, a General Ulysses S. Grant, an inept and irresponsible ignoramus. And Adlai Stevenson was rejected when an astute choice of opponent revealed the acumen of self-appointed President-makers — so much so that there was justice in the charge that the elections of 1952 and 1956 were no more than popularity contests.

A study of the 1952 campaign demonstrates the enormous effect of General Eisenhower's personality as well as the fact, be it remarked, that "candidate appeal would appear to be the most susceptible to the vagaries of public sentiment." [48] Sentiment, be it noted, not reason! Because the President is expected to play a dual role, demigod and astute politician, the voters disregard the immensity of the responsibilities with which he is vested as they seek to assess his charm. This matter is all the graver in the present age of television and the hidden persuaders.

Once elected to office and given tremendous decision-making

power, the President loses something of his mortality; the role of demigod dulls the cutting edge of criticism. "There is a divinity which doth hedge a king." In England, the monarch makes no political decisions; Queen Elizabeth reigns but she does not rule. The cabinet and the prime minister decide all issues as long as they hold the confidence of the electors and the houses of Parliament. The principle is this: the Crown is morally perfect and innocent. The Crown can do no wrong *because it has no power to do so*. The nakedness of the cabinet subjects it to every severity, indignity, and vituperation — no holds barred. Having observed American politics at close range for thirty-five years, I do not argue that opponents of the President, the "outs," fail to criticize his policies (especially since privately owned media of communication allow one-sided campaigns of disparagement); they do; the vilification of Franklin Roosevelt and Harry Truman was often vicious. Yet it cannot be denied that the President is criticized with bated breath. Punches *are* pulled; the critics feel, or they sense that the voters will feel, it unfair, undignified, to accuse the President in terms harsh enough to match his mistakes. For such criticisms seem to be an attack upon the President's failures of character, his mind, even his physique. The President, simply because he is Chief of State, is allowed mistakes for which he would be soundly and rightfully damned in Britain. The combination of the two roles, national symbol and political leader, is too emollient, too disarming, to be healthy for the mightiest democracy in the world.

Once he is elected, the historic eminence of the office allows to the incumbent all the possibilities of the "cult of the individual." He has the press, television, and radio at his disposal, without the shadow of rivalry from the men who fought him during the campaign and those who will challenge him at the next election. He possesses the nation, and he has a fixed term. So large does he loom over the land through all the processes of magnification and beneficent distortion that he is almost certain of renomination and re-election, slight as his merits may be. He has the right to free time on television and radio, ostensibly to "report" to the nation, but, all the same, he is a party chief, briefed by party colleagues for party advantage. In the competitive submission of the political case to the public he is given a preference on the networks, even when the Speaker of the House is refused time to discuss pending legislation. His oneness cannot be matched by the singleness of an opposition, for Congress is a Babel of voices. This is a gross liability for the nation's welfare, for history has shown us that the man who is President can be at one and the same time a popular celebrity and an officious or supine ass. My country, right or wrong, becomes My President, right or wrong.

Absence Abroad

In any account of the burden of the Presidency in our time it has become impossible to omit the wear and tear, the adverse affect upon his conduct in office, produced by the foreign travel the President may believe he must undertake. President Wilson began the practice when he traveled to Paris to negotiate the Treaty of Versailles. Exhaustion made serious inroads upon his health, his absence from Washington lost him public support and perhaps ruined the fabric of international agreement he had helped so laboriously to weave. His visits to other countries, his pilgrimage on behalf of the Fourteen Points, his missionary zeal to represent the best of American idealism to the Old World — surely these cost Wilson his life. During World War II Franklin Roosevelt continued the practice. Eisenhower, upon the death of Secretary Dulles, followed suit in so-called summit conferences, general good will tours in Europe, India, the Pacific, and Latin America.

The practice has grave consequences for the efficient conduct of the duties of presidential office. There may be occasions when the one man who symbolizes the American people must travel to distant lands and confront other chiefs of state, to show himself as America incarnate, to flatter the peoples of other nations, to show them that the devil has not got horns. The President's impatience with the processes of diplomacy may urge him to try his hand. A vain President, loving adulation and public applause, may be tempted to travel to lands where American economic aid makes a wildly enthusiastic reception a certainty. But the consequences are serious. Suppose Truman had been in India or

Venezuela when the Korean invasion began? Dean Rusk, who distinguished himself in the State Department, has put the issue vividly and realistically:

> The President is as mobile as a jet aircraft, but it is not clear that the Presidency is equally so. One can accept the pleasant and necessary fiction that the White House is wherever the President happens to be and still recognize that prolonged absences from Washington impair the effective performance of the office. Unless the President is accessible decisions on important matters are postponed by sympathetic subordinates or settled at the level of the common denominator among the departments and agencies concerned. On his own side, the President will be partially cut off from his cabinet offices, his personal staff, his usual flow of information, the leaders of Congress and of his own party. In addition he cannot act with regard to many of the formal and informal aspects of his office. . . . A President must be free to leave Washington, on business or on vacation, but the effect of his absence is greater than his personal staff would have him believe. . . .[49]

If the President *must* be absent, it is all the more necessary that he leave behind him in Washington colleagues with equal authority and electoral responsibility to assume the executive function in his absence.

Criticism of the President Necessary

There are occasions in the government of nations when men in responsible positions must be candidly, sometimes brutally, attacked for their *personal* unfitness. They must be exposed as lazy, inept, feeble, cowardly. It is dangerous when a nation becomes committed to a perpetual honeymoon with its Chief Executive, only punctuated by lovers' tiffs, a honeymoon maintained by "sweetheart contracts" of the most elusive sort. The nation desperately needs that men shall have such a standing, such a belief in their own authority, and be so unencumbered by the holy aspects of the state as to be able to say what L. S. Amery (echoing Cromwell to the Long Parliament) said to Neville Chamberlain in the House of Commons: "You have sat too long here for any good you have been doing. Depart, I say, and let us have done with you. In the name of God, go!" Yet, time and again, presidential spokesmen in the Senate seem to expect Congress to bow to the President's policy, declaring that otherwise they may anger the President.

Two quotations signalize the enormous power granted the President. The first, from John Adams, second President of the United States, appears in a letter he wrote to Roger Sherman in 1789:

> The duration of our President is neither perpetual nor for life; it is only for four years; but his power during those four years is much greater than that of an avoyer, a consul, a podesta, a doge, a stadholder; nay, than a king of Poland; nay, than a king of Sparta. I know of no first magistrate in any republican government, except England and Neuchatel, who possesses a constitutional dignity, authority, and power comparable to his. . . .[50]

The second quotation is from the British prime minister, William Ewart Gladstone, in an article written in the eighties:

> The head of the British Government is not a Grand Vizier. He has no powers, properly so called, over his colleagues: on the rare occasions, when a Cabinet determines its course by the votes of its members, his vote counts only as one of theirs. In a perfectly organized administration, such for example as that of Sir Robert Peel in 1841–6, nothing of great importance is matured, or would even be projected in any department without his personal cognizance; and any weighty business would commonly go to him before being submitted to the Cabinet.[51]

But the powers of the American President are mighty and sole, eased only somewhat by the President's discretion in the delegation of business. The President is an autocrat, the prime minister is a colleague among colleagues; the one is aloof, the other, immersed.

Independent Strength of the President

We have seen that the President has an independent strength nourished by the powers the Constitution vests in him and colossally enhanced by the play of modern politics. I talk of independent strength, meaning powers which no one else can exercise or control, or only under extreme circumstances. The President has all the power to do right or commit wrong, bringing irredeemable grief upon the people of his nation and other nations of the world.

These are the powers that make for independent strength of tremendous effect:

1. Control over the entire administrative personnel and operations;

2. Power to act, almost regardless of statute, in any emergency;

3. Power to initiate laws and exercise the power, both positive and negative, of the veto;

4. Budget-making power;

5. Power to conduct diplomacy and make treaties, committing the nation to agreements with other nations, disposing of American troops, etc., in such a way as to court or avoid war;

6. Power as Commander in Chief;

7. Exercise of considerable patronage;

8. Prestige and influence as leader of his party;

9. Glamor as Chief of State, the nation's symbol;

10. Access to the public by means of press conferences, where he alone determines what he shall say and what self-praising excerpts shall be flashed on the screens of television sets and theaters;

11. Access to television and radio to tell his side of any political story, with no equivalent right conceded by the networks to other branches of government, say, the Speaker of the House, the opposition party, or the majority leader of the Senate;

12. Role as the most important source, and object, of newspaper stories; ubiquitous and incessant if compared to other elements of the nation (perhaps with the exception of sports personalities) and far superior to the amount of attention given Congress.

A President commences with an enormous advantage in the opportunity to make his personal convictions prevail: He has status, and status backed by the whole history of the United States, all its patriotism, its glory. If, in addition, he has conviction and will, and, as it were, professional skill, few men around him can withstand his command or refuse to submit to his persuasions.

There is no independent or collective challenge of any real substance to the President's power. The President alone is charged with a prodigious and perilous enterprise, the highest temporal power on earth. Surely, after a sober and earnest view of our nation's obligations, this is a situation which must fill us with apprehension. It is impossible to suppress the question of whether any one man, no matter how brilliant he may be, should enter into possession of this might, this unobstructable power for good or evil. The presidential office is no trifle, light as air, no bauble; it belongs rightfully only to the offspring of a titan and Minerva husbanded by Mars. Is there a mortal we can name who can exercise this office both beneficently and responsibly? It is not a trust to be treated with flippancy. We have a responsibility, to discover how to regenerate the Presidency so that several men together may fill it as no one man can — a responsibility fearful and imperative indeed.

III

The Qualities of Political Leadership

To become President a man must possess the qualities necessary to win elections. But, once elected, he should possess the attributes proper to the conduct of that supreme office. The two sets of qualities are not quite the same thing. It is possible to be elected President without having the talents necessary to fulfil presidential responsibilities. Or a man may have all the talent required of a distinguished President but lack the faculty to win elections.

What qualities should men in positions of leadership possess? How should they be judged for their leadership? Are there general qualities common to leadership, applicable at every level of responsibility? I believe there are — and each notable and re- membered leader has had these qualities in ample measure to carry out his responsibilities.

But we must focus our attention on the particular qualities required for the conduct of the office of the Presidency of the United States. Each will be required, at one point or another, in the course of the President's week; all of these qualities will be called upon in time of emergency; and some, perhaps all, perhaps each with a different stress, will be evident from moment to moment in the conduct of the office, according to the furies or zephyrs of circumstance. There will be times when the tasks of office will be light, when no howling wind stirs the sea and no raging waves buffet the ship of state. There will be other times, "grand" times, "historic" times, when the hazards will be appalling and the vocation exalted, when all the latent powers of the office of President will be called out in heroic measure.

We appreciate political leadership by how well a man responds to his constitutional duties and how well he responds to his heroic opportunities — how well he behaves in the face of destiny. The twentieth century (let us say, since 1912) has called for a President with heroic attributes, and there is no reason to believe that the need for heroism will grow less in the years ahead.

I have contrived a list of qualities I believe essential to the office of the Presidency after close study of men with whom I have worked at various levels of government. I have asked myself, for what qualities did I admire them? I list twelve but it would be as easy to give twice that number. Some Presidents have had all these qualities in high measure. Some have had but few and have had to suffer (as the nation suffered) for lack of the rest. And once or twice, God help us — and He must have, for we survived — we have elected men who had none of these qualities:

Consciousness	Cleverness
Conviction	Coherence
Command	Constancy
Creativity	Charm, or Captivation
Courage	Conscientiousness
Conciliation	Constitution

I am only too well aware that all attempts at the dissection of character must meet the charge that one cannot divorce one quality from another, that all are intertwined, that none can be severed. I agree. But this will not prevent me from making the attempt to catch the qualities of presidential greatness in action.

Consciousness. — knowledge or perception of the facts involved in presidential decisions. No one expects the President to have independent knowledge of every facet of American life — for example, on such issues as whether the wild horses remaining in Nevada are being killed inhumanely, the subject of a bill in Congress. But surely his education and experience should have given him rather more than an average knowledge of the main facts of the nation's economy, international position, and defense needs, and this understanding should be in some depth and with recognition of their interrelated intricacy. He ought to have a sound grasp of the objectives of social policy and the role of each of the government departments and the co-ordination required for their fulfilment. He must be particularly knowledgeable about his constitutional position, especially of his legal and tactical relationships with Congress.

He must have enough consciousness of the facts to be able to say: We will make the atom bomb now; or, Our frontier is on the Rhine; or, Labor unions have and need a certain status in the economy; or, The average American family requires a government-supported health service; or, Soviet economy is making such strides that we must be spurred on to a competitive response, and the chief means by which this can be done are thus and so; or, Conditions of modern American strategic action for national survival require the co-ordination of the three defense departments and scientific and technological research and inventiveness in such wise as I ordain; or, It is time we designed an atomic-powered submarine; or, Slavery in the southern states consists of these particulars; or, A tariff will have such and such an effect on certain industries; or, Develop and stockpile missiles as fast as we can, regardful only of survival and regardless of expense.

We have examples to spare of Presidents who made the wrong proposals. Think of Truman, who proposed that Nationalist China troops be used in Korea at the outset of the "incident," failing to consider their lack of training and their poor equipment and the political complications that would ensue. Or consider the ignorance displayed by President Taft when he signed the Payne-Aldrich Bill, even as he confessed that everything about the high protectionist tariff was "just like Choctaw to a man who is not an expert." Yet he consulted no one before signing.[1] Truman became a capable President, but his ignorance of foreign affairs had serious consequences for the United States. Consider Truman's China policy: How inept was the mission on which General Marshall was sent, to seek a "democratic solution" for the conflict between Mao Tse-tung and Chiang Kai-shek. And the invasion of south Korea was in part due to an ignorance which muffled what should have been a clear voiced announcement of America's perimeter of defense. Truman let himself be opportunistically misguided by the Joint Chiefs into pushing too far north in Korea.

The minimum independent knowledge a President should have must be sufficient to enable him to call in expert advice and the ability to ask searching questions that test the expert's truthfulness and good sense.

This may seem a counsel of perfection. It is, of course it is; and no less essential for that. To require anything less of the President would be frivolous. But a counsel of perfection leads to this question: In the present magnitude and complexity of government affairs, can one man be presumed to have the minimum basic knowledge we expect of the President? My own answer is that it is impossible, and it would be incredible if he should claim it or if his publicity officers should claim it for him. I do not forget in any wise the assistance he obtains from his cabinet officers and from civil servants and the many agencies whose advice and expertise he has at his command. But he personally must have enough understanding to receive their reports intelligently, and he must be able to react with his own evaluation and choices of policy to put that knowledge into action. If it should be decided that the function so ascribed in this observation is unrealistic, then the theory of presidential responsibility as held hitherto, as sensed, or as assumed, is a hollow mockery.

Wilson was weak in knowledge of foreign nations, economics, and military affairs; Harding and Coolidge in almost everything; Hoover was knowledgeable in old-fashioned economics and rather primitive in foreign affairs; Truman was seriously weak in an understanding of international politics; Roosevelt had little sound grasp of national economics; Eisenhower was educated in an army barracks. Most of these men improved while in office the measure of their convictions, political experience, and ability to learn. But to say in June, 1959, that an obstinate-looking steel strike must be left to "the free forces of collective bargaining" shows a culpable lack of understanding of the simplest economic truths.

The want of a true perception of the nature of America's government accounts for the contemptible fiasco suffered by the President on January 17, 1957, at the hands of his own Secretary of the Treasury, a man in whom the President had exceptional faith, indeed, to whose views and character he clung. The President found himself confronted by a budget much in excess of that which he had requested and violating his election pledges that the budget would be balanced. The promise should never have been made in the cocky way it was. The President pusillanimously allowed his friend to conduct a press conference to explain the unfortunate state of affairs instead of facing it himself and plainly admitting that he had been in error. The Secretary of the Treasury lost control of his fuming subconscious and said that if the "terrific" tax burden were not reduced he would predict that "you will have a depression that will curl your hair." He added that the budget could be cut in many places — a direct contradiction of what the cabinet, with the President presiding, had just announced.

Executive responsibility would seem to be more practically secured and would be more credible if twelve men shared the task now imposed on one man. Meanwhile, we may reasonably ask how the public is to learn whether the candidates put before them have the requisite knowledge. If one of the answers to this question is that the selection process in the nominating conventions (and in secret conclaves preceding the nomination) takes care of that, the next question must be, How well does the selection process do this? Are the highest leaders selected in a responsible way?

The electorate may find it impossible to distinguish a candidate's true consciousness from what is really conceit or dogmatism. Almost every Western politician who talked with Khrushchev reports that he knows all the facts about the Soviet Union (but gives little evidence of an understanding of the United States) and is never at a loss in talking policy because he has the knowledge necessary to do this intelligently. American journalists report, with apparent amazement, that President de Gaulle can explain French policy lucidly, elegantly, and *of his own knowledge*. Of course he can! and so can his colleagues. This is the ability I have in mind in assaying the consciousness of the American President. The Presidency is clearly no place for an amateur.

Convictions — a conscientious adherence to certain policies, a personal philosophy of the national way of life and the rights and obligations men and women owe to each other, taking forms appropriate to the social and economic and international structure in which we live. It is difficult to dissociate convictions from consciousness; for convictions, according to their intensity, lead to an acquisition of knowledge and understanding; and right knowledge tends to evoke moral response productive of policies of conservatism or change.

Not to be separated from conviction, that is to say, loyalty to certain causes, are passion and will, a man seized in all the intensity of his being, to have no other interest and spiritual impetus until his vision is fulfilled. It is drive, the drive of self and of others. It is an error to believe that political leadership consists only of beckoning or teaching; it is moral fervor, driving all others and all things to the goal. It is *his* goal, passionately willed at the outset, using his own power to overcome the dead weight of others, until they catch aflame. The idea is nicely embodied in Winston Churchill's tribute to Roosevelt, his wartime colleague: "This formidable politician who imposed his will for nearly ten years upon the American scene . . .". As Hegel rightly said, "We may affirm absolutely that nothing great in the world has been accomplished without *passion*." He emphasized the last word. A leader is justly characterized by the intensity and persistence of his will. This element, conviction, passion and will, is not to be divorced from the quality of conscientiousness.

Conviction, I would say, is the fundamental quality of a statesman. It has certainly been that which has most enduringly and most unerringly distinguished the "great" President from others. In a poll conducted in 1948 by Professor A. M. Schlesinger, Sr., six American Presidents were judged to be great. They were Lincoln, Washington, Franklin Roosevelt, Wilson, Jefferson, and Jackson. When the respondents were asked what quality constituted "greatness," the answers amounted to what I have styled *conviction* of an intense and elevated moral order.[2] Schlesinger found that the qualities common to men of the most diverse personality and temperament were these: Each was identified with some crucial turning point in the nation's development, and each had established a new conception of America's destiny. Each had sided with whatever was understood in his time and circumstances as progressivism and social improvement. They were loyal to "great ends," having a vision of a perfect society, a worthier way of life. Or, as Franklin Roosevelt once said, "The Presidency is pre-eminently a place of moral leadership." This, too, was Truman's expressed conviction. Each of these men left a permanent mark on his time; each voiced his moral vision. Thus, Washington on "party" and "entangling alliances"; Jefferson on the rights of the majority and the minority; Jackson, "It is to be regretted that the rich and powerful too often bend the acts of government to their selfish purposes" (in his veto of the Bank of the United States bill), and "Our Federal Union, it must be preserved"; Lincoln's Gettysburg Address, a vindication of and a full expression of the democratic system, and his admonition that the Union could not continue half slave and half free; Wilson's "The world must be made safe for democracy"; Roosevelt's New Deal, "the forgotten man," the Four Freedoms, and so on.

None of these, as it happened, was a cliché borrowed from popular conviction; but it must be admitted that in our own time the electoral method encourages candidates to borrow phrases (or to suffer them at the hands of press agents, public relations men, "buddies," and political confidants). Candidates find themselves bolstered by flashy generalizations ("moral crusade," for example) and have no idea of the origin, purport, or consequences entailed. But the Presidents we have named sought only to express their own convictions as clearly and warmly as possible, even when, like Jackson, their spelling was not all it might have been.

It is impossible in this essay to recapitulate the social philosophy of Presidents great and small. We can point to the influence of each of the great Presidents. Andrew Jackson's determination that the common man, the rising middle and working classes, should not have their opportunity of economic and social advancement throttled by private control of credit; that careers in the public service should not be closed to ordinary men because they lacked social privilege. Lincoln's noble and merciful message of the equality of all men, regardless of color or previous servitude, and his determination that the Union must be preserved. Wilson's conviction that big business must be controlled in its coercion of smaller competitors, its attitude toward labor, in its "dollar diplomacy," and his attempt to embody a new vision of the world (no less striking because wise and saintly men had entertained it before him) in the Fourteen Points and, above all, in the League of Nations — making him and the creation that attended his vision immortal. Franklin Roosevelt's flamboyant and gay restoration of the courage of a nation terrified by the immensity of its economic disaster, his elevation of labor unions to their rightful place, his gift of social security to the distressed and the aged, the introduction of the concept of *positive* freedoms in addition to the protective ones, and his support of the democratic cause in World War II, his emphasis on human salvation in international affairs through the United Nations Charter, permanent alliances (reversing George Washington's doctrine, for the world had shrunk, become very acquisitive, and discovered nuclear power) with the democracies and a "good-neighbor" policy to all nations and especially to those south of the border. Truman's continuation of these principles, yet forced to invent out of his own convictions America's responsibility in the use of nuclear weapons; the "cold war" with Russia, entailing a philosophy of alliances, economic aid, military aid, and recognition of the consequences of international strength in a time of extreme peril; and a sustained and explicit support of the United Nations.

Other, lesser Presidents stood for nothing in their own persons, or very little, unless prompted by men and events; they were less creative, apt to be passive; they were not, as Hegel would say, "persons." But how can it be conveyed to the modern voter that when a President's philosophy of government is announced it is the work of a team of ghostwriters and no more than a combination of popular, carefully tested clichés?

A glaring example of lack of conviction was Eisenhower's gingerly treatment of the Supreme Court's decisions on desegregation. The use of troops at Little Rock became necessary because he had too-long-failed to champion the moral basis of the Supreme Court decisions. Of course, the President's aloofness may be defended with the argument that such an expression of conviction would exacerbate southern feelings of disunion.

We have raised a serious problem; rather, the conduct of presidential elections and the service of the men who have attained the office have raised the problem for us. How is a man of conviction discovered and brought to the Presidency, and does the process lead to the reliable judgment that the candidate's convictions are his own convictions, that he is sincere and to be intrusted with the sole responsibilty for the exercise of so life-giving, so lethal, a power?

One of the most remarkable phenomena of modern presidential electioneering, especially when candidates are entering the race for the first time, is that instead of attempting to make clear their convictions they are deliberately advised to hide them. The surest way to the Presidency is to remain calculatedly silent about one's political philosophy. Of course there are many different ways to say nothing — the ever-open mouth and the dashing pen may be instruments of concealment. In the American system, it is better for a presidential candidate to say nothing at all; he will make fewer enemies, alert fewer rivals, and will be able to make an overwhelming assault on public sentiment in the six weeks of the election campaign when the cards are stacked against reason and sober, penetrating criticism. Silence also provides the least embarrassment to party tacticians, ghostwriters, and newspapermen. Silence will get a man the nomination, without convictions.

Here it is pertinent to observe that some Presidents with firm convictions have held them at a time when they were irrelevant: Hoover once complained that what he believed was sound but that the people wanted "dramatics," which he could not give.

One final observation must be made on the nature of conviction as an essential of leadership. Conviction ought not to be confused with "smart politics," by which I mean that widespread notion that "politics" signifies nothing more than to say or do whatever is necessary to capture votes or prevent votes from going to another man. Cunning is not conviction; indeed, it is often its destroyer. Nor should voters believe that pious platitudes, bombast, sentimental sermonizing, fanatic declarations, or an *idée fixe* are signs of genuine conviction. The messianic faith in France and hostility to de Gaulle manifested by Franklin Roosevelt in World War II was conviction run wild and of no help to the Allies.

What we have said may be summed up in an observation made by Truman:

> All presidential messages must begin with the President himself. He must decide what he wants to say and how he wants to say it. Many drafts are usually drawn up, and this fact leads to the assumption that presidential speeches are "ghosted." The final version, however, is the final word of

the President himself, expressing his own convictions and his policy. These he cannot delegate to any man if he would be President in his own right.[3]

Does the American political system encourage selection according to conviction? Is the contemporary system of selection the best conceivable? I will attempt to answer these questions in a later chapter.

Command — the ability to decide that at a certain moment all the choices available shall be brought to a head, one be preferred over all others, and that action be undertaken on it.

Government is not merely contemplation; it is action, the solution of problems and the subdual of difficulties. Conviction and consciousness propose the direction and suggest the means. A leap is required from these partly kinetic and partly potential energizing elements in leadership — it is the decisiveness of desire and will. It is an artist's response, the leap over doubts and fears, having its expression in commands to colleagues and subordinates.

That decisiveness is nine-tenths of government may account for the strong inclination of the common man to favor a military candidate for office, though so much in the soldier's life is disqualification for the office of the Presidency. An army exists to act and its officers to command action and seek decisions. An analogy of the army and civil government is farfetched, but there are sufficient apparent similarities to mislead the electorate, accustomed to thinking that government is action, existing only to do something, to make things happen. The field of battle is very different from civil politics and government. Without conviction and consciousness, command is unhinged, at sea. To make a decision calls for more than the soldier's prowess and courage.

Command does not mean that the impetus must or will come only in the form of an order, for it might function more effectively, according to circumstances, through persuasion and argument; for example, in the relationship between a President and his cabinet, as described in a later chapter. Yet, behind presidential persuasion looms his vested authority — he plays his role with the influence of his constitutional status bearing down on the minds of other men.

No conviction, no decisiveness; no decisiveness, no command;

no command, no government. But not all command is the off-spring of conviction; sheer officiousness and snap judgments may look like decisiveness, and some decisions may be foolish.

Creativity — the ability to apply convictions inventively to the newly emerging problems of government, to the end that the problem is solved for the national benefit. A brilliant example is Alexander Hamilton's creation of young America's new political economy as Secretary of the Treasury under Washington. The creativeness of the President is not to be tested by congressional acceptance or rejection, for a President is expected to have more political imagination, both valid and ingenious, than that commonly expected of a congressman. The League of Nations and American participation in world affairs as expressed in the Treaty of Versailles were creative acts. They were defeated, to the ultimate damage of the United States and the world, by men of narrower mind than President Wilson. He was a prophet. The evolution of foreign policy under Truman was a wiser creativeness, the adoption of principles to meet an evolving situation, than that offered by the right wing of the Republican party, even of its moderates as redeemed by the leadership of the convert, Senator Vandenberg.

Theodore Roosevelt's mediation between warring Russia and Japan in 1904 was a creative stroke that produced the Treaty of Portsmouth and preserved China's integrity against Japan. If Japan was angry, that anger was mollified in part by Roosevelt's "gentlemen's agreement" permitting some immigration to California; and Japan was overawed by the presence of the U.S. fleet in coastal waters.

Another prime example of political creativity was Franklin Roosevelt's decision to mobilize all resources, human and material, needed for the making of the atomic bomb at a time when even the scientists involved could not be certain of success. The President grasped at once the political implications of the news of advances in Germany, and his decision is presumed to have saved half a million American casualties in World War II. Other examples of creative mind and conscience in the Presidency are the Truman Doctrine, the Marshall Plan, the Brannan Plan, the Berlin airlift rather than the plan of the Joint Chiefs of Staff to challenge the Russians on the ground, and Truman's decision to order the making of the H-bomb. In Eisenhower's tenure, the most notable acts of political creativity were rapprochement with Khrushchev and the USSR and the beginning of a policy of "massive deterrence."

An example of creativity *missed* was the failure to mobilize science and education in the period 1952–57 to develop the intercontinental ballistic missile before the USSR could use its own success in this field as an immense force in diplomacy, not least to bend the American will. Another is the boycott of Red China by both Truman and Eisenhower, as if thereby Red China would cease to exist.

Courage. — The life of a leader is lived under three permanent stresses, omitting the danger that some lunatic will seek to settle a grievance against the world by attacking a representative of its authority. The President must face opponents and their calumny. He must undertake actions which may benefit the majority but bring hardship on a few. And he must suffer the pangs of uncertainty until a decision is seen to be a cause for rejoicing (or to be buried as a mistake).

A leader must brave the calumny of his opponents. Wilson fought the bosses of New Jersey who had nominated him for the governorship so that he need not compromise when he appealed to the legislators and the electorate for the reforms he had at heart. Wilson had rare courage in challenging Bryan, who might have failed to support him at the 1912 Democratic nominating convention. His courage was further manifest in the resumption of personal messages to Congress, a practice avoided by Presidents since the time of Jefferson. Wilson, against advice, decided to take part in the Paris Peace Congress in 1919. He fought a battle against Henry Cabot Lodge and his associates in the Senate in order to carry the Treaty of Versailles to acceptance, and he fought to final physical collapse in a nationwide tour to rally popular support. He defied those who circulated rumors of an illicit love affair; he defied the slanders of George Harvey, breaking with him when Harvey demanded concessions to "Wall Street interests." He made concessions to Britain regarding tolls on the Panama Canal in the face of Irish-American and German-American opposition and congressional uproar; he met treaty obligations, and he apologized to the government of Panama for an insult of which he was guilty. He sponsored notable tariff reductions in the Underwood Tariff Act of 1913 by appealing to the public over the most violent attacks of the lobbyists. These are but a few instances of acts of signal presidential courage.

Republican and southern opposition to Franklin Roosevelt's policies was determined, and he was reviled as a traitor to his class. The slanders about his person and the hatred evinced at mention of his name were shrill and foul. Invective in politics has been more rancorous, because more robust, in America than in other countries, including France, and rising to intensities seldom surpassed except in German extremist circles. The chief mitigation when a President suffers slander and obstinate opposition is the intensity of his convictions. It must be admitted that the President often accepts this burden genially enough. A leader is apt to relish his achievement of political change, which is his métier, and enjoy "making things happen," which is his delight, and will not shrink from inflicting pain on real or imagined enemies, since to see them squirm is one of the compensations of the game.

A President is obliged to make decisions that are painful to some. Modern representative government, vesting responsibilities in legislators and executives which in more primitive societies are borne by the population as a whole, transfers the terrible burden of conscience from the masses to the few; and in the democratic system the transfer is very largely to one man. His courage is sustained by his popular election, which re-places a measure of responsibility on the electors. Yet he must sign death warrants and refuse to grant mercy to convicted traitors. He must refuse men the offices they seek. He must dismiss men (for example, Truman's dismissal of General MacArthur) in spite of popular clamor and threats from Congress. And he must act, whatever the judgment or bias of the press, which in some instances may oppose malevolently any policy he champions.

It was an act of political courage on Eisenhower's part to refuse to prime the pump with public works during a time of serious unemployment in 1958 (brought on, in part, by the mistaken policy of his own financial advisers) and to have faith in the prognostications of his economic aids who believed that an upturn would come about without pump-priming and without attendant inflation. The President had to hold out against charges of having an insensitive conscience and a tough hide, against labor leaders and some congressional leaders who urged immediate action. The President took the only course open to him, recommendations for small increases in unemployment benefits. Within six months the economy had begun to right itself, though Eisenhower's prediction that it would improve by April or May was wrong; it lasted into 1959. Moreover, Eisenhower's appointment and unyielding support of Ezra Taft Benson and his agricultural policies through eight hard years was an act of signal courage, though it must fairly be said that the wisdom of the policy is sharply disputed. However, the President believed he had a good man and stood by him under heavy fire.

A President must take his courage in both hands and give orders for American troops to go into action.[4] Truman's decision to fight in Korea was a hard decision to make; it was, he said, the most agonizing day of his life. The dropping of the atomic bomb in 1945 was to end a war; but the decision on Korea in 1950 was to begin one — and the agony was, where might it end?

And other acts of courage: Truman's seizure of the steel mills; Eisenhower's action in regard to Suez (crassly and damagingly mistaken as I think it was); the landing of troops in Lebanon (beneficient as I believe it to have been). Courage of another sort might have been shown had the President been willing to "get in the gutter" (in Eisenhower's words) with men like Senator Joseph McCarthy in time to stop the incalculable mischief which such a rogue could do. It might have meant the hostility of some congressional friends of the senator, but this would have done the President no great harm. Instead the fight was left to private citizens (above all, Edward R. Murrow). Faintheartedness, want of conviction, want of consciousness of the situation, are too often mistaken for "wisdom" and "dignity."

Among examples of modern courage of a tenacious kind must be reckoned Franklin Roosevelt's purge of the Democratic party to remove certain dissentient congressmen. It had never been tried before, and this unsuccessful action may have given pause to those tempted to thwart the plans the President laid before Congress. Another notable example was Truman's defiance of the Dixiecrats; such a stand as his might well be the purification of the Democratic party, to the immense benefit of the nation.

Courage was much discussed by the ancient philosophers. It is not foolhardiness, they said, but a realistic understanding of the terror to come, coupled with the fortitude to take the spiritual and physical pains consequent on action in the face of it.

I understand the professional *sang-froid* a statesman (like a surgeon) is obliged to adopt if he is to continue his painful duties; but to maintain this prayerful combination of self-possession and dispassion is a strain on a man's courage. A surgeon will confess that he dies a little when he loses a patient, and a President when he loses a bill, a friend, or an appointment he proposes. But neither will break down. Max Weber says that one of the marks of a politician is a "sense of proportion." By this he means, "ability to let realities work upon him with inner concentration and calmness. . . . For the problem is simply how can warm passion and a cool sense of proportion be forged together in one and the same soul?"

We confront Lord Acton's misleading dictum, now something of a cliché, "Power tends to corrupt, and absolute power to corrupt absolutely." Of course; if a man is a coward, power magnifies his cowardice; if he is noble, as Lincoln was, power magnifies his nobility. What was but of small dimension in the man becomes gigantic through the exercise of the powers the nation has vested in the office. He may seem to be forced to act out of character, but he cannot act as he is not.

The President may be a kindly man yet find himself using some form of blackmail against an opponent in Congress or even in his own party.[5] It is difficult to tell when courage becomes callousness or secret cruelty. A leader can be too kind for the needs of his office. Eisenhower relied on Sherman Adams far too long (using him, by the way, as "hatchet man" for acts for which he lacked fortitude), even until the coming 1958 congressional elections cut short this indulgence. Truman was far too blind to some of the men around him, men who betrayed his trust and tarnished the Presidency.

It would be an injury to the nation not to be able to discriminate between a cruel man or a vulgar ruffian and a man of courage, yet the electoral system scarcely permits the discrimination to be made. Also, rashness looks like courage sometimes.

Can a man's potential courage be assessed before he is endowed with the authority which will demand its exercise? It is assessable in the selection process, to a certain extent; but can it be discovered under the present nominating process? It is doubtful. The candidate is not seen in roles which might allow us to make an intelligent guess. Is a better process of discernment conceivable? Yes. And it need not be anything like the brutal selective process used in the Soviet Union, where no leader's hand has been unstained by the blood of comrades who failed to shed his. Something like the selective process used in the British parliamentary system would be helpful.

The third type of stress a statesman must be willing to suffer is, on his own initiative, to dare to contradict his close advisers, his most intimate friends, because he believes himself to be right, and to endure the agony of waiting until his calculated risk is attended with success.[6] Not only must he wait, but he is obliged to continue, to add resources and personal energy to a policy under fire, and to present a smiling, unperturbed face to a wolfish world. All political decision is a calculated risk; it is an attempt at prophecy. Reputation is dear to those who have thrown their whole identity and meaning into the climb to the top. It is Aristotle's error, although an amiable one, to argue that the best statesman is likely to be the man who does not want office; such a man might have the wisdom but he would seem to lack the will and the convictions that governing requires. Bismarck has expressed the agony of holding firm until the results are in:

> For a Minister who completely identifies his own honor with that of his country, the uncertainty of the result of each political decision has a most harassing effect. It is just as impossible to foresee with certainty the political results at the time when the measure has to be carried, as it would be in our climate to predict the weather of the next few days. Yet we have to make our decisions as though we could do so, often enough fighting against all the influences to which we are accustomed to attach weight. . . . The consideration of the question whether a decision is right, and whether it is right to hold fast and carry through what, though upon weak premises, has been recognized as right, has an agitating effect on every conscientious and honorable man. This is strengthened by the circumstance that often many years

must elapse before we are able in political matters to convince ourselves whether our wishes and actions were right or wrong. It is not the work which is wearing, but rather doubts and anxieties: the feeling of honor and responsibility, without being able to support the latter by anything except our own convictions and our own will, and this is more especially the case in the most important crises. *The intercourse with others whom we regard as similarly situated helps us to overcome these crises.*[7]

I have italicized the sentence above. The responsibility of the President is solely his; surely he must crave others to help him overcome the crises he faces?

To a man of conviction this is the most wearing aspect of the office; to a man, indeed, who recognizes his responsibility to serve the people who elect him, who has an informed mind as well as a sensitiveness about the effect of his actions on his nation's future; and it is a dreadful burden, wearing on health no less than on nerves. (Psychosomatic medicine seeks to demonstrate that each is a factor in the other.) Such a man in such an office must have courage.

Conciliation. — It is generally agreed that a good President should be able to unify the nation as he tries to unify his party. Whatever differences may antagonize and cause conflict among citizens, it is desirable for the larger interests of humanity — for peace and order, above all — that the disgruntled, the wounded, shall not be pressed too hard, that they shall be appeased. Justice often throws a sharp sword among the masses of the nation and cannot avoid doing so, as the policy, the noble demeanor, and the suffering of Lincoln show. Conviction will clash with conciliation. Some Presidents have been praised for producing a "concert of interests" in the nation; others, Truman, for example, have been accused of exacerbating dissension, by their very personality. The particular instance may be valid or not. But any peace-loving nation will benefit from the solicitude of a conciliator, and cleverness and charm can make the bitter more palatable. Yet unanimity is not to be expected, not even in the course of a war for survival. And conciliation can be exerted at the cost of civil rights and with burdens placed upon the underprivileged by a President who is not merely without conviction of civil rights and wrongs but is, by nature, incapable of such conviction. Ignorance and false good nature often masquerade as conciliation before the vast electorate. The self-satisfied smile, and the attempt to appease, must be challenged in debate from time to time to test its purpose or its hidden vacuity.

Cleverness — an adroitness, a daily resourcefulness in surmounting obstacles. An early example is Polk's agility when, though an expansionist candidate, he allowed Congress to take the onus of accepting the 49° parallel instead of 54° 40′ as the Oregon boundary. Consider how Franklin Roosevelt played upon Secretary Ickes' ambition to head a Department of Conservation. Roosevelt needed Ickes but had no need of a new department, and he managed to keep Ickes without yielding to him. Again, consider Roosevelt's manipulation of public opinion by means of his famous "fireside chats," and the tactics he used to secure the repeal of the Neutrality Act in October, 1939. ("I am almost literally walking on eggs. . . . I am at the moment saying nothing, seeing nothing and hearing nothing.") And all the while the votes in Congress were being lined up by every device available to the President.

A President can be too clever. Roosevelt overreached himself in attempting to reform the Supreme Court. Surely this was, and is, so hallowed an American institution that nothing less than open and frank action (if anything at all) would have succeeded? A surreptitious course brought suspicion of his purpose and increased distrust of the man.

Roosevelt was a past master of the degree of cleverness needed for success in the American system; Woodrow Wilson was not clever enough. Roosevelt was sensitive to public opinion and knew how to manipulate it; he was quick to comprehend the almost inconceivable amount of detail which determines the balance of votes and influence, and he learned to deal with intragroup factions in order to sway the group to his policy without becoming embroiled in their quarrels. He was a prince of correct timing. Through thirteen years of leadership he displayed his skill. During the campaign for a third term in 1940, he secured Republican support for his foreign policy in spite of isolationist opposition to war, and he fortified the social and economic gains of the New Deal.

Hoover lacked a dramatic and flamboyant personality and was not clever with words. He could not create the phrases that sway men. He was unable to announce himself "too proud to fight"; he had no gift for a soothing "There is nothing to fear but fear itself"; he never boasted of our "manifest destiny," though this was a journalist's phrase, not a president's invention; nor did he dub Al Smith "the Happy Warrior," or belabor "economic royalists," or view with shame "one-third of a nation ill-housed, ill-fed." Men who are not clever with words are usually not clever with ideas and imagination.

One of Roosevelt's clever traits was his ability to anticipate public response to events; he could guess the moment when a telling phrase would find its mark. He spoke of "a rendezvous with destiny," and the American people recognized it to be true. Courage backed by cleverness will draw from an apathetic or reluctant people reserves of loyalty and effort unsurmised by the sceptics. It was a very shrewd decision to send American troops to North Africa in 1942. Americans had a need to do battle after a depressing year of forced surrenders and defeats. To some extent, the invasion of North Africa delayed preparations for the invasion of Europe, and military advisers opposed it; nevertheless, the President insisted and proved to be right.

A pusillanimous President, on the other hand, is not able to inspire, nor can he set in motion important events. He complains irascibly that the people will not follow him and that his critics are unfair.

Wilson would have been a failure as President, and perhaps would never have become President, had it not been for the cleverness of his friend and confidant "Colonel" Edward M. House, one of the most astute connoisseurs of human nature, American variety, in politics. Was it cleverness or some instinctive affinity that produced the "strangest friendship in history," between a Presbyterian minister become President and a consummate Texan and political manipulator? An unusually clever stroke to be attributed to Colonel House was the "leaking" of the contents of a secret note from the German ambassador Zimmerman offering to cede American territory to Mexico in return for Mexican support against the United States in World War I. This maneuver aroused war sentiment and made more palatable Wilson's announcement of our entry in the war.

Truman blundered when he failed to be suspicious of a speech on U.S.–Soviet relations prepared by Henry Wallace. Then again, Truman showed cleverness in choosing General Marshall for a mission to China (even though the attempt to reach a settlement misfired), and even more so in sponsoring the Marshall Plan of economic and military aid.

The qualities of leadership I have listed would be ineffectual in the American political system, so disrupted by the separation of powers, geographic diversity, the broken history of political parties, and the ferocity of pressure groups — all amiably called "American pluralism" — if the kind of cleverness I have sketched here were lacking. But all the cleverness in the world, without other qualities to restrain it, would be equally vain. The American system is more prone to reward cleverness in office than to encourage and recompense the substantial qualities of conviction, creativeness, and consciousness. The American is more disposed to applaud cleverness than greatness, for greatness by its nature is remote from, alien to, his everyday life: men who "play it smart," men who "get by," men who "put it over."

How a President behaves in the course of a press conference is a gauge of his cleverness. It is reported that Franklin Roosevelt, who held press conferences on the average of twice a week (!), had four categories of answers: direct quotation on special occasions, indirect quotations to be attributed to the President himself, background information to be presented as under the reporter's own authority, and off-the-record comments that could not be used at all.[8] Roosevelt, ardent fisherman, played the various categories with tremendous skill. He delighted in composing news stories for the correspondents and, many have admitted, he had a sure eye for a striking lead.

Truman, enjoying press conferences, accepted them as a challenge to a contest of wits between reporters and himself. He made frequent use of ridicule, pretended anger, and was not above blaming reporters if a trial balloon collapsed. His most serious fault was a failure to examine the phrasing of a question and parry in kind. More than once he was trapped by an insinuation. Douglass Cater asserts that Truman's extremely costly observation that the charge that his administration was soft on communists was a "red herring" was in answer to the mild question,

"Mr. President, do you think the Capitol Hill spy scare is a red herring to divert public attention from inflation?"

Mr. Truman was unguarded in issuing a statement to the press that he had "always under consideration" the use of the atomic bomb in Korea. Some newspapers omitted the word "always" — and Prime Minister Attlee hurriedly crossed the Atlantic (November, 1951) to make certain that the bomb would not be used before consultation with America's allies. Reporters had tried to alert Truman to the gravity of his statement, but he chose to misunderstand them.

It is difficult to know whether Eisenhower's red-faced anger, often reported by White House correspondents, and his indulgence in folksy homilies should be considered cleverness or not, for they both hide and reveal him. Early in office Eisenhower employed a skilled actor to coach his television appearances.

Richard M. Nixon's visit to Russia and the demeanor he preserved during rioting in Latin American are prime examples of consummate political cleverness. Polished behavior says nothing of convictions; varnish is not philosophy; it gives no clue to policies; it is composed of gestures and phrases to which measured dissent (or reasoned assent) is next to impossible. Adlai Stevenson's depiction of Nixon during the 1956 presidential campaign suggests one of the doubts cleverness may raise: "This is a man of many masks. Who can say they have seen his face?"

Probably our "cleverest" President, in the unpleasant sense of the word, was Martin Van Buren, known as the "Red Fox," the "Magician," whose cleverness brought him to office where, at length, his feebleness was revealed.

Cleverness may be revealed as cunning and trickiness. It is, in fact, an exploitable quality in campaigns lasting but six weeks. If it is something more devious than resilience of reaction and quick-wittedness under fire, it may be a disadvantage to a presidential candidate.

How can the voter be assisted to discriminate more nicely between cleverness as an asset and cleverness as a liability? The Constitution might have given Congress the task of judging candidates. Congress contains professional politicians accustomed to judging the soundness of men and as alert to sham as they are able to appreciate the skilled tactician and campaigner. There is a good deal of truth in the proverb, Set a thief to catch a thief. But Congress was abruptly excluded from the process of presidential selection. The original electoral college was vested with this function, but party caucuses and conventions have assumed the authority. Should it be restored to the electoral college? I say, on the sober grounds of efficient and responsible government, it ought to be.

Coherence — that quality of leadership which recognizes that one segment of policy cannot be pursued without regard for the claims of the rest. At a certain juncture in a nation's affairs it is madness to rage over an unbalanced budget when the need of military strength for survival is paramount. If to defend the nation it is necessary to allocate huge sums for munitions and science, one may require a balanced budget only if ready to increase taxes to compensate; and taxation and a defense program may call for the government to intervene in industry to maintain an expanding rate of production. The relationship of Charles Wilson, Secretary of Defense, and George Humphrey, Secretary of the Treasury, to Eisenhower's policies from 1953 to 1958 may well have weakened disastrously the nation's position in the balance of world power, led to the loss of the Middle East to the influence of the USSR, increased the pressure for the surrender of Western rights in Berlin, and prepared the way for the evils yet to come by reason of our paucity of military strength. Another illustration was Hoover's inability to make his gold standard policy cohere with the need for federal aid when unemployment struck the nation. Another example, Roosevelt's acceptance of the advice of the Joint Chiefs of Staff, who urged him to allow Russia to participate in our invasion of the Far East.

A particularly grave example of lack of coherence at the presidential level was noted by Walter Lippmann during the steel strike in 1959. The main weight of the President's economic policy had been the acceleration of national production in a battle against inflation. The steel strike meant the loss of production in an industry indispensable to the productivity of many others; about 700,000 men were thrown out of work by the strike, and in other industries another 100,000 were affected. There was danger of greater unemployment should the stockpile of steel be exhausted before the strike was settled. The interdependence of all industries is an elementary fact in all countries with a modern economic structure. The outbreak of the strike in June, 1959, was greeted by the President with the observation that it must be settled by the "free processes of collective bargaining." It was not until the strike had lasted over two months that the President exerted himself slightly to arbitrate, saying that he was "sick and tired" of the lack of progress, and pleading "in the national interest." [9] The cost of indecisive action was shocking. At last a provision of the Taft-Hartley Act was invoked, calling for resumption of work in eighty days because "national health and safety" were endangered.

Since the President is vested with final responsibility, his is the function of securing coherence among the many departments and conciliar bodies. Far too much, I think, is demanded of one man. If his cabinet were composed of men drawn from a well-developed party with a well-defined program, the cabinet might provide coherence. To be single in responsibility is not necessarily to be coherent in relating one phase of policy to another. Congress does not supply coherence; the parties do not do so. How can one man, beset with so many tasks, make a whole of a thousand separate parts supplied by sources of vastly different status and competence? The men chosen by Franklin Roosevelt for his first cabinet and "brains trust" were of an impossible and damaging heterogeneity, and some of the policies pursued in the course of the first four years were shockingly wasteful and in conflict one with another.

It is to court disaster and waste resources not to have a collective body able to achieve coherence. What are the chances that the electorate, without careful guidance, will recognize that what the candidate for President may claim to be a coherent policy is nothing but superficial formalism or bland officiousness? Coherence is far from easy to descry.

Constancy. — The public has moods; Congress has moods; pressure groups fluctuate in their interests; yet all demand leadership that is constant — ever-present, ever-alert, ever-prescient and presentient, always touched in conscience by what may happen if those responsible fail to act. [10] This demands of the Chief Executive exceptional qualities of spirit. It invites national disaster if the President's body and nervous system are not more than usually excellent. The President must undertake exceptional measures of diet, rest, and exercise to meet his obligations. Wilson fought a losing battle against arteriosclerosis, Franklin Roosevelt against the effects of polio. Roosevelt's superhuman bravery at Yalta may not have offset his failing strength when he needed all of his energy and militancy to cope with Stalin. The harm done the nation since 1955, especially by omission to act, by the presence in the White House of an ailing President is incalculable. As an image of the presidential candidate is flashed on the screen, can the viewers say whether it is constancy they see or a want of inspiration, a dull mind, the self-preoccupation of the invalid?

Conscientiousness — a quality closed allied to conviction, being the willing commitment to act on one's beliefs. If leadership were only a game, a pleasant pastime, a lively gamble, it would pall in the course of time and be pursued only in spurts of passion. But consider an observation made by Woodrow Wilson in 1914, when foreign affairs began to press upon him as they had not in earlier years:

> When I think of the number of men who are looking to me as the representative of a party, with the hope for all varieties of salvage from the things they are struggling in the midst of, it makes me tremble. It makes me tremble not only with a sense of inadequacy and weakness, but as if I were shaken by the very things that are shaking them and, if I seem circumspect, it is because I am so diligently trying not to make any colossal blunders. If you just calculate the number of blunders a fellow can make in twenty-four hours if he is not careful and if he does not listen more than he talks, you would see something of the feeling that I have.[11]

Wilson was speaking to some journalists. A little later he confessed that the pressure of responsibility was "unconscionable."

Truman, dwelling on the establishment of the Strategic Air Command, argued:

> I do not believe that the President is well served if he depends upon the agreed recommendations of just a few people around him, boiled down to a brief statement submitted to him for approval. This may be efficiency in military administration, but not in government at the top level.

In the long run the best results come from intensive study of different viewpoints and from arguments pro and con. I have spent many hours, late at night and early in the morning, poring over papers giving all sides. Many times I was fairly convinced in my own mind which course of action would be the right one, but I still wanted to cover every side of the situation before coming to a final decision.[12]

I am persuaded that it is assurance of this degree of conscientiousness that the public would like to have from its leaders; and only conscientiousness as rigorous as this bodes well for the interests of the nation. The more sophisticated public is not reassured when a reporter announces that the President is doing a better job in his seventh year of office because he has begun to read the newspapers. The public has a right to be anxious when it learns that the President relies to excess on oral reports. It is true that some men learn by listening to others, but, as Francis Bacon observed, it is writing that maketh an exact man. If a man can read and knows how to think he may learn more swiftly alone than in company.

Conscientiousness, like a sense of conviction, is the trigger that sends men on flights of surmise and speculation toward understanding and action. For example, Roosevelt's creation of the PWA and the WPA. An omission may be costly to the nation: Eisenhower arranged for a special briefing on the intercontinental ballistic missile and preparedness to meet missile attack only after being urged to do so by the chairman of the Joint Committee on Atomic Energy and the chairman of the Senate Military Applications Subcommittee. Earlier proddings seemingly went unheeded.[13]

A false impression of conscientiousness may be gained by the public when it is, in fact, a prudish temperament, timidity, or an officious nature in command or asking election.

Charm — a quality known to all statesmen and rhetoricians, an endearment in the man himself, in his body, eyes, and expression, perhaps some physical or spiritual attractiveness, a degree of magnetism, that inspires a following, generates trust without making explicit promises. It was known long before Max Weber, drawing attention to a link between charm and charisma, brought it to the attention of sociologists. Shamen and prophets enraptured by epilepsy have led men by its influence, often to a shared doom. From sublime eloquence to ranting is often but a note in the voice to a mass of listeners, sometimes only a borrowed metaphor beautiful enough to be mistaken for reality. It is not, then, an unmixed blessing to be captivating, to have charm.

Woodrow Wilson possessed charm through the force of prophetic utterance, an enormous power; but, as he admitted, until he spoke his face was against him. He was lucky to have Colonel House to offset his somber appearance and his self-consciously labored jokes. Theodore Roosevelt had a personal force of energy and robustness — to the point of caricature; it was effective for his purposes. The most charming President, if we except Andrew Jackson's lively ways, was Franklin Roosevelt, who combined good nature, affability, wit, an attractive voice, and infectious smile (calling to mind the psychology of sympathetic action adduced by Adam Smith), and a prankish sense of humor. Of course he failed to charm the sort of men he called "economic royalists." Charm is President Eisenhower's chief asset.[14]

There is a peril in a politician's charm when he has at command the mass communications, particularly the television networks which bring him into every corner of the land. Appeal becomes less and less rational; the appearance of good humor, confidence, and, let us say, "a famous grin" are set above intelligence, conviction, and conscientiousness. It is possible to envisage a day when a wax dummy, controlled by Univac, will be capable of gaining our confidence and winning our votes. This is, of course, *reductio ad absurdum*; may it continue to be so.

A one-man Presidency puts a premium on charm. In the history of the American Presidency the most damaging aura of charm has been that of military figures encouraged to enter politics. But worse may come, as mean cleverness conspires to hoodwink mass communication. It is quite possible for charm to be simulated long enough to deceive the voters; they may choose a play-actor rather than a Lincoln and a genius at chicanery rather than a Washington.

Constitution. — Let this be summed up in a remark made by Woodrow Wilson: "The office of President requires the constitution of an athlete, the patience of a mother, the endurance of an early Christian."

The possession of cleverness and charm and constitution are the special marks of the politician, concerned as he is chiefly with the gathering of votes in order to impose his will on his followers, outwit his opponents, and offset and neutralize the forces acting against him. In an earlier work I stressed the politician as broker, that is, a go-between, gathering the ideas, values, philosophies, interests of others, and matching, compromising, and enacting them. The observations were addressed less to the Chief Executive and his cabinet than to the numerous members of the legislatures. Even in their case, I would now more emphatically stress an independent, imaginative, creative role — that they add something of their own personal view of the nation's interests and destiny to the sum of their responses to the crude importunities of the individuals and groups in the populace. But this creative element, the transmutation by the power of a man's morality of *what is*, and *what is demanded*, into *what ought to be*, is pre-eminently the responsibility of the Chief Executive, be he President or represented by a cabinet. This it is that distinguishes the statesman from the politician.

The mark of the statesman is the possession of convictions which determine the advancement of the destiny of his nation. He is conscious of the human and physical phenomena he must master and utilize, is capable of solving problems as they develop, of using foresight to invent ways and means; he has courage to endure opposition and slander, the pain of decisive firmness, the tension of risks; he appreciates the need for a coherent policy embracing all the various aspects of the social and economic present and future; he has constancy and devotion to responsibility that is continuous and solicitous; he takes upon his conscience all the burdens of office. These qualities he has with which to exercise the authority vested in him and to interpret that authority according to the nature of the emergencies he is called upon to meet.

It is impossible to teach these qualities to men who have not got them when they are born; men with these qualities have to be found. The problem of any society is to recognize the necessity of such men at the helm to help solve the public problems that agitate the nation. It is to develop the institutions and systems that make their recognition the more probable, the possessors of these qualities the more likely to be discovered, the suitable candidates encouraged to come forward, and the best among them to be elected to wield the nation's highest authority and fill its highest office. The qualities, I repeat, are inborn, for they are not mere qualities of received knowledge but the sudden impulse and comprehensions of the artist. And we know that the number of artists in any profession or vocation is but a tiny percentage of the total number of those who profess to practice. The Presidency deserves only the distinguished artists of political life.

In sober truth, no man alone has all of these qualities in the degree necessary to fulfil the obligations required of him by the Constitution to which the President pledges himself in taking the oath of office :

> I do solemnly swear that I will faithfully execute the office of President of the United States, and will, to the best of my ability, preserve, protect, and defend the Constitution of the United States.

IV

The Surrender of Efficiency
and Responsibility

I have sought to demonstrate the weight of responsibilities and the immensity of the authority resting in one man alone, the President of the United States, and the historic response of the men who have held the office to tasks imposed by the many-dimensioned growth of the nation.

The office is man-killing, or the man is office-killing; there seems to be no other choice.

Let us consider the tenability of the ideas the founders of the Republic entertained about the fundamental principles of the presidential office. It is necessary to appraise their judgment from two points of view, the first, How far was their reasoning sound for their own time? and second, How far is what was then sound appropriate to the responsibilities of statesmanship in the supreme offices of American government today?

The President Shall Be One

The founders of the Republic proclaimed that the Chief Executive, whatever his powers (and to a large extent they were vague), shall be one person. Their justification of this stand was complex. For one thing, they feared a collective body. Such a body, some feared, would be divided in its membership, made up of men representing all the diverse geographic areas of the United States. There would be elements of discord in the councils and rival demands made upon the Chief Executive. Yet it ought not be forgotten that there were men attending the Constitutional Convention who believed that a collective body would give to the executive the possibility of sharing the onerousness of the task and of contributing wisdom to decisions. But the First Congress would consist of only 59 representatives and only 22 senators, and an assembly as small as this seemed to be adequate to participate in the highest leadership.[1]

The positive theory of the single-headed executive was summed up most cogently by Alexander Hamilton in the *Federalist* papers.[2] A comparison of his exposition and the observations of the members of the convention and the congressmen participating in the debates of the First Congress, determining whether the President should alone have the power to remove officials and sundry matters, permits us to say that the Hamiltonian exposition is a fair covering, no more and no less, of the prevalent philosophy of government in this context and will serve for analysis.

Hamilton and the Federalists defended the unity of the executive on two grounds: Unity would secure "*energy*, or vigor, and despatch," that is, speed, in decision and action, and unity was essential if *responsibility* of action was to be secured. These, of course, are the indispensable requisites of the highest statesmanship, even more necessary in our own time than in the largely rural America of the late eighteenth century. But the meaning intended by such words as energy and responsibility demands a close examination. It will be recognized that some serious gaps exist in the Federalist proposal; it can hardly be considered a theory valid for all time if it admits of alternatives and is not applicable to human nature in all circumstances.

"Energy," it was said, "in the Executive is a leading character in the definition of good government." To protect the nation against foreign attack, it is essential to secure the steady administration of the laws. The same steady administration is needed to protect property against combinations that might interrupt the ordinary course of justice and to secure liberty against ambitious men, against factions and anarchy. "A feeble execution is but another phrase for a bad execution; and a government ill executed, whatever it may be in theory, must be, in practice, a bad government." In assessing the general validity of this theorem, in approving of it as I do, I keep in mind the crushing nature of the duties which now devolve on the President.

For energy in the executive office four ingredients are needed — unity, duration, adequate supports, and competent powers. We have dealt with the President's powers and, by inference, his "support," which means finance. I shall not review them at this juncture. Yet I pause to suggest that when, as now, the President's powers are sufficient to make him strong in leadership they may be of such a weight as to enfeeble him and overtax his single strength, overstimulating him to "off the cuff" decisions, perhaps thwarting the likelihood that he will pause to take calm thought.

Why should unity be conducive to energy in the executive office? And of what does energy consist? It connotes "decision, activity, secrecy, and despatch." And there follows a warning note: "In proportion as the number is increased, these qualities will be diminished."

How can unity be destroyed? You can divide power among two or more men of equal dignity. Or you can give it to one man, subject to the control and co-operation of other men who act as counselors to him. Roman history (for the founders of the Republic were far more willing to learn from experience than is the present generation) is adduced to demonstrate that a government, divided, falls. But Hamilton turns away from the "dim light of historical research" (a pity, since addiction to it might have produced a valid theory) to "the dictates of reason and good sense," that is, the psychology of decision-making and command.

The Federalist argument proceeds in this fashion: Wherever more than one person is trusted with a common enterprise, there is the danger of rivalry, even animosity, and therefore dissension and, at critical moments, the defeat or delay of important measures. Dissension might split the community into factions. Hamilton most penetratingly explains how men come to differ out of vanity, conceit, and obstinacy; or because someone else has been the first to propose or adumbrate a question or pose a proposition.

Divisions of this sort in the legislature, a "numerous body" proper for a legislature, are dangerous enough; introduced into the executive branch, dissension would be fatal to the welfare of the nation.

Let me pause for one moment and put a no doubt disturbing question to any contemporary Hamilton among those who have read so far. Is not the President in our own time a "legislative body"? Both those who rhapsodize upon the magnitude of presidential statesmanship and those who regard the present aggrandizement of the office with anxiety agree that the President is Chief Legislator. Ought not Hamilton's defense of differences of opinion in the legislature be adapted, perhaps with caution but in essence, to the President who has become Chief Legislator? On this theme Hamilton says:

> The difference of opinion, and the jarrings of the parties in that department of the government, though they may sometimes obstruct salutary plans, yet often promote deliberation and circumspection, and serve to check excesses in the majority.

Just so may differences of opinion and the jarring of the parties promote deliberation and circumspection in the President's office, if the President had true and equal colleagues.

The word "parties" may have a sinister ring for some defenders of the status quo; but I think it at least tenable that Hamilton did not mean by "parties" what we mean today; he may have meant no more than "other people." To "check excesses in the majority" is to regard the President himself as constituting the majority. Hamilton sharpens the point of his argument, as we would do today, by observing that the conduct of war requires "vigor and expedition," that the energy of the Chief Executive is "the bulwark of the national security." Yet modern warfare requires wisdom as well as energy, a wide network of minds in combat, national logistics, indeed a many-nationed logistics, and, above all, especially in a long-enduring "cold war," wisdom, foresight, imagination, planning, and a probing mind to forestall the vicious politics of bitter enemies unsleeping in their preparation to undo the American Republic. It is unreasonable to suppose that this is within the capacity of any one man, and it is not supplied by the

President's cabinet or by other conciliar devices, not even by the National Security Council.

There are sensible alternative ways of constructing the executive so that it may enjoy the benefits of good counsel and a sharing of an otherwise intolerable burden. Excess of responsibility saps the unity of the executive in fact (if furtively in manner).

Hamilton cites another argument used by the founders of the Republic to promote a single executive rather than a collective body — to secure a responsible executive: "But one of the weightiest objections to a plurality in the Executive . . . is that it tends to conceal faults and destroy responsibility." Hamilton and his colleagues were exercised by the need to secure a responsible government, responsible to and held responsible by the "nation," "the people." But how can the people constrain the executive branch to accountability unless it can identify the author of decisions and of action, unless it can locate the source of achievement, the origin of mistakes? Identification *places* responsibility. It is to be achieved by oneness of the executive, the Chief Executive, about whose identity no mistake can be made. The fundamental theory must be quoted:

> But the multiplication of the Executive adds to the difficulty of detection. . . . It often becomes impossible, amidst mutual accusations, to determine on whom the blame or the punishment of a pernicious measure, or series of pernicious measures, ought really to fall. It is shifted from one to another with so much dexterity, and under such plausible appearances, that the public opinion is left in suspense about the real author. The circumstances which may have led to any national miscarriage or misfortune are sometimes so complicated that, where there are a number of actors who may have had different degrees and kinds of agency, though we may clearly see upon the whole that there has been mismanagement, yet it may be impracticable to pronounce to whose account the evil which may have been incurred is truly chargeable.

The campaign against the policies of George III, and the War of Independence itself, protested a system of government which obscured responsibility. Burke's *Thoughts on the Present Discon-*

tents denounced the British system on the same general grounds as did the founders of the Republic who suffered its injuries and insults, and they spoke with the same eloquence and high spirit he used to defend the American cause in his speeches on conciliation. This is what they read in the pamphlet of their champion:

> . . . two systems of administration were to be formed; one which should be in the real secret and confidence; the other merely ostensible, to perform the official and executory duties of government. The latter were alone to be responsible; whilst the real advisers, who enjoyed all the power, were effectually removed from all danger.[3]

The basic theory of the Federalists was right: If responsibility is to be exercised toward the Republic, given the nature of the common man's mind, confused and with many preoccupations (and they knew much about this), it was essential to identify, to single out, to determine responsibility. It must be made as easy, as unmistakable, as possible. Oneness in the executive branch would secure this; for surely then there could be no mistake. There he was, he could be seen.

Is identification today of the hero or the culprit as easy as Hamilton seems to have thought? Of course, he would turn the argument by suggesting that it is never easy but that it would be even harder to do so with a plural executive. Yet we hope to show that Hamilton's rejoinder is not crushing. Let us beware the ocular fallacy in government, for *seeing* may not be believing.

Hamilton continues:

> It is evident from these considerations that the plurality of the Executive tends to deprive the people of the two greatest securities they can have for the faithful exercise of any delegated power: *first*, the restraints of public opinion, which lose their efficacy, as well on account of the decision of the censure attendant on bad measures among a number as on account of the uncertainty on whom it ought to fall; and *secondly*, the opportunity of discovering with facility and clearness the misconduct of the persons they trust, in order either to their removal from office, or to their actual punishment in cases which admit of it.

If this passage is scrutinized with the same care that Alexander Hamilton lavished on the ideas of others, it will be observed that if the restraints of public opinion are to be effective there is need for a vastly different organization than that provided by the Constitution. The present system is no longer such as to admit of the clear discovery of the extent of responsibility of those at fault, those deserving of praise, those who would best be removed from office.

Hamilton concludes this part of his discussion with the assertion:

> I rarely met with an intelligent man from any of the States, who did not admit, as the result of experience, that the UNITY of the executive of this State was one of the distinguishing features of our Constitution.

The unity of the executive branch, when embodied in the person of one man, does not necessarily guarantee the qualities of efficiency intended. Whether the executive branch will be efficient depends not alone on whether one man will conduct it but far more on the personal qualities of that man and his ability to handle the duties of the office. Mind, not number, is the decisive principle. It is the theory of my present essay that the single President, no matter who he is, is faced by an impossible task. Surely this has been demonstrated in the pages I have devoted to a reasonable description of the President's authority and responsibilities in the several spheres of his office. Consider further the variety of situations a President must meet, the many diverse tensions relieved or intensified by his every decision. Consider the sudden onset of crisis, a diplomatic stroke which threatens the international balance of power, a strike which threatens to slow or paralyze the nation's economy.

The Work Load of the President

The routine work load of the President is extremely heavy and it is unremitting. Look at the chores of a single day, a record made available in an issue of *United States News and World Report*.[4] Let it be remembered that it does not include a number of the regular meetings and conferences which the President attends during an average week. For example, on Tuesday he has a conference with House and Senate leaders; a press conference on Wednesday; the National Security Council on Thursday; a cabinet meeting on Friday. Each of these meetings requires a considerable amount of preparation if necessary "homework" is done. The press conference is never a spontaneous attempt to answer unexpected questions. The President's press secretary undertakes to anticipate the questions to come. He briefs the President and coaches him before the conference — and sometimes mis-coaches him.[5]

March 4, 1958 — An Average Day for President Eisenhower

7:00– 7:55 a.m.	Dressed, ate breakfast, and read one Washington and two New York newspapers.
8:00– 8:22	Quick look at morning mail and conference with Assistant to President Adams and Secretary of Labor Mitchell.
8:22– 8:27	Received overnight intelligence reports from the Central Intelligence Agency. Also sheaf of documents, including a proclamation for National Defense Transportation Day, a directive on military housing, and papers covering the nomination of 339 postmasters.
8:27– 8:29	Met magazine editor and photographer.
8:29– 8:35	Read mail and intelligence reports.
8:35– 8:41	Worked on documents with his special counsel.
8:41– 8:55	Discussed legislative matters with Deputy Assistant and administrative assistants. Was briefed by Appointments Secretary on day's visitors.
8:58– 9:02	Talked with Vice-President Nixon.
9:02–10:46	Meeting with Republican legislative leaders. Among topics discussed: the President's view that a constitutional amendment is need to clarify the issues of presidential disability and succession; possible increases in highway-con-

	struction program as an anti-recession measure; postal rate and pay increase bills; and statehood for Alaska and Hawaii.
10:46–10:53	Discussion with the minority "whip" of Congress, and a White House legislative aide.
10:53–10:56	Read memos at desk.
10:56–11:08	Received and spoke briefly to 4-H Club delegation. Had picture taken with award winners, with whom he exchanged gifts. Returned to office with Secretary Benson and 4-H award winners.
11:08–11:12	Dictated to secretary.
11:12–11:25	Visit from former staff member and the Eisenhower "official biographer."
11:25–12:15 p.m.	Discussed with press secretary what White House should do about announcing the launching of second U.S. earth satellite.
12:15– 1:55	Lunch in bedroom and an hour's rest, prescribed by physicians.
2:00– 2:15	Returned to office; discussed coming appointments and dictated letters.
2:15– 2:37	Met with Secretary of State Dulles and newly appointed disarmament negotiator. Pictures by press photographer.
2:37– 3:29	Dictated more letters (a total of 35 during the day) and worked on speech to be given in a few weeks.
3:29– 3:37	Conferred with Assistant to the President Adams on three major policy matters.
3:37– 3:55	Worked with his staff secretary.
3:55– 4:29	Dictated to secretary, outlining forthcoming speech.
4:29– 5:00	Returned to living quarters in White

	House, dealt with personal business for next half hour.
5:00– 6:20	Saw an important "off-the-record" visitor in his study, on government business.
6:20– 7:30	Watched TV news shows, read newspapers.
7:30– 8:30	Dinner.
8:30–10:15	Studied official documents; read transcript of Secretary of State's news conference, magazine articles suggested by staff.
10:15	Went to bed, read western novel until sleep.

In addition, there were telephone calls selected for the President's attention from among 286 calls received by the White House staff during the day — not many, but some of an important or confidential nature.

Political scientists sometimes speak of an administrator's "span of control." [6] They mean that there is a limit to the number of persons any director or supervisor can effectively inspire, animate, direct, and co-ordinate. If he supervises six men, he has thirty-six interrelationships to watch; if it rises to ten his vigilance must rise to one hundred crisscrosses of policy and action, and so on. But, if he shares the responsibility with men close in colleagueship and tried and tested by long experience, then his intensity and width of attention need be much less. And supervision does not connote merely a looking-on but the exertion of pressure. For how long can a single man in the Presidency continue pressure on the executants? How can he remember to ask whether his wishes have been carried out? Speaking apropos of one of the most forceful men in the headship of a government agency, Jesse Jones of the RFC, Jonathan Daniels, an intense and alert observer of Presidents, said:

Half of a President's suggestions, which theoretically carry the weight of orders, can be safely forgotten by a Cabinet member. And if the President asks about a suggestion a second time, he can be told that it is being investigated. If he asks a third time, a wise Cabinet officer will give him at least part of what he suggests. But only occasionally, except about the most important matters, do Presidents ever get around to asking three times.

How many activities a President can span effectively depends on his knowledge, his realism, his speed of assimilation, his memory, and the "cleavage" power of his mind as it probes a political situation.[7] Men vary tremendously in these respects, but even the most gifted President finds a limit to his span. "Getting things done," or, as Woodrow Wilson said, "making things happen," is the prime responsibility of the President, for he is not only a thinker and a contemplator but an enforcer.

Ought we not to launch on the waters of managerial theory a new term, "the surfeit of simultaneous stimuli" — implying a limit to the number of agonies and incitements a man can be expected to face at one time? Clearly, men differ in the degree of their receptivity, to the point at which they feel that the surge of events is too much for them. The great juggler was Franklin Roosevelt; but other men have again and again cried out, "This is too much!" They were not always vocal, but they greeted with relief the proposal that they delegate some of their responsibilities to others.

The "Responsibility" of the President

Two meanings, not one, lurk in the word "responsibility." One may mean that the President feels his duty to be such and such, that he takes upon his conscience the burden of performance. This may be called moral responsibility. The other, that there is a clearly established agency to which he must render account, and which can bring effective and sanctioned pressure to bear on him through its authority over him. This may be called, using Alexander Hamilton's term, censorial responsibility, that is, a censoring body to establish principles of acceptable performance and exert itself to compel the President to act accordingly, with unpleasant sanctions if he fails to do so.

The founders of the Republic said that the President would and ought to be responsible to the nation and to the public, but they did not make clear whether they meant moral or censorial responsibility and whether agencies of government were empowered to enforce censorial responsibility.

If the President commits high crimes or misdemeanors while in office, impeachment is possible.[8] Impeachment is the ultimate political punishment in a democracy. It can hardly be used, for its severity is such as to frighten men from entering government, where the ascription of guilt may be made by political foes, where the chance of bona fide mistakes is enormous, and where the imputation of incompetence and even of sabotage, rather than honest error, is intolerable. Men under daily threat of impeachment might become timid, reckless, or dishonest in self-defense.

Censorial responsibility means the ability of the people through their representatives to influence in strong measure the actions of the President and allows for his impeachment if he persists in a wrongful course. The price of power is the continued beneficial employment of it, as determined by those who grant that power.

Some students of the Presidency are content to say that the President cannot become a dictator, satisfied that Congress is empowered to obstruct a would-be dictator. But this is a hopelessly limited response to the problem of presidential responsibility. The President, without becoming a dictator, has powers which, if used incompetently or maliciously, could ruin the nation. Let us consider errors in strategic imagination, bear in mind fumbling efforts to avert mass unemployment, clumsy efforts to match wits in international diplomacy. Of course we abhor dictators; but it is as necessary to abhor fools.

When the President is Chief Executive (chief legislator, chief diplomat) and Commander in Chief, Congress cannot assert control even if, in the age of the H-bomb, he commit the nation to perdition! And certainly Congress is not able to exert with ease what I have called the rescue-facient function. In effect, Congress is prevented from exerting influence upon the President. The debaters in the Federal Convention and the First Congress insisted that the President be free of legislative influence except for certain specific functions, the power to appoint and the power to make treaties. The founders of the Republic would neither allow nor require the President to take the advice of senators or congressmen. The President's cabinet was not to be made up of congressional legislators, and rejected was the proposal that the President himself be elected by the legislature, lest its members thereby acquire and exert influence upon him in his official capacity.

Were not the founders of the Republic afraid that a man might be chosen for the Presidency who would be unable to exercise its authority? They were. But they conceived an instrument which could exact responsibility from him and sanction it: the instrument they believed would secure responsibility was the peculiar presidential electoral system they chose.

The Virtues of the Electoral College

The appointment of the President of the United States was confided to the electoral college, composed of electors chosen in each state by enfranchised citizens, a comparatively small body of men: in 1789 there were only 69; in 1792, only 132; today, there are only 531. What qualities were expected of these electors? They would be capable of analyzing "the qualities adapted to the station"; they would be "acting under circumstances favourable to deliberation" and to a "judicious combination of all the reasons and inducements which were proper to govern their choice." They would have the ability to discern, and the settled knowledge to enable them to choose, among the contenders those men possessing qualities of leadership, with an eye to the President's responsibilities while in office. Hamilton said: "A small number of persons, selected by their fellow-citizens from the general mass, will be most likely to possess the information and discernment requisite to such complicated investigations." [9] This Arcadian simplicity, so noble and so trusting, may come to mind when we see the hucksters and politicians at nominating conventions and manipulators in smoke-filled rooms as they trade votes for the contending nominees. Consider the phrases "capable of analyzing the qualities adapted to the station"; "circumstances favourable to deliberation"; "judicious combination of all the reasons and inducements"; "information and discernment." And use these phrases to measure the men who select and nominate our candidates for President, and those who "direct the choice," the electorate, 103,000,000 men and women, scattered over three million square miles, and the public relations "men"!

This was by no means all that Hamilton said in vindication of the invention of the electoral college. For the electors in each state were to vote in each state by sending their ballots to Washington. "This detached and divided situation will expose them much less to heats and ferments, which might be communicated from them to the people, than if they were all to be convened at one and the same time in one place." [10] But what the electoral college was designed to avert, political parties have brought about through insufficient application of the principle of party loyalty, responsibility, and organization. "Heats and ferments" are communicated by campaign managers — precisely the words to describe modern mass elections and the unscrupulous manipulation of votes practiced by politicians on the advice of their "psychological warfare" consultants, bent, as such men are, on victory at any cost.

The electoral college, if called together, would have been excellent for the choice of a President for a first term, and even more so to judge whether the President should have a second term if he wished it. If it were a small and select conclave close to the President, the electoral college would better know the considerations that contributed to each presidenial decision and so could be just to the inevitable imperfections of the man in office.

How idealistic were the hopes of Hamilton during the first fine rapture of the Republic when seen in the light of current practices! Hamilton sought to convince others to accept the Constitution, on the grounds that "there will be a constant probability of seeing the station filled by characters pre-eminent for ability and virtue." And again, he believed:

> Talents for low intrigue and the little arts of popularity may alone suffice to elevate a man to the first honours in a single State; but it will require other talents, and a different kind of merit, to establish him in the esteem and confidence of the whole Union, or of so considerable a portion of it as would be necessary to make him a successful candidate for the distinguished office of President of the United States.

We would not wish to say that Hamilton was right in believing that men of little merit may rise to state governorships; but sometimes he has been right. Yet he was certainly too sanguine when he spoke of the method of selection of the President. And more certain is this: The original method of sifting candidates was discarded even before the Jacksonian revolution of 1828 because party organization outside Congress became necessary to produce concert among the electors. All the safeguards for rational choice were cast down. Even if the electoral college had remained intact and entire, it would not have answered the necessity of securing the candidate's accountability to the people and the nation. Even if we should suppose that the true hope of the majority of the founders of the Republic was that the House would most usually choose the President, as in 1825, then they still looked to a knowledgeable selective body.

The Fixed Term of Four Years

Hamilton believed that to strengthen the office of President the incumbent should remain in office at least four years. Thus the principle of the fixed term for the executive office was established. Some opponents of the Constitution feared that so long a tenure might encourage tyranny. Hamilton is to be applauded for his proposition, "The republican principle [democracy] demands that the deliberate sense of the community should govern the conduct of those to whom they intrust the management of their affairs." Surely this is a sound statement of responsible government and censorial responsibility. And he continued:

> It does not require an unqualified complaisance to every sudden breeze of passion, or to every transient impulse which the people may receive from the arts of men, who flatter their prejudices to betray their interests. . . . When occasions present themselves, in which the interests of the people are at variance with their inclinations, it is the duty of the persons whom they have appointed to be the guardians of those interests, to withstand their temporary delusion, in order to give them time and opportunity for more cool and sedate reflection.

So much for the fixed term of office as expressed in the doctrine of the founding fathers. But sound as it is, it does not anticipate all contingencies. The people may be right; the President may be wrong; and, if not the people, then a select body of legislative mentors may be wise when the President is unwise. Surely it was placing a good deal of trust in the personal ability of the President to allow him a four-year term chiefly on the ground that the *people* might be wrong! The fear to be stilled by Hamilton and his colleagues was that a long term might justify alarm for the public liberty. Yet it may happen — indeed, it has — that liberty is preserved, and with it, when the office for a fixed term is held by a man of feeble character or a man of ignorance, incompetence is preserved as well, incompetence every bit as dangerous to liberty as tyranny would be.

Lincoln, in his first inaugural address, said:

> While the people retain their virtue and vigilance, no administration, by any extreme of wickedness or folly, can very seriously injure the government in the short space of four years.

Yet it is implied that some injury would be done. And is four years such a short time in this rapidly changing world? Think of the speed, the momentum of modern economy, and, in contrast, the time it takes to fashion the blueprints of modern warfare. In four years a civilization or the entire world can be destroyed if power should fall into the hands of incompetents or vulgarians. Think of the proofs we have today of the might of other nations.

Re-eligibility, said the founders of the Republic, would give the people the opportunity to retain in office a man who has served his country well, "in order to prolong the utility of his talents and virtues" and to secure the virtue of permanency in a wise system of administration. We know, in our time, that re-eligibility increases the President's sense of responsibility, though some critics believe that in the final term, whatever it may be, the authority of the President, especially in relation to Congress, tends to weaken. More important than the anticipation of re-election in increasing the sense of responsibility are the conditions under which the President may appeal to the people for a second term. His monarchical glamor as Chief of State, the tremendous powers of the office, his priority in all means of rhetorical communication, tend to make it less easy for the mass electorate to judge him and to "reason in the approval of his conduct." Their judgment will act only under strong impulse of despair as that which rejected Hoover in 1932.

Lack of Intermediate Official Bodies

The American Constitution allows for no intermediate bodies with an independent base of power, bodies so constituted as to bring to bear on the President the principle of censorial responsibility in such wise as to oblige him to justify himself to them. My emphasis is on the fact that such institutions as there are do not have the appropriate and effective power to *exact* responsibility. I am fully aware of the institutions and procedures which are intended to influence the President to act wisely. I will list those that may be supposed to exist, those that would be adduced by defenders of the present status of the President. First, the President is besieged and importuned by pressure groups. Would any of these imposing organizations, involved in election campaigns, linked with this party or that in frequent bipartisan alignment, ever allow the President to be ignorant of the limits of policy they believe to be fair? If he is not responsible, at any rate he is responsive. Their electoral threats cannot always be effective; they may be defied, and they sometimes cancel out, giving the President his liberty. Second, the custom of weekly or bi-weekly press conferences which has developed since Woodrow Wilson's accession is thought to be a force. If the President fails to appear, he may become unpopular with the press, a powerful agency for creating the public image of the President, able to make him seem a hero or a pusillanimous fool. The press has a certain leverage, and the President, however reluctantly, responds to it. Roosevelt averaged one hundred conferences a year, Truman about fifty, and Eisenhower about twenty-five. But appearances mean neither commitment to responsiveness nor commitment to what is responded. The President is able to evade the questions he does not wish to answer by refusing "in the public interest," or he may simply ignore the question, parry it with an innocent confusion, or splutter with indignation. He may favor some reporters and ignore others. His answers are not subject (though they ought to be) to cross-examination so that plain content — and misunderstandings caused by bad grammar — may be cleared up. Since the President is under public scrutiny, some responsibility is exacted by the fear of loss of prestige should he be exposed as ignorant or incompetent.

Of recent years much has been made of the number of letters and telegrams that flow into the White House, the implication being that these must effect the President and determine his response to the mood or demands of the nation. If this is not the implication, I find it hard to imagine why statistics are quoted, except possibly to demonstrate that the nation looks to the President to do something when something needs to be done. In Theodore Roosevelt's time, the President received some four hundred letters a week; in Franklin Roosevelt's time the number had risen to five thousand a day, about eight times as many. On exciting occasions the President receives as many as 460,000 letters (as, for example, on the day Roosevelt proclaimed "We have nothing to fear but fear itself!"). The rate of five thousand a day seems to be continuing. But what can this prove of presidential responsibility? Only that he is being asked to make a response. Surely these five thousand letters must be uneven in quality, message, and appeal; above all, they cannot compel. They are probably even less of a spur than the press conferences at which the President meets his interrogators face to face.

Third, the party organization may appeal to the President to mend his course for the sake of the reputation of the party and its future fortunes. How much the President is likely to do this is dependent on his loyalty to and affection for the party. Influences of this kind may be powerful, but they are not continous nor are they clear to the public. The President is allowed enormous discretion in policy, without rein of public responsibility. External influence is at best sporadic; sometimes the two, party and President, are totally at odds, as it would seem from occasional disclosures, for example, the remarks made in July, 1959, by Thruston Morton.[11]

Fourth, in the course of deliberation Congress may make clear to the President's emissaries, his congressional liaison between the White House, the Hill, and the "big four" — the Speaker of the House, the Vice-President, the majority leaders, the ranking congressmen of the minority — that, in their judgment, the President is not acting responsibly. This may be effective from time to time, depending on the President's degree of conviction. But it is not a certain influence; Congress can be ignored; and on major issues it has not only been ignored but insulted, sometimes with a direct appeal to the public. And when there is a difference of opinion between the Chief Executive and Congress, the President has the upper hand. In August, 1959, the major television networks refused to give Speaker Rayburn equal time to answer President Eisenhower's address on the labor bill.

Although each of these so-called devices of restraint is sometimes effective, together they do not exert an integrated, continous pressure upon the President. They do not share a fairly settled standard of responsibility to which he is to be held. What is lacking is a consistent and systematic pattern of national principles and integrated national policies. Above all, none of these spheres of influence has substantial force to overrule the President's obstinacy or lethargy. He can, within the broadest limits, do whatever he personally wants to do, just as the founders of the Republic proposed when they planned a four-year term to give the President his own way against the "ill humours, however transient, which may happen to prevail," either in the public or in Congress. As long as the President was chosen by the rational processes expected from the electoral colleges in each state there might have been value in this proposal. But today the electorate is an inchoate mass whipped up by artificial and factitious storms only to subside into quasi-apathy.

How important a role did these informal "institutions of responsibility" play in the policies of Truman and Eisenhower? In Truman's tenure, such matters of grave responsibility as the dropping of the atomic bomb, the agreements at Potsdam, the H-bomb, the assumption of leadership in Korea, the establishment of NATO, the development of the Marshall Plan and the Truman Doctrine, the organization of the National Security Council and the establishment of the Department of Defense, the prosecution of cases against labor unions, the veto of the Taft-Hartley Act, the maladministration of certain government departments, among them Internal Revenue? And what influence did they exert during Eisenhower's tenure upon missile policy, education policy, credit policy, inflation *vs.* housing policy, economic policy, general policy in the Middle East, especially during the Suez crisis of 1956–57, the foreign economic aid program, neglect of and later frenzied intervention in the steel strikes of 1959, the feebleness of the FCC and FTC in policing malpractice in television and radio, the slackness in insuring safety in air travel, above all, the curious, bland evasion of questions at press conferences? No, in neither administration did "institutions of responsibility" shape and influence presidential decision.

That is not all. Suppose the fault of a President is inaction masquerading as masterly knowingness at a time when foreign dangers and social cataclysm demand intervention? The prodding action, the rescue-facient function, of governmental responsibility was not anticipated by the founders of the Republic. Yet it is the ever-present dangers of inaction which the Republic must face.

Since the President's responsibility is the very core of democratic government, let us review briefly the course of one well-remembered attempt to fix presidential responsibility in a matter touching upon the survival of the nation. My purpose is not indictment; but I discern a pattern here, a pattern to be seen at one time or another in every President's administration. It is the fault of the system but can be aggravated by the man.

Over a period of several years expert witnesses have demonstrated to Congress that the United States is losing the missile race to the Soviet Union — missiles capable of carrying H-bombs to targets seven thousand miles away. The President first replied that we were not in a race with the Soviet. Later, under fire, he insisted that the nation had sufficient deterrent forces of *other* kinds to warrant confidence that the Soviet Union would not dare an attack. Nonetheless, the administration did not seem to believe in its own argument, for it then proceeded to "repair the gap" by changes in personnel, organization, and appropriations.

Critics charged that the President's replies were misleading. He retorted that he was a general and knew more about military strategy and arms than any of his several military experts, whom he now denigrated as capable of only a "parochial" view. At once it is rebutted that "parochial" is an odd term for men who are specialists; the President himself is not and cannot be so skilled as they in special technologies which, in any case, are beyond his personal experience in war and his military studies before and since. At the suggestion that the President's military talent is not unassailable, an unusual note of *lèse majesté* is interjected by his faithful leader in the Senate, who expresses anger and deep shame that "disrespect" has been shown to so great a wartime leader and to the President of the United States! He proceeded to insist that the morale of the nation is injured by such criticism, that thus the Soviet obtains material to encourage its belief in the inferiority of the United States, and that all the President is doing is trying to save money to keep the nation from bankruptcy. The specific charges of a missile lag are bypassed.

Congress and the press will not desist, for the nation's safety does not allow it. This nettles the President, who conveys to his Senate leader a taste of temper described by that master of subtle language and curious humor as "angry, but not mad." The charge is now advanced that Congress is being given pessimistic figures in private committee sessions by the director of the Central Intelligence Agency, while the public is simultaneously receiving optimistic reports from the President and his spokesman. The newspapers report that at press conferences the President is irate, angry, and icy, denies that he is "deliberately misleading," and cries out that such a charge is "despicable." The opposition observes, correctly, that the charge of "misleading" was never made; and the adverb "deliberately" begs every important question of responsibility in political leadership. For it may be worse for the nation for the President to mislead "undeliberately," unintentionally, than with knowledge. A President may be ignorant; he may not have done his "homework"; he may have done it but without understanding the problem and the facts; he may have learned the truth but been incapable of grasping its significance.

In part inspired by the fact that it is an election year, the critics persist, though it is on record that they began the crescendo of questions and objections at least as far back as 1955, an outcry rising in anxiety with the mounting evidence of Soviet successes. To overcome public dismay, the President makes his first visit to Cape Canaveral and tours the base for somewhat less than four hours. Then, to reassert his stubborn views, he picks a farewell television speech on a propitious Sunday evening and in a talk on South America insinuates that the nation's defenses are "awesome." His Senate leader then repeats that the "package of weapons" — not missiles — is, indeed, "awesome." Almost simultaneously, the Vice-President (a candidate for the Presidency) indorses the President's announcement, and this is not to his own disadvantage since his prospects are boosted by publicity that he participated in sessions of the National Security Council.

Yet this mechanism, this procedure of charge and counter-charge, tort and retort, has not pinned responsibility or elicited the truth. To avoid the opposition's scalpel, the administration shifts grounds, makes an abrupt change in its measurements of Soviet missile strength. McElroy, the Secretary of Defense, who resigned in December, 1959, measured Soviet strength by a calculation of Soviet production capacity. Now Gates, the new Secretary of Defense, discards this yardstick and speaks instead of "Soviet intentions." The former secretary was sick at heart at the prospect that the Soviet would have a three to one advantage by 1962; his immediate successor has no such figures for the public. The issue is altogether confused. Military experts observe that to guess at an enemy's intentions, especially when decision-making is utterly secret, is the way to military disaster.

Thus, at every item in the dialogue, in an admittedly intricate field, the ability of the Chief Executive to escape criticism and correction leaps to the eye. It is simply not possible to pin him down, to fix responsibilty, for he cannot be forced to meet his critics face to face and answer under exhaustive cross-examination. The mechanism of interrogation is a clear failure. If the example given is believed to be appropriate only to a President like Eisenhower, let us be reminded of the humorous tergiver-sations of Theodore Roosevelt, of Franklin Roosevelt, or the per-emptory and snappish self-righteousness of Truman. Each in his own way, so different in their concepts of what constitutes presi-dential leadership, could not be brought to book in the system as it prevails. Even over the U-2 *gaffe*, a screen of smoke was wafted.

Lack of Concerted Opposition

One of the most striking facts about American government is the absence of an opposition at every important turn of public affairs. Its absence will be noted, for example, in such routine matters as expenditure and taxes, in farm support policy, in the handling of unemployment, in education, and in such far from routine subjects as foreign affairs, when mistakes lead to the most severe consequences. Congress is torn among its members and within its parties on every major issue, just as it disagrees upon what constitutes constructive legislative leadership. During the Suez crisis in 1956–57, during the Chinese–Soviet pressure on Quemoy and Matsu in 1958, during the Berlin crisis in November, 1958, public opinion was in complete disarray, corresponding to the confusion of Congress and the voices that spoke so variously in administrative circles.

The nation is in need of a sober, energetic, collective voice to review, assess, and sometimes check leadership in the White House. The electorate has a right to be informed. Opposition serves to benefit sound policy. Because there are so many alternatives, so many nuances, in every policy, it is next to impossible to make all these clear to the public unless the major alternatives have first been expressed. Let me offer in example current practices. The President and the Secretary of State make statements of policy. Their statements are not challenged for many days, perhaps for weeks. Press "handouts" appear, with a certain amount of editorial comment. Editorial comment is not generally considered responsible appraisal of foreign policy and for various reasons is most questionable as a main source of popular opinion on current issues. Days, weeks pass; the diplomatic situation is brewing, and there is no word from Congress as a single body nor from either political party. Then separate voices begin to be heard — Knowland, Bricker, Goldwater, Humphrey, Mansfield, Fulbright, Dirksen. None are in agreement; nor do they agree with the policy statements of the President, the Secretary of State, and the Chiefs of Staff. Congressional voices are single voices and not in the tradition of the party or its platform; they do not commit the speakers to hold to their views in subsequent proceedings.

The lack of a concerted, responsible opposition is a grave deficiency in a democracy. In this respect our government is almost as wanting as is that of France, so blithely maligned, for decades the subject of derision and scorn from political scientists and writers of newspaper editorials. In France there is no single opposition and too many oppositions, formed, dispersed, and re-formed — a kaleidoscope of contradictory opinion. The French can point to the existence of many political parties as the cause; in the United States there are alleged to be only two parties. It is boasted that we are more sensible and have only two—when the question seems to be whether we have any parties at all! The leaders of the French government never know from day to day which groups will coalesce into an opposition. Here, we have reasons to believe there is nothing to coalesce.

It is in England that the institution of a loyal opposition began and operates in most accomplished fashion, followed in quality by the governments of Canada, Australia, and New Zealand. The leader of the minority party is chosen by vote of what is virtually the party caucus. He is flanked by a dozen or so leading members of the party. The leader of the opposition receives a salary from the government to enable him to devote all his time to his duties. This taut organization of about a score of men leads their party in the Commons and relies on a steady vote. (Some may occasionaly and almost by consensus abstain on conscientious grounds.) The government is confronted by a planned, continuing, and inescapable criticism from those who have assumed the responsibility of opposing the government's policy. Whatever the government proposes to do, the opposition, speaking with one determined voice, suggests an alternative. "Opposing" means posing an alternative to, not simply caviling, carping, and vilifying. The government cannot propose policy on any subject, or omit to do so, before the opposition, officially and in debate, offers a constructive alternative fit to be a responsible commitment—in a sense proposing what the rival party would promise to undertake were it in office. This is a sobering check upon rash action.

In a democracy, especially in so vast and conglomerate a nation as the United States, comparison is the intelligent way to popular knowledge. If democracy is to persist the voters must have a chance to choose between alternative proposals. Such a contrast is not likely to be absolutely and academically true to the nature of the problems at hand, but the average voter is not so skilled in political dialectic that he can follow all the controversies that arise—or even a few of them—unless they are expressed in black and white. Democracy must allow this, or it may be nothing. Such a congressional or extracongressional organization does not exist in the United States. Still less, then, is the President subject to check and balance by an assembly having an independent base of authority and power enough to compel him to reconsider his decisions. Because Congress is distraught, the way is unencumbered to presidential aggrandizement and, indeed, encourages it.

As Clinton Rossiter, in a dashing and remarkably cheerful essay on the Presidency, has said:

> In the end, of course, the checks that hold a President in line are internal rather than external. His conscience and training, his sense of history and desire to be judged by it, his awareness of the need to pace himself lest he collapse under the burden — all join to halt him far short of the kind of deed that destroys a President's "fame and power." He, like the rest of us, has been raised in the American tradition; he, perhaps better than the rest of us, senses what the tradition permits and what it forbids in the conduct of high office. If he knows anything of history or politics or administration he knows that he can do great things only within the "common range of expectation," that is to say, in ways that honor or at least do not outrage the accepted dictates of constitutionalism, democracy, personal liberty, and Christian morality.[12]

In this inspiriting message it would seem that, for the purposes of the present discussion, all the significant questions are begged. "If . . ."; "perhaps better than the rest of us. . . ." But we are grateful that Rossiter reviewed all the phenomena that tend to limit the power of the President before coming to the conclusion given above. He was led by his own arguments to acknowledge that every check on the President could become an opportunity for the exertion of power.

The one power to secure responsibility we have not paraded is "power of the purse," that is, the power of Congress to deny the President appropriations when his proposals displease. We have not called attention to it because the Budget and Accounting Act of 1921 gave this power to the President. The present essay is not concerned with whether a President may become a dictator. We are concerned with the far more subtle and realistic problem of efficiency and responsibility; not whether the President goes beyond the limit of the permissible, but how clever, how imaginative, how creative and serviceable he is, and to whom, if anyone, he renders account.

It is helpful to realize that others emphasize the belief that "In the end, of course, the checks that hold a President in line are internal rather than external." For this reinforces the need for us to turn our attention to how the President is chosen and the conditions under which he is expected to work.

Moral Responsibility

At present, the Chief Executive's responsibility is very largely, almost entirely, moral responsibility. Conscientiousness differs with each man, in the objects of policy to which it is addressed and in the intensity with which it is felt. It is precisely this variation in response to the claims of conscience which makes it far from unfair to characterize the presidential role as a gamble and excessively personal in the abruptness of its zigzagging policies. It is in no way a compromise between the extremes of the wings and middle of a political party, nor does it tack and veer within a collective cabinet as a moderator of extremes. The tasks of modern government have made the Presidency excessively personal. Observe the tremendous swing of the Stock Exchange when there is or is about to be a change of Presidents or when there is concern for the President's state of health.[13]

The almost exclusive reliance on the President's sense of moral responsibility has produced statements from the President himself that would be considered strange if made by the leader of any other democratic country — that is, statements concerning how far he believed his authority could go. In France, England, Germany, and in other lands with a collective cabinet system, the prime minister may say "I can go as far as the National Assembly, the Commons, the *Bundestag* will tolerate as the result of direct debate with them and/or discussions behind the scenes if there is not time to debate before the legislature. And I must carry the rank and file of my party, the members in the legislature, the militants outside."[14] But the President can offer only the kind of justification that would have met the pleased approval of a Bismarck or be aped by a Khrushchev when deigning to contend with the Communist Party Presidium or the Central Committee about the freedom and limits of his power, that is, that the nation may put its trust in his moral self.[15]

Stewards vs. Supervisors

Presidents have been classified on the basis of their views upon the limits within which they can initiate and sometimes consummate personal policies — the stewardship theory of Theodore Roosevelt as opposed to the restrictive theory of William Howard Taft. The stewardship theory holds that it is legal for the President as administrator to do anything that is not expressly forbidden by the Constitution, provided, in his opinion (in *his* opinion), that it is in the interests of the people. The restrictive theory (the term is mine, for want of a better) holds that the President must have specific permission or command in the words of the Constitution or by act of Congress before he proceeds. It is conceivable that a President may hold the stewardship theory, but, by temperament, be disinclined to initiate and fulfil his policies. Or he may accept the view that his scope is restricted, yet, like Taft, be an energetic governor in matters he believes to be constitutionally within his province.

I would propose another divergence between Presidents according as they accept an "immersive" responsibility or a passive-post-facto responsibility. By the immersive I mean that the President conceives his responsibility to begin from the first moment that issues (indeed, he may invent them) arise for solution, that he participates actively in each, at every stage, until a solution is found. By the passive-post-facto, I mean the President who awaits the counsel of his advisers, the President simply signing his name to a decision that has been made outside his ken and without his participation. Or perhaps alternative views are presented to him at the end of the same kind of process, when the grounds for judgment have been narrowed in such a way as to make unnecessary the exercise of his own choice on the policy proposed. I pair these forms of moral responsibility, human nature being what it is, the strong with the strong, the weak with the weak: stewardship and immersive responsibility, restrictive and passive-post-facto responsibility.

Stewardship may be illustrated by a classic utterance from Theodore Roosevelt's *Autobiography:*

> The most important factor in getting the right spirit in my Administration, next to the insistence upon courage, honesty,

and a genuine democracy of desire to serve the plain people, was my insistence upon the theory that the executive power was limited only by specific restrictions and prohibitions appearing in the Constitution or imposed by Congress under its Constitutional powers. My view was that every executive office, and above all every executive office in high position, was a steward of the people bound actively and affirmatively to do all he could for the people, and not to content himself with the negative merit of keeping his talents undamaged in a napkin.

I declined to adopt the view that what was imperatively necessary for the Nation could not be done by the President unless he could find some specific authorization to do it. . . . Under this interpretation of executive power I did and caused to be done many things not previously done by the President and the heads of the Departments. I did not usurp power, but I did greatly broaden the use of executive power.[16]

This is stewardship with a vengeance, it would be said by those who fell foul of it.

Another expression is a passage already quoted, Franklin Roosevelt's message to Congress on price controls in 1942. Still another is Truman's justification of the seizure of the steel mills in 1951, as given in his *Memoirs:*

In my opinion, the seizure was well within my constitutional powers, and I acted accordingly. The Constitution states that "the executive power shall be vested in a President of the United States of America." These words put a tremendous responsibility on the individual who happens to be President. He holds an office of immense power. It surely is the greatest trust that can be placed in *any man* by the American people. It is a trust with a power that appalls a thinking man. There have been men in history who have liked power and the glamor that goes with it: Alexander, Caesar, Napoleon, to name only a few. I never did. It was only the responsibility that I felt to the people who had given me this power that concerned me. I believe that the power of the President should be used in the interest of the people, and in order to do that the President must use whatever power the Constitution does not expressly deny him.

When there is danger that a vital portion of the economy will be crippled at a time that is critical to the nation's security, then, in my opinion, the President has a clear duty to take steps to protect the nation.[17]

(The italics above are mine. This means any *one* man, does it not?) Truman quotes with approval the famous passage in which Abraham Lincoln justifies his suspension of the writ of habeas corpus. Thus we see that Truman presses the stewardship principle far indeed. He claims that whatever the views held by the Supreme Court upon his intended seizure of the steel mills (and, as I have said, the court's views were heterogenous at the very least), the President "must always act in a national emergency." Truman points out that it is not realistic for the court to admit such sweeping powers only when "a war has been declared or when the country has been invaded." He observes that modern hostilities may begin without the polite exchange of diplomatic notes; that sharp distinctions no longer exist between combatants and noncombatants, military targets and civilian sanctuaries; that the economic facts cannot be separated from provisions for defense and security. And from this situation he draws conclusions regarding the extent of the President's authority and responsibility.

It is for us to reflect that Truman speaks in a time that may well demand of the United States the initiation of a so-called preventive war, or surrender in the event we are attacked, or collapse of a friendly nation makes our own destruction seem imminent.[18] Truman writes:

In this day and age the defense of the nation means more than building an army, navy, and air force. It is a job for the entire resources of the nation. The President, who is Commander in Chief and who represents the interest of all the people, must be able to act at all times to meet any sudden threat to the nation's security. A wise President will always work with Congress, but when Congress fails to act or is unable to act in a crisis, the President, under the Constitution, must use his powers to safeguard the nation.[19]

No one, surely, will accuse Truman of a wilful disrespect for Congress, though it is not always a guarantee of respect that a man has been a member of that body. But Truman has enormous admiration for Congress. Woodrow Wilson, never a member of a legislative body, despised most of the members of the New Jersey legislature and of Congress.

Truman's interpretation of stewardship is almost unlimited. It is doubtful whether an ineffective President, so ignorant of the Constitution as to be incapable of understanding the scope of his constitutional responsibility — and there have been such Presidents — could afford to take this view, considering the ever-critical nature of government's contemporary problems.

No one will argue, surely, that Grover Cleveland was a man of dictatorial temperament? Yet his experience in the Presidency — marked by his command (July, 1894) to American soldiers to clear the way for trains carrying mail to Chicago, the focus of strikes and civil disorders leading to riots and bloodshed, over the protest of John Altgeld, governor of Illinois — compelled him to undertake many vetoes of congressional legislation, and to conclude:

> In the scheme of our national Government the Presidency is pre-eminently the people's office. Of course, all offices created by the Constitution, and all governmental agencies existing under its sanction, must be recognized, in a sense, as the offices and agencies of the people — considered either as an aggregation constituting the national body politic, or some of its divisions. When, however, I now speak of the Presidency as pre-eminently the people's office, I mean that it is especially the office related to the people as individuals, in no general, local or other combination, but standing on the firm footing of manhood and American citizenship.[20]

Cleveland was one of Wilson's mentors. From his youth, Wilson nurtured the ambition to be President and tried to fit himself for the office by his studies. Wilson's temperament, and temperament plays a vital part in the way a man interprets the authority of the Presidency, was that of a shepherd guarding his flock, a prophet ready to lead men, and drive them if necessary, to their salvation, a theologian, as John Maynard Keynes judged him, making the tenets of his theology come true by way of political leadership, a leadership he could visualize only in terms of fervent moral rescue. What Wilson believed, he said:

> That part of the Government, which has the most direct access to opinion has the best chance of leadership and mastery; and at present that part is the President. . . .
>
> The President is at liberty in law and conscience, to be as big a man as he can. His capacity will set the limit; and if Congress be overborne by him, it will be no fault of the makers of the Constitution; it will be from no lack of Constitutional powers on its part, but only because the President has the nation behind him, and Congress has not. He has no means of compelling Congress except through public opinion.[21]

And again:

> The President is also the political leader of the nation, or has it in his choice to be. The nation as a whole has chosen him, and is conscious that it has no other political spokesman. His is the only national voice in affairs. Let him once win the admiration and confidence of the country, and no other single force can withstand him, no combination of forces will easily overpower him. . . . He is the representative of no constituency, but of the whole people. When he speaks in his true character, he speaks for no special interest. If he rightly interprets the national thought and boldly insists upon it, he is irresistible. . . . [The nation's] instinct is for unified action, and it craves a single leader. . . . A President whom it can trust cannot only lead it but form it to his views.[22]

Wilson's is the prevailing doctrine of presidential responsibility — the stewardship principle. The Constitution permits the President anything that crisis, and his personal assessment of crisis, demands in the protection of the welfare of the people. It is an awesome authority that is claimed, an awful responsibility assumed; even twelve men of character, closely associated and inspired by the general policies of a single political party, might well quail before such a prospect, and the nation might well blanch at the thought of admitting (not, perhaps consciously, committing) such dreadful control of its fate to a group of men, much less to one man alone.

On the other hand, a restrictive interpretation of constitutional responsibility might well err in an emergency. Its standards are those pronounced by William Howard Taft:

> The true view of the executive function is, as I conceive it, that the President can exercise no power which cannot be fairly and reasonably traced to some specific grant of power or justly implied and included with such express grant as proper and necessary to its exercise. Such specific grant must be either in the Federal Constitution or in an act of Congress passed in pursuance thereof. There is no undefined residuum of power which he can exercise because it seems to him the public interest, and there is nothing in the *Neagle* case and its definition of a law in the United States, or in other precedents, warranting such an inference. The grants of Executive power are necessarily in general terms in order not to embarrass the Executive within the field of action plainly marked for him, but his jurisdiction must be justified and vindicated by affirmative constitutional law or statutory provision, or it does not exist.[23]

In the same work, Taft refers to Theodore Roosevelt's principle of stewardship as the view that he, as President, is privileged "to play the part of a Universal Providence and set all things right. . . ."

It is not possible for the electorate to inquire beforehand what view candidates for the presidential office take of stewardship versus the restrictive principle. They hardly care. What individuals and special-interest groups want of the candidate is a pledge that he will increase their happiness and reduce their burdens; his constitutional right and means to do this are secondary to them. If the American people had some acquaintance with constitutional law, I would venture the guess that, considering the temper of the electorate, the majority would favor the stewardship principle. Once the candidate is elected, in any case, no one can do anything about his choice of one or the other principle. He cannot be restrained; he cannot be urged to hedge; he cannot be dismissed within the term of his four years unless he gives cause for impeachment.

Is not the present system far too personal for efficiency and for responsibility? Is it not an enormous gamble, a double gamble? A gamble on the view that the President takes of the scope of his powers, a gamble on his ability and convictions in matters of domestic and international policy?

Let us for a moment turn back the pages of history to the President who wrote some of its most glorious pages. Abraham Lincoln's most characteristic utterance on the powers of the President's authority as it applies to the function of Commander in Chief is in a letter he wrote to A. G. Hodges in April, 1864:

> My oath to preserve the Constitution imposed on me the duty of preserving by every indispensable means that government, that nation, of which the Constitution was the organic law. Was it possible to lose the nation and yet preserve the Constitution? By general law life and limb must be protected, but a life is never wisely given to save a limb. I felt that measures otherwise unconstitutional might become lawful by becoming indispensable to the preservation of the Constitution through preservation of the nation. Right or wrong, I assumed this ground and now avow it. I could not feel that, to the best of my ability, I had ever tried to preserve the Constitution, if to save slavery or any minor matter, I should permit the wreck of the government, country, and Constitution altogether.[24]

And elsewhere Lincoln wrote:

> No organic law can ever be framed with a provision specifically applicable to every question which may arise in a practical administration. . . . The whole of the laws are being resisted and all will be destroyed if not protected. . . . I am to sacrifice one law in order to save the rest. . . . The Constitution is silent on the emergency.[25]

It is not for us to argue at this juncture whether Lincoln was right or wrong in the interpretation he put on his powers; he had an oath to preserve the Constitution, and he tried to do this according to his own convictions. There is the point that the President's personal convictions are at the heart of the matter.

Let us turn for a moment to another pair of opposites in regard to presidential responsibility — the immersive view and the passive-post-facto view. The immersive corresponds to what we usually consider leadership, the passive-post-facto is nearer acceptance or quiescence. Let us illustrate the contrasted views with appropriate quotations from the writings of Truman, Frank-lin Roosevelt, and Eisenhower.

Truman wrote:

> The Presidency of the United States carries with it a re-sponsibility so personal as to be without parallel. Very few are authorized to speak for the President. No one can make decisions for him. No one can know all the processes and stages of his thinking in making important decisions. Even the closest to him, even members of his immediate family, never know all the reasons why he does certain things and why he comes to certain conclusions. To be President of the United States is to be lonely, very lonely at times of great decisions.[26]

(The motif of loneliness, of grave importance to the theme of this essay, was remarked upon by Taft, a "restrictive" President.) Truman continues:

> Within the first few months I discovered that being a Presi-dent is like riding a tiger. A man has to keep on riding or be swallowed. The fantastically crowded nine months of 1945 taught me that a President either is constantly on top of events or, if he hesitates, events will soon be on top of him. I never felt I could let up for a single moment.
>
> No one who has not had the responsibility can really understand what it is like to be President, not even his closest aids or members of his immediate family. There is no end to the chain of responsibility that binds him, and he is never allowed to forget that he is President. . . .[27]

Truman acted in the spirit of these words. He neither slumbered nor slept — except, to his bitter regret, on one occasion when he signed the order terminating Lend-Lease. The number of resignations he secured for cause, e.g., Byrnes, Wallace, Mor-genthau, and the hundreds of decisions of major and minor im-portance initiated by him, watched over by him, exemplify his avowal, "As long as I was in the White House, I ran the executive branch of the government."

Franklin Roosevelt displayed much the same élan. He saw to it that the government of the United States was conducted in the White House. Just after his election in November, 1932, Roosevelt said:

> The President is not merely an administrative office. That is the least part of it. It is more than an engineering job, efficient or inefficient. It is pre-eminently a place of moral leadership. All our great Presidents were leaders of thought at times when certain historic ideas in the life of the nation had to be clarified. . . . Isn't that what the office is — a superb opportunity for reapplying, applying in new conditions, the simple rules of human conduct to which we always go back? Without leadership, alert and sensitive to change, we are all bogged up or lose our way.[28]

Then, in December, 1940, at a press conference, Roosevelt said:

> There were one or two cardinal principles; and one of them is the fact that you cannot, under the Constitution, set up a second President of the United States. In other words, the Constitution states one man is responsible. Now that man can delegate, surely, but in the delegation he does not delegate away any part of the responsibility from the ultimate responsibility that rests on him.[29]

And this was the spirit in which Roosevelt acted. I was a witness to his handling of one administrative item, the Tennessee Valley Authority, during a particularly revealing time, 1937–38, and can offer evidence of his active responsibility. He was present at the conception — or let us say, as we would say of any President of immersive persuasion, he conceived — the TVA and wrote in his own hand the first drafts of policy. He presided at subsequent reappraisals, on guard all the time, calling for reconsideration, demanded statements of progress from his trusted experts, until the moment of maturity. And even then his stewardship was not ended.

This degree of presidential immersiveness, where the President is creator, was exercised by Polk in a fruitful and forceful

Presidency. Men of this kind never delegate responsibilities to others. They do not relax their vigilance, nor do they expect others to initiate policy and carry out each project on the agenda.

In contrast to the immersive view of the Presidency is the notion of responsibility expressed by Eisenhower on one of the few occasions when he has been known to speak of such matters. I would classify his remark as passive-post-facto:

> I would like to make one thing clear: no President can delegate his constitutional duties. How can he do it? He has to sign the papers. He has to sign them, and he is responsible for them. I am the responsible head of the Executive part of this government, and there is no more chance of me delegating away the responsibilities. I might delegate someone, "You take the action but I will take the gaff," you might say. But that I have to do, and I expect to do it, and I should do it.[30]

This is part and parcel of an attitude toward leadership which, when affairs have been alleged to have been mismanaged, defends itself by blaming the people. It is a singular notion of responsibility, and it deserves to be documented. At the President's press conference of February 3, 1960, the following exchange took place. The questioner was a representative of the American Broadcasting Corporation, and the question is reproduced in full. The answerer was President Eisenhower, who at that time had been over seven years in office, and his answer is reproduced in its chief sections.

> *Question:* Have you considered the possibility that the American public may be confused by a psychological aspect of our struggle with the Russians? They may have more missiles than we. They did beat us to the moon. Their rate of economic growth now is faster than ours, and they are now turning out, for example, more trained engineers than we do. Now, individually, none of these factors is decisive. But cumulatively, is it not possible that a state of mind, a dangerous state of mind, is being created under which we would be in a position or be forced into a position to accept a posture of second-best in everything or anything?

Answer: . . . Now, we have a free enterprise, we place above all other values our own individual freedoms and rights, and we believe, moreover, that the operation of such a system in the long run produces more, not only more happiness, more satisfaction and pride in our people, but also more goods, more wealth. . . . Now, let's remember that dictatorships have been very efficient. Time and time again, look how we were overawed, almost, by Hitler's early years in his war against overrunning Poland. . . . This is dictatorship. If you take our country and make it an armed camp and regiment it, why, for a while you can — you might do it with great morale, too, if you could get people steamed up like you did in wars; you might do this thing most — well, in very greater tempo than we now are doing it. . . . I would like to see our people — and I admit that there's — that they get disturbed, and probably at times alarmed about something, particularly when the headlines make it, give it an interpretation far beyond its true meaning, like hitting the moon. I've heard people say: "Well, soon there'll be colonies on the moon and they'll be shooting at the earth from the moon." I saw that in one story. . . . Now, what we should think about and talk about more in the world are the values on which we set — on which we do treasure. They don't have them. And since we believe in the long run — in the long run, men do learn to have this same belief about the same values I believe that there is just as much of the seeds of self-destruction in the Communist system as they claim is in ours; because they claim the inherent conflicts in our system have been destroyed. . . . Now, I think our people ought to have greater faith in their own system, go ahead in their own — because, let's remember, you people are the bosses of the American government. You are the people, by your votes and your representatives, and so what do you want? All right, you can make the decisions. All you have to do is to inform yourselves and you will make good decisions. And that is exactly what we are doing . . . We want these things or we don't want them. So let's just be sure that we don't kid ourselves that somebody else that, different from ourselves — because people in government are just you people. All right, then it's your responsibility to make sure that you are secure, that you are not alarmed and certainly not hysterical.

Question: Then, sir, you don't feel that there is a basic danger of defeatism under the present circumstances?

Answer: Not as long as I can keep — put it this way: None in my soul; I'll tell you that.

Thus, government responsibility is not to "steam up" the people; the government is not the government, "you people are the bosses"; *you people* being the reporters or the nation? and it follows, "All right, then it's *your* responsibility." The question is forced on the sober onlooker, If the people are the government, what is the need of a government, or a President?

In Eisenhower's statement there is hardly a trace of the understanding or the initiative visible in the statements of the men quoted earlier. Some opponents of Eisenhower have dubbed him a "rubber-stamp" President. Eisenhower's record, as set out in R. J. Donovan's *The Inside Story,* bears out the presumption of quiescence, a President waiting for ready-made decisions.[31]

Kitchen Cabinets

The President cannot exercise his "energy" as a single executive in the way the founders of the Republic calculated. He escapes from the burden of work and the pressure of responsibility, from the pangs of conscience, by going in search of the personal kind of help he needs. He craves friends, friends to help him bear the moral and spiritual burden of the Presidency. Alexander Hamilton performed indispensable services for George Washington, virtually putting the President into the position of reigning monarch and himself that of ruling prime minister. With this experience began the long line of companionships between Presidents and special friends, irresistibly forced upon the Chief Executive by the unreasonable demands of the Constitution. Therewith the President ceased to be "one," in the sense used by the founders of the Republic. Hamilton held a formal position; others after him have held similar public position, but equally important have been more who have not been on the official payroll. None was elected. They were not the chosen of the people; they could not be censured or dismissed; often they were "appointed" from the shadows to hold high office in the shadows.

These men provide the President with the warmhearted companionship for which he hankers. Their encouragement helps the President discharge his duties and relieves him of some of the moral burden of sole responsibility.

When the Hoover Commission's report on departmental management refers to members of the cabinet as the President's alter ego it is mistaken. The President looks elsewhere for his "second self" — to cronies of long standing, to men who share his tastes and prejudices, to men of the same background and experience; in short, to men as much as possible like himself, or the self he would like to be, or the self he knows he needs but was not given at birth — men in whom he can trust. If he had no such friends, the Presidency would be unbearable.

Jackson appointed to his kitchen cabinet two extraordinarily able newspaper men, Amos Kendall and Francis Preston Blair.[32] They helped him to compose his thoughts and write his speeches and affirmed his conscience in his policies. He took them to himself, he said, because the nationally known politicians who worked in the cabinet could not meet "the necessary standards of selflessness and candor," the essence, it may be said, of collective responsibility. William J. Duane referred to Kendall and Blair as "an influence in Washington unknown to the Constitution and to the country." Accounts of this kitchen cabinet, by two of Jackson's contemporaries, might have been written yesterday:

> He [Kendall] is supposed to be the moving spring of the whole administration; the thinker, planner, doer, but it is all in the dark. Documents are issued of an excellence which prevents their being attributed to persons who take the responsibility of them; a correspondence is kept up all over the country for which no one seems answerable; work is done, of goblin extent and with goblin speed, which makes men look about them with a superstitious wonder; and the invisible Amos Kendall has the credit of it all.

In the House of Representatives, Henry A. Wise complained peevishly:

> He [Kendall] was the President's *thinking* machine, and his

writing machine, ay, and his *lying* machine! . . . the chief
overseer, chief reporter, amanuensis, scribe, accountant
general, man of all work — nothing was well done without
the aid of his diabolical genius.

What a remarkable precursor of Harry Hopkins, Sherman Adams,
and James C. Hagerty! "Goblins" instead of "ghosts."

Without the support of Colonel House, Wilson would have
succumbed to the burdens of office; he would have failed to keep
faith in himself and to make the political adjustments necessary
to such success as he had. Louis D. Brandeis and a few others
formed Wilson's "tennis cabinet."

Franklin Roosevelt conjured up a changing group of confidants
to which was given the fanciful soubriquet of "brains trust." The
group included at various times professors, journalists, and
lawyers like Raymond Moley, Rexford Tugwell, A. A. Berle, Jr.,
Judge Samuel Rosenman, Thomas Corcoran, and Ben Cohen,
and political impressarios like Charley Ross, Louis Howe, and
Marvin McInytre. But, above all, Roosevelt owed his aid and
comfort to Harry Hopkins, deviser of public works and social
services and security, adviser on foreign relations, party tactician,
"trouble shooter," special agent of the President in delicate relations with delicate allies during World War II. Other officers of
the government credited Hopkins with the power to exert a
baneful influence upon the President, compelling him to take
action against his better judgment and personal inclinations:

> Indeed, that overworked scholar, the historian of the future,
> reading various memoirs of this era, may come to the per-
> plexed conclusion that Roosevelt never did anything on his
> own — that everything good that he accomplished was done
> at the instigation of the authors of the memoirs, and every-
> thing bad was due to "other influences," which usually
> meant Hopkins. Hopkins always laughed at the suggestion
> that he was a Svengali, for this implied that Roosevelt must
> be a sweetly submissive Trilby. Roosevelt was many things,
> but he was not that.[33]

And we pass to the cronies who surrounded Truman, and, more
recently, to Eisenhower's golfing, bridge, and canasta companions
(including Sherman Adams, followed by General Persons).

In comparison with the power held by the personal confidants of earlier Presidents, the power of Sherman Adams, and thereby the surrender of responsibility by President Eisenhower, is the most remarkable in American political history, exceeding the trust placed by President Harding in that shady character, Harvey Daugherty. Adams began his service to Eisenhower from the moment he became floor manager at the nominating convention in 1952; he graduated from that tactical role to become chief of Eisenhower's campaign staff. Adams began his career by entering local and provincial politics to become the governor of New Hampshire. To him Eisenhower delegated virtually all the domestic business of the federal government by naming him Assistant to the President, a power in his own right and as head of the tightly knit White House staff. Scarcely a document demanding the President's signature reached Eisenhower unless it had been okeyed by Sherman Adams. In private conversation Adams once described his role: "I have done whatever the President has not done," and, on another occasion, "I only say what the President thinks," an ambiguity worthy of the Delphic oracle. Adams' reference to the Soviet *sputnik,* and our failure to launch one of our own, as "nothing more than an interplanetary basketball game," is a significant example of this thinking, and suggests the sort of negative influence Adams brought to bear on the President.

As Eisenhower's chief assistant, Adams sat in the cabinet and the National Security Council, prepared the agenda of the cabinet, achieved interdepartmental agreement leading to and following from decisions, and took responsibility for dealing with whatever matters of policy and administration he thought might overburden a President whose time should be free for higher things. When the President was stricken with a heart attack, Sherman Adams was the channel of business from all the departments and agencies of government, except foreign policy, and from the cabinet officials and the little group of politicians centering on Nixon — even, it has been said, fending off Nixon's efforts to encroach upon the authority of the Chief Executive. A White House official is quoted as saying, "The President has great faith in Adams and has told me many, many times that with Adams as his assistant he can sleep better at night. He finds it a great relief to have Adams around — to know that no one is going to come knocking at the door to make a deal." [34] Eisenhower himself once said: "The one person who really knows what I am trying to do is Sherman Adams." How reassuring to the nation, if the nation had only known!

When it became necessary for the two to part company, Adams being accused of using his influence to obstruct administrative action by the FTC and the SEC and accepting gifts from the potential beneficiary, the President pleaded that he be allowed to keep his right arm: "I personally like Governor Adams. I admire his abilities. I respect him because of his personal and official integrity. I need him.[35]

Adams was replaced as Assistant to the President by General W. B. Persons. From 1933, Persons served as liaison office with the House of Representatives for the then Secretary of War, Dern, and later H. W. Woodring. He continued in this role until 1949, with increasing responsibilities. For many years he maintained an army friendship with Eisenhower, for some time as his subordinate at NATO headquarters. He worked for Eisenhower during the campaign of 1952 and was appointed to the White House staff. Persons is on better terms with Congress than was Sherman Adams and is accurate in his estimate of sentiment and the direction of votes. One of his associates has said: "Jerry [Persons] made it clear to Ike that you can't move down the road unless you've got an engine. Congress is the engine in our government. Now the President is more at ease with congressmen. He listens to them with interest. He has been well briefed on their problems."

Not only does the President have a kitchen cabinet and assistants like Adams and Persons, he maintains special friendships with men in the cabinet, submitting to their judgment (notably, Eisenhower's trust in George Humphrey). Outside the government he has friends and cronies on whom he relies for the warmth of private pleasure and comfort, and these, assuredly, help to fashion his mind and reassure him.[36] Indeed, like Grant, he is mesmerized by the myth of the talent of the businessman. Eisenhower has delegated a part of his immersive responsibility to his brother Milton, who has been in constant attendance on him.

The most astute member of Eisenhower's kitchen cabinet is James C. Hagerty, who is also Press Secretary and member of the White House staff. During an interview Hagerty made it plain that he believed it a part of his job as Press Secretary to put the President in the best possible light. *Time,* in an article on Hagerty, reported Sherman Adams' observation, "Jim [Hagerty] has been largely responsible for the complexion of the administration." [37] And a journalist in the same article is reported to have said: "Jim Hagerty holds a lens ground to his own prescription over the White House — and outsiders have little choice but to look through it. . . ."

Hagerty has centralized government information to the most extreme degree ever known in American government; he is the one, and almost the only one, to whom the press must repair for news of the highest moment. As the Crown in England is the fountain of honor, so is the White House Press Secretary the fount of news. Douglass Cater reports that, because Hagerty maintains such strict control of press relations, "At least one major United States newspaper felt obliged to cut down the number of front page stories coming out of the White House because they judged it was causing a false public impression of the President's activities." [38]

Certainly advisers are essential to a President's formation of decisions and his peace of mind, considering the enormous burden he must bear. The makers of the Constitution thought to secure energy and vigor and dispatch — and sole responsibility. The responsibility was to be assured by a oneness that made identification simple. Yet the President's need for moral support has made the American executive branch plural in fact, the formal oneness masking its plurality. The founders of the Republic denounced the obsfuscation of the two British cabinets functioning under George III. How right they were in their discernment. But the President today demands collective counsel. The President, whether he appears wretched (Polk, Eisenhower, Harding), stalwart (Wilson), or gay (Franklin Roosevelt), is alone and needs the moral backing of others.

Under Eisenhower, the imputation of responsibility for actions taken and decisions made is, correctly or incorrectly, directed other than at the President. No one seems to know exactly where responsibility lies. *The Invisible Presidency,* the title of a recently published work on the occupants of kitchen cabinets over the generations, is most apt.[39]

Responsibility Remains Sole

Something more must be said on this theme to draw from it its significant lesson. The solitary nature of presidential responsibility, the feeling entertained by the man in office that the burden must come back to him in the end, no matter how he may delegate authority to others, is to be recognized in the public career of Woodrow Wilson.[40] In 1900, still holding to the convictions he had formed as a youthful admirer of the British cabinet system, he thought that, for "harmonious, consistent, responsible government," America's dire need, the only way was to connect "the President as closely as may be with his party in Congress." Wilson thought that the natural connecting link was the cabinet, which should be the President's responsible party council made up of representative party men with long and honorable public service as a certificate of reliability. After another decade of reflection, Wilson abandoned this idea and believed that the cabinet should consist of a number of advisers skilled in law and administration, representatives, it is true, but not necessarily representative of the President's party.[41] When Wilson became President he adopted the latter opinion. He wished to have around him men who served his will and mind alone. He placed first value on loyalty to his own ideas and purposes. And this a President is forced to do if he is to act effectively.

President Polk said:

> No President who performs his duty faithfully and conscientiously can have any leisure. If he entrusts the details and smaller matters to subordinates, constant errors will occur. I prefer to supervise the whole operations of the government myself than entrust the public business to subordinates, and this makes my duties very great.[42]

President Taft on the day of Woodrow Wilson's inauguration told the new President: "I'm glad to be going — this is the loneliest place in the world!" [43] It was not long before Wilson was confiding in those around him: "The responsibilities of the President are great, and I cannot perform them alone. If I can't have the assistance of those in whom I have confidence, what am I to do?" Franklin Roosevelt was frank to confess:

> The Committee has not spared me; they say, what has been common knowledge for twenty years, that the President cannot adequately handle his responsibilities; that he is overworked; that it is humanly impossible, under the system we have, for him fully to carry out his constitutional duty as Chief Executive, because he is overwhelmed with minor details and needless contacts arising directly from the bad organization and equipment of the government. I can testify to this. With my predecessors who have said the same thing over and over again, I plead guilty.[44]

President Truman relates how bitter was the lesson he learned when he did not exercise responsible vigilance; as he calls it, "my first bad experience in the problem of delegating authority." His foreign economic administrator, Leo Crowley, and Joseph C. Grew, acting Secretary of State, saw him after a cabinet meeting in May, 1945, and asked for an order to reduce Lend-Lease, an order which had been approved by Roosevelt but had not been signed at the time of his death. They told Truman that now that Germany was out of the war it was time for reductions to start. Satisfied with their "briefing," Truman signed the document without reading it. This action had a most adverse effect on America's relations with the Allies, the British being especially hard hit and the Soviet Union protesting; more serious still, it increased Stalin's suspicions of American intentions. Let us observe that this matter could have been discussed in the cabinet; indeed, in England, France, or West Germany it would have been.

> That experience (that I must always know what is in the documents I sign) brought home to me not only that I had to know exactly where I was going, but also that I had to know that my basic policies were being carried out. If I had read the order, as I should have, the incident would not have occurred. But the best time to learn that lesson was right at the beginning of my duties as President.
>
> This was my first experience with the problem of delegating authority but retaining responsibility. The presidency is so tremendous that it is necessary for a President to delegate responsibility. To be able to do so safely, however, he must have around him people who can be trusted not to arrogate responsibility to themselves.

Eventually, I succeeded in surrounding myself with assistants and associates who would not overstep the bounds of that delegated authority, and they were people I could trust. This is policy on the highest level: It is the operation of the government by the Chief Executive under the law. That is what it amounts to, and when that ceases to be, chaos exists.[45]

It is in the most difficult decisions that the President's responsibility comes home to him with most tragic poignancy. For weeks, Wilson did not go to bed without fear of news that the United States had been drawn into war. He wrote the note to the German government on the sinking of the "Lusitania" in his own hand because he felt the issue too solemn to be shared with others. He warned his military leaders not to talk or act in a way that might be misconstrued as political. His note to the Mexican dictator Huerta in the spring of 1914 he himself composed and typed; it was not discussed with the cabinet because it involved the President's personal responsibilty for peace or war.

Truman required from Secretary of State Byrnes a report on foreign affairs every twenty-four hours, and when Byrnes failed to obey he was told to resign. "The Secretary of State should never at any time come to think that he is the man in the White House, and the President should not try to be the Secretary of State." [46] Henry Wallace, as Secretary of Commerce, made highly embarrassing speeches on American foreign policy, sadly lacking in prudence and wisdom.[47] Before making one of these speeches in September, 1946, he told Truman he intended to do so and sketched the tenor of his remarks. Truman agreed to its delivery without reading the text — another clear failure to gauge his responsibility as President. When Wallace allowed newspapers to print a letter on the same subject he had written to the President in July of that year, he was called into session with the President, in the presence of Charlie Ross, the Press Secretary. Wallace was told of the effect on America's friends and enemies of his cozening speeches, and that his speeches were undermining the negotiations Secretary Byrnes was conducting in the Council of Foreign Ministers in Paris. Byrnes had complained to Truman that his position was being made untenable. In conclusion, Truman asked for Wallace's resignation. Only one voice could speak for America —

the President's. Only to Byrnes had he given the right to speak for him in Paris.

Truman was alone in his decision to drop the atomic bomb on Japan. Against this was the possible cost of half a million American lives to force Japan's surrender, according to the advice of General Marshall. Truman has said, "I had told Stimson that the bomb should be dropped as nearly as possible upon a war production center of prime military importance." [48]

These are some of the grave consequences of the sole responsibility of the President.

The President as Unifier

Government officials and agencies are many and far-flung, under constant tension, and tempted to throw off the reins of central direction and responsibility. The President's responsibility makes him the only unifier. Whatever is not acceptable to the people, or to the aggrieved heads of departments, is certain to become a reproach to the President. I have shown the grave responsibility he bears in overcoming the squabbles of the branches of the military and pacifying the Joint Chiefs of Staff, the Secretary of Defense, and the Bureau of the Budget. Truman while in office was highly conscious of this responsibility. To avoid contention, Forrestal, then Secretary of Defense, advocated the adoption of the British cabinet system. Truman, though he acknowledged the superior efficiency of the British system, demurred: "Under the British system there is a group responsibility of the cabinet. Under our system the responsibility rests on one man—the President." [49] Truman preferred to stay with the existing system because he thought the United States was doing well under it.

Truman could not leave the problem of Israel to the State Department and think his responsibility was fulfilled. Officials below the rank of secretary were not sufficiently controlled by their own chief to draw them into the magnetic center of the President's sole responsibility. The President had to overrule them. Nor could he surrender his position as unifier to anyone in the issue of the Korean campaign. Nor could he ask anyone else to reprimand the rebellious MacArthur. "Of course, I would never deny General MacArthur or anyone else the right to differ with me in opinions. The official position of the United States, however, is defined by decisions and declarations of the President. There can be only one voice in stating the position of this country." Truman pointed out, quite justly, that it was necessary to listen to more than military judgments in order to make policy in the field of foreign relations.[50] The President alone establishes basic principles: "We will not buy an armistice by turning over human beings for slaughter or slavery." [51]

Sole Inspirer of Administration

The President's role as inspirer of thought and action was perhaps most clearly evident during Wilson's terms of office, but of Franklin Roosevelt's cabinet meetings Harold Ickes writes: "You go in tired and discouraged and out of sorts and the President puts new life into you. You come out feeling like a fighting cock." [52] Wilson, in undertaking the role of enthusiast, offered these reflections:

> I cannot choose as an individual what I shall do; I must choose always as a President, ready to guard at every turn and in every way possible the success of what I have to do for the people. Apparently, the little things count quite as much as the big in this strange business of leading opinion and securing action. . . . The President is a superior kind of slave, and must content himself with the reflection that the *kind* is superior.[53]

Presidential Impact is Abruptly Personal

The conduct of national affairs is subject to zigzags of policy, largely because the moderating influence of a cabinet is lacking, and perhaps because the political parties have no coherent program or continuous organization. The consequences are serious; America's allies and the American economy and fate of thousands of military and civil career and non-career officials are at stake. It is almost a psychological necessity for an incoming President to seek to distinguish his own personality from that of the man he has replaced and from the candidate he has beaten. Thus, the abruptness of Dulle's advocacy of a "massive retaliation" and satellite policy shocked allies and enemies alike and caused grave anxiety, suspicion, and misunderstandings within the government itself. As Truman said:

> ... it is one of the facts of American foreign policy, and one
> that those in responsibility must bear in mind, that an im-
> pending change in Washington makes our friends abroad
> anxious and our enemies hopeful. They all remember what
> happened when Harding replaced Wilson, and what a
> calamity it meant for the world.[54]

It is true that abrupt reversal of policy hurts the rest of the
world more than it does the United States, but to be considered
unstable and capricious is equally harmful to our relations abroad.

I do not intend to say that political or party change is undesirable; it is necessary for the health of a democracy. The difficulty of American government is to maintain policy on a fairly
even keel from one President to the next.

Yet Bradford Westerfield, for another reason than mine, fears
that the presidential election is an occasion when partisanship in
foreign policy may be particularly displayed, with necessarily
injurious consequences.[55] But it is not so much that partisan feelings may be displayed during election campaigns that gives me
cause for worry. Rather it is the vastly more important fact that
however much changes in foreign policy may be muted in the
campaigns, it is, after all, inevitable that a President shall be
elected on the basis of their consideration. Or is the nation to be
discharged from a choice between alternatives by unvoiced con-
nivance?

Consider the startling reversal of foreign policy when power
passed from Acheson-Truman to Dulles-Eisenhower on the lib-
eration of the Balkan and Baltic satellites, the wobbling on
Berlin, the harshness toward Israel very nearly reaching sanctions (with a subsequent steady kindness toward Nasser), and,
again, the sudden policy of peacefulness (on Dulles' death) and
an acceptance of summit meetings, more recently scouted. The
President, an unknown factor at the time he becomes President,
appoints another, relatively unknown, to be his Secretary of
State. The abrupt expression of conviction, presented to the
world with the announcement of a new foreign policy, is bound
to come as a surprise.

Energy Impeded, Responsibility Untethered

It seems to me that the foregoing analysis of the office of President of the United States warrants certain reasonable conclusions, conclusions serious enough to become the basis for substantial reforms of the executive branch.

1. The physical burden of the office is far too racking and perpetual for one man, if we accept the view that the reliability of the President's response to problems of policy and administration is of first importance.

2. The range of responsibilities in almost any one of the segments of the President's authority — strict executive and administrative action, general executive power in both normal and emergency government; the conduct of foreign policy; the initiation and enaction of special projects, including the budgetary function; responsibilities as Commander in Chief; the exercise of party leadership, the mustering of like-minded forces and the gathering of electoral strength; the functions of Chief of State and national symbol — the weight is beyond the reliable power of decision of any one man.

3. It is no longer tenable to operate on the basis of the belief of the founders of the Republic that "energy, despatch, vigor and promptness" will issue from the unity of the Chief Executive. On the contrary, one man is so taxed that efficiency is to be found not in unity but only in collectivity. This truth has been explicitly and eloquently admitted with the establishment of all sorts of conciliar and delegated executive bodies as auxiliaries to the President, but they remain at a tangent and are not and cannot be blended with the single executive. His own personal powers cannot make them blend, cannot make them a part of his mind and body, and, morally, his sense of responsibility inhibits delegation.

4. It is no longer possible to be satisfied with the idea that responsibility to the people has been instituted. Responsibility for what? brings a hollow answer. Responsibility to whom? brings the same ghost of a voice: for vague purposes and to vague entities. Furthermore, there are no institutions of responsibility intermediate between the President and the people, to be at once the sieve, the focus, the informed discriminating body that, at the minimum, makes clear the merits and demerits of the President's actions.

5. A vast and scattered population, as in the United States,

needs a strong stimulus to think, feel, and act politically. To be effective, legislators, particularly the President, must be unusually stimulating. A man of strong character can make problems and proposed solutions clear to the public before a crisis has arisen. The phrase "strong character" is not intended in any way to suggest arbitrary power; it is intended to suggest conviction and ability and, for the rest, all those qualities we praise in the man we acknowledge as a leader of men. The present tendency in American government is for each branch to wait for another to make the first move. The temptation is for each member (House, Senate, the President) to "Let George do it," sometimes to request it of George, and all too frequently to avoid its own obligations.

6. We are thus left with a single man who, to a frightening degree, is alone in his decisions on what he believes the Constitution permits him to do; and what he believes to be his responsibility — immersive and bold, conceiving and constantly constructive, or permissive, quiescent, passive-post-facto in his conduct of the office — and a man with a fixed term, shielded by the glory of being the nation's representative, not subject to account to anyone but himself, not, at any rate, through the conveniently and flexibly operating criticism of a loyal opposition with independent authority to force him to take notice.

All our respect must go to President Truman for the motto emblazoned on his desk: "The Buck Stops Here!" In this way he acknowledged that all responsibility converged on him, that all obligations flowed from him and that he would meet both in his own person. The legitimate doubt is whether any single person can shoulder the obligations, even with all the appointed persons that assist the President. His constitutional and moral responsibilities are his alone.

Can a genius be found for the Presidency, a man who will give us a more reliable guarantee of the qualities the founders of the Republic sought than we now have? What methods are needed to obtain such a genius, and are the present methods of choice the best conceivable for his discovery, selection, and election? If the answer to these questions is in doubt, given the governmental problems of the age, what alternative can be invented?

V

The President Needs Rescue

By the terms of the Constitution and the demands of the office the President is in sole charge in all important affairs. It is useful to think of him sitting at his desk in the White House, just returned from a meeting of the National Security Council or the cabinet, and to see his predicament, alone as he is, as he looks out at the wide, wide world. What are his connections with it? When does it give him the signal for action? Who provides a timetable and from what source do the deadlines appear? How imperative are they, how far are they permissive? At least four great sectors of reality converge on him, vast sectors that come to a pinpoint at their sharpest angle, the President's mind. One is the nation to which he made promises, demanding firmer fulfillment than the shape they took in the party platform and in his personal obligations, the insurgent pressure groups, the claimant individuals. The second is the busy, jealous, and powerful Congress and the great corps of officials, his help but also his gadfly. Third, he owes something to his party since he is concerned with its policies and the continuation of its success, and he is obliged to look for its help to turn his persuasions into enactment and law enforcement and favorable public morale. Fourth, being the supreme political authority of the most powerful democratic nation in the world, he finds that the whole world looks to him on every occasion that it looks to America, and he himself is beholden to that world because his own nation, his trust, requires the assistance and admiration of it. He sits there, for most affairs, strange and alien to the clamor, and it requires months, even beyond the compass of a year, to enter into rapport. By what instruments?

To govern, Mendès-France has said, is to choose, to choose between alternatives of direction, effort, money, and time-priority. To choose it is first necessary to know. Who will feed into the funnels that lead to the President their demands, the force and validity of their wants; the state in which they are received; the process of their appraisal and cogitation; their respective time-positions on the agenda; the discovery of the answers, their scope, their content, their fiscal provision, their timing, and the follow-up of their execution? Not one of these elements of government is dispensable; all are relentless; none can be ignored or slighted without exacting a revenge. All affect each, in quality and effect; the subjects of government have a natural intertwinement with each other.

What apparatus will remind the President of the realities and appetites of the outside world, set his program so that he even stumbles into it whenever his gaze is too distant, force him to meet the deadline imposed by the laws Congress has enacted? Enable him meetly to discipline his time and his output of energy so that he may do one of his duties properly, namely, respond to felt and expressed needs, and the other, perhaps the greater, initiate those things which are very personally his own, such as Point Four with Truman and "Atoms for Peace" with Eisenhower? What apparatus will magnify his own personal power to make certain that what is commanded, or what is agreed to after presidential persuasion, shall be carried out?

It is a tenet that the President needs help; it will be shown in this chapter that the help that has been provided does not satisfy the needs of the twentieth century; and it will be suggested that the President needs rescue.

The founders of the Republic provided assistance for the President in his work, but not in his responsibility, by establishing the elements that came to be a cabinet, the "principal officers." His executive power allows him to seek the assistance of officials employed in the public service as well as various special advisers, confidential colleagues, and agents. In the course of time there developed an enormous apparatus. It did not burgeon into anything extraordinary in numbers and organization until the advent of Franklin Roosevelt (especially after 1937). The apparatus for presidential assistance has given rise to what political scientists have come to call "the institutionalization of the Presidency." It has impelled some of them to talk of "The Presidency," meaning not the role of the President but of this large and intricate instrument, as something almost if not quite independent of the man himself.

"Institutionalization" offers something of an escape hatch from the grave problems of the President as statesman. It tends to have the same falsely benign effect on listeners as the experience reported by the lady who sedulously attended chuch and when asked what so fascinated her in the sermons replied, "Ah! that blessed word, that *blessed* word, Mesopotamia!" And a superstitious reverence for the power of a word like "institutionalization" disguises the gravity of certain disturbing problems that should be pondered, not evaded.

The use of the word "Presidency" can have the same effect, blinding the observer to the weaknesses of the man as mortal. The word has at least two meanings which offer opportunities for a pea-and-thimble game or a game of Cox and Box. It may mean simply the office, in the sense of the job, of the President. If used in this way, we know where we are. But it is sometimes used otherwise to represent all the agencies which assist the President, offering advice, drafts for discussion, decision, and action, facts, "briefings," liaison with Congress and the departments and agencies to see that the President's decisions are carried out.

The President is assisted by thousands of men and women of special expertness and continuous activity, but in the public mind this is forgotten and there is imputed to the President himself a wisdom and skill at deliberation that seem miraculous, tending to inspire trust that all is well. This is specious. It darkens truth because it is always less than true.

The apparatus of the Presidency has come to stand for the man, and yet one man's responsibility and efficiency are at the heart of the executive branch of the government. It is not my intention here to analyze the purposes and composition of the many agencies assisting the President. Years of study of the assistance the President has to draw upon enables a certain number of general conclusions.

The Presidency "Institutionalized"

The executive office of the White House (405 members), the cabinet (10 members), the Bureau of the Budget (437 members), the Council of Economic Advisers (31 members), and the National Security Council (about 12) assist the President in making and enforcing decisions of every kind within the range of his constitutional and statutory responsibilities. (The figures in parentheses indicate the size of personnel of each as of July, 1959.) Impinging on them, and linked through them to the President himself, is a vast miscellany of departments and agencies, with millions of officials, incorporating some 15,000 different skills in the physical sciences, the social sciences, and in administrative science.

It can be said at the outset that, generally speaking, the White House is now more amply and efficiently manned than it was even in the early thirties, that the laudable change that has come over the provision of auxiliaries to the President is due to the initiative and constructive energies of Franklin Roosevelt. Before him, practically no steady assistance proper to the President existed. The system was further developed by Truman and given some additional touches by President Eisenhower.

The executive office of the President consists of the White House staff, most directly and continuously in contact with the President; and in regular touch are the National Security Council, the Bureau of the Budget, and the Council of Economic Advisers.

The little group of men, Louis Brownlow, Charles Merriam, and Luther Gulick, who were responsible for bringing to President Roosevelt the help he needed, deserve well of their country.[1] They diagnosed the helplessness of the Chief Executive, the colossal burden thrust on him by the modern economy with its precarious equilibrium, and America's precious destiny in the wild world of turbulent nations. The White House staff began with their proposal for six assistants to the President to help him secure pertinent information needed in the making of responsible decisions and to see that the decisions were made known to every administrative department and agency concerned. They were to be "possessed of high competence, great physical vigor, and a passion for anonymity."

Today, according to the *U.S. Government Organization Manual, 1959–60,* there are some forty principals — the Assistant to the President, three deputy assistants, two secretaries, three special counsels, three administrative assistants, nine special assistants to the President, four special assistants in the White House, some special consultants, and several persons with such titles as "assistant to the deputy assistant to the President." They are variously concerned, with the cabinet secretariat, the press, interdepartmental affairs, the National Security Council, personnel management, congressional liaison, foreign affairs, economic affairs, army, navy, and air force, and so on. With their staffs, they numbered 405 in July, 1959.

This is the group at the President's beck and call when he is in need of information and advice, available to him at any moment if he has an inspiration, an inkling of a doubt, or the energizing perturbation of an inventive political impulse. It is in continuous being to stimulate his thoughts, to prepare his program and help him make up his mind, to hold him to regularity and punctuality in action (at its discretion under the watchful eye of the Assistant to the President). It links the teeming, ever-mobile, far-ramifying apparatus of government to the President. Only the intellect and the character of the President are to blame if he remains an uninformed and uninspired executive. Even if the group is unable to give a passive-post-facto President qualities of conviction and courage, it seems likely (who can say for certain?) that the United States is better off with such an assembly than without it. The President's assistants have acquired a rescue-facient function of a minimum order; and better to have it in this fashion than to have none at all. Yet it would be much better if the function were exercised by men who owed their authority to public election, for these now do not.

The President, at will, is briefed on the economic situation (sometimes at a regular appointment each week), congressional affairs, the march of science, the state of the budget, and matters contingent, as, for example, a steel strike or what is occuring in Algeria. The Secretary of State briefs the President on foreign affairs, and a special assistant provides interim briefings. The special assistant on the National Security Council keeps him in touch with matters of defense. It is at once manifest how much the utility of this advice and prompting depend on the wisdom and the sense of responsibility of the Assistant to the President — John R. Steelman for Truman, and for Eisenhower, first, Sherman Adams and, later, Wilton B. Persons. (Adams promised much when he announced that the staff system would function so smoothly that "the Chief Executive will only have to make three or four major decisions a year.")[2]

When the Hoover Commission of 1949 proposed that the President have an assistant, it offered a naïve description of the limited responsibilities the job would entail:

> At present there is no place in the President's Office to which the President can look for a current summary of the principal issues with which he may have to deal in the near future; nor is a current summary of the staff work available on problems that have been assigned to his advisers, his staff agencies, or the heads of departments and agencies.
>
> To meet this deficiency, the Commission proposes the addition of a staff secretary. He would not himself be an adviser to the President on any issue of policy, nor would he review (in a supervisory capacity) the substance of any recommendation made to the President by any part of his staff.
>
> The Commission believes that this recommendation will facilitate teamwork among the President's staff, the agencies of the President's Office, and any Cabinet or interdepartmental committees which are studying problems for the President.
>
> If possible the staff secretary, like the executive clerk, should be a career public servant.
>
> The staff secretary should keep the President currently informed of the work which has been undertaken by various parts of the President's Office, by the Cabinet committees, or by interdepartmental committees or special advisory committees. He should inform the President of any diffi-

culties which have arisen because of the overlapping of assignments or conflicts of policy.³

Of course it seems incredible that such an assistant would not "himself be an adviser . . . on any issue of policy." How could he fail to inject his own values and verbal coloring into the briefings he is called upon to give the President?

R. E. Neustadt, an experienced and subtle observer of the presidential office at work, has observed:

> The President in person needs help more than he did in 1937, but he is far less equipped to get help for himself. What he needs most is help in gaining personal perspective on and personal control over the issues that ought to be decided by nobody but himself. Eisenhower seems to have less help of that sort than Roosevelt did. His Executive Office, including the White House, has become an agglomeration of agencies and committees existing at least as much to serve other purposes as to serve the President in these personal terms.⁴

If such is the case, I can offer an explanation. A man's convictions and political knowledge will lead him to the help he needs; but if he is too little possessed of these, he will either get no help at all, since he does not know what to ask for, or he will get help that is useless to him, that clutters up his mind.

The assistants surrounding the President may involve him in time-consuming routines that represent someone else's ideas of what the President's role should be. He may reach the point where he is over-loyal to his assistants in order to insure their loyalty to him.

Why do we hear the frequent plaint that conditions must be established to give the President time to think? In a "letter to a friend" describing his views of the duties of a "first secretary of the government," Eisenhower wrote:

> This officer — who in this case would be Mr. Dulles — would be responsible to the President for co-ordinating and directing the efforts of the State Department, the USIA, the ICA and the international activities of the departments of Commerce, Agriculture, Labor and the Treasury. He [the

President] would be relieved of the chore of meeting with committees and long hours of detailed discussion and argument — he would be given time to think. . . .[5]

How curious — to believe that mastery of policy is possible without immersion in its tangled affairs! The truth is that the President needs advisers but cannot assimilate all the facts they tell him. An elected, collectively responsible Presidency, that is, a plural executive, might manage to do so by sharing the chores of office.

This brings us to a second possibility, that the President may be so assailed by the many briefs hurled at him that he becomes unheedful even as he pretends to be listening. He will be Rodin's "Thinker," a lonely figure, solitary, crouched as though in deep thought, green (but not of bronze), giving answers to questions that other people have posed in terms others have suggested, and worrying about his far-flung responsibility and what other people (who keep bothering him) are doing with it. . . .

President Eisenhower, of course, comprehends this very well. At a press conference in May, 1958, he said:

> I do not believe that any individual, whether he is running General Motors or the United States of America, his phase of it, can do the best job by just sitting at a desk and putting his face in a bunch of papers.
>
> Actually, the job, when you come down to it, when you think of the interlocking staffs and associates that have to take and analyze all the details of every question that comes to the Presidency, he ought to be trying to keep his mind free of inconsequential detail and doing his own thinking on the basic principles and factors that he believes are important so that he can make clearer and better judgments. And, I tell you, that is the problem of the Presidency, not to give all the details of why some man was fired for this or some other little thing, but to make clear decisions over the best array of facts that he can get into his own brain.

Receptivity determines what is received, but what is selected for attention is determined by and depends on one's convictions. In the light of this observation, one wonders whether the White House staff and other components of the executive office have offered the President assistance to overcome the long delay in emphasizing science in the curriculum of our schools, the disastrous loss of time in the missile program in spite of repeated congressional prodding, the abandonment of Indochina, the pretended surprise at Britain and France's expedition to Suez, followed by panic-stricken diplomatic expedients, the misinterpretation of America's attitude to "neutrals" throughout the world, with Dulles and the President announcing disparate views, two economic near-crises in two terms, that of 1958 being extremely serious. Was the flight of the U-2 "inconsequential detail"?

Let me add another example from Truman's administration of the unreliability of "institutionalizing" the Presidency. James Reston, Washington correspondent for the *New York Times,* asserted (July 30, 1950) that the National Security Council had failed to appraise correctly the Korean situation:

> The feeling here now, however, is that the council fell down on the task of thinking through and arguing out, before the moment of crisis, all aspects of policy before that policy had to be put into effect. And one reason for this was that it was composed of Cabinet members with other urgent decisions that they had no time to think through or argue out all aspects of long-range policy.

Two further observations concern the Operations Co-ordinating Board and suggestions designed to assist the President (made by Clark Clifford and John Steelman, aids to President Truman).

The Operations Co-ordinating Board is supposed to see that the policies recommended by the National Security Council and approved by the President are fulfilled. The purpose is to secure that the various government departments that have foreign duties, intelligence and defense, labor, immigration, atomic energy, agriculture, commerce, the State Department, information, function energetically and in mutual helpfulness. Its members are the Undersecretary of State (chairman), the special assistant to the President for security operations co-ordination, the deputy secretary of defense, the director of the International Co-operation Administration, and the special assistant to the President for national security affairs. The institution was begun under Franklin

Roosevelt, developed by Truman, and still further adapted by Eisenhower. The board makes a progress report to the National Security Council and to the President at least once every six months and calls for redefinition of policy when it seems obscure in practice.

Yet there is widespread belief that the co-ordinating board wastes everybody's time because it cannot bring any real force to bear on the officials concerned. Again and again there are complaints that the departments and agencies go their own wilful way and that the President does not have time to read progress reports. When it was suggested that Vice-President Nixon be given charge of the board, the proposal was jettisoned at the insistence of the Department of State. Why appoint another co-ordinator for a department which itself is intended to co-ordinate?

Having said as much long ago, I was dismayed to learn from no less an intimate authority on presidential behavior than Arthur Krock of the *New York Times* that the Operations Co-ordinating Board, one of the vaunted agencies of "institutionalization," was indeed feeble.[6] He reports that "many months ago" its chairman, W. H. Jackson, an undersecretary in the State Department and so occupying a secondary position in one executive unit, was required to bring into line with high policy all the operations of his superiors in the executive branch. Jackson reported that success was impossible without a chairman of a status that would command prestige. On January 13, 1960, Gordon Gray, special assistant to the President in national security affairs, one of the President's immediate officers in the executive office of the White House, was made chairman of the co-ordinating board. Mr. Krock admits that the organization has suffered "fundamental weakness" hitherto. Is this not very, very late to be attempting to remedy the matter? It is confessed that the board never has had the voice of command it needed. The informant asserts his belief that now matters will be better because the chairman stems directly from the President's own office, but only "if the President will fully support his own assistant in seeing that the President's high policy decisions in the National Security Council are put into operation throughout the Administration."

I do not believe that the fecklessness exposed will be remedied, for the *if* contained in the above proviso cannot be fulfilled while one man alone has all the multifarious and pressing responsibilities of the President. It seems that Mr. Krock is doomed to continue to see what he seems to deplore and has witnessed "for years": "the constant recurrence of conflict between the policies set by the President and their translation into Executive acts. . . ."

When British, West German, or Scandinavian cabinet ministers disperse, they know what they have decided or can be reminded by the cabinet secretariat. Each member is responsible for the obligations of his own department, and when co-ordination is essential each member consults equally authoritative ministers in other departments. All begin with the firm presumption that they work with solidarity, in and to the same plan, all of them being *elected* and equally responsible to the legislature, the party, and the people.

The Hoover Commission proposed to Congress the establishment of an administrative Vice-President. It was a confused suggestion, but in essence a number of minor functions were to be surrendered in this way. The suggestion was resisted by several experts (among them, especially, the late James K. Hart, one of America's foremost constitutional lawyers and an expert on the Presidency) as likely to produce a "plural executive" — or rather the evils of a plural executive without the gain of its efficiency.

The most interesting evidence came from two men who had served as close assistants to Truman. I quote Clifford Clark:

> I was familiar with the method that President Truman used. He felt that he did better and he maintained a more personal knowledge and contact with a problem if he was able to talk personally with the man to whom he had assigned the problem. He did not use the staff system. If he had ten or twelve men working for him at the White House staff he found he did better if he talked with those men personally, with reference to their reactions to a particular problem, rather than having them produce reports and referring them to a chief of staff who, in turn, would digest them and pass them on to the President. . . .[7]

Clark continued to propose a "more fundamental and elemental approach to the problem," which was "to change the concept of the function of the Vice-President."

> *I believe that the Vice-President could be moved from the legislative branch, where he now is, to the executive branch.* It would take a constitutional amendment. But I believe the enormity of the problem is such that it is going to take far-reaching measures to satisfy anything like the need that exists at this time.
>
> . . . I think the Vice-President could be the second officer in the executive branch of the Government. He could take over from the President a vast amount of administrative detail. And it would help the President immensely if you had that kind of arrangement. I believe, too, you would get the sort of man that you wanted for the job, because when the great parties met in convention they would know that they were nominating the two men who were to guide the destinies of the nation. I believe that the Presidential nominee would be one with whom he could work. . . .
>
> Also, you would be preparing in the process a man for succession to the Presidency.

(The italics above are mine.)

Clark pointed out that President Eisenhower was called upon to make 245 speeches in 104 weeks. Even if someone else did the necessary spadework, the presentation of the speeches took the President's time and energy and put him under tension each time he delivered a speech. If the Vice-President were qualified, as Clark proposes, he could relieve the President of many onerous duties, not least of which would be speechmaking. The Vice-President would also be valuable at meetings and in negotiations with political officers of his party — "again, it takes stamina, it takes time, it takes the strength of the President." Clark believed that the Assistant to the President should not be authorized to handle important political duties that belong rightfully to the President, but that the Vice-President, allowed a more responsible role, could do so. "The Vice-President can relieve him of many ceremonial and political burdens . . . so he can do the real job that the Constitution has in mind for him to do."

Let the essence of Clark's proposal be observed closely. It requires that the Presidency cease being unitary; it introduces the principle of shared or collective responsibility. It is prudent, because it acknowledges the impossibilty of easing the awful burden unless it is distributed among elected colleagues of the President. *But now suppose that instead of one Vice-President there were eleven?* That would give us, at least, a cabinet with collective responsibility, owing its authority to election by the people.

I turn to John Steelman's proposal presented at the same hearings at which Clark appeared. Steelman is well entitled to comment since, under one title or another, he served as assistant to President Truman from 1945 to 1953. His first considerable power was exercised as the director of the Office of Mobilization and Reconversion and helped to return the American economy to a peace time footing, an operation that required the action of more than half of the departments of the federal government. Direction of the Office of Mobilization and Reconversion, said one Chief Justice of the Supreme Court, was "the most powerful office ever created by the Congress, a power next to that of the President himself." In this position Steelman was given power to issue directives to the members of the cabinet. Steelman recommended to the President that the job be abolished, on the grounds that, "In peace time, certainly, I do not think the President needs anybody with power to act between the President and his Cabinet or the President and anybody else who is supposed to report directly to the President." It is, of course, not surprising that Truman was astonished to see Steelman relinquish such power, and teased him with the observation, "You are a peculiar bureaucrat." Consequently, Truman made Steelman "Assistant to the President" and allowed him to amend the title by prefixing the definite article. Henceforth the President's authority was paramount; Steelman was the executant at the President's direction. This was as wide an authority as the President wished to make it, or as narrow, depending on the problem to be solved. Sometimes the assistant and the department heads would settle a matter among themselves; at other times, Steelman showed himself extremely sensitive to the President's constitutional and political responsibility:

> Many times I have said something to the effect that there is a problem that I do not believe I have a right to decide. I think I must tell the President about it — depending on what

it was. But the staff people have to be careful about making some of these decisions. *Nobody has ever voted for members of the staff to be where they are.* The President put them there and he is responsible for them — responsible for their activities.

And so you may call in representatives of several different departments and thresh a problem out and then later decide to discuss it with the President or get a committee to go see the President about it, depending on what it is.

But the final responsibility is the President's, and nobody else's. We cannot take any of the responsibility away from the President. You can take some of the paperwork and some of the time for discussion, and so forth.

(The italics above are mine.) Steelman, under cross-examination by Senator Norris Cotton (New Hampshire), was emphatic in saying that one of the difficult problems faced by the White House staff was that too many people expected the President to do everything:

If you take any staff member and build him up to where the public thinks he is running the White House, or any part of it, it is bad. . . . The things done at the White House are the President's responsibility, and he does them. The rest of us just work there.

This is an honest, modest, and loyal statement. Indeed, Steelman claims that as director of War Mobilization and with all the publicity the office entailed, he played down his role deliberately so that the public might not worry about who was responsible.

Steelman suggests that matters be left as they are so that the President is free to delegate business to his assistants. He rejects the suggestion that there be an administrative Vice-President, appointed by the President and confirmed by the Senate, for he is convinced that presidential responsibility must be preserved intact.

Steelman suggests that the President be allowed to judge how much business (with its attendant power over persons and property) can be delegated to others, with the attendant responsibility of making certain that the delegated power is exercised in a way to satisfy his conscience.

Is there no cause at all for profound misgivings for the nation's welfare and security when officials in intimate touch with the operation of the Presidency make this appraisal of the present system: "The President approved the decision to put up Vanguard rather than the Army's faster, less-complex satellite. However, it is somewhat doubtful that he even knew the details of both of the projects."[8] (The real decision probably was made by the Department of Defense.) Or, again:

> The President says he did not know the Russians were ready to send up a satellite. Yet General Lauris Norstad, Supreme Allied Commander in Europe, says he reported to the heads of the Allied governments just a few days before Sputnik went up, the fact that Russia was to launch a satellite. Apparently the word didn't get through.
>
> At high official levels there was little knowledge of this country's satellite program. There was no realization of its prestige value and there was not very much noticeable enthusiasm for the whole project. It is doubtful Mr. Eisenhower was at all concerned that the Russians might make gains with a satellite of their own, because he had not been alerted to the importance that might attach to a Russian launching before the U.S. was ready with its satellite.

The same commentators explain how the conduct of the civil rights policy and the treatment of the Little Rock affair devolved so largely (almost exclusively) on Attorney General Herbert Brownell. And when asked if Sherman was not, in effect, an Executive Vice-President:

> The reply: Yes, he is. *But the need is for three Sherman Adams.* He simply does not have enough hours in the day to do all that is required. He has done a remarkable job, by sheer ability, but he cannot possibly do it all. It may be that some day we will have to come to a Vice President for domestic affairs and another for defense and foreign affairs.

(The italics above are mine.) The reporters were apprised of a serious choking of the channels between the expert and operating officials and the President himself:

> Within the White House whole layers of people stand be-

tween those who do things and the man who makes the final decision. This makes it increasingly difficult to reach the source of authority. It is thus next to impossible to pinpoint responsibility for decisions that resulted in the defeat of the U.S. by the Soviet in the launching of a satellite.

All the praise lavished on Sherman Adams only make the issue of the location of responsibility more parlous and, from the standpoint of a democratic Constitution, more grave. It is a matter for serious concern when the President's assistant grows as powerful as the President himself:

Sherman Adams alone is the judge of whether he is to consult the President before giving an opinion. There is not time enough in the day to get approval of the President himself for all questions that arise. However, Mr. Adams never uses the President's name on any specific subject unless the President directs it. It isn't necessary to do that. It is assumed that Mr. Adams, in giving an opinion, reflects the President's views.

How did Adams achieve the confidence to undertake decisions for the President? Under what circumstances does a President abandon so large a part of his responsibility?

But Mr. Adams is a scrupulous New Englander. He checked into the General's views, satisfied himself that he could square his own political beliefs with the middle-of-the-road views of the prospective candidate. . . . Later, in the White House as the President's assistant, Mr. Adams made a point of acquainting himself with Mr. Eisenhower's stand on a great many problems. The President's staff chief kept up with Mr. Eisenhower's attitudes by attending all Cabinet meetings, most Security Council meetings, all important staff conferences and by studying every word that the President spoke or wrote. Mr. Adams came to learn how Mr. Eisenhower's mind worked, in detail.

Now what becomes of the theory of responsibility devised by the founders of the Republic? And, if it is not impertinent to ask, *did* Sherman Adams learn how the President's mind works? And, if he did, is this enough to justify the transplantation of powers?

The President is alone but he must seek moral and intellectual support. If his cabinet and the National Security Council do not give it him, he will choose his own "kitchen cabinet." When that happens, and it always does, the nation has a right to ask, Who is governing us? Who is responsible? The President can buy efficiency at the cost of responsibility, or he can maintain responsibility at the cost of efficiency, or both may suffer, but under the present system it is all but impossible to have the degree of efficiency *and* responsibility required for the welfare, progress, and survival of the nation.

From time to time we are given an intimate view of the nature of a presidential decision. In July, 1959, the Director of the Budget told the Senate in closed session that it had been recommended that Congress not be asked for an appropriation of $260 million for a new aircraft carrier and had been overruled by the President, who wanted the carrier. Pressed, the director said that the Bureau of the Budget watched carefully the estimates proposed by the Secretary of Defense and made recommendations to the President based on a weighing of the Defense Department's claims and those of other departments. "We do not make the decisions; the President makes the decisions. We are a fact-finding and recommending staff for him. We are one cog in a process of presidential staffing. We are not the exclusive cog on which he can rely." The director went on to say that there was disagreement among top advisers over building another big aircraft carrier, but the navy was insistent that the carrier "was a very important adjunct to their force." The Bureau of the Budget suggested to the President that the navy might have a lower priority than a number of other programs. The President made the decision in favor of the carrier, overriding the recommendation of the Bureau of the Budget. And next? The House of Representatives refused the appropriation, but the Senate restored it and increased the amount to $380 million, thus making possible the building of a nuclear-powered carrier instead of the conventional one.

The President and the Cabinet

Until Franklin Roosevelt developed several agencies of personal assistance, the cabinet was, from Washington's time, the President's principal council of political advisers and collaborators. The President obtains help from many agencies, but with the possible exception of the National Security Council, his most steady collective public political council remains the cabinet, however unsteady it may be. We are interested in his relationship to the cabinet for three reasons. Of what value is it to him personally? Of what value is it to the nation at the highest council of supreme leadership? What light does its operation throw on the Presidency's efficiency and responsibility?

The cabinet in the United States is modeled on that of the British government, of which American government is a lineal descendant; but British government continues to be a cabinet government, American government is presidential. In England the cabinet is collective in its authority and responsibility, in the United States the President may choose to summon the cabinet as he sees fit. Here, the cabinet's authority and responsibility are not collective, for its members are an assemblage, not a board, council, or commission. In America, only one man has political responsibility — the President. The office of prime minister in England is not to be compared, for he is simply first among equals and, under certain circumstances, may have less authority than his more able colleagues. In England, the several members of the cabinet constitute an organic body, each insignificant without the rest; in America the cabinet remains, constitutionally and practically, superfluous to the Presidency. The founders of the Republic did not wish to create a council that would share the President's power, fearing it would impede his energies and obscure his responsibility. But they provided him (weakly) with permission to "require the opinion, in writing, of the principal officer in each of the executive departments upon any subject relating to the duties of their respective offices. . . ."

George Washington, with practical good sense and an equable temperament, found it necessary to call in his chief department heads to personal and common counsel, state, treasury, and war, later joined by the Attorney General. By 1793, the term "cabinet" was freely applied to this body.[9] Even so, Washington kept the power of decision for himself; often he decided interdepartmental matters without cabinet advice; and departmental matters were settled by the heads of departments in consultation with the

President. John Adams followed suit, but under more difficult and complicated circumstances. After leaving the Presidency he published a justification of his conduct in 1797 and 1799, when he reopened negotiations with France without consulting his cabinet. The result was a quarrel in the cabinet, which Adams settled by dismissing two of the chief participants. It is the position taken by President Adams that crystallizes the superior and detached role of the President to this day:

> Here, according to the practice, if not of the Constitution, the ministers are responsible for nothing, the President for everything. He is made to answer before the people, not only for every thing done by his minister, but even for all the acts of the legislature [*sic*]. Witness the alien and sedition laws. In all great and essential measures he is bound by his honor and his conscience, by his oath to the Constitution, as well as his responsibility to the public opinion of the nation, to act his own mature and unbiased judgment, though unfortunately, it may be in direct contradiction to the advice of all his ministers. . . .[10]

Alexander Hamilton could hardly disagree with Adams, seeing how strongly he himself had advocated a powerful Presidency with sole responsibility. In a pamphlet on "The Public Conduct and Character of John Adams," Hamilton wrote:

> A President is not bound to conform to the advice of his ministers. He is even under no positive injunction to ask or require it. But the Constitution presumes that he will consult them; and the genius of our government and the public good recommend the practice. . . . As the President nominates his ministers, and may displace them when he pleases, it must be his own fault if he be not surrounded by men, who for ability and integrity deserve his confidence. And if his ministers are of this character, the consulting of them will always be likely to be useful to himself and to the state. . . .

There is no doubt, even with Hamilton's demurral on behalf of the cabinet members, that the President is all, that the rest are but his minions, and necessarily so, when the President has a mind and a will. They are not rooted in independence that derives from popular election or support within the party, even if they are men of strong character like Ickes, Dulles, and Brownell; it is not the *President* who has to give in or get out.

The growth in the number of the departments by congressional enactment and appropriation did not mirror the personal policy of the Chief Executive but resulted from the sporadic growth of government responsibilities. From 1829, under Andrew Jackson, the Postmaster General was included in the cabinet. A representative of the navy was added in 1798. Today, it is the custom to call into the cabinet the Secretary of State, of the Treasury, of Defense, the Attorney General, the Postmaster General, the Secretary of Agriculture, of the Interior, of Commerce, of Labor, and of Health, Education, and Welfare. From time to time certain other persons are invited, almost always some of the other department heads — and, under Eisenhower, the Vice-President. From the standpoint of numbers, the cabinet is a wieldy body; if only it *were* a body. It must be remembered that the ten secretaries mentioned above are members of an administration which includes over sixty departments and agencies.

The better to appreciate the characteristics and spirit of the President's cabinet, it is illuminating to glance at the British system. There, the cabinet is nominated by the prime minister and its members are formally appointed by the Crown. The prime minister is commanded to form a cabinet by the Crown, and the Constitution requires the Crown to send for the recognized leader of the party that commands a majority in the House of Commons. The recognized leader is chosen by party caucus, his colleagues in the party, some of whom were, for many years on the way up, his close rivals for the top position. All, prime minister and cabinet ministers, are bound together by loyalty to the outlook, purposes, policy, and program of their party and as members of the House of Commons. (Exception is made of two or three rather minor ministers and one, more important, who together lead the House of Lords.)

The American cabinet system differs markedly. Its members are banned (by custom) from participating in the deliberations of Congress and (by law) from being members of Congress.

When Alexander Hamilton, a genius in the realm of political science, was appointed Secretary of the Treasury, the statute passed by Congress (September 2, 1789) required the secretary only to "digest and prepare plans"; Congress had stricken the word "report," to avoid admitting cabinet officers to the floor of Congress. Nevertheless, Hamilton assumed a leadership in Congress that seemed to grant him the role of prime minister. He was immensely active, organizing, conspiring, planning the fiscal progress of the nation through his friends in the legislature, and at first he was welcomed. In this capacity he wrote his famous reports on public credit, a national bank, the encouragement of manufacturing, and so on.

At that time the office of the British prime minister had not resumed all of the formal characteristics it had possessed between 1707 and 1760. Since 1760, George III had played the role of prime minister. The men closest to the king were only rarely called by the title of prime minister; instead they were "First Lord of the Treasury." No doubt Hamilton, an admirer of English genius in government, would have wished that he could grant the office of Secretary of the Treasury the functions of the British First Lord of the Treasury. It was impossible because the powers of legislation and of the Chief Executive were separate in the American system and, specifically, Article II prohibited persons holding office from being members of Congress. Hamilton's resignation was speeded by congressional hostility; in March, 1794, the House decided to make its own reports through its ways and means committee and, later in the year, accused Hamilton of fiscal operations without authority of law or presidential sanction.

Several incidents led to the loss to government of Hamilton's talents, the main cause being the unwillingness of Jeffersonians to tolerate the verbal presentation of administration policies in Congress, lest they influence congressional deliberations and "clog the freedom of inquiry and debate." Madison supported the ouster of department heads from Congress. Oliver Wolcott, Hamilton's successor in 1795, was not made of the same stuff but resembled the typical cabinet member — not, of course, those like Albert Gallatin or Elihu Root. Congress believed that the President's responsibility could be controlled if executive officers were not permitted to lead the congressional program or take part in its deliberations. To be invited, even compelled, to appear before committees, legislative or investigative, was quite another matter, for then the executive officers would appear as subordinates of Congress.

Cabinet members are appointed by nomination of the President (as are the heads of non-cabinet departments), subject to the consent of the Senate. From 1789 to 1959 the consent of the Senate was given on all but eight occasions. Consent is given after a process of consideration which makes the prospective cabinet member realize that, to some degree, his authority is dependent on the Senate as well as on the President.

The only member of the cabinet to hold elective office is the President; the rest are his appointees, his creatures. They have no independent authority equal to his and none even approaching his. They have only a departmental authority unless the President permits supradepartmental influence. The President may undermine the departmental standing of each by using his authority to see that the laws are faithfully executed. (Sometimes he is forced to waste his time and energy in backing their authority against the inertia or ill-will of their subordinates.)

There are slight variations in practice among Presidents, but the main lines are plain: In his choice of cabinet the element of party membership is evident, but only feebly, as feeble as the party organization happens to be and, as so often happens, dependent on whether the President is at odds with factions in the party. Generally speaking, a Republican President will not appoint to office a Democrat. In 1953, Eisenhower appointed Martin Durkin, considered a Democratic labor union leader, in an attempt to offset the charge that he had chosen a "businessmen's cabinet." Durkin soon left, pleading he had been misled in assuming that it was the President's intention to modify the harshness of the Taft-Hartley Act against the labor unions. A Democratic President will not appoint a Republican except in time of national emergency (Roosevelt appointed Stimson and Knox on the outbreak of World War II, and they were soon read out of the Republican party!).

What have I said when I assert that the President appoints his cabinet from members of his own party? What is his party? Is it a united body? Not when it contains rivalries of outlook and ambition. Cabinet members, usually, have taken no part in politics at the national level; and neither the public, congressmen, "party leaders," nor they themselves know for certain their relationship to that amorphous entity called party. The President may not have met them before he begins his campaign; and he may have no chance to know them, let alone their minds and characters, until he has entered office. Nor do they know him, as a party leader or as a man. Most do not know each other!

Some are appointed in return for specific "political" (it can be called "party") service in the nominating process and during the campaign. The office of Postmaster General may go to the chairman of the national committee, the office of Attorney General to a man who has held a similar position (a Howard McGrath, a Herbert Brownell). Some are appointed in return for financial donation to party coffers. Some are appointed because they are close personal friends of the President (such as John Snyder by Harry Truman, Harry Daugherty by Harding, Henry Morgenthau and Harry Hopkins by Franklin Roosevelt). Under Wilson, Edward M. House would have qualified in this category, but he, very wisely, refused to enter the cabinet. Some men are commended for certain posts by their administrative expertness; there prowls the amiable ghost of a principle that "the best man" ought to be appointed to head an important department. L. L. Strauss, at the head of the Atomic Energy Commission, was nominated as "best man" to be the Secretary of Commerce but was rejected by the Senate; A. S. Flemming was made Secretary of Health (and perhaps Charles Wilson, of General Motors, appointed as Secretary of Defense, falls into the same category).

There are other considerations that determine cabinet appointments. The nation's regions must be represented for the information cabinet members can bring on prevailing conditions in their regions and because, to some extent, regional political loyalty to the President will be assured in this way. The East, the West, the Middle West, and the South are accommodated, yet not in set proportion to population or wealth. Thus, the "first-best" as "best man" may be passed over in favor of a nominee from a region not otherwise represented; and the flimsy link of party may become flimsier still because regionalism has frayed it. Some particular states are election kingpins and must be rewarded with cabinet posts — New York always, and Illinois, Ohio, and Pennsylvania as a general rule.

The President yields to the pressure of certain interests in making appointments. Sometimes the Secretary of Agriculture is appointed to satisfy the appeals of farm organizations, and promises to this effect are made to attract votes. In making appointments, the President has regard for the future "political" support a member will bring him. Thus, Wilson's appointment of Bryan, whose command of the vast and passionate loyalty of millions won him a most incongruous office, that of Secretary of State, an office concerned with war as well as peace, though the Great Commoner aspired to think away war from a wicked world. Other choice examples are men who have a power in Congress (Cordell Hull and Franklin Roosevelt); Truman's appointment of two active representatives, one former representative, and a former senator; Woodrow Wilson equaled that number. Only the Eisenhower cabinet among those since 1900 lacked an elected member of Congress and had greater need than most, considering the political inexperience of the President.

The President is not able to surround himself only with the men he would like to have. The United States does not possess a considerable number of public-spirited men devoted to the service of government. Those who might be called often refuse because they may not be offered a post best suited to their talents. They realize that their authority will not extend beyond the department; they are not being invited to participate in the fashioning of the general leadership of the nation. They remain at the mercy of presidential whim and congressional intrusions.

What is the significance of these truths about the composition of the cabinet? The men chosen are not always most fit for the jobs they are to undertake.[11] They are not likely to be talented in general counsel on national and international policy of the most elevated and profound kind.[12] They are not likely to be truly competent in the special responsibilities of their departments. They are unlikely to know each other's ideas and character. They are likely to be men with separate ambitions; they have not known and may never know the President well. They are not united by party principle and program. If they are ever united it is by the personality of the President. But the usual situation of an American cabinet is that of a group of relative strangers meeting reluctantly with a chief they do not know, the group presenting, as in Roosevelt's first cabinet, the most striking contrasts of social and economic philosophies. One reason given for Roosevelt's habit of assembling a roaring collection of heterogeneous characters in his cabinet is that he was stimulated by the diversity of contradictory opinion when it was necessary to make a decision. I am disinclined to believe this explanation and still more disinclined to believe in its effectiveness for the selection of a cabinet. And yet, just possibly, it might be true. It may be that some approximation of truth is come upon if one listens to many diverse minds and many contending interests, since no single view is entirely trustworthy. For this, the President needs a first-class brain.

Some re-emphasis is needed: When the cabinet is called into session the men may not know each other; may never before have seen each other; they may never before have seen the President, and the President may have not the slightest idea of who they are or what they think. This leaves much to chance in the government of the nation, if the cabinet is its highest council.

It is the crassest of all mistakes to believe — I almost said, affect to believe — that men who emerge from the professions or industrial or commercial occupations, in which they have been immersed for personal profit, can adapt themselves to the requirements of the life political in the space of, say, four years. Actually, cabinet members rarely stay more than two. The standards of government are very different from those followed in the pursuit of professional success and profit; the motivations of public officials and of congressmen are very different from those of customers and business competitors. Sinclair Weeks could not understand the reasoning of Dr. Astin of the Bureau of Standards who had declared useless a certain additive to motor fuel, or the outraged clamor caused by his attempt to force the resignation of Dr. Astin on the grounds that government officials should not be allowed to interfere with the activities of private enterprise. Charles Wilson could not understand the indignation caused by his statement, "What is good for General Motors is good for the country." There are beneficent coincidences, it is true, but there are many more profound differences between business and government. One of these Wilson overlooked. As Secretary of Defense (May, 1953) he declared that theoretical research and development should be classified as "boondoggling" — unnecessary and wasteful projects. The budget for research funds was slashed from $1.6 billion under Truman to less than one billion in 1952.

In February, 1957, Wilson admitted: "I don't know how anyone can be sure what the Russians are doing, and so accurately predict what the situation will be ten years from now." The Russians, later that year, showed us what they were doing, with a report on intercontinental ballistic missiles and a satellite weighty enough to support their claims. Political leadership, as I have said, is prophecy of a sort, and as such very different from the marketing of automobiles (though automobile makers might find to advantage a simpler gift for prophecy). It is precisely the business of political leadership to look into the future and take calculated risks. Did Wilson as Secretary of Defense have no information from the Central Intelligence Agency? Was he not informed of Soviet advances by the National Security Council? And what contact did he have with the Department of State, which surely must have had some idea of what the Russians were doing? And where was the President, the center of the teeming congeries of auxiliary offices and institutions? The President had many reports on his desk from scientific advisers, all stressing the fact that the Soviet was overtaking the United States in research and the recruiting of trained personnel; and so fearful was he that he refused to publish the Gaither report.

Austere principles of the balanced budget are proper and good; but they cannot be the sole standards of public policy. George Humphrey based public policy on the principle that had made him rich in private business. The Atomic Energy Commission treated Robert Oppenheimer not as one of the great physicists of the world but as a kind of felon. Those trained in government service would have found a way to use Oppenheimer's strengths for the national benefit and to safeguard the nation against his weaknesses. If the cabinet had been staffed with politically experienced men, it would have been wary of a contract with Dixon-Yates which cost the President prestige when he admitted he knew nothing about it. But the executive office staff may have involved him in this, for in June, 1953, Eisenhower preached, "In the last twenty years, creeping socialism has been striking in the United States." It is a brilliant phrase, uncharacteristically so; and Eisenhower named the TVA as one example.

A notorious case, illustrating the damage to a President's policy and standing resulting from the capricious heterogeneity of his cabinet, is furnished by Secretary of Commerce Sawyer, who delayed the action required of him in the seizure of the steel mills because his loyalty to the business world from which he came made him reluctant to perform with celerity those measures demanded of him by President Truman.

I am not arguing that cabinet members are invariably selected from big business. This is not so. But cabinet members are selected from diverse walks of life, and they have little or no experience of government and still less of government at the highest level, still less in common policy-making. They are appointed by the President, they are his personal choice. They are not chosen in accordance with the specific requirements of the departments to which they are to be assigned; they do not reflect the general policy of the President; and they have had no experience in collaborating with Congress or anything like it. The members of the cabinet are a gamble to the President who has appointed them; and a risky bet to the nation that elected the man who appoints them. The majority are not even part-time politicians, that is, men who, pursuing their careers, have yet given a large part of their time to national affairs or to local politics.

One of the most critical appointments is the Secretary of State. In almost every case (I do not forget men like John Marshall, Charles E. Hughes, John Foster Dulles — yet they were political men), the Secretary of State, since the appointment of Thomas Jefferson, has been a man much devoted to national political life. In the main, the office has gone to the second most important politician in the country (in some cases, to the most important), e.g., Van Buren, Webster, Buchanan, Cass, Seward, Blaine, Sherman, Bryan, and Hughes — to the advantage of the nation. The names of Jefferson, Madison, John Quincy Adams, Clay Webster, Calhoun, Seward, Hay, Hamilton Fish, Root, Hughes, Stimson, Hull (and perhaps Dulles) will evoke the gratitude of those who concern themselves with the nation's diplomacy in peace and war. But more remarkable still is that in all important issues the capable Presidents have themselves conceived, initiated, and decided the foreign policy of the nation. The capable Presidents have not looked to their secretaries for a world outlook; that they themselves have supplied. From their secretaries they receive information of events abroad, technical advice on international law and procedure, the conduct of negotiations, the execution of their policies through all diplomatic procedures, the drafts to fill out and bolster presidential conceptions — and, if the secretary is good enough, another view of the merits and ways and means of their policies.

Where the President is weak in intellect or character, the Secretary of State is of immense importance to the interests of the nation: John Quincy Adams and Monroe in the recognition of Latin American republics, the acquisition of Florida, and the liquidation of the problems of British-American relations following the War of 1812; or Webster and Tyler, making the Canadian settlement with Britain in 1841–43; Hamilton Fish and President Grant, especially the Alabama arbitration and resistance to those Americans who clamored for intervention in the Spanish-Cuba conflict.

The gamble with the nation's welfare involved in the appointment of the Secretary of State is not entirely upon the personal decision of the President; electoral and congressional forces must be taken into account (e.g., Franklin Roosevelt's appointment of Cordell Hull, Eisenhower's tardy appointment of Herter).

Cabinet members and heads of departments are constrained to take care of their self-respect and their public reputations. Constitutional separation of powers forces them to take orders from Congress. They need appropriations; they must expect to submit their actions for the approval of Congress. Loyalty to their own department causes them to dissent when they object to the President's general policy. But if the members of the cabinet, in some cases, are forced to flee the President, the President must attempt to win them back to his policies.

The President cannot be sure of having his own way when he himself has reached a decision (or when the cabinet has resolved on a line of action, in the rare cases in which it does so) because each cabinet member has taken an oath to carry out the responsibilities of office as he interprets them; it is his conscience that he must satisfy. A President without firm character, knowledge, charm, or courage is put at some disadvantage by this conscientious effort of cabinet members to fulfil their oath of office.

The Cabinet in Operation

The President decides if and when a cabinet meeting is to be called; no one else can do so. But the President finds that his own need requires him to call regular meetings frequently. Polk, who had what I have called a sense of immersive responsibility, called regular meetings. Lincoln and Wilson preferred occasional meetings. It is worthy of note that the stronger the convictions of the President, the less likely he is to rely on the cabinet; more modest and uncertain men put their faith in cabinet meetings.

Some Presidents have met twice weekly with the cabinet; it varies from time to time and with the pressures of circumstances. Until the coming of President Eisenhower, cabinet meetings had no fixed agenda. The meeting was for presidential convenience; he would bring to the attention of the cabinet such anxieties as he wished. None could press him to make policy collective; none dared do this; few wished to. The Eisenhower cabinet resembled the top-level army staff meeting to which he was accustomed, the military practice of the top command, who depends upon his staff officers to make preparatory studies and brief him. The President wanted to know what was to come in order to avoid painful surprises such as he has suffered all too often at press conferences.

In the Eisenhower cabinet, in spite of much-wanted procedural changes, as in other cabinets, the operation is, and most assuredly will continue to be, marked by certain cardinal (and questionable) characteristics. The cabinet is rarely used as a common council to make the highest policy decisions of the President.[13] In any case, the cabinet as a group cannot decide policy against the will of the President. If a vote is taken, and it sometimes is, the responsibility remains with the President, and he goes his own way. There is a famous story told of Lincoln, who, finding his cabinet opposed to him, announced, "Seven nays, one aye — the ayes have it." Sardonic, perhaps apocryphal, but true to the situation most common in cabinet meetings. . . .

No subject of high foreign policy is submitted to the cabinet for decision (and, rarely, for discussion). The members do not, as do British cabinet ministers, receive State Department papers. No subject of domestic legislation of high import comes to them.

Most of the items on the agenda are trivial. When subjects of any moment are broached, individual members of the cabinet, overwhelmed by departmental affairs and heterogeneous as party members or as nonpolitical men, are silent or perfunctory in their comments or bicker to no purpose. But the general tendency is to evade matters of common policy. Nor do they bring departmental problems with them, fearing interference in their several departments.

How does the President deal with divergent answers he receives to the problems he has raised? Refuse to make a choice that is counter to colleagues sitting before him? Be evasive himself? Take dissidents to task, as Wilson sometimes did? Joke about the differences, as Franklin Roosevelt did? What is served if the cabinet members raise questions of common concern when they lack authority to do so and cannot be held responsible for the results of their advice?

It is in these respects that the President's cabinet normally differs so markedly from the British cabinet, the latter normally a full sharing of authority and responsibility, the former become an instrument of only minor and casual usefulness, unfairly leaving to the President the task of finding answers to the nation's plight, leaving to him the burden of responsibility and the burden of conscience.

The British cabinet is a truly collective executive body. It has several imperfections, but it has merit as the highest national leadership. It supplies cogency of thought, that is, intense consideration and analysis of current problems, a deliberate examination of alternate courses of action, the weighing of all clashing elements involved.

British cabinet ministers cannot, as can their opposite numbers in the United States, keep secret departmental affairs and problems demanding the consideration of the cabinet. The cabinet is the place where the cards of all departments must be dealt face-up, where no member can play his cards close to his chest or hide them up his sleeve. They cannot evade the challenge of their colleagues. Each department is a concern, in some way, of all. What we might label "interference" enables each minister to know whether or not his colleagues support him, share his responsibility, and will help him to carry out his job, offering moral support, assistance, and interdepartmental collaboration.

The President's cabinet is still dispersive rather than collective. It lacks the collective policy and principle and budget-deciding power that the British cabinet has, and general discussion is commonly regarded as interference. Whereas the British cabinet is an instrument of co-ordination, the American cabinet tends to increase departmental antagonisms. Both reports of the Hoover Commission on the reorganization of the executive branch are witnesses to this regrettable truth.

It is essential that some incidental, eccentric consequences of the anarchic operation of the President's cabinet be indicated. Only (almost) at cabinet meetings do members, and sometimes the heads of other agencies, learn whether the President will have time to spare them in the near future. They may believe they discern a favorable or unfavorable attitude toward their department and request the opportunity to approach the President in private. (The cabinet member has the customary right to ask for an audience, though he does not always obtain it; the head of a non-cabinet agency is far less certain to be able to arrange one.) A private discussion is often of more efficacy than a request that the matter be put on the cabinet agenda and more likely to secure a decision from the President. Why should the President bother to put these matters on the agenda when the deciding choice and the responsibility are his alone? Should he make a decision at once? But if he does his decision may be mistaken.

Cabinet members are of less value in council than they might be because they are overburdened with administrative detail as heads of large departments. They would be able to devote more of their time to national policy if they were relieved of the burden of detail. But the American system does not assign to career officials the responsibility to make decisions based on the general policy of their department heads. Each department is comprised of a number of bureaus; the head of the department and his many assistants must spend time and energy trying to weld these together, allowing the department head less time for the cabinet, indeed fretful at the time the cabinet consumes. He is glad to rush away when it is over, especially if there may be an opportunity to buttonhole the President on a departmental matter. Of course he does not view his cabinet colleagues' anxieties as his own.

If only those who joined the cabinet stayed to help the President, but their tenure is shockingly brief. The various incumbents leave at odd times; subsequent personal and administrative adjustment is painful and confusing to those left behind and expected to carry on.

The second Hoover Commission pointed out that the average tenure of cabinet members during the recent Democratic administrations was about forty-two months. If the long tenures of Ickes, Frances Perkins, and Henry Morgenthau are not considered, the average tenure was much less. Average tenure of undersecretaries was twenty-three months, of assistant secretaries, about thirty-two months. Let it be recalled that Franklin Roosevelt served for thirteen years, and Truman for seven, yet many of their chief assistants served only two-year periods.

It has been admitted by a fair sample of those who have been questioned that cabinet members need a considerable time to become oriented to the departments, and, indeed, some never feel themselves to be at home. And yet these are the men who are intrusted with the infusion of the presidential policy into their departments and those who are to advise the President of what their segments of government need. Below cabinet rank, some executives have had experience in government, but cabinet members and department heads are usually unfamiliar with government service and its attendant problems. Robert A. Lovett, once Secretary of Defense (1951–53), a man of exceptional intelligence, business experience, and years of military service, told the Senate subcommittee on national policy machinery (February, 1960): "It takes a long time for an able man, without previous military service of some importance and experience in government, to catch up with his job in this increasingly complex department. At a guess I would say he could pay good dividends to the government in about two years."

In March, 1957, one-fifth of the subcabinet positions in executive departments were listed as vacant.

> In the forward echelons of government, including Cabinet and sub-Cabinet positions, there are 750 offices of excep-

tional political and executive responsibility. These jobs deal with continuing and long-range problems — national defense, foreign aid, atomic energy. They demand men of high talent, ingenuity, and determination to foster and administer the programs by which the Administration stands or falls. . . . Yet it is an accepted fact of life in Washington that fully one-third of the officials holding these posts today (October, 1957) may be gone a year from now. In some agencies, including some of the most sensitive, the proportion of departees will be higher. But it is safe to say that, twelve months hence, 250 of these highest offices will probably be in new, and ofttimes inexperienced, hands. When one considers the cumulative effect of this turnover in two or three years, or in an Administration's four-year term of office, the results are startling.[14]

Startling is not the word; the facts are alarming. The cardinal question is not whether the administration stands or falls, but whether the nation stands or falls. It is most alarming to realize that between 1947 and 1959 seven different men have served as Secretary of Defense. (Deputy secretaries — there have been eight since 1949 — have each served little more than sixteen months.)

Tethered to these several hundred top political executives, the alter ego of the President, are some 2.3 million career officials of all levels and varieties of skills. Upon their proper integration and energizing depends the efficiency of the government. The recruitment and morale of these men and women pose serious problems. Let it be said that all is far from well. Some solutions might be devised if the President alone did not have to bear all of the anxieties of the executive branch. If there were colleagues to assist him, with equal responsibility for the success of the nation's leadership, the corps of officials in each department, even as constituted today, would perform more responsively and efficiently than they do.

Finally, when assistants to the President have reported to him, what have they given the President? Not a decision but the material for a decision; a proposal which he must evaluate. We are back at the sole responsibility of the President for government action, and the man who takes the office seriously, as Truman did, will ruin his eyes reading the "fine print" of all the memorandums.

Robert Sherwood gives an interesting insight into the relationship of presidential decision to cabinet counsel, and, indeed, the dubious value of the "institutionalization" of presidential authority. Referring to Harry Hopkins, Sherwood writes:

> This was the first time [on board ship, at the Atlantic Conference] he had seen both the President and the Prime Minister [Mr. Churchill] in operation away from their own home bases. He remarked on the fact that whereas Roosevelt was completely on his own, subject only to the advice of his immediate and self-elected entourage which advice he could accept or reject, Churchill was constantly reporting to and consulting the War Cabinet in London, addressing communications to the Lord Privy Seal, who was then Clement Attlee. During three days more than thirty communications passed between the [battleship] *Prince of Wales* and Whitehall, and the speed of communication and of action thereon was astonishing to the Americans.[15]

Sherwood stresses the solitary responsibility of the President and the collective responsibility to which the prime minister must bow. How easily this difference could become that between personal whim and collective thought!

Is the cabinet of any use to the President? The answer is yes, occasionally, but not nearly as much as it might be. It gives him some conception of departmental hopes and anxieties; it enables him to learn the value of individual members, and from these he may choose one or two as his special advisers outside cabinet meetings (but, perhaps, as with George Humphrey, former Secretary of the Treasury, to become overborne by their influence). The cabinet is an instrument of information, especially for the President who has come to depend in his earlier career on the exchange of opinion and ideas during group discussions. The cabinet aids the President in gauging public opinion and in evaluating the opinion of special groups. The cabinet gives the President a measure of moral support — for example, when Wilson was concerned about relations with Germany (1914–17); or

Franklin Roosevelt at the meeting in November, 1937, with signs of returning depression; or the immediate problems created by Germany's invasion of Poland in 1939; or the somber meeting called on November 7, 1941, to discuss the probability of war with Japan.

All of the benefits the President derives from cabinet meetings do not compensate for their failure. Co-ordination of all policies into a flexible, integrated program is not achieved. They do not provide for the execution of measures decided on during cabinet meetings. Above all, they do not relieve the President of his sole responsibility to make decisions or of the weight of seeing that his decisions are carried out.

Defense and the National Security Council

When the deficiencies of the cabinet are exposed it has become a recent custom to dwell with some satisfaction on the assistance the President obtains from the Secretary of Defense and the National Security Council. But an examination will demonstrate that the President is not relieved of his responsibility to make decisions, and though he is responsible for policy-making, he is hardly in a position, alone, to do so soundly.

Perhaps the most serious example of fissiparousness of policy and administration is in the relationship of the three armed services, the Secretary of Defense, and the President, a theme given profound examination in the first Hoover Report on national security organization (January, 1949).

First, the Secretary of Defense. Who is he? There have been seven secretaries, Forrestal, Louis A. Johnson, General Marshall, Lovett, Charles Wilson, Neil McElroy, and his successor Gates. From what sphere of civilian life were they drawn? Forrestal had considerable government experience; Marshall, military experience; Lovett, law, military service, government office; Johnson, a similar short preparation. Wilson, McElroy, and Gates were drawn from big business, McElroy and Gates from Procter and Gamble, the soap manufacturers. But none had had a career in politics at the national level from which they could have acquired an understanding of the strategic interests of the United States throughout the world; the relationship of existing and developing weapons systems for defense, deterrence, and assault; American foreign policy; the plans and logistics of the armed services; and the relationship of defense in all these phases to other broad policies of the United States.

The statutory organization of the Department of Defense militates against the right kind of man doing the proper kind of job — and gives no indication of the personal qualities the job requires. It is impossible here to summarize recent congressional-executive battles over government defense mechanism, so vast an apparatus that it is rightly considered a "defense government within the national government," spending some $70 billion a year. Here are some of the questions argued: Were the Joint Chiefs of Staff to dictate fiscal demands? Were they to advise the President as a group or singly?

The Joint Chiefs of Staff come within the administrative hierarchy of the Department of Defense, first set up in 1947; before that date they were not geared to any department but worked solely through the President. The Joint Chiefs are not only under the "authority and direction" of the Secretary of Defense, they are also under the President; and they are advisers to the President and the National Security Council. A fourth military expert, a chairman, has been added to the Joint Chiefs of Staff; generally he sees the President for briefing once a week. He must then return with policy suggestions or surmises of presidential expectations that will give them the backbone to face the Secretary of Defense. The purpose of this intricate structure is to make possible a coordinated view of America's requirements so that they may be reconciled with the nation's economic strength and civilian consumption. This requires, it would seem, far more ample independent resources of strategy-making in the Department of Defense if the President is to be well advised and the three services controlled and yet encouraged to devise working strategy. The position of the Secretary of Defense is weakened in his own department because the National Security Council functions as a supreme strategy board.

The preservation of a clear and demonstrable civilian control over the military is not left to the President alone. The Defense Department has an economic controller who functions with a strength similar to that which the Bureau of the Budget exerts upon the government itself. The Bureau of the Budget and the controller join in fiscal control of the military and in proposal provisions for the national forces. This internal control is justified by the immensity and the intricacy of modern military technology.

The power given the controller, who is subordinate to the Secretary of Defense, would not be tolerated in the British cabinet system. It would not be tolerated if the controller, on his sole authority, reduced the total service estimates between 1950–54 from $273 billion to $211 billion (some 22 per cent); and yet exactly this was done by the controller working with the Joint Chiefs of Staff, not by the President himself!

The function of the Secretary of Defense is to advise the President on the defense establishment, managing a judicious blending of military and financial consideration. Under Louis Johnson, a lawyer by profession, and Charles E. Wilson, economic considerations became paramount. The President himself must be blamed if economic considerations obscured a realistic assessment of the nation's peril. The President did not try to make himself a strategist by seeking independent advice. Charles Wilson's concept of his role was "to get more defense for less money" and to reduce the national deficit insofar as it was increased by the Defense Department; but of strategy he had not an inkling. Between 1955 and 1956 the air force was reduced, at a time when the Strategic Air Command was beginning to be vaunted as our principal weapon of deterrence.

Two men who served as Secretary of Defense operated as strategists in order to fulfil the duties of the office. They were James Forrestal and Robert Lovett. They, at least, attempted to see the problem in the correct light. President Truman insisted on a very strict budget, regardless of what might be funneled to him from the Joint Chiefs. Lovett began with the Joint Chiefs' proposals for the right force levels, persuaded the National Security Council that these were correct, and asked for $71 billion, but Truman and the National Security Council said, "Try to get what is needed for $45 billion." The Joint Chiefs responded with a proposal for $55 billion; and Truman gave them $52 billion, against Lovett's views that air power was being dangerously starved. Forrestal and Lovett felt hampered because they had no independent military staff as advisers and as verifiers of the advice of the Joint Chiefs of Staff.

Lovett pleaded for complete subordination of the Joint Chiefs to the Secretary of Defense; but if this were done the President would have no direct communication with the Joint Chiefs. This the President might favor if the Secretary of Defense (as well as other secretaries) shared his collective responsibility in the cabinet, but as it is the President feels he must know all that the Secretary of Defense learns from the Joint Chiefs of Staff. The Joint Chiefs are supported in their reliance on the President rather than the Secretary of Defense by the National Security Act of 1947 (amended in 1949), which places them under "the authority and direction of the President and the Secretary of Defense," a curious conjunction. The statute has not been amended to enhance the secretary's authority, though some interpreters believe him to have full power over the Joint Chiefs of Staff. Nor is the clause that designates the secretary as "principal assistant to the President in all matters relating to the Department of Defense" adequate to give him full control at the top of the military pyramid.

Why are the statutes worded so ambiguously? It is to be explained, in part, by a fear of giving any one person total authority, especially if that authority is military, and in part as an attempt to preserve the President's authority from all dubiety or encroachment. But how ridiculous it is to leave the Secretary of Defense without a strategy-planning staff.[16] If he cannot be a strategist there is little else he can do but concentrate on tightening the military budget.

A President may not have political stature, that is, the ability to sway the people, or the personality, the imposing character, to carry out the plans proposed by the National Security Council. Truman must fall in this class, at least when pre-Korean military preparedness is discussed. Responding to the fact that the Soviet Union had exploded an atomic bomb, the National Security Council planned a very considerable strengthening of forces during the winter of 1949–50; the State Department and military officers in the Department of Defense strongly supported these proposals. Louis Johnson, then Secretary of Defense, was less enthusiastic, and the Bureau of the Budget lodged stubborn objections. The President adopted both views, as it were, supporting strategic requirements which demanded additional appropriations, yet not to go beyond the $13 billion earmarked for defense.

But when fighting in Korea began late in 1950 nothing of importance had been done. The National Security Council's advice to the President had been frustrated by the President's preoccupation with the budget. His responsibility was exercised wrongly; the National Security Council's assistance was seriously impaired.

Huntington, to whom reference has been made, deplores the fact that men of a stature equal to that of those men who, as Secretary of Defense, conducted American diplomacy in its rich years are not appointed to the office today. The Secretary of State "must be a man of policy. His greatest needs are breadth, wisdom, insight, and above all, judgment. He is neither operator, administrator, nor commander. But he is policy maker." [17] He must have some familiarity with the problems he is to face, and this is "best achieved by service in one of the subordinate secretaryships within the Department." But how can a President arrange for it, still less find a nominee with the elevated qualities Huntingdon wishes? The Secretary of Defense must command the admiration of informed public opinion, but will this be given to someone who has come up through the ranks? Huntingdon would wish the Secretary of Defense to be "nonpolitical in the partisan sense." But if he is "nonpolitical," what becomes of his political tendencies which enable him to win the admiration of "informed public opinion" and to find a clue to strategy, which must depend in large measure on international political convictions and comprehension?

The problem is not solved when highest policy is the responsibility of the President alone. It was a wise plan to transfer general responsibility for strategy to the National Security Council. The only trouble is, and it is a desperate trouble, the council operates but feebly, as fumblingly as very large committes usually do.

Once again, where is the ultimate weakness? It is in the failure to create a presidential council or ministry to act as the collective President of the nation, containing some eleven or more heads of departments and some general counselors who trust each other and who can share the burdens of office without fear that any will be given too much responsibility and be expected to endure far more intellectual and spiritual strain than mortal man can bear.

The lack of cogency in contemporary government is shown

with clarity in the arrangements for policy decisions assigned to the National Security Council. It is a prime example of the attempt to govern by committee when the committee has an advisory capacity but must leave decisions to the President.

Senator Henry W. Jackson has offered the best analysis of its functioning, and we must take his comment as being the most authoritive revelation of the internal affairs of the National Security Council. Jackson argues that more than enough committees have reported on strategic policy, with no tangible results — the Finletter Committee, the Gray Committee, the Paley Commission, the Sarnoff Commission, the President's Committee on Scientists and Engineers, Citizen's Advisers on Mutual Security, the Gaither Committee (the President refused to permit the publication of its findings, though the main conclusions were made known), the Draper Committee, the Boechenstein Committee, the reports of the Committee on Economic Development, and the Rockefeller reports. Jackson observes that not since the Marshall Plan, which sought to strengthen and unify the Western democracies, has anything been done to mobilize the nation's understanding and co-operation in the interest of national security.

> The Planning Board of the National Security Council plans and proposes new policy and programs. These go for consideration to the heads of Departments who are members of the National Security Council. An agreed paper is approved by the National Security Council — which serves as an advisory board to the President. The President decides. The policy is then implemented under the watchful eye of the Operations Co-ordinating Board. And the President has a clear and consistent policy to spell out for the American people.[18]

But, in fact, the system does not work as smoothly as this would imply. The choice among immense strategic alternatives should be made by the President himself (as in 1941: Which is to be tackled first, Germany or Japan?). Following the President's decision, the National Security Council undertakes to establish the military and civil consequences and plans objectives, calling upon the various executive departments and their planning staffs to provide more detailed implementation. The President is kept posted on the feasibility of objectives. At present the system is reversed; the departments influence the National Security Council, with the usual compromises of will and intention. The image placed before the President is blurred. Often no plan is agreed upon and all decisions are deferred.

Cabinet officers are far too busy to stimulate and support their policy-planning officers. Senator Jackson may exaggerate in his description of a cabinet member's week, but it can hardly be a serious exaggeration: "Seven formal speeches, seven informal speeches, seven hearings on the Hill, seven official cocktail parties, seven command dinner engagements. It is a schedule which leaves no time for the kind of reflection essential to creative thinking."

A decision must be based on a weighing of all factors and a consideration of the means available and practical to solve the problem in question. Only the President is in a position to do this; the departments, even the National Security Council, can see some of the parts but never the whole.

In May, 1944, I was secretary at a meeting of the governing board of the International Labor Office. The board met to draw up a policy for postwar social reform. The director-general submitted his recommendations, to which the representatives of several countries began to offer diverse and far-reaching amendments. He answered them with an analogy relevant to the present discussion: If it were necessary to compose a poem, he said, several excellent poems on the same theme might be written, each different from the others in every particular because each the result of a different inspiration, elaborated and embellished by the poet's vision. But to assemble a poem composed of bits and pieces submitted by a dozen men of distinct vision is impossible. And yet this is the method used by the National Security Council-cum-President when it produces a plan of strategy. Furthermore, the allocation to the council of responsibility for military planning tends to diminish the efforts of other departments of government. Each department says, "Let George do it," and yet George (in this case the National Security Council) is not prepared to play George.

No doubt the ineffective planning of the National Security Council has resulted in the organization of the special advisory committees mentioned above; but inertia at the center renders pointless the reports as they are made, and they become so many soot-laden gravestones of policy.[19]

Senator Jackson's statement of the problem before the United States deserves to be quoted:

> Can we organize such an effort without the stimulus of War? This is the heart problem of our time. Can a free society organize itself to plan and carry out a national strategy for victory in the *cold* war?

The word "stimulus" is at the core of this observation; for it is energy and purposefulness, a goal, that makes for cogent thinking. War provides a people with the "necessary enemy" — supplies, in a sense, a common incentive lacking when self-interest rules.

Jackson's proposals are in the form a series of targets to aim at — rapid progress toward an "invulnerable" military deterrent; expansion of the economy at a faster rate (5 or 6 per cent a year instead of 1 or 2 per cent); the strengthening of education, especially in the fields of the sciences and foreign languages, though without consequent neglect of the social sciences; an increase in technical co-operation and development loan programs; a dramatic expansion of the economies of backward countries; efforts to rally the best minds to the public service. . . . However, each of Jackson's proposals requires conviction, energy, and thought, and the guiding force of an able and intelligent President.

Jackson asks why it was necessary for Congress to spur the President to his first full-scale briefing on our lag in ballistic missiles? Did the National Security Council consider the blow to our prestige abroad when the Soviet Union announced the first ICBM, the first satellite in orbit, the first rocket shot beyond the moon? Did the council consider the need for and the means of expanding our economy? Has the council decided the budgetary limits on American arms? Has it pondered the use of nuclear weapons in a "limited" war? Has it considered the best ways of developing our crop of scientists and engineers and how best to make use of them?

Jackson proposes policy-planning staffs for each department;

continuing staff relations between Defense and State departments; a thinking, planning body similar to the Rand Corporation, answering directly to the President; an Academy of National Policy, like the Gaither Committee, composed of experts in defense, the natural sciences, the social sciences, and the humanities, and leaders from private life, to think for the President. He proposes that the National Security Council sharpen policy choices for presidential decision; that the Secretary of State be the principal initiator of policy before the council; that the departments (not an independent director, as now) supply the planning staffs so that the National Security Council is faced with clear-cut alternatives and not a lukewarm porridge of strategy.

Yet we must draw attention to Jackson's earlier observation:

> Over and over again, vital questions never get before top officials in such a way that those officials have to face them, take responsibility for them, and decide them — one way or the other.

Turning now to another witness, the exceptional governmental experience of former Defense Secretary Robert A. Lovett gives unusual pungency to his evidence on the operation of the National Security Council.[20] Lovett reports that the original intention was to have a small number of persons on the council in order to encourage incisive and frank debate. "It was an attempt to translate into our form of operation some of the benefits we saw in the British system." However, the number of persons attending have increased since Truman's time until the National Security Council resembles a mass meeting. (Other sources have indicated that on some occasions as many as seventy-three people have attended.) The council has lost its character as a court presided over by the President listening to vigorous arguments. Furthermore, with so many persons attending, the original intention, that only important subjects be discussed and that "whatever number of hours were necessary in order to exhaust a subject," is thwarted. If the President is not able to hear a frank and full debate, ". . . it is a real disservice to the President . . . because it denies him . . . the possibility of seeing an alternative or an obstacle. It forces him to look down the full length of the hard road and not simply the first few steps of it."

The President ought to be present, not merely to act on the reports of compromises arrived at, but "because so much of the feeling of the intensity of the support comes through when you sit and listen to it yourself." Cross-examination is a way toward truth.

The comment I am bound to make on Lovett's proposal is that it calls for a President who can and will be present to thresh matters out; but that requires inclination and, given that, time. With only one man having the responsibility to make decisions, something in the range of government is bound to be neglected. The help the President is given is not only inappropriate, it is insufficient. Lovett deplores and thinks dangerous attempts to "protect" the President from information. He is right; and yet, *there is so much information!*

Dean Acheson, former Secretary of State and once Undersecretary of State and Undersecretary of the Treasury, draws attention to the dangers of institutionalization:

> What has just been said underlines . . . the great importance of interplay between head and staff at all stages in the development of decisions. By this I mean that the chief must from time to time familiarize himself with the whole record; he must consider opposing views, put forward as ably as possible. He must examine the proponents vigorously and convince them that he knows the record, is intolerant of superficiality or of favor-seeking, and not only welcomes but demands criticism. . . .
>
> Through this judicial function, through pondering what has been read and heard, and suggestion or decision that one of several lines is the one to be pursued, the chief makes his most valuable contribution to thought and policy. It takes work and it takes time.[21]

Yes, it takes time. Time, set by Nature herself, can only be multiplied by increasing the executive from one to several, from one self to a collective self, to an elected collective self. The ascription to his colleagues of the authority that comes from election is some guarantee that unity will come of the multiple body.

To add a staff to the National Security Council, as Acheson

pointed out, would be to require the President to talk to an even greater number of people, but the "wrong people," because a "staff cannot add knowledge, which remains in the departments, or responsible advice to the President, which is the duty and right of his cabinet secretaries. More bodies only clutter up a meeting and strain a flow of communication."

Cogent thought and decisive will are intimately bound together. In the presidential system they tend to draw apart unless a genius emerges during the gamble of nomination and election.[22]

The truth is that only by entering deeply into detail is the President likely to gain sufficient understanding of the facts and the alternatives open to him; but this is asking too much of one man. The nature of presidential decision, given the scope of the nation's business, requires that several men, not one man alone, be vested with responsibility.

It is a fair commentary on the priority of brains to "institutionalization" that the Marshall Plan, until the time of NATO (which followed it) the most distinguished foreign policy decision since the end of World War II, did not emerge from the National Security Council, for that body did not yet exist.

The Bureau of the Budget

The budget of a nation ought to be planned — not by one person, for that would be impossible and undesirable — but by "one mind," a collective body capable of adjusting appropriations for the two thousand items of government to the revenue of the nation and the national income from which it is obtained. Against this general principle, accepted by economic experts the world over, the budgetary system of the United States offends grievously.

It should be said that on the day in 1921 when Congress ceded to the Presidency the preparation of the budget it relinquished an enormous degree of its own legislative independence and leadership, for the power to propose expenditures and taxes, coupled with the right to appeal to the public, to defend proposals as reasonable, and backed by the veto power, is far more than half of the authority of governmental command.

Before the establishment of the Bureau of the Budget, federal financial provisions were almost entirely in the hands of Congress — and in truly lamentable state. Congress received a flood of unintegrated demands from various departments and from the Treasury proposals for taxation. Congress alone is vested with the right to legislate bills for raising revenue; no power to raise money is given the President; his obligation is to inform Congress of the state of the Union and recommend the measures he judges expedient. Largely as a result of professional recommendations, the power (virtual, under Woodrow Wilson) to prepare a so-called executive budget was by statute assigned to the President. Briefly, the President is given the responsibility of presenting to Congress a budget which is truly a budget and not simply a collection of unco-ordinated estimates of expenditure from the many departments. Departmental needs are adjudicated by the President, juggled, balanced, increased or decreased as circumstances demand, subject to presidential calculation of the relative importance for the national welfare of each demand. Together they are considered with reference to the total amount the President believes the nation can afford to spend; and the total the nation can afford to spend will exert its compromising and integrating pressure on the specific amount allotted to each of the thousands of various demands. Whatever the faults in practice of this procedure, the theory is sound. The Bureau of the Budget is the hub of this budget-making function.

The process of preparing the annual budget, until it has been accepted by the President and introduced to Congress, takes eighteen months. It depends on the detailed and intricate co-operation of the Bureau of the Budget and the staffs of the various spending departments. Some months before the President presents the final budget the director of the bureau submits tentative figures to him. The President consults with the National Security Council, the Treasury, and trusted advisers before proposing a maximum appropriation for each department. The Council of Economic Advisers is obliged to have a say in this as well. Estimates are returned to the departments and the bureau for revision in accordance with the tentative ceilings proposed, From the departments they are returned to the director of the Bureau of the Budget and to the President. Figures indicating revenue expectations are developed by the Treasury (based on the forecasts of the Council of Economic Advisers) in some relationship to the whole complex of economic conditions and predicted development. This annual forecast is a major political fact because it depends on party guesswork (optimistic or pessimistic) and because it poses the most serious final decision for the President, his party, and the leaders of Congress.

A director of the Bureau of the Budget once informed me that the forecast was made by "looking into a crystal ball." And this ability to make an intelligent guess about the future is the highest function of political leadership. Another of the most serious problems of American government is this: Can the President think out the major fiscal and departmental problems in the face of an enormous variety of conflicting demands? Is he not apt to be confused by the far-too-detailed parade of estimates and the claims of highly contentious rivals? To achieve coherence is his task — avowedly, with assistance in the matter of detail. Until the budget reaches his desk, the choices (and necessary co-ordination) occur at the career-official level by departmental "push and pull." The President has no assistance from his cabinet. The philosophy that governs his choice is, of necessity, largely personal, insofar as there is a choice. The system demands much of a conscientious President and far too much of the ignorant one. The financial issues to be decided are many — so interdependent, so inclusive, and so in need of integration that the preparation of the budget ought to be made a cabinet responsibility, if we had a true cabinet.

It must not be forgotten that a budget is an expression of the relative importance we assign to social, economic, and cultural desires, representing a fundamental pattern of values in the guise of a parade of figures. The political heads of the departments of expenditure should be held accountable, and should be aware constantly of their collective responsibility for settling the lineaments of the budget for which, at present, the President himself is alone responsible. In such a collective body the Secretary of the Treasury would participate, since he proposes taxation, estimates how much the nation can afford to raise, and, when necessary, what modification of expenditure or taxation must be made.

The budget, resting finally on the predilections of one man (or on those of non-elected, unknown, and non-responsible officials in the obscurity of the departments), is submitted to Congress.

Congress does not consider the President's budget as a whole, nor do the appropriations committees. The subcommittees prepare separate appropriations bills in a welter of confusion, turmoil, and cross-purposes. Subcommittee hearings on the budget produce transcripts, something like 25,000 pages of discussion each year. Committee members flash from questions of major policy and principle to trivialities in a single breath. (The agriculture subcommittee is an exception, for here the members have a powerful interest in government subsidies, an interest unspoiled by serious party differences, and considerable socio-technical knowledge.) Generally, congressmen are baffled in an attempt to understand what they are supposed to be doing, in spite of the competent exposition and justification presented to them by the various department heads and their skilled assistants.

The Budget Act of 1921 emphasizes the responsibility of the bureau; it must produce something like rational harmony among competing claims. Budget-making power is a mighty arm for the integration of administration and policy, and the act of 1921 added much strength to the presidential office, but the bureau can exert its authority on behalf of the President only if the President is equipped to discipline departmental chiefs — and this he is not in a strong position to do, unlike the British and West German prime ministers, though vastly more able than is the French prime minister. The Bureau of the Budget gives a lively and intelligent President a splendid instrument for progress, welfare, and good sense in national policy and in administrative cohesion and tempo. Yet this is not proof against the disruptions of Congress when the budget passes through its deciding hands, nor against the surreptitious appeals of department chiefs to congressional friends for support when protesting the Chief Executive's decisions. Since 1933, and especially under the impulse of recommendations by the President's committee on administrative management, the bureau has become a comprehensive engine of presidential control, especially under the direction of Harold D. Smith, appointed by Franklin Roosevelt. It greatly increased its staff and recruited special talents.[23] In the armory of several instruments recommended between 1933 and 1937 it was not foreseen that the Bureau of the Budget would emerge as *the* outstanding weapon of the President. The only serious doubt entertained about the Bureau of the Budget concerns its possible intervention in policy-making to fit its fiscal prejudices, and this can occur only under a weak President. Only then would it attain authority without responsibility, and instead of being the financial expresser of policy would become a maker of policy — without the authority to do so.

The Council of Economic Advisers

In 1946 Congress was compelled — by the sentiments of economic improvement nurtured by experience of a war and the economic and social ideas clarified by arguments which emerged from it — to set up the Council of Economic Advisers to the President. (Indeed, some politicians had proposed a committee of cabinet members to work with an advisory council.) The general political purpose was to use government to provide "full employment" and to attain higher standards of living. Congressional opposition succeeded in qualifying these clear objectives to read:

> . . . creating and maintaining, in a manner calculated to foster and promote free competitive enterprise and the general welfare, conditions under which there will be afforded useful employment opportunities, including self-employment, for those able, willing and seeking to work, and to promote maximum employment, production and purchasing power.[24]

All the agencies of government would be utilized and co-ordinated for this purpose, as a continuing policy and responsibility. To enable the President to play his leading and commanding part, a council of three advisers was established in the executive branch, to be appointed by the President so that he need not be beholden to any other body for the formulation of his economic policy.[25] To enable Congress to play its co-ordinate part, Congress established its own joint committee. In January, at the beginning of each regular session of Congress, the President transmits to Congress an economic report setting forth an account of current conditions of employment, production, purchasing power, and the trends of these factors, together with a review of the government economic program and the relationship of all these matters to the responsibilities for economic prosperity imposed on the government by statute. It is the joint committee's business to report to Congress its "findings and recommendations with respect to each of the main recommendations made by the President in the Economic Report."

The economic report is the President's; it is not produced by the Council of Economic Advisers, although it is based on their findings as well as upon the assistance and advice of the President's cabinet and of various departments. The council consults with a number of advisory committees in which business, labor, agriculture, consumers, state and local governments, and educational and research institutions participate. But then how can we reconcile the statement, "The ultimate judgments entering into the Economic Reports to the Congress rest with the President"? All it can mean is that the President has accepted the advice of others and agrees to assume responsibility for the analysis and suggested recommendations for action.

The Council of Economic Advisers keeps fairly strictly to a detached advisory-analytical, professional role and does not attempt itself to plan public works and programs of conservation that under certain circumstances might seem advisable. Of course, it may be asked by the President to co-operate with the Bureau of the Budget to do so, or to implement a general policy formulated by the President. It is most careful to refrain from proposals of policy.[26] So important did the first chairman believe this to be that he expressed the view that members of the council should not be required to appear before congressional committees to express views on pending legislation. In this way council members would not find themselves in the position of advocating or disagreeing with the policy the President had decided to follow. Other members of the council disagreed with the chairman and felt that they ought to extend assistance to the congressional joint committee when it was in process of considering the material contained in the economic reports, and this is what they do, to mutual advantage.

Although the council is advisory, it remains in close co-operation with the Bureau of the Budget, which values the economic analysis provided by the council, especially since it is responsible for gathering and sifting for the President the year's proposals for legislation and can funnel to the council those that require the comments of economists. As President, Truman had the council appear at a cabinet meeting each quarter to present for discussion a survey of economic development and related problems. Yet, even so, one must remain skeptical when one hears that, after less than two years of effort, "The result of the Council's participation in cabinet meetings has been to help bring the thinking of department heads to a more unified consideration of the central economic problems faced by the President." [27] The Hoover Commission, for one, did not believe in the council's efficacy and proposed that the council give way to a single economic adviser.

In recent years the chairman of the council has become a constant and close adviser to President Eisenhower. With such support to rely on, the President and Congress should be able to take the best measures that economic science can suggest to assure economic prosperity. Whether the advice is taken depends, once again, on the political considerations which induce men to act — that is, on the balance of group wills in the community. In 1951, under Truman, and in 1956, under Eisenhower, it was necessary for the Chief Executive to take steps to resolve tension between the Council of Economic Advisers and the Federal Reserve Board, an independent agency, regarding the latter's raising of the discount rate, and though the Federal Reserve Board has indicated its willingness to co-operate with the President in seeking full employment, a choice between board and the Council of Economic Advisers may still be imposed on the President, who will then look to his political aids to assist him in exercising his sole responsibility.

How the political considerations he faces are to be weighed is the business of the President. And here, precisely, the President is without the assistance he needs as a creator of policy, a sufficient number of equal colleagues sharing equal elective responsibility for a common end of which all are conscious and to which all are loyal.

Political and Career Executives

How is modern government to balance the two major forces that guide and assist the democratic masses, the impetus and direction of democratic leadership based on the aims and wills of the community, and the benefits of science, natural, social, and administrative? It was expressed most aptly by a noted French official of the last generation: how to bring into co-operation the law of number and the law of science. In a democracy the majority determines policy but must learn not to speak until it has the counsel of the laws of knowledge furnished by the scientists.

Policy, we have seen, is represented at its highest level by the President. Information is channeled to him by his advisers. If co-operation is lacking, information is useless. To disregard or misinterpret available information is to blind and deafen the nation, to live again in the murk of a benighted Middle Ages. If the President does not have the attributes of leadership, unrest is rife and the nation in danger of civil disturbance, as is inevitable when right knowledge is not called upon to answer the statesman's problem of the best means to serve the nation.

The problem is how to link these two forces, and it is here that the United States in dangerously weak. Testimony is available; the reader need not depend solely on my own research.[28] Examine the reports and the recommendations of the Hoover Commission and the data furnished by its special task forces! I will attempt to define the problem as they see it. They believe that the nation needs party executives at the head of each department and of each regional organization. It needs, as well, an adequate number of the most qualified career experts to assume the administration of each department. The latter will provide the benefits of the various kinds of science, natural, social and administrative, on which progress in the modern world depends. The former will provide the drive and the direction as members of the same party as the President in office, who is responsible to the nation. Senior career officials in large number are needed to direct the work and to see to the efficiency of the hundreds of thousands of lesser officials, keeping them energetically, responsively, economically, and efficiently at work. This, the bureaucracy, a word too often interpreted in a derogatory sense, is absolutely indispensable to the modern state. It should remain ready to serve any group in the community that at some time or another will demand that the federal government, empowered by statutes passed by Congress, undertake social or economic programs which will be of benefit to the special group.

All nations have forged such career services, though quality and nature vary immensely. At the head of government departments, serving under a few representatives of the party in power, is a corps of senior officials, senior civil servants, to advise the political appointees and to carry to fruition the intentions and will of Congress and the President or cabinet.

It is not possible in the space of this essay to adumbrate the many expedients adopted in various democratic countries to secure these ends.[29] But there is no doubt that on the rightful solution of this problem the nation's welfare depends. Indeed, the United States, more than any other democratic nation, needs about 4,000 top civil servants. The one grand and beneficent bridge between Congress and the President, the one bridge that might compensate for the shortsighted view of transient members of the House, Senate, and executive branch, would be such a permanent body of senior civil servants. Yet it does not exist.[30]

No one can mistake the Americanism of Herbert Hoover and his colleagues. This is what the Hoover Commission of 1955 proposed:

> What is needed is recognition of the difficulty, importance, and manpower needs of top management in the national administration, and specific steps to supply and utilize the managerial talents needed. The task force recommends the following steps:
>
> 1. To make a clear division of functions between the political executives who are publicly responsible to the President for the executive departments and agencies of the Government, and the career administrators whose duty it is to assist the political executives in a nonpartisan spirit and to serve them in operating the machinery of Government.
>
> 2. To concentrate the political executives, who are properly political appointees serving at the pleasure of the Chief Executive or his agency heads, at the level of departmental management. . . .

8. To create a Senior Civil Service of 1,500 to 3,000 career administrators, selected solely on the basis of demonstrated competence and integrity from the ranks of the career civil service, to serve in positions of administrative assistant secretary, deputy heads of staff offices concerned with questions of substantive policy, bureau chiefs, assistant bureau chief, division chief, regional or district office director, and as technical or professional assistant to political executives.

Senior civil servants could be transferred to any post where they were needed. They would be chosen from among those men and women of competence, integrity, and qualities of leadership who have a minimum prior service of at least five years; and those selected would be expected to remain politically neutral in all their official acts.

Proposals of this kind are by no means new; similar proposals have been advanced for over thirty years. Some years ago, indeed, a small step toward the creation of what seems necessary was taken with the establishment of the administrative rank of junior administrative assistant, recruited in the main from academic circles. American scholars, imbued with a profound interest in American democracy, realized that the political chiefs of the departments, appointed for political reasons, were not always knowledgeable about the responsibilities they were to assume, had little or no understanding of the relationship of one department to another and no continuing interest in the work of government when they had completed their time in office, and as a result did not assist the President in the formulation of policies and the making of decisions. Many officials in the body of the administration are "political," a number so large that it can be inferred that political executives, as they have come to be called, play far too important a part in the administrative hierarchy for the good of the nation.[31] They are not in office long enough to conceive or master the policies for which the department is responsible or to learn the process of the march of administration within the department. They are not involved in their tasks long enough to have opportunity to think. They can neither advise cogently nor keep a steady and corrective hand on the fulfilment of presidential and cabinet purposes. It is not alone the 1,100 top executives, including members of the cabinet and subcabinet, deputy chiefs and assistant chiefs of executive departments, agencies, boards and commissions, but many others in positions allegedly confidential or "policy-making" who meddle with the work which should be assigned only to career officials.[32]

Of course, in a democracy the heads of departments may be appointed and removed when political considerations demand it. The President has his commitments, and his personal program as well as his party's program requires that the levers of policy and enforcement be in the hands of trustworthy friends. Yet many office-seekers are foisted on the President against his will by party machine headquarters. Often, a pressure group will batten on the party in office and demand the appointment of representatives to departments and bureaus having jurisdiction over the laws important to special interests, and these demands cannot be ignored.

The Hoover Commission proposed a distinction be made between "political" and "career" executives. Now, since we are political scientists of the twentieth century, not schoolmen of the fourteenth, let us make a commonsense calculation. The British government manages with, at the maximum, three or four political executives in each department. These are the men and women appointed by the party in power for the period the administration lasts or at the discretion of the prime minister if the appointee proves incompetent, is unsatisfactory politically, or if it pleases the prime minister to "reorganize his team." Roughly speaking, the British Home Office is the equivalent of the Department of the Interior in Washington. Its political chief sits in the cabinet, and with the prime minister as junior ministers are two joint undersecretaries. The total number of career officials at all levels in that department is 24,000, and the number at the top level, the administrative class, is 93. The same is more or less true in each of the departments of the British government.

The body of 700,00 British civil servants of all classes, from the administrative class to the messengers, is under the direction of 19 cabinet ministers, 13 non-cabinet ministers (equal to department heads in the United States), 7 ministers of state (junior ministers under a chief minister), 12 undersecretaries, and 17 parliamentary secretaries; in all, 68 political executives (as of October, 1959). Sixty-eight in Britain, as compared with 1,100 or more in the United States! What is the secret of the difference in organization? It lies in the general nature of the British and the American political and social systems and, I regret to say, in certain irrationalities committed in the name of principle in the United States.

The British cabinet (with responsibility equivalent to that of the President) can rely on the competence and lifelong devotion of its civil servants, especially of the 3,000 men and women of the so-called administrative class. They serve each change of government with equal loyalty — or they resign. The resignations of civil servants over the past decades have been infinitesimal; their fidelity and competence are enduring and lauded by all political parties. How is it possible that the British cabinet relies on men in a position to sabotage their policies, who instead give them the most expert advice, the most faithful co-operation in devising laws and executive orders, and manage the rank and file of the service in such a way that the will of Parliament and the cabinet is carried out according to law and the creed of the good administrator and the loyal citizen, with devotion, enterprise, and patriotism? It came about because some time in the middle of the nineteenth century the British government concluded that such a service was necessary for the national interest, and they deliberately built it, sacrificing the advantages of patronage and spoils. They enlisted educated men from the universities, and the universities, having a decent conception of public service, inculcated such a spirit and provided a proper education. The government supplied prestige and honor (and moderate salaries) in exchange for some of the finest minds nineteenth-century England possessed.

Why cannot the United States do the same, or similarly? Many political scientists have come to regard a senior civil service as indispensable for the continuance of efficient and responsible government. Former President Herbert Hoover unhesitatingly agreed to name the most important of the 314 reforms recommended by his second commission: "The recommendation of the setting up of a senior civil service . . . the nearest to my heart."

Since the President does not have the assistance of eighteen cabinet members in the same way as the prime minister, why not create a senior civil service to aid him and his cabinet members? Reluctance stems from several causes imbedded in the minds of the various actors on the American political stage. There are no environmental, historical, geographical conditions that would make it unsuitable, as might be argued if attempts were made to reform American political parties. "The cause lies in ourselves and not in our stars. . . ."

American party leaders fear that the parties will be sabotaged by career executives who stay in office after a change of President; they may become political enemies or deadwood to the succeeding administration. The answer is that hundreds of thousands of British career servants in permanent positions have remained efficient and ready to change the direction of their professional efforts when instructed to do so. There is far too little trust in these fellow Americans. And this is extraordinary, since, of all democratic nations, in the United States the cry is most frequent that "politics" ought not to enter into the determination of grave issues of farm, business, foreign policy, and national defense, and that it is here the structure of political parties is most flabby. It would seem to an innocent that if party structure is not firm, and if the parties have no decisive differences in their pattern of a good society, why the bother about administrative sabotage? I am persuaded that the outcry comes from party headquarters, and the motive, "jobs for the boys." And this is why I say that the arguments against a senior civil service are factitious.

Government career service should be supervised at the apex of each department by an administrative assistant secretary. The secretary would have under him a staff of about 75 (on the average; it would vary from department to department) senior civil servants — senior not by age or length of service, but in authority and in weight of responsibility. This staff would form the "brains trust" of every political executive from cabinet member downward and be his adviser, his confidant. It would be the duty of the corps to see that what had been decided by the President, the cabinet, and the National Security Council was carried out. The corps would be responsible for what exists too feebly in our government, cogent thought about America's present and future.[33]

If such a corps of career administrators became the connecting link between political chiefs and scientists (including social scientists), and through them to all the wealth of expertness in our universities, this same corps would serve as well as a buffer, averting misdirection and abuse of scientists by politicians. They would extract from the Robert Oppenheimers their genius in science for government use and return to them any irrelevant political philosophizing. Such an administrative corps, it is clear, would be composed of men of general sagacity — humanists, in short. Their learning would be in the liberal arts and the social sciences; and whatever their education, it would be as minds liberally and humanely formed that they would function. In the jargon of the schools of public administration, they would be "generalists," not specialists.

If such a senior civil service were constructed, cabinet members and department heads could work with fewer political appointees, could devolve to administrative assistants in the career service all the detail and forethought and the multitude of administrative procedures with which they themselves are now bothered. With such competent assistance, cabinet members and department chiefs would find their own responsibilities clearer, and they would be able to attend cabinet meetings and appeal to the executive office more inventively, more comprehensively, and more incisively. On the best evidence available, the activities of the political executives in the departments show that they are confused, never fully oriented, plunging into affairs they know too little about, more apt to obstruct than to facilitate, and obliged to appeal to career administrators for instruction. They soon quit, to make room for others.

Recent Reform Proposals

American statesmen are still trying to square the circle of political leadership by a series of desperate half-measures, "institutionalizing" the President while attempting to leave his responsibility and authority sole and unitary. Institutionalization has proved, overwhelmingly, to be an impasse — or worse, an added avalanche under which to bury the President.

Suggestions for institutionalization have come from two sources. One was President Eisenhower himself.[34] He repeated an earlier proposal, that a new and superior cabinet post be established, to be called First Secretary of Government, with more power than the present Secretary of State and a rank higher than other cabinet secretaries. The First Secretary would have authority to supervise the State Department, the foreign-aid program, and the international operations of a dozen different departments and agencies, with the authority to negotiate for the President at international meetings.

Insofar as the new post would co-ordinate policies and activities in the field of foreign affairs this reform would be useful. But it is a mistake to believe that thereby the President would be relieved of his responsibility for policy. It would be a greater mistake to believe that a President who takes his responsibilities seriously would allow the First Secretary to negotiate agreements abroad with any more authority than the Secretary of State now has. This desperate expedient cannot meet the needs of the modern President. If the Secretary of State, with other cabinet members, were elected on the same slate as the President, presidential responsibilities might be truly shared; short of this, inefficiency and irresponsibility cannot be eliminated.

A variety of suggestions come from the subcommittee on national policy machinery of the Senate Committee on Government Operations (interim staff memorandum, December 4, 1959). The subcommittee complains of the lack of a unified defense policy in the National Security Council in spite of the establishment of a planning board to work with the President through his special assistant for national security affairs. Some observers favor shifting the "center of gravity" in national security policy-making from the department to the White House. "In essence," says the memorandum, "they would have the White House or Executive Office play a much larger part in the detailed formulation of policy. They argue that such a step is needed to overcome the parochial views of the departments and agencies."

This function and responsibility belong to the executive branch under the Constitution; to talk of "shifting" it is to misread the problem. The difficulty comes in electing a President with (in the words of the subcommittee) "the wisdom and courage necessary to acquit the responsibilities he already has."

The memorandum continues:

> Outside of the President, the Secretary of State is the official mainly responsible for formulating our national security goals. It is less and less possible, however, to divorce ends and means in security planning. The relationship between our political objectives and the military, economic and other capabilities needed to achieve them is increasingly intertwined.

This is true and of such significance that the creation of a Minister of Foreign Affairs under the Secretary of State, to relieve him of chores at conferences abroad but in charge of diplomacy, information, and economic matters, will not serve the purpose. What might help would be a collective cabinet with the President at its head. The very argument of the memorandum carries me to this conclusion. Examine the first paragraph in the statement of the problem:

> In the fourteen years since the end of World War II the traditional distinction between peace and war has been obliterated by a contest which knows no boundaries and no limits except those imposed on world communism by expediency. The competition is total — it is military, economic, scientific, political, diplomatic, cultural, and moral.

The collective minds of some twelve men in a single cabinet, elected to office, would be needed to represent all the facets of government involved in this sweeping and accurate statement, the minds "collectivized" so that various factors and forces were harmonized in a way that one man alone, the President, cannot succeed in doing when forced to rely on sundry institutions established to assist him.

The memorandum proposes a co-ordinated relationship between the Secretary of State, the Secretary of Defense, and the Joint Chiefs of Staff. Elsewhere it asks for a more integrated budgetary process between these offices and other departments so that defense spending and other spending may be considered in relation to the nation's economic strength and development. It also suggests that proposals for scientific development be integrated therein. It points out the past shortcomings of government science-planners, especially in the development of weapons. These demands indicate the need for cabinet co-ordination and an intermeshing of all departments, functions which cannot be left to the mind of one man alone. A collective mind is necessary, a collective conscience and imagination is necessary; collective decision is necessary; short of this, the co-ordination between departments so far achieved is sure to lapse.

There are certain ineluctable demands imposed by certain inexorable facts of national survival and progress; a committee might succeed in meeting some of them, but for success a more enterprising regeneration is essential. Clinton Rossiter is of the same opinion, though he does not draw the same conclusions:

> Yet if it has become a twelve-hundred-man job in the budget and in the minds of students of public administration, it remains a one-man job in the Constitution and in the minds of the people — a truth of which we were dramatically reminded when the President fell ill in September, 1955. Since it is a one-man job, the one man who holds it can never escape making the final decisions in each of the many areas in which the American people and their Constitution hold him responsible.[35]

All experience of presidential "institutionalization" has demonstrated that, no matter the number, homunculi cannot combine into one political *Homo sapiens*.

Cogency and its Lack

The very essence of the function of government is cogency of thought, the combination of thinking with drive or will, well-mediated and well-directed impulse. But in the presidential branch of government there is only a loose association between deciding what ought to be done and the act of seeing that it *is* done. Responsibility for decision and command stimulates the individual to search for what ought to be done; the act of thought gives direction to the will to act. A responsibility incurred is a goad until that responsibility is fulfilled. It was astute of the founders of the Republic to center both functions in one man. They themselves were men of vast and intense practical experience, tried in council, experienced in diplomacy, trained by the emergencies of war. As Alexander Hamilton wrote to George Washington: "It may be interesting for the President to consider . . . whether there ought not to be some Executive impulse. Many persons look to the President for the suggestion of measures corresponding with the exigency of affairs." [36] But today, as we have shown, the two functions can be fulfilled only feebly by one man, or they are divorced and disjointed. The departments, whether cabinet or not, the department committees, and the interdepartmental committees number hundreds, not scores. The main lines of policy decided by the President (if he has the capacity to do so) are outlined by the President, who gives to the departments the task of advising him and relating the scientific and technical possibilities and economic alternatives involved. Their advice often induces an alert and knowledgeable President to revise that plan of action he at first deemed desirable. From these miscellaneous agencies arise numerous suggestions that one day may reach the President's desk, to be pondered and, perhaps, to become a part of major policy.

In the American system a serious loosening of the ties between presidential decision and departmental thought and stimulation has occurred. Often the two are worlds apart; they clash and produce confusion and frustration.

A frequently quoted passage (Truman's) is symptomatic:

> And people talk about the powers of a President, all the powers that a Chief Executive has, and what he can do! Let me tell you something — from experience!
>
> The President may have a great many powers given to him in the Constitution and may have certain powers under certain laws which are given to him by the Congress of the United States; but the principal power that the President has is to bring people in and try to persuade them to do what they ought to do without persuasion. That's what I spend most of my time doing. That's what the powers of the President amount to. [37]

Truman sounds very small, very remote from the levers of control. Once out of council, whether cabinet or on affairs of national security, what was he, what could he be? His advisers and aids were all dispersed. On whom could he rely for reconsideration of the most desperate problems? Whom could he telephone, whom summon to command that certain decisions be carried out? He stood in need of equal co-adjutors, but the Constitution did not supply them.

To secure co-ordination of thought, decision, and execution in the American system, what is necessary? One ought to begin with a comprehensive policy, a tendency, a purpose; it could come from the President alone or from a party-based cabinet. To have it come from a single man is asking the impossible if it is expected at all times; but in government *each* time is integrated with *all* times. Eisenhower's press agents announced that he would construct a "team," the "Eisenhower team." Headlines soon reported a series of clashes between cabinet and department chiefs and the President, and of exits from the administration. Co-ordination cannot come about by whim or chance; it demands organized communication between the departments in a collective body, amplified by agencies to help the members of the cabinet. My discussion of the President's cabinet has suggested that the members operate at a tangent, with a definite disposition to speed off on their own concerns. The instruments of co-ordination established outside the cabinet are of considerable value but of minor political effectiveness in the perspective of national and international statecraft. Their relative ineffectiveness stems from the solitariness of the source of authority and responsibility, the impossibility that one man alone can provide the energy and continuing initiative to animate auxiliary agencies in their work of prompting the cabinet and other departments to combine and carry out common policies.

The resolution of difficulties between departments requires a pattern, a principle, for the determination of a choice between who is right and who is wrong and in what measure. The application of a principle is the essence of such decisions regarding department policy conflicts; it is to be provided by the party or by the President. But the present parties do not provide it; and a single man cannot invent and apply principle in a field so enormous as that of modern government.

No matter how energetically the President has attempted to create a structure for the discovery of the principles of national statesmanship or the integration of policy-fulfilment by the numerous departments to produce a team of mind and will and executive purpose, he has been unable to do so, in spite of the variety of apparatus proposed by the committees that have cogitated upon these matters.[38] With the constitutional authority vested in one man alone, the government remains and must remain a mere assemblage of virtually separate policy-making bodies and policy-executing agencies. The magnitude and variety of the task defeats the President's strength, the strength of any President, the strength and virtue of any one man.

VI

The Gamble on a Solitary President

To carry the argument that the Presidency is in need of regeneration to the next stage it is necessary to draw together the threads so far woven. It is clear that the way a President is selected does not provide the highest level of statesmanship for America amid the burdens and terrors of the twentieth century.

Either the man chosen as President is able to immerse himself in each and all of his duties, and so keeps his official oath, or he is unable to do so. If he is responsible he may be inefficient; or he may be both irresponsible (to a degree only, of course, for someone will wrap him on the knuckles if his fecklessness goes too far) and incompetent. Yet he is now, and has been from the time of Andrew Jackson (always excepting the weak Presidents) the single most potent force, initiatory as well as co-operative, in American government, the most potent force in American society. During the administrations of Lincoln, Cleveland, Theodore Roosevelt, Wilson, Franklin Roosevelt, Truman, and even at times of Eisenhower, the President has been by far the major element in the conduct of the nation's highest leadership in every sphere of domestic and international anxiety. He acts on his personal decision, however much he is briefed; this is true or the responsibility vested in him by the Constitution is a fiction.

The President needs help, but it is useless to offer him the help of "institutionalization," for he is left with the crushing weight, the travail, of making the final decision. It is this that is unbearable. As an aspirant to the office, Adlai Stevenson, with experience of a governor's responsibilities, said: ". . . the burdens of that office stagger the imagination. Its potential for good and evil now and in the years of our lives smothers exaltation and converts vanity to prayer."

It is not a valid answer to say that, after all, Lincoln, Wilson, Franklin Roosevelt, and Truman bore the office. They did not do so without excessive, even killing, strain, and Wilson and Roosevelt, with all their prowess, had their sharp failures. The urgent question arises: Can the nation continue to rely on the advent of such men in time of crisis?

It is true that ill-health, aggravated if not brought on by the strains of office, leads to serious failures of policy — Wilson's loss of the Treaty of Versailles, perhaps Roosevelt's errors in strategy at Yalta. It is also true that, since the Civil War, the Presidents we have elected have been younger than those who served before the war, yet (with but three exceptions) all died before they were seventy; and those who survived to retire did not match the longevity of earlier Presidents. John Adams lived to be ninety; Madison, eighty-five; John Quincy Adams, eighty; Van Buren, seventy-nine; Jackson, seventy-eight; Buchanan, seventy-seven. The expectation of life has increased since those days — why do our Presidents fail to live out their span? The Metropolitan Life Insurance Company reports that of thirty Presidents only twelve surpassed the expectation of life at the time of their inauguration according to then-current actuarial calculations of mortality; and omitted, of course, are Harrison, who died a month after taking office, and the three Presidents who were assassinated. Before 1850, the Presidents surpassed life expectancy by an average of three years; between 1850 and 1900, they fell short by three years; since 1900 they have fallen short by eight years. Furthermore, they defeated candidates who lived longer than they did. Or was the shorter life the effect of the strain of office? Aware of the burdens of the Presidency, I am suspicious of a President who leaves office healthier than when he entered it.

Risk-laden Choice and Election

The process of selecting the President (Seward called him "a king for four years, with absolute power within certain limits") is one of the riskiest, most ramshackle arrangements devised by the mind of man, the only exceptions being the hereditary succession of a king or the way French prime ministers were chosen between 1875 and 1959. The number of elements ("variables") entering into the result is frightening to contemplate if the electorate truly hopes to choose the "best man."

An element of serious risk enters in at least five particulars: (1) the lack of a reservoir of able men devoted to national political leadership; (2) the process whereby candidates are selected; (3) the hazards of the election campaign; (4) the possibility of winning the Presidency with a minority of popular votes; and (5) the fortuity of the succession of a Vice-President.

First, the nation lacks a large enough reservoir of men devoted to political service and leadership. (If it were not likely to be received with prejudice, I would speak of a "political class.") In American society the reputation of the professions, especially law, is very high. Success is worshipped in every field. After reputation and successful accomplishment, wealth is looked upon as a most impressive symbol of personal virtue. But in politics it is otherwise: Political life is looked upon as corrupting, few young men will devote themselves to it, and few wives will encourage them to chance the slings and arrows of outrageous fortune.

I am not to be taken as facetious, hypercritical, vindictive, or utopian when I suggest that American politicians are the toughest and the least inclined to ethical scruples in the world — with the exception of communist politicians, and here the gulf is wide and deep. There is, of course, a significant difference in the methods of communist politicians and American politicians; we have renounced murder and imprisonment as instruments of the political battle for "the public good."

Again, the authority of American government is dispersed throughout the federal system and opportunities for office are available locally. I do not intend to criticize the institution of federalism; I am, up to a point, its vindicator, as I am one of its historians.[1] But federalism in America has done much damage to the national government, and this must be set against its un-doubted value to the state, the city, and the individual.

The opportunities for political office, the attraction of local responsibility, the pleasure taken in the conduct of legislative or party or executive office, the personal popularity to be obtained in leading and advancing public causes, even the satisfaction of defying opponents when one is in a permanent minority — the sweets of office, let us say, can be indulged locally in sufficient measure to satisfy men who might otherwise play their part on the national scene. Offices are convenient as mayor, governor, member of the state assembly, and as party committeeman.

The usual answer to the lament that a potential reservoir of national leadership has been drained is that municipal and state service is a valuable training ground for national leadership. But training in local leadership is, at best, training in local leadership — I recall a proverb, "Home-keeping youths have ever homely wits." To have mastered the problems of Seattle, of Houston, of Abilene, of Boston, is no apt education in national and inter-national affairs, certainly not adequate to prepare a man to assume responsible word in decisions for a nation, though it may be an education in the tactics of winning popularity in lesser circles. Federalism, especially in an area as vast as the United States, immensely depletes the character and brains at the service of the nation, to its dire loss. Many American Presidents have had humble beginnings, but they rose to eminence in a less complex age. We are not so certain today that genius will emerge; we are far less certain that there is a mute, inglorious Milton on every rural route. Can we leave the discovery of a talent for politics to chance?

Comparatively speaking, in other democratic systems top lead-ership is attained, in normal times, by a most careful process of competitive selection. In the United States the President is not chosen as a candidate of his own party, nor does he enter the con-test with the opponent chosen by the other party, after a period of close public competition with rivals sufficient to allow skilled people to gauge the worthier candidate, the abler contestant.

In order to make my meaning clearer, and in the spirit in which the founders of the Republic adduced the experience of Athens and England to clarify America's problems at the Federal

Convention in 1787, I am obliged to sketch the normal course through which a British prime minister and his cabinet ministers pass to achieve top positions as statesmen. A potential prime minister is elected as an ordinary member of Parliament from his own constituency. (Before 1886, an occasional peer, a member of the House of Lords, could become prime minister.) Nowadays, only a member of the House of Commons, a popularly elected person, is likely to be considered for office. The embryo prime minister, far from optimistic at the time of his first election however ardent his ambitions, is adopted by the local committee of one of the political parties and is indorsed as acceptable. To obtain this acceptance he must subscribe explicitly to the constitution and bylaws of the party; that is, he begins with an act of political faith.

From his entry into the House of Commons as a novice, at about the age of thirty-five if he is a Conservative member or forty if he is a Labour member, he will be immersed in the conduct of the government of the nation, day in and day out (about 160 days in session each year), either as member of the government "back-benchers" or as one of the rank and file of the opposition. In either case he will be a follower and a contingent supporter of the little body of men at the head of his party in the daily conduct of the nation's business. If his party has command of the government, he will support the prime minister and the rest of the cabinet, some twenty members, and fifteen non-cabinet heads of departments, usually supporting them enthusiastically in their contests (*his* contests) with the opposite party. He has the opportunity to challenge the policy and actions of his leaders in caucus meetings, and he will have a chance to discuss special policies in the committees that are formed within the party. He will be in close liaison with the ministers who attend these committees. The committees, generally, are steered by members likely to challenge the prime minister's policy. In effect, the new member is learning constantly. If he is a member of the opposition his situation will be much the same, for the opposition is a responsible body of members not yet in office, but hoping to be, and their words of opposition to the party in power are weighed carefully.

In the course of time, the member, according to the qualities he has demonstrated in caucus debate, at committee sessions (formal standing committees and party committees), at the annual conference of the party, and in emulation of his fellow members, all with an eye to reputation and eventual preferment for national ministerial office, will rise in esteem and responsibility. He may be elected to the twelve-man executive of the Labour members in Parliament; or he may be chosen by the leader of the Conservative party to be a part of the entourage of leadership. The party leader will select those who have shown clear ability for the so-called shadow cabinet or shadow government. Only a few men are chosen, some twenty or so who are thought capable of occupying a position as head of a department and as a member of the cabinet as soon as the party attains office; for the shadow government, those who will head departments, the party leader selects another fifteen or so, who will be ministers but not members of the cabinet. When the member of Parliament has reached this point in his career, he will have been assigned by his leader to a slightly more specialized responsibility in a special field of national affairs, with the foreign minister, the defense minister, the home secretary, the minister of education, and so on. I am anxious to emphasize that the field in which he specializes does not subtract one whit from his collective interest, authority, and responsibility for the general policy of leadership. Collective responsibility begins before ministries are formed; it begins when a man joins a party, becomes firmer when he becomes a candidate, and firmer still when he becomes a member of Parliament.

Having attained the upper circle of leadership by election and upon being named for demonstrated ability, he is now in line for appointment as a junior minister, full minister, or cabinet minister when his party attains a majority in the House. He will have spent many years, it may be anywhere from ten to twenty according to the political chances of his time, in hard work and incessant, fierce competition with scores of others. He will have taken part in debates in the House, in party caucus; he will have experienced uninterrupted collaboration with colleagues and will have had opportunity to test the resources of his rivals; he will have taken part in questioning the prime minister and cabinet ministers in the House of Commons, and will have been seen by others to be clever, a fool, wise, imprudent, resourceful, or dull. Moreover, the House of Commons, unlike Congress, is more than a legislative body; it is sovereign in the making of law, the provision of finance, the control of the executive in its day by day administration, in its general policy of action, in the development of foreign policy. All of the members are participants in the proceedings of the House. The members, face to face with each other and with cabinet ministers, who sit continually in the House, are flesh of its flesh. Moreover, the actions of the House are not obscured or monopolized by the chairmen of committees, as happens so frequently in Congress.

What is the significance of this process of selection? First, it is a lengthy apprenticeship. Second, it is a competitive trial of extreme severity. Third, it is a selection based on rivalry on common ground, subject to a well-defined and genuine standard. Fourth, those who apply the standard are deeply, intimately, involved in the same policy-making as the people to whom the standard is applied; they are immensely knowledgeable. Fifth, the standard of merit is applied by examiners who share the same ambitions; there is rare praise in their admission of another's superiority. The continuous assessment of top performance is an affair of conflict as well as collaboration; it is candid, to the point of brutality, even when it is couched in the language of gentlemen. Sixth, the competition occurs before the eyes of the public and, to a considerable extent, for the eyes of the public; the procedure of the House, compared with other legislative assemblies, can be watched by all. Seventh, the business undertaken in Parliament covers every field of concern, domestic and international. Eighth, the House of Commons is the *only* channel by which men can reach the highest political offices.

The parliamentary method of selection of top statesmen has been in operation, with occasional ups and downs, since the last half of the sixteenth century, more reliable and routine since 1689, and more regularly still in the nineteenth and twentieth centuries. It has screened from the many who have offered themselves in public service of the nation's good such men as Hampden, Cromwell, Coke, Walpole, Fox, Burke, the Pitts, Canning, Palmerston, Peel, Gladstone, Disraeli, the elder Chamberlain, Balfour, Asquith, Lloyd George, Baldwin, McDonald, Neville

Chamberlain, Churchill, Attlee, Eden, and Macmillan. Some were superb, many excellent, some poor — but they were the best of their group in their time and the product of closely competitive choice. It must be remembered that they had as their close collaborators a dozen or more colleagues, two, three, possibly four, very nearly equaling the prime minister in character, ability, and the qualities of the highest statesmanship. It must not be ignored that the quality of British leadership is not to be attributed to one man alone, the prime minister, nor does it depend on him alone, for he and his cabinet form one body, all members being collectively responsible for decisions.

In Britain the picture the public has of the prime minister is almost fully on canvas in heavy oils long before he is called to enter office; in the United States the character and abilities of the President are unknown and, indeed, cannot be known, are deliberately veiled, until after he enters office.

For an island that is one of the smallest countries in the world, and with no great store of natural resources, England's leaders were capable of making excellent use of government and of the forces that have risen in the nation, its learned men, advances in science, innumerable acts of economic innovation and invention, and the advantages of its geographic position.

Compared with the taut process of selection in England, the American system for selection of a President is loose enough to be called a gamble. There is a general popular lore of the "availability" of candidates that requires notice. The elements of chance are at work even before the nominating process gets under way. It is calculated that to insure election the candidate must be of good American stock, that is to say, Nordic.[3] He stands a better chance if he is Protestant than of another faith. He is at a great advantage if he happens to reside in a state with a large electoral vote, e.g., Ohio, New York, California, Illinois, especially if the state teeters between one party and the other at time of election. As a governor of one of these states, with a machine at his disposal nourished by state patronage, he is a likely candidate. He must be well-known as a personality outside his state, his face and figure must be familiar. His ideas did not count for much, though he must not be passionately opposed to popular beliefs or in favor of a policy that might alienate delegates and voters. What is not required of a candidate is what would make him an able President — character, an established record, and clear policies for America's welfare and survival. If the candidate can prove these positive elements, and has a good moral reputation, then, as Sydney Hyman believes, the nation has only about one hundred men to choose from.[4]

The selection process reveals some extremely dubious characteristics. First, candidates are not chosen as routine from members of Congress, nor is selection exercised by the electoral college. The same absence of a selective mechanism is seen in the appointment of members of the cabinet and the heads of departments. If the President and cabinet members attained office only after years of capable service in Congress, we would have greater assurance of their skill in domestic and foreign affairs. The electorate would come to understand that a quick trip to Russia is no substitute for daily study of world affairs. Furthermore, if it were known that the only way to the top in American government was through Congress, it is probable that Congress would attract more good men that it does, its quality would improve, and a larger number of capable men and women would be willing to devote their lives to national politics. It is one thing to expect a man to devote the whole of his life to public affairs when there is only one office as Chief Executive; it is another and a far more attractive risk when thirty or forty places, each having a full share of the highest responsibility, are the prizes that beckon him.

Some Presidents have made a career of being statesmen and have attained high office after service in Congress or its equivalent; it is true of what I like to call America's first generation of gentlemen politicians, which Burke called a "natural aristocracy." Jackson served in Congress and between terms was engaged in every form of politics. Van Buren served seven years in the Senate and was for four years Vice-President. Harrison was in Congress, so was Tyler. Polk served, Taylor did not. Fillmore, Pierce, Buchanan, Lincoln, and Johnson served. Grant did not. Hayes and Garfield served, Arthur did not. Benjamin Harrison did; McKinley did. Theodore Roosevelt did not, Taft did not, Wilson did not. Harding, of "unblessed memory," served six years in the Senate. Coolidge, Hoover, and Franklin Roosevelt did not. Harry Truman did, Eisenhower did not. We cannot know what membership in Congress did for each of these men — made them dull, awakened them? We can draw no conclusions from the past because the opponents of the men who won nomination and the election were never in direct and open competition with them in a forum in which the plentitude of government powers were disputed by rival parties, and particularly by the leaders of opposing parties, each representing a firm fellowship determined by political conviction. Instead, each candidate represented a momentary issue. They were not concerned to defend or uphold general policy, and personal qualities of leadership were not judged in comparison to the abilities and characters of others contending for the same political role. Irrelevent comparisons decided the issue of nomination and election.

Hence, those who would denigrate Congress as an exclusive forum of selection of the presidential candidate cannot argue that so many of those from Congress who won election were in the second, third, and fourth rank as President. But service in Congress certainly prompted the choice of some men who served with ability; among these must be accounted Tyler, Polk, Lincoln, Johnson, McKinley, and Truman. To his experience in Congress, Truman ascribes a remarkable broadening of mind and a tempering of character, and alertness to the whole range and interdependence of the major problems a President must face.

Twenty-three Presidents were lawyers or closely involved in the legal profession. Eight were educated in the humanities or some branch of natural or social science: Washington, mathematics and surveying; Madison, theology; Harrison, medicine and military tactics; Taylor, Grant, Eisenhower, military science; Garfield, education and theology; Hoover, engineering; Harding, liberal arts and journalism. Johnson was a tailor, without formal education, before entering politics.

Among the Presidents have been five who served as Secretary of State (Jefferson, Madison, Monroe, John Quincy Adams, and Van Buren); three as Secretary of War (Monroe, Grant, and Taft); one Secretary of Commerce (Hoover); twelve who served in the House of Representatives; ten senators; fourteen governors; eight who served in city government.

Fifteen presidential candidates were men of military experience. Ten of these cannot be counted as professional soldiers, that is, their military service was not their primary occupation: Washington, Jackson, Harrison, Pierce, Fremont, Cass, Hayes, Garfield, Harrison, and Theodore Roosevelt, who exploited his service in the Spanish-American War. The professional soldiers were Taylor, Scott, McClellan, Grant, Hancock, and Eisenhower. Cass, Scott, Fremont, McClellan, and Hancock were defeated. None of the professional soldiers elected came near to being a great President. Analysis of Eisenhower's elections demonstrates a substantial vote for him as a personality, without regard for his program, his party's program, or the records of the Democratic and Republican parties. The glamor of his role as military hero played a vital part in Eisenhower's success.

If the barracks world does not fit a man to be President, how did so many professional soldiers become candidates? Party leaders calculated that they possessed certain qualities that would win the electorate once they had impressed the nominating convention — and the winning of the office was considered more important than political talent and the character necessary to guide the destiny of the nation. Also, the soldier's life is supposed to warrant the power of decision, and decision is what many people wish in a President.

An exhaustive study of presidential nominating politics offers us a key to the gamble by which the Chief Executive is chosen.[5] Six different basic patterns of leadership succession are to be distinguished in political parties as well as other organizations:

1. Inheritance of leadership by an understudy selected by the previous leader.

2. Inheritance without a contest by a secondary leader whose "right" to succeed has come to be generally accepted.

3. Selection by an inner group from within its own ranks.

4. Selection by an inner group from outside its own ranks.

5. Advancement through successful leadership of an insurgent group or faction that wins in a contest with the faction previously holding leadership.

6. Advancement through successful leadership of one of several co-existent groups or co-ordinate factions, no one of

which has been clearly in possession of the leadership, but one of which eventually wins leadership in the contest.

Presidential choice by an inner group seems to be missing on the American national scene. A President may select his successor according to his own quality and way with his party; if he does not, rarely is there an inner group, formal (like the British House of Commons), or informal (like the British party caucuses), to do so. When there are inner group conclaves to prepare for the national convention of a party out of power, they are variable in their composition, seldom representative of the party as a whole, and are rather centers of negotiation among agents of competing fashions than "a place where unified decisions can be made with some degree of unanimity representing a true party consensus."

But what of the sixth pattern, an active contest among several factions for party leadership?

It probably does not occur as often elsewhere as it does in the United States. . . . In this country, such contests are favored in our national parties by the continental scale of our politics, the federal nature of our parties, and perhaps most of all by the absence of any assured means under our system for providing in a formal and well-recognized manner for the effective leadership of a national party when it is out of office.

But what are the consequences? Out of such contests both great Presidents and at least two or three of the weakest have emerged. Some scholars believe that the quintessence and greatest virtue of the American party system is its occasional ability to discover a leader like Franklin Roosevelt — but, say the authors, "Benjamin Harrison and Warren G. Harding were equally products of the American party system." They devote five volumes to an analysis of the gambits in the battle of factions which elected President Eisenhower, a close contest between regions and states rarely in touch, with a concatenation of innumerable minor hazards and turning points, few of which had any relation to or were revelatory of Eisenhower's qualifications as Chief Executive.

The process of pre-nomination and nomination selection in 1952 is a revelation of the gamble in assigning political responsibility, of democratic participation as it has come to be, casting grave doubt on those who are proclaimed to be competent to conduct the nation's affairs.

Only a few men — Thomas E. Dewey, Henry Cabot Lodge, his brother, the then president of Doubleday, the then president of International Business Machines, and some few other businessmen and financiers — determined to nominated General Eisenhower. That choice, considering the legislative and executive experience of these men, could not have been founded on belief in his talent as a statesman. How could it be, if they knew the demands of the Presidency (and Roosevelt's and Truman's terms must have opened their eyes) and had reflected on the innocence of political conviction shown by their candidate? What then influenced them to persist in the face of Eisenhower's apparent reluctance? Could they have been dazzled by his glamor, knowing the questionable quality of glamor? Did they believe his demonstrated skill in matters of military organization and decisiveness and the co-ordination of diverse and egocentric services would serve in the White House as well as it seemed to have served in World War II? Or did they focus their interest on the bet that a reputation as a hero and a universally recognized grin would decide millions of votes?

If they loved their country, and understood the pressures of government in the White House, did they not weigh the fact that their favorite had almost always been wrong in the strategic decisions in which he had participated during World War II, that his success in logistics had been faciliated by the willingness of the commanders of Allied armies to avoid a repetition of the lack of co-operation evident during World War I, and that the United States (1941–45) always had the last word because it had the most arms and men? Was it not their patriotic duty to take these facts into account?

By October, 1950, Dewey had reaffirmed his intention, declared a year and a half before, not to run as a candidate. During an interview in October, 1950, Dewey announced his support of Eisenhower:

> Well, it's a little early, but we have in New York a very great world figure, one of the greatest soldiers in history, a fine

educator, a man who really understands the problems of the world. . . .

I draw no special attention to the phrase "a very great world figure"; I skirt the fallaciousness of "one of the greatest soldiers in history" for its irrelevance to the competence of a presidential candidate. But when Dewey blandly speaks of "a fine educator" one is entitled to wonder just how qualified he is to choose the nation's Chief Executive. Eisenhower's record at Columbia University in no way supports Dewey's optimism. Nor can it be neglected that it may well have been electoral strategy that a man may appear less unqualified as a candidate if he emerges from a scholar's cap and gown than from a military uniform.

I advance the belief that behavior such as this has become the pattern of selection, promotion, propaganda, nominating convention tactics, and campaign appeals for the Presidency. The occasion is no longer a time for "talking sense." It is certainly far from the careful process of matching several candidates against each other in order to judge their relative fitness for the job.

No doubt the purpose of Eisenhower's sponsors was victory at any cost over the Democratic party, especially as represented by Truman. They also intended to dish their own party's chief contender, Senator Robert Taft, who had aroused much personal and political antagonism. Taft made the mistake of not only having convictions but stating them publicly. When active citizens pointed out that Eisenhower knew next to nothing of political and economic problems and possessed no experience in dealing with legislatures or pressure groups, that he was an utter amateur, the stock answer was: "We'll provide him with the experts." The answer is not forgotten; but it was not enough. A man can be helped only if he knows what help to ask for. Sherman Adams, Dulles, Charles Wilson, and George Humphrey relieved Eisenhower of responsibility but could not help him to fulfil it. From the moment he accepted the nomination, he was forced to rely on "ghosts."

How can the decisions of military life fit a man for the labors of a statesman, unless, like George Washington or Napoleon, he is a statesman first and a soldier second? The military man's outlook was well expressed in the 1956 campaign when Eisenhower responded to a matter of the highest importance with the refrain: "I have said my last word on the subject." It hardly fits the ethos of democratic government, though it does reveal an instinctive ability to arouse the latent antipathy of the crowd against an apparently impertinent egghead who dares to ask questions of a military hero.

How soon the plain lessons of history are forgotten or deliberately flouted! The most insistent and reasoned teaching of political science, learned from centuries of political practice, is that a soldier is not, as a soldier, fitted to govern a nation's civil destiny — or even its military strategy. The soldier is a specialist; he may have an inborn talent for civil policy, just as a lawyer, a surgeon, or a carpenter may have; but that must be proven in each case. It is suggested that this warning was not brought to the attention of the electorate in 1952 and 1956. The point should have been made.

During World War I, a dismayed Georges Clemenceau said, "War is too grave a matter to be left to generals," a judgment echoed by Lloyd George, the wartime prime minister and comrade in arms of Clemenceau. What did they mean, speaking so from bitter experience? That policy embraces faraway ends and distant places and times, built on a nation's history and economics and social character and projected as a vision of its destiny. This alone gives birth to military strategy and tactics. The general is the professional man, the instrument of policy, not its generator. He has not been trained to the breadth, the humanity, the synthesis required of the statesman. And that is not all: Top military officers, promoted to high command, spend a good deal of their time "fighting the last war over again," with all the old familiar weapons, the old familiar tactics. They are not normally gifted with inventiveness and are puzzled or angered when new arms and new tactics are furnished them by other and younger minds. The history of the use of tanks, machine guns, airplanes, and missiles is only partial witness to this. When will military glamor be recognized for what it is, best allowed influence only in its own narrow field? Has it been learned now? If de Gaulle is cited as the exception, I must point out that de Gaulle is a historian and statesman, a military leader only second.

Now let us remember the part played by the allegation of the

"Texas steal" against the Taft forces, the superb management of the issue by Henry Cabot Lodge, to benefit Eisenhower against his fellow party member, Senator Taft. Or the tactics of Stassen and Governor Warren at the same convention, to gain political leverage, without hope of winning the nomination, and the confusion produced in party ranks by such maneuvers. The "Texas steal" issue drew attention from what Eisenhower thought about economic, social, and foreign policies; according to the unkind judgment of a zealous Taft supporter, Congressman Carroll Reece, "It looks like he's [Eisenhower's] pretty much for mother, home and heaven." But the nominating convention did not ask the candidate to reveal more specific convictions. The candidates were not judged on their convictions. Nor were the Democratic contenders in 1952; there was no pitting of mind against mind, character against character, among Kefauver, Russell, Harriman, Kerr, Stevenson, and Barkley.

Others may affect to see in this kind of process some invisible hand, some divinity which, in angelic mercy for the deserving American people, contrives to nominate the best man in the United States. I do not. The process is a gamble, with the odds heavily against discovering and nominating a capable man.

The governorships of the major states are much more likely to nurture presidential candidates of caliber and appropriate orientation than are the armed services. But the office of governor will not keep the candidate close to decisions in foreign affairs as longish service in Congress will do if the candidate is a truly hard-working member. Many of the qualities among those we have listed as indispensable to the proper conduct of the Presidency are developed in the gubernatorial chair, but there are some that are not. Nothing can make up for a lack of continued interest in politics and political theory, reading, talking, traveling, and the other experiences that mature political judgment.

The present discussion of how candidates are nominated was undertaken to demonstrate how a very few men, a handful of men, can control the sifting when there is no clear and open competition to demonstrate leadership and conviction. The outcome is a gamble when the nominating convention meets, and it continues to be so during the campaign.

As for the use of the primary to test the candidates of each party, the sponsors are forced to select candidates by process of divination. Since primary campaigns occur long before the presidential campaign itself, the issues debated are largely theoretical, have slim connection to the problems besetting Congress, and are unlikely to be planks in the platform to be presented in the critical November.

It is, of course, a noble principle that the Presidency is open to any natural-born citizen who proposes himself for nomination. It has, no doubt, inspired many a youth. The Republic needs such inspiration. Yet it must be acknowledged that there are some ambitions to which some men should not aspire if they have given proper consideration to the responsibilities and to the binding character of the oaths of office. Ambition is a passion that conceals much dross; it is not the sole index to a man's right to aspire. This might be better brought home to the youth of America if Congress were the sieve through which one must pass, the test of merit to prove oneself prepared for the Presidency.

To the grave fact that presidential candidates are not drawn from a significant, sagacious forum of national purpose and policy (and there is nothing better, even if Congress is not as efficient as it might be), thus offering us what the founders of the Republic called "men most capable of analyzing the qualities adapted to the station," must be added a second element of risk — successful nomination at the party convention, followed by arrival at the Presidency with a distinct minority of popular votes.

What terrible risks were run in Lincoln's contest with Seward and Chase (not to mention the other contestants, Bates and Cameron). "If you can throw the Ohio delegation to Lincoln, Chase can have anything he wants." Or consider the machinations of Mark Hanna to insure McKinley's nomination on the first ballot in 1896. Or the drama of Wilson's nomination over Champ Clark after forty-six ballots; fortunes ebbed to and fro, William Jennings Bryan was on hand to be the candidate nominated in the event of a deadlock and held a substantial number of votes until the fourteenth ballot. Clark won a clear majority of the delegates' votes, but the two-thirds rule was in operation. Or consider Roosevelt's first nomination in 1932; failure to have the two-thirds rule repealed; the risky cunning of Farley in winning over promises for Roosevelt; the challenge by Garner, a nonentity when judged by the criteria of national leadership in spite of thirty years in the House; the office of the Vice-Presidency to Garner to release Texas votes to Roosevelt; persuading Sam Rayburn to persuade Garner to this course; a process described by J. M. Burns as "nomination by a hairsbreadth."

In 1844, Van Buren was defeated after eight ballots; he could not muster the two-thirds majority then needed in Democratic conventions, and a "dark horse," James K. Polk, won the nomination. Knowledgeable politicos inquired, "Who the hell is Polk?" (Perhaps the historians Rhodes and Fiske invented this story, being Whig-Republicans.) He was a good President, but was he a better choice than Van Buren would have been? The selection process offers no valid clue; a William Henry Harrison preferred to a Henry Clay. In 1924, the leading candidates killed each other off, and after more than one hundred ballots a bland nonentity was nominated, J. W. Davis, who pleased nobody.

Let us dwell for a moment on the gamble in 1940 — Wendell Willkie's candidacy, a candidacy that gave tremendous anxiety to Roosevelt in the midst of preparations for war. This completely unknown outsider, a utility tycoon, "the barefoot boy from Wall Street," had never fought a primary, and his politics were a mystery. He was believed to be a conservative, a champion of free enterprise, at war with federal projects like the TVA. The sponsors of Willkie dazzled the nation with stories of his virtues. At the Philadelphia convention, Dewey and Taft led by 330 and 350 votes, respectively. In a Gallup poll, Dewey was accorded 47 per cent of the votes and Willkie only 29 per cent. On the first ballot Dewey had 360 votes, Taft 189, Willkie 105. Stassen, then governor of Minnesota, a fresh and vigorous force in Republican politics and keynoter at the convention, sided with Willkie. Taft and Dewey obstructed each other by refusing to come to an agreement that might have shut out Willkie. The "floating" delegations were captured by the Willkie forces. The shrieks from the gallery, "We want Willkie!" — most sonorous of electoral alliterations, akin to "I like Ike!" — increased the possibility of a landslide. Willkie beat Taft on the third ballot and Dewey on the fourth, and on the sixth romped home, a candidate for the Presidency — and his convictions, his policies, his governmental abilities entirely unknown.

The closeness and unexpectedness of various other nominations have been demonstrated time and again. Byran was nominated on the strength of a single speech coming at the end of the debate on the silver plank. Consider, also, the unexpectedness of Horace Greeley's nomination in 1872, or Garfield in 1880 — they had not been reckoned with until the convention. In 1952, Adlai Stevenson, the governor of Illinois, emerged from truly outer darkness as the Democratic candidate. He might have made a very worthy President, yet he did not pass through the preliminary stages of trial and choice. Four years as governor, demanding as they might have been, were not in themselves assurance of talented leadership.

Eisenhower's nomination in 1952, contested by the Republican right wing supporting Senator Taft, was clinched not by a shred of evidence of his ability to make a good President but by some twenty state Republican party governors who controlled convention delegates by offering to give or threatening to withdraw patronage. Among the twenty were Pennsylvania and New York. Governor Dewey told his delegates that he had a long memory and reminded them that his term in office had two and a half years to run.

It is argued in some quarters that the present method of choosing candidates increases party unity, drawing together all the factions, regions, states, and interests into a single front. It is, to my mind, a spurious unity, as I have demonstrated; indeed, the simulation of agreement may be responsible for presidential irresponsibility. The process is sometimes glorified by those who believe with Hegel that "all that is real is rational." The party convention is seen as a brokerage which brings together diverse interests and values, regions and peoples of a pluralistic society. But agreement upon a candidate is momentary at best; the delegates do not support the candidate because they share his national vision, his sense of national purpose; they have had no chance to learn *what* he believes in. The conventions themselves, with thousands present, have been properly dubbed "unwieldy, unrepresentive and unworthy," by a committee of the American Political Science Association.

The risks involved in the nominating convention or the primaries are compounded by the gamble of popular balloting and want of responsiveness of the electoral college. Hayes, through most unusual circumstances, defeated Tilden in 1876 by a margin of one electoral vote but trailed behind him by a quarter of a million popular votes (of the little more than 8,300,000). In 1888, Harrison had 233 electoral votes against Grover Cleveland's 168; Cleveland had 100,000 more popular votes in a total of about 11,000,000, but they were, unfortunately, in the "wrong" states. A switch of 700 votes out of 1,284,500 cast in New York State would have given the victory to Cleveland. This aberration is due to the method of giving electoral votes to the winner of the plurality of popular votes; the minority in the electoral college gets nothing, however large it may be.

Omitting Hayes and Harrison, seven Presidents have been supported by only a minority of popular votes: Polk (1844) polled 49.5 per cent of the popular vote; Taylor (1848), 47.4; Buchanan (1856), 45.3; Lincoln (1860), 40; Garfield (1880), 48.3; Cleveland (in two terms) 48.9 and 46; Wilson (in two terms) 41.8 and 49.3. In each case three or more parties were contending in election years. This would be a minor cause for criticism if other elements of the gamble were not present. The endemic possibility of repetition of a minority choice cannot be ignored in evaluating the argument that the President is "the choice of the nation."

The process of nomination is invested with a mysticism which is calculated to set at rest all doubts of its utility. Harold Laski is quoted as an authority. When attention is drawn to worthy men who were defeated, such men as Henry Clay, Daniel Webster, and J. C. Calhoun, Laski's argument is introduced: "In each case their failure is explicable in terms of defects of character that, on the whole, is a tribute to the delegates who decided against them." [6] The speciousness of this dictum is enough to fill with dismay those who have studied the careers of these men. Granted that they had "defects of character," it will not be denied that their successful rivals had similar defects. Does the record show that a comparison of defects caused the losers to be ousted? Or did the interest-begotten prejudices of the nominator decide in favor of Van Buren (known to his generation as a cunning politician of dubious honesty!) and not his rivals; W. H. Harrison rather than Clay or Winfield Scott; the Taylor-Fillmore ticket rather than Webster; Adams and Jackson rather than Henry Clay? Calhoun, far too extreme in his theories of southern and states' rights, declined to be nominated in 1844. Webster fell foul of the tensions between North and South over slavery; Clay fell foul of the rising tide of the West and the increasing popularity of Jackson; moreover, Clay's preference for Adams over Jackson was used against him by men of inferior character to his own.

In accepting arguments like those advanced by Professor Laski, the issue itself is confounded. It is particularly difficult to apply this Pollyanna theory of the virtuous candidate to the nomination of Warren Harding, that strikingly handsome, dissipated politician. His sponsors were known as the "Ohio gang," notorious scoundrels headed by Harry Daugherty. Daugherty's promise that his protege would be nominated after a deadlock in the convention by "a little group of Republican leaders in a smoke-filled room" was punctiliously kept; Harding was chosen by a group presided over by Colonel George Harvey, whom Wilson had had the courage to repudiate as his sponsor in 1912. The tragic consequences, the Teapot Dome scandals, the Prohibition administration, the way the United States turned its back on world responsibilities, are too well known to require repetition.

By far the most serious aspect of pre-nomination activity is that the candidates create a thoroughly false view of themselves. The gravest element is their failure to explain what they believe, what they reject, what they hope, and what they will do if elected to office. They draw attention to every aspect of their persons except their convictions. The public is not given a chance to know under what circumstances the candidate would exert his energies, give his life. And if commitments are made, they stress no more than a single point, e.g., ending the war in Korea, a promise so dazzling as to make the electorate blind to every other facet of national welfare. The most cunning deception practiced is to conceal, as far as is humanly possible, any mention of the domestic, economic, and social issues which are the causes of dispute and conflict between the many individuals and groups in the nation, promising, instead, prosperity. Candidates are even praised by some of the public and certainly the politicians for their carefully calculated silences. The candidate may make easy and noble reference to international peace and the superior, i.e., "inside," knowledge he has of the nature of our relations with other nations; but this is as far as we will go.

Sometimes there are exceptions to this rule of deliberate muteness, this caginess — for example, when several senators are in competition for the nomination. Laudable as it may be, it will not be the comprehensive revelation of mind and character, specific and incisive, that is enforced by the British method of selection through the House of Commons. For the senators have not been in open competition. All the same, it is praiseworthy; and it would be desirable to encourage and strengthen this element in presidential selection. It is particularly deplorable when one party's choice has been maneuvered into the sole candidacy without a public rival or the need to explain himself early enough for people to know him.

Douglass Cater, a highly skilled Washington correspondent, reviewing a half a dozen "campaign biographies" in March, 1960, quotes approvingly Justice J. D. Voelker of Michigan in a biography of Governor Mennen Williams:

> If democracy depends on choice, and choice upon accuracy of data, then I suspect our country may be in the hell of a fix. For it seems that today the more we hear about our public figures the less we really know them.

Cater continues:

> We have entered the stage of the campaign that might be called the period of the mask. Despite all their public posturing, the candidates are taking on a frozen-faced similarity as each recites his collectively composed speeches and carries out his collectively conceived maneuvers.[7]

When the candidate has been nominated — not on the basis of what is the best self of party policy for the good of the nation, but the minimum that state and regional and pressure-group delegates will concede in order to collect a majority of votes (it is not much!) — the election campaign begins. It is not my intention to offer a description of campaign methods; it is necessary to consider only their essential character.[8] All democratic elections are, to some extent, a deception of the masses of voters — even if they are, or can be, a way toward political education. The deceptions are shaped by three variables: the nature of the political parties; geographical conditions; cultural mores. The first and the last are in the power of men and women to change, and this can be done to make the most of geographical advantages and to minimize disadvantages. If there are two political parties, the deceptions practiced by one party can be exposed and checked by the efforts of the other. But for this to insure enlightenment, these parties must be fellowships consciously and sincerely imbued with a pattern of a good society. Political parties in the United States are not built and do not function on this basis, in part for geographic, ethnic, and historic reasons, but in the main because the will to subordinate self to a conception of the public good is not strong. The public good is regarded as that which satisfies special loyalties, but these are like pieces of a jigsaw puzzle that must be shaped before they will join.

I have said that democratic elections are more or less a deception of the masses of voters. Most if not all politicians seek office by persuading the electors that the policy they advocate (if only the policy of "standing pat") will bring more profit for everyone, and that the payment in taxes, effort, and obedience to the law is a small, if inevitable, price. The deception is all the more venal if the public is unsophisticated and if the country is so vast that candidates can make contradictory promises in different regions without the danger of prompt exposure.

We may, if we wish, list political gambits which have become subjects for laughter; campaign biographies, making each candidate a saint; baby-kissing; dancing polkas; claiming to be exactly like the audience the candidate is addressing — if rural postmasters, then a rural postmaster, if sports fans, then a sportsman; using the language of an ethnic group, with a laugh at one's mispronunciation, as if to yield superiority by saying, "After all, I can't do everything!" with the clear implication, "I almost can!"; straddling policies before large audiences containing more than one economic group; false logic, deliberately expressed; information withheld; identifying oneself with noble leaders of the past; attacks on the record of the other party without suggesting practical alternatives that might serve as a commitment; striking phrases which brand opponents with the sins of his party — "The Democrats are the party of war!", "Hoover caused the Depression!"; false accusations of communist sympathy or corruption; terrible boasts that the candidate has it in his power to end a war or prevent a war; rousing pronouncements likely to win votes at home and lose respect abroad; the candidate who scoffs at the advice of military and political experts and brands as "the numbers game" advice that the Soviet Union is drawing ahead of American missile production; candidates who declare in martyred tones that they will not respond in kind to "name-calling," usually somewhat after they have called the first name; candidates who "play with statistics," implying much, until statistics are demanded and the data shown to be false.

In 1956, Adlai Stevenson, the Democratic candidate, attempted to escape the noisy and misleading babble of electioneering; he held the view that for the highest temporal office in the land men ought to talk sense in the process of selection. He issued a series of "program papers," his policy on each great segment of national affairs, explaining his views in specific terms and making commitments. Never was there such a failure in an appeal to understanding and reason! The public ignored the papers; Republican candidates were not to be drawn; the popular press reported the events of the campaign without mention of these important publications.

No, candidates do not come to grips with each other over their practical proposals or the application of their convictions. Every known trick of nonrational inference comes into play. There are balloons, pompoms, campaign buttons, bands, parades, drum majorettes, songs, euphonic and specious slogans, "I like Ike," a winner, and that cacophonous flop, "Madly with Adlai!" If it is impossible to make election campaigns more rational and sober, one is faced with the need of submitting to the public two rival teams chosen by a more serious and thoughtful and comparative process than that of the nominating conventions alone.

All this as the process of choosing between two candidates to become for four years an autocrat was dubious enough in the past, but television, that new medium of wholesale rhetoric, has aggravated the potential injury to the nation. A word on this is surely essential? Television minimizes the effect to be gained by the cross-country speaking tour. The candidates are saved from local heckling. Television has made possible nationwide deception at one fell stroke. It makes it quite feasible to sell to millions, the decisive millions, an effigy in place of a man. Camera magic can emphasize his most attractive feature, that smile, the whimsical twitch of the left nostril, the majestic frown, and wipe out the low forehead and the clear and expressive ignobility of a common jowl. Unnecessary eyeglasses lend sobriety and maturity to the appearance of a vulgarian. A candidate can be coaxed into postures which are taken for signs of elegance and nobility. The candidate can be given the requisite lines to speak, although he will not be able to read them without stumbling, has no idea what they mean, and on his own could not compose one hundred words on any subject of American policy without committing innumerable bloomers and exposing his lack of judgment. It has happened that a presidential candidate has announced on television "the principles by which I have always lived" — and been so uncertain of them as to be forced to rely on a teleprompter. Is it possible to make a candidate seem alert and wise by assembling flunkies to ask him questions which he answers by reading prepared statements printed on blackboards out of sight of the camera? Is it possible to choose these questioners for their social, artistic, or athletic fame in such wise that the public falls victim to logical fallacy, accepting a person as an authority on a subject of which he knows nothing, e.g., a baseball player's wife commenting on the gold standard? Yes, it has happened. The public can be thoroughly swindled by television rhetoric, whereby something less then a chimpanzee can be made to look like something more than a man.

In 1952, Republicans proposed a beautifully planned strategy for an "all-out saturation blitz — radio-television spot campaign," focused on forty-nine counties in twelve states.[9] In 1956, the winning candidate was assisted by the televising of the convention, for the roars of the crowd had an irresistible influence on viewers.

The expense of network time is a serious problem. It could be a decisive handicap to the candidate with the least funds for such a campaign. At $70,000 for a half-hour program, the candidate or party with the greatest amount of money can smother his rivals. In 1956, the Republican party spent over $4 million on television time, the Democrats somewhat less than $3 million. Moreover, to restrict election discussions to half an hour does not allow more than a summary view of serious policy. And how dangerous the artful dodge of catching viewers between programs with "spot" slogans. Look at the success of the one-word slogan, "Liberation!" for the Hungarian patriots.

What ought the nation to do to guard itself against suasive fraud? We are, let it be remembered, pondering a grave problem in desperate times. Television networks are presented with a fortune by Congress; they are awarded licenses to broadcast. In return, should they not be required to insure political processes first priority? (The same would apply to radio.) Candidates could be given equal and ample time. As for the candidates, it might be required that they speak only in the presence of the other candidates; none be permitted to read his speech or use notes; and each have the right, nay, the obligation, to answer the arguments of contending candidates.

Would it not be for the good of the nation, in the highest sense, if the tradition of the Lincoln-Douglas debates were resumed? What a demonstration of resourcefulness and character, convictions, consciousness, and sense of responsibility! What a test this would be of rival candidates! What fears this would engender in the sponsors of unlikely candidates! What an instrument for the deflation of windbags and humbugs! What a stringent governor of rational responsibility! This procedure could hardly do the nation any harm, and it might do democracy a great deal of good.

If, as I have argued, and as so many others have argued, the office of the President is so powerful that its misuse jeopardizes the nation's welfare, then there ought to be some surer way than the present one of selecting the man who will be given the office. It is dangerous to increase the risks of the gamble on character and personality by failing to curb the extravaganzas in the name of politics on television. If the President is the sole representative of the nation and is responsible to the nation, is not the first requisite that the nation be apprised of his personal and political identity?

It is relevant to recall President Eisenhower's surprise when the electorate returned a very considerable Democratic majority to Congress in 1958. It would seem that if he did not know why a Republican Congress was repudiated, he may have been as easily misled about the reasons for the great Republican majority in 1952 and 1956.

> *Question*: On another aspect of the election, what do you think was the primary reason that so many Democrats were elected? Was it local issues or perhaps disenchantment with the Administration locally?
>
> *Answer*: Disenchantment with what?
>
> *Question*: With the Administration.
>
> *Answer*: Well, so far as I know, I have never varied in my basic convictions as to the functions of the Federal Government in our country and in my beliefs as to what is the great, broad, middle-of-the-road that the United States should be following. I have preached this as loudly as I could for six years. . . . Now, after four year of that kind of teaching, the United States did give me, after all, a majority of I think well over nine million votes. . . . Now, here, only two years later, there is a complete reversal; and yet I do not see where there is anything that these people consciously want the Administration to do differently. And, if I am wrong, I'd like to know what it is; but I am trying to keep the fiscal soundness of this country and to try to keep the economy on a good level keel and to work for peace. Now, if they want me to do anything else, I don't know exactly what it is.[10]

Eisenhower did not appreciate that the public was just as much at a loss about what it did as he was, and for much the same reasons.

Enough has been said to demonstrate that the selection and election process that produces a President is a gamble, a risky undertaking for high stakes, that may reward us with a President of the highest talent or penalize us with an inept, feckless, lackadaisical glad-hander.

In only one other country among the mighty in the world — the Soviet Union — are the talents and policies of the aspirant for highest office such a mystery to the public as are those of candidates in the United States. The candidate for the Presidency who has the best chance of being elected, other things being equal, is the one who keeps silent before the election. Of course, he cannot be mute; he is bound to make a gesture or breathe a hint of opinion from time to time; but revelations and commitments are not expected of him. And the result? Whatever is, is good! Anyone the dice of the nomination procedure shakes from the dark cup is good! What else can be said? To produce a capable President there must be adroit competition, rivalry of character and brains, open candidatures openly arrived at. But the American system inhibits this process in many ways.

Some onlookers are prepared to accept the results with pleasure. The *Economist* commented in this manner on the nominating conventions of 1952:

> Europeans, viewing the clumsy chaos of the nominating conventions, . . . yet resulting in the nomination of two such admirable teams as General Eisenhower and Senator Nixon, Governor Stevenson and Senator Sparkman, will be moved once more to reflect that God moves in a mysterious way his wonders to perform. . . . The great strength of the people's choice can go deep into the barrel and pull out the best men available — in the present case, a man who has never played a part in Federal politics, and a man who has never held elective office at all. . . .
>
> In either of these hands, the leadership of the free world is safe. Those of us who have no votes, but whose lives and liberties yet depend upon the policies of the United States, can settle back to watch the show with the comfortable knowledge that we shall be able to cheer the winner in all sincerity, whoever he may be. . . . May the best man win.[11]

In the years that followed there was less reason to cheer. I draw attention to the hidden trap contained in the phrase "to pull out the best men *available*."

But let us return to two continuing problems, not merely to find a good man, but to be confident that a better man cannot be found; and when the nominating convention selects the best for its party, the hazards of the campaign, and the hazards of the choice of the Vice-President who may succeed to the Presidency, lie ahead. And that is far from all. When the people of the United States elect a President, they have not they slightest idea of the sort of man they have chosen. He will not be able to conduct the government by himself; he will need twenty men or more around him, each intrusted with a great responsibility. And there is no way of knowing how well the President will choose.

In the light of the serious deficiencies of current methods of selecting candidates, the preoccupations of some scholars with lesser aspects of the process cause profound dismay. They give excessive attention to the mechanism of presidential primaries, the distribution of voting power at the conventions, the status of the electoral colleges, and the problem of the representation of the minority vote in each state. I deem these largely irrelevant, for they do not consider the most critical problem — how to encourage good men to enter American politics and how to choose from among them the one who is the possessor of the qualities of leadership the office of President requires.[12] It is of no consolation to quote Hamilton, as some have done, on the impossibility of electing to office a knave or a scoundrel as if it applied to current practices. The quotation deserves to be repeated in full:

> The process of election affords a moral certainty, that the office of President will never fall to the lot of any man who is not in an eminent degree endowed with the requisite qualifications. Talents for low intrigue, and the little arts of popularity, may alone suffice to elevate a man to the first honors in a single state; but it will require other talents, and a different kind of merit, to establish him in the esteem and confidence of the whole Union, or of so considerable a portion of it as would be necessary to make him a successful candidate for the distinguished office of President of the United States. It will not be too strong to say, that there will be a constant probability of seeing the station filled by characters pre-eminent for ability and virtue.[13]

Hamilton was not speaking of nominating conventions, primaries, smoke-filled rooms, the appeal of television and radio; he was speaking to a pastoral America and of a very small electoral college so constituted as to exercise discrimination among well-known candidates. Indeed, this quotation, taken in its time and context, serves not to support the argument of those satisfied with electoral methods today, but rather the opposite, quite definitely the opposite.

The Vice-President as Successor

Is it not reasonable to expect, especially in a democratic government, that reliable arrangements will be made for the proper replacement of the Chief Executive in the event of his death, disability, or resignation? Surely a successor must be at hand and fit to wield the power and take the responsibility in an age when neither delays nor errors of judgment can occur except on pain of internal collapse, violent disruption, and atomic war? The provision of a successor is often praised as one of the superiorities of democratic government over dictatorships, where, most probably, force will be used to secure the succession.

The number of times the Vice-President has assumed the Presidency gives some index of the gamble involved in the choice of the President's running mate. Of the thirty-three men who have been President, ten were former Vice-Presidents. Of these, seven arrived at the highest office in the nation upon the death of the Chief Executive. The other three were elected to the Presidency. The ten served as President a total of fifty-one years, or about one-third of the time between 1789 and 1956. The seven who succeeded upon the death of a President and completed his presidenttial term held office for twenty-three years. From 1900 to 1955, three Vice-Presidents succeeded to the Presidency. Following their succession to the office, Theodore Roosevelt, Coolidge, and Truman were elected in their own right. They served for a total of twenty-one years, nearly 40 per cent of the time.

These figures do not represent the full measure of risk. Once a man becomes President, he assumes the right to the symbolic advantages of the Presidency, the exercise of influence, the donation of offices and patronage and honors, leadership of his party, that make his subsequent election a virtual certainy.[14]

Some other particulars are relevant. In 1881 there was no responsible person in the White House for a period of eighty days as Garfield lay dying of an assassin's bullet. Wilson suffered a stroke on September 2, 1919, and was incapacited until March 4, 1921. In 1955–56, Eisenhower was incapacitated for nearly five months following a heart attack.[15] Franklin Roosevelt was said to have been ill when he met Stalin at Yalta; he died some three months later.

I have already drawn attention to the average age at time of inauguration; inaugurated at fifty-one, the President dies at sixty-three. I attribute this short span to the immensity of the burden of the office.

There is another risk. The world is full of deranged persons for whom the times are out of joint. Garfield was assassinated by a disgruntled office-seeker; and McKinley was assassinated by a young anarchist. Attempts were made to kill Franklin Roosevelt and Harry Truman; threats against Eisenhower have been reported.

The founders of the Republic were unusually casual in establishing the Vice-Presidency. Probably it seemed of less importance to them than their earlier intention to have the President elected by Congress, for succession would then have been quite simple in method, if no less hotly contested. Later, the electoral college was established to choose the President and the Vice-President, to be elected together. Moreover, as agreed at the Philadelphia Convention, the President and Vice-President were not to be specifically designated on the ballots; whichever obtained the greatest number of votes would become President, the next highest would become Vice-President.

Electors dared not vote for a person believed to be second-best, for he might become President. Hence the first Vice-Presidents were men of presidential caliber, Adams, Jefferson, Aaron Burr. This system led to a tie-vote in 1800, and was abandoned in favor of the present method of designating candidates for the Presidency and the Vice-Presidency. Until that time it seemed as if a healthy precedent was developing; both Adams and Jefferson, having served as Vice-President, were elected to the higher office.

Later, the Vice-Presidency degenerated into what Wilson called an office of "anomalous insignificance and curious uncertainty." The Constitution charged the Vice-President to preside in the Senate but otherwise gave him no duties. Should the President die, resign, or be unable to discharge his office, the Vice-President was to succeed for the remainder of the term.

For decades the Vice-Presidency was a kind of geriatric refuge, a home for the ailing and the senile. Yet there was a potentiality in the office. As Vice-President, John Adams said: "I am possessed of two separate powers, the one in *esse* and the other in *posse*. I am Vice-President. In this I am nothing, but I may be everything." The office became a plum, useful to attract voters for the presidential candidate by appealing to a region, a state, of which the campaign managers were not sure. John C. Calhoun was offered the bait, in 1824 and again in 1828, to relinquish his southern claims and leave the path to the White House to Jackson. As Governeur Morris had warned in 1802, the separate vote for the Vice-Presidency had converted it into "a bait to catch state gudgeons."

Two unfortunate political consequences followed. First, the Vice-Presidency was not weighed as an office which might lead to the higher one, a prospect which would have required the nominators in smoke-filled rooms, or standing at the bar of an aromatic tavern, to pick a man with presidential qualitites. Second, because the candidate was picked to "make weight" for the presidential candidate, or to head off someone else, he served as a decoy, taking the voters' minds from a clear and objective judgment of the President himself.

Rescue-facient forces intervened, for the most part inadequately. The election of G. A. Hobart, Vice-President under McKinley, was a signal that political campaigners were prepared to consider the Vice-President as a potential President. But if the names of those who have been elected Vice-President in the twentieth century are recalled, those who may be considered distinguished happen to be those who did go on to become President, not those who did not; the rest have a curious air of being insignificant and ghostly strangers. Thus the robust Vice-President is exemplified by Theodore Roosevelt, Coolidge, Truman. But how much character do we grant Thomas R. Marshall, Charles Dawes, and to Garner, who became a thorn in the side of Franklin Roosevelt?

The President, from McKinley on, began to use the Vice-President to assist him in one way or another, thus giving each some glimmer into the executive responsibilities of the highest office. Marshall, in his second term, was Wilson's hard-working and effective liaison with the Senate and presided at cabinet meetings when Wilson attended the peace conference at Versailles. Harding, the most handsome "hollow man" ever to become President, invited Coolidge to sit in the cabinet and thus unwittingly introduced Coolidge to presidential anxieties. Dawes refused to sit in Coolidge's cabinet and, far from being the President's link with Congress, balked his program, especially with farm legislation.

Franklin Roosevelt established a precedent in this context as in so many others. Garner became his pipeline to Congress. Garner had been Speaker of the House, a past master of parliamentary tactics, and *persona grata* in Congress. But the President was not happy to have Garner in the cabinet, for he could not be trusted to keep secrets. Moreover, the Vice-President had political ambitions, and the two soon clashed violently over matters of policy.

Truman, who served both offices, has pointed out that if the Vice-President is invited to sit in the cabinet he is not prepared thereby for high executive responsibility, since the cabinet does not discuss matters of high moment and does not make decisions. We cannot disregard the President's sole responsibility under the Constitution. He cannot take the Vice-President into his confidence for fear of a leakage on politics and intentions which might suffer ruin if disclosed prematurely. It is difficult to find a place for the Vice-President in the echelons which the President has created to suit his tactics. The Vice-President, depending on his standing with congressmen and senators, may be of value to the President if he has the skill to influence opinion and increase support for the President's legislative and financial program.

The President may delegate many important matters to the Vice-President. He may find it wise to do so if he himself is relatively inexperienced in national politics and government. (Eisenhower allowed Nixon to bear the brunt of campaigning in 1952, 1954, and 1958.) The President may look to the Vice-President for advice on the development of the party and its relations with the public. If the President has had spells of serious illness, he may wish to train a younger man to take office in the event of his own incapacity. Thus, as Eisenhower has done, the President invites the Vice-President to cabinet sessions, allows him to preside in his absence, makes him deputy chairman of the National Security Council, and sends him to visit other countries. The President may wish the Vice-President to be his successor, though unwilling to make a public announcement for fear of stirring up opposition among factions in the party.[16] Because the President needs help, he looks to the Vice-President, giving him responsibilities now which brighten his political hopes for the future. "Dick," President Eisenhower has said, "is the most valuable member of my team."

For all this, the Vice-President is a political makeweight. An unqualified man may succeed to the Presidency, as would have happened if Franklin Roosevelt had died while Henry Wallace was Vice-President.[17] Although the Vice-President is a very busy man, his potentialities cannot be appreciated because he is given no executive responsibility for decision and command.

There is a glimmer of new doctrine requiring that the Vice-President "should stand for precisely the same policies as the President," or at least come from the same "wing" of the party as the President. It was first stated by Henry Wallace: "We [Americans] owe it to the world not to open the door to a sudden shift in our course as the result of the death of a President." Eisenhower urged the same principle, "where abrupt changes could make so much difference." Will it be implemented in the future?[18]

Other democratic systems make more prudent provisions for succession. Where there is cabinet government, with all members of the cabinet collectively responsible, all the members share, year in, year out, in making decisions. Those next in line to the prime minister or chancellor are prepared to substitute for him when he is ill or absent, and at least one man is prepared to take over the office if the prime minister should resign or die. There is no difficulty in arranging the transfer of authority, though there may be some turbulence within the party as factions contend for their favorites. But the transition itself is smooth.[19] Collective responsibility furnishes a second, a third, a fourth candidate, each with substantially the same experience of executive responsibility in domestic and foreign policy as the man who is to be replaced. This stability and efficiency are impossible in any arrangement so far suggested for the improvement of the American Presidency.[20]

Every fresh experience of the relations between a Vice-President and the President reveals some new and unfortunate aspect, judged by a criterion of efficient and responsible leadership. Nixon and Eisenhower offer a case in point. Although Nixon is included in the councils of the President, no one can judge how effective or ineffective he has been. At least one question was planted by Nixon's office with a reporter at one of the President's press conferences shortly before the 1956 campaign: How well had the President thought Nixon had done as Vice-President?

The participation of the Vice-President in cabinet meetings and the National Security Council is often used to suggest that he has had a share in executive responsibility, has shared in making decisions; and this may be publicized whenever the decisions have been favorably received and are considered intrinsically sound. It also enables the Vice-President (especially if he has ambitions to the Presidency) to benefit from the popularity of the President.

When the Vice-President is challenged by opponents on the failures of the administration, he can suggest that he is not the President, with the implication that, had he been, he would have behaved differently. When the President has incurred criticism, the Vice-President may suggest (probably he will not do this loudly) that he ought not to be regarded as culpable for situations out of his hands. Thus in 1959–60, Nixon has not made a clear statement of just how far he supported the unpopular farm program of Secretary of Agriculture Ezra Benson, nor has he answered public criticism of American missile policy since 1953, though he has dismissed warnings as part of "the numbers game."

At the same time, it is possible for the President to help forward the candidacy of the Vice-President if he so chooses. In February, 1960, Eisenhower said at a press conference that he had never disagreed with Nixon on any subject in seven years.[21] What an ambiguous statement that is! Just what subjects? Personal or political? How candid was each? How clearly were subjects expressed? Agreed in every particular? Agreed after exhaustive discussion? Or is this a Delphic communication, to be interpreted as it suits those who are impressed by it? The electorate, in any case, is not in a position to exercise judgment.

In other democratic systems the gamble for a talented statesman is the chance men suffer that such a man is available; in the American system to this inevitable risk is added the necessity of accepting the Vice-President for better or for worse.

The Two-term Limitation

Since 1789 it was the tradition that no President should seek to serve more than two terms, though it is true that President Grant tried for a third term, unsuccessfully. Theodore Roosevelt fell just within the tradition since his first term came to him on the death of McKinley. The case for tradition, omitting the jealousy of the ambitious, would have it that excessive tenure produces stagnation, a touch of despotism, and a want of responsiveness to the people and to Congress. The Constitution itself does not limit the number of times a man may be elected President; the founders of the Republic held that if a man were good enough to be elected he could do the country no great harm no matter how many terms he sought to serve.[22]

Franklin Roosevelt broke the tradition by asking for a third and fourth term in a time of international crisis, the gravest through which the United States had passed. In 1947 a Republican Congress set out to make certain that no future President would seek a third term. With little debate, the Eightieth Congress passed the necessary resolution for the Twenty-second Amendment. Its intention was "to forestall dictatorship!" The amendment was adopted in February, 1951.

The arguments in favor of abolishing this restriction are clear. First, it introduces inflexibility where there was flexibility; the electorate's judgment is estopped. Second, during the President's last term in office he will be considered a "lame duck" and lose what influence he has over Congress, party, and officeholders. Third, it makes it impossible for political leaders to re-intrust the office in a national emergency to a man of proven worth. George Washington said:

> I can see no propriety in precluding ourselves from the services of any man who on some great emergency shall be deemed universally most capable of serving the public.

The Gamble of the Presidency

I believe I have shown how serious is the gamble the American people take in looking to one man to give them supreme political leadership. Let us sum up the argument of this chapter with those observations needed to accentuate its significance.

The thrusting of the burden of the Presidency on one man very probably contributes to the strain which may cause his collapse. The nation lacks a reservoir of candidates devoted to public life. The process of selection of candidates is obscure and without the application of competitive standards of talent and character conducive to rational and responsible choice of an appropriate man. The election campaign is a species of continental plebiscite, marked by vagueness and hedging on major issues, confusion, demagogic argumentation, and rowdiness, encouraging the abuse of a major media of communication, television. The choice and succession of the Vice-President is exceedingly fortuitous; in other words, the nation hardly knows what it is getting or for what purpose it is choosing the man. A President who has demonstrated his ability in office is not allowed to continue for more than two terms.

The personal gamble is enhanced by the fact that the President's advisory bodies depend on his selection for their value to him and to the nation. I have shown that they sometimes are not councils of cogent thought, that they leave the burden of personal and solitary decision upon the President as well as the chore of command, persuasion, and enforcement, unless he is willing to have his policies ignored, thwarted, or perverted. All these characteristics damage efficiency and weaken responsibility. Finally, responsibility wavers because the President is forced to fall back on the advice of his kitchen cabinet, men unknown to the public or, at any rate, not elected; this compounds the gamble.

What a multitude of hostages the American people offers to Fortune in the manner in which it chooses and composes its highest political leadership in this century of total war! How shall the nation assure itself of the statesman it needs to apply the gift of mind and the command of men to appropriate policies for social welfare and the preservation of human nobility?

VII

The Indispensable Solution

I have argued, and I believe that I have established, that certain features of the authority, structure, and operation of the Presidency give cause for serious civic concern. Our sober criteria are the nation's economic, social, and cultural needs, the needs and aspirations of many representative groups and thoughtful men and women, the reliable protection of the nation's interests and honor abroad, and the assurance of the nation's survival as a power for moral good.

1. In our time, the qualities demanded in the presidential office, with no foreseeable easing of responsibilities, are those of a genius; and how rarely a genius is found!

2. The President is required by oath to bear too heavy a burden. The weight of office is impossible; the intellectual demands are unfulfillable; the charge on the conscience is too exacting for one man alone.

3. The selection and election of the President is a gamble on folly, genius, and all the stations between.

4. The President's responsibility is demagogic rather than democratic, for he is not subjected to the continuous scrutiny and influence of a body intermediate between him and masses which can exercise a discriminating surveillance from a foundation of

300

independent power. American government is a government by quadrennial plebiscite.

5. The President and his cabinet are not selected by a process of intense and close competition before a discriminating forum. Once elected, there is no concerted opposition to offer alternative constructive policies expressed with responsible vigor. The Presidency becomes "a privileged sanctuary," in part because the President is a symbol of the nation, however inept a Chief Executive he may be.

6. The speeches and reported actions attributed to the President are too frequently public deception. So demanding is the presidential office that even a relatively unsophisticated voter must realize, at least from time to time, that "someone must be doing it for him behind the scenes." The President becomes a "ghost," supported by ghostwriters, thinkers, and deciders. If it is rejoined that the "ghosts" have a mighty effect on the United States, I heartily agree. It remains a deception in which it becomes almost impossible to "talk sense," but this augurs badly for the future of the Republic.

7. It has become difficult to provide adequately for the succession to the President in case of disability or death. If the electorate keeps its eyes on the President at the head of the ticket, the Vice-President becomes nothing but a vote-catching makeweight, and the nation courts trouble, already reaped on several occasions.

8. The President has a fixed term and for at least four years can damage the interests of the nation with impunity and, in the international hostilities of today, damage them irrevocably. He can be ejected only by impeachment. But impeachment is of little help when the President is likely to be a fool, an ignoramus, listless, or irresponsive to the changing mood and needs of the nation. It is presidential incompetence, not criminality, that urges an appropriate instrument of correction.

9. The prohibition of more than two terms takes away from the American people and from the burden and discretion of the political parties the continuance by successive re-elections of a man who proves to be competent. It subtracts from his power, and it reduces his responsiveness to his tasks. If the knowledge that his second and last term is about to end makes a President

feel strong in his own right, having nothing to gain or lose by concern for either the electorate or Congress, and causes him, as he would say, "to do only what is right," such highhanded behavior cannot be condoned by any view of the democratic principle.

10. The separate elections of the President, the Senate, and the House of Representatives fractures the nation's vision and will, destroys cogency of thought, and pits legislature and executive branch against each other.

11. The lack of a collective executive, a responsible body in which the members share in all national policies as well as the major policies of separate departments, robs the American nation of an organ of ordered, continuous, and cogent thought and persisting will. A one-man executive has not the brains, the vision, the patience, or the mental and physical capabilities to draw intellectual and spiritual nourishment from a multitude of sources.

Drastic changes are needed in the Presidency, far more drastic than the provisions for auxiliary institutions enable the office to have. As much thought should be expended on the regeneration of the Presidency as on the creation of a modern weapons system or progress in the direction and structure of the nation's economy.

Many scholars have been disturbed by the inadequacy of the Presidency to discharge the responsibilities with which the office is charged today and have made various proposals to regenerate the political leadership of the nation. It is convenient, however, to relegate an account of the more important proposals to an appendix, although two comments on these proposals deserve to be made here.

First, the criticism of existent practices made by their authors tally with my own, and, indeed, some are more severe.

Second, and more important, their recommendations do not go far enough. They propose — to summarize with extreme brevity — these various courses:

Congressional-presidential leadership should be linked by simultaneous elections of both houses at the time of the presidential election and for the same term. Linkage could be further developed by having cabinet members participate in congressional debate and answer questions in Congress.

Presidential leadership could be strengthened by joint council of legislative leaders and the President, promising co-operation and a clearer definition of the business of both branches.

Institutionalization, already embarked on, should be further developed and improved wherever it is found to sag and to be ungeared to policy-decision and command.

To provide responsible, concentrated, and harmonious advice and will, to get more cogency of thoughts and a firmer execution of decisions, it is deemed important to have President and his immediate colleagues nominated and elected on the same ticket.

Finally, recognition is given to the value of a coherent and continuously organized opposition around the defeated candidate or an alternate nominee of the party.

All of these recommendations have merit, but I believe that their intentions cannot be fulfilled by the measures so far proposed. I am persuaded that tinkering is ineffectual and may do harm. A thoroughgoing reform is indispensable.

To achieve their full value, the recommendations about to be advanced for the reform of the Presidency would be facilitated if certain proposed reforms of Congress were undertaken at the same time. Some of these are suggested in an appendix to this volume.

The following reforms are put forward on their own intrinsic merit to improve the Presidency, for the reasons adduced in the foregoing chapters. They could not fail to bring about a measure of improvement in Congress as a consequence of their implementation. The problems that beset the American executive might be solved by the following recommendations:

A President and Eleven Vice-Presidents

The President and a cabinet of eleven Vice-Presidents shall be elected on the same ticket every four years, without limit on the continued eligibility of any or all of them. The ticket of candidates shall be named, without instruction by primary election, by the nominating conventions of each political party. The election shall occur on the same day as the elections for the House of Representatives and the Senate whose members shall be elected for the same period as the President and his cabinet. No other elections shall be conducted on that day, or within forty days before or after, for any other public offices.

The Vice-Presidents, or any single Vice-President, will not serve in the Senate as its presiding officer. Their attention and experience will be concentrated on executive responsibility.

The recommendation of eleven Vice-Presidents is not arbitrary; it represents the minimum number of men required to handle the most important government departments and is not too large a number for cogent discussion in cabinet. Some of the Vice-Presidents (as in the Soviet Union's Presidium of the Council of Ministers) will not be assigned to a specific department but will be available as deputies of the President and concerned with the main lines of policy as well as general counseling. In the British cabinet two or three members are not required to head departments and so are free from the intensive daily attention to the administration of policy and can be utilized for more comprehensive deliberation.

A four-year term of office is suggested because, though modern political executives need a longish period to acquaint themselves with their responsibilities and to develop working relationships, this desideratum must be weighed against the need for popular responsibility. Furthermore, I am inclined to a four-year term and no longer because I do not believe the legislature should be granted the right to demand the resignation of the President and his cabinet, though the executive branch should have the right to resign if it wishes to challenge a deadlocked legislature. The truth of the matter is that where the party system has become stabilized into a two-party system (or virtually so, as in Britain and in West Germany) the term of office of the cabinet resting on the majority party has become to all intents and purposes a fixed one, though dissolution is possible and has an influence upon the actions of all concerned.

I do not think that a presidential-cabinet will harm the nation if its fixed term in office is four years. Congress need not be granted the power to oust it, as long as there is collective responsibility in the executive. The cardinal fact that frightens me in the present situation is that *all* responsibility falls on one man, who may be inept politically.

The President and his cabinet may be re-elected, and no limit is set on the number of terms they may serve. The arguments set forth by the founders of the Republic in favor of permitting the public (and parties) to judge their need of the services of the candidate without limit of terms are fully persuasive. The argument that the Presidency is too heavy a burden for one man for a long times does not apply when, in effect, twelve men shoulder that burden in a collectively responsible cabinet.

I do not recommend that Congress choose the President and his cabinet. The nation should choose, assisted by the usual nominating machinery of the several parties. This gives the cabinet an independent basis of authority with which to fulfil its functions and to face Congress. It is not my intention to reduce the dignity or the powers of Congress — far from it; but the development of political parties, in the United States as well as in other Western democracies, makes them paramount in the selection and nomination of political leaders and the management of election campaigns. In other nations, more so than in the United States, it has resulted in the maintenance of a strong, supple, and responsible link between the local party organizations, pressure groups, and individuals and the party itself as it is represented and active in both the legislature and the executive. I am inclined to believe that to intrust the parties with the nomination of the cabinet, as I propose, would have a consolidating and clarifying effect on their deliberations and on their platforms at the time of nomination. They might have far more trouble than they have now in finding a common denominator, but they would find a way of doing so. A politician accepts more than the usual number of headaches and gains his satisfactions in the discovering of remedies.

I would ban primaries, for they are internal subverters of the unification of each political party. Primaries are most unfair, and sometimes mortifying, to the incumbent President. Primary contests are far removed from the national vision as it will be on the day the candidates for the legislative branch and the executive branch come up for election. The idea of the primary was a noble one in the eighties, to remedy the worst tactics of the city and rural bosses; but that day is over. The primary is at best irrelevent and at worst injurious to the democratic system.

Local and state elections are banished from the scene of national election day and for long enough before and after to avoid mixed motivation, mixed ambition, and mixed patronage. It is good that the nation be as clear-headed as possible on the one day in every four years when it reflects and acts upon federal government candidates and their policies.

Equal Electoral Terms for President and Congress

Congress and the President should have the same term of office — that is, four years. This would have several implications. First, that the term of the House be raised to four years; that the term of the Senate be reduced to four; and no off-year elections, for then there would be no "off-years."

To expect the electorate to supply national leadership for Congress every two years, for the Senate every two years (but only to the extent of one-third of the senators), and a President every four years is to result in no clearly visible line of authority, responsibility, or concerted policy. It splits the power to make policy, disperses it, obscures it. It splits the voters' acknowledgment of their own duty to accept the consequences of their choices and thus to be sensitive (in anticipation) of their own duty to accept the consequences of the leadership they have chosen, or rather the leaderships, rival and clashing leaderships.

Why should the House be granted a four-year term? In order to relieve congressmen of the anxiety of re-election in such a short period as two years, when after only three months in Washington he begins to look homeward to every pressure group, lest he be rejected. Congress is far too subservient to local and immediate views. A four-year term would give definite assurance, and we hope that this will fortify independence of mind for a more deliberate view of the national good, a broader view of the nation's policy, and a higher view of the nation as a community of more importance than the local district. The two-year term is one of the most antiquated political devices in the modern world. No nation today has less than a four-year term. Above all, the longer term is necessary to give a chance for an understanding of the nation's foreign policy. In four years a man will learn much by a process of trial and error, combined with reflection, provided he is not overly preoccupied with mending his fences.

The politician's independence of mind is one of the most important ingredients for able political leadership.

Let all senators be judged by the electorate on the day the House and the President are judged. Let them account for their filibusters and tergiversations and their stratagems of debate in and out of committees. If it be thought that four years is too short a term for the Senate, then a five-year term might be prescribed for all, House, Senate, and the President. The purpose is to confront the nation with slates of candidates that combine legislative and executive office, or rather legislative-executive office, the Congress, and executive-legislative leadership, that is, the President. So combined, so synchronized, it would be much more difficult than now for any candidate to speak other than a common language on a common program to solve the nation's problems.

More sober and concerted care would be devoted to the common platform. It is possible that the title of each party would acquire a firmer meaning in the minds of the candidates and in the minds of the voters. Less would be heard of the excuse that only the President represents the nation, the Congress represents only the constituencies.

They would be compelled by the need of victory, much against their presently divided will, to meet and consider what House, Senate, and presidential candidates are to promise. There could hardly be as many open or mental reservations as there are today, that we can "change all this" in two year's time in the off-year elections, or "We can be careless and evasive, promise everything and nothing."

The presidential platform would have to be harmonized with the platform of House and Senate — or in time those who evade issues would be discovered and labeled as such. The platform would serve the President, and the electorate, as a definite commitment; the President, House, and Senate would be more bound than now within their own political parties. The need for consultation on a program and a campaign would add impulse to nationwide party organization, and a sensing that the stakes were far greater than where power is seriously divided might impose, in time, a new and substantial sense of responsibilities on the candidates, the parties, and the electors.

In proportion as a well-integrated program was developed, the party caucus would strengthen its power in Congress and form a firmer link with the Chief Executive, now almost certain to be supported by a majority in House and Senate.

It is the error of those who seek the good of their nation to refuse to acknowledge the need for reform if hallowed institutions may be altered in the process. It must be risked if the issue is vital.

With equal terms of office, both executive and legislative branches would appeal to common experience and commitments, and they would feel the necessity to present a united front at the next election with a record of shared achievements. The simultaneity of the elections, the banishment of the possibility of alibis during off-year elections, would assist in the reconstruction of parties as entities, each with a well-integrated program.

It has been suggested that if there were a fixed date for national elections, an enemy equipped with ICBMs or submarines carrying H-bombs might plan an assault on the nation during the campaign period or on election day. But there must always be an election-campaign period, an election day. Of course, if instead of a single President and Vice-President, as now, there were eleven Vice-Presidents, with one, two, or three in immediate line of succession should the President be killed, then at least one part of the hazard would be reduced. But is not this theme so speculative as to border on fancifulness? If there are fears of attack during a campaign, then all our precautions for defense against surprise attack need reconsideration. It was not because the Japanese attacked Pearl Harbor on a Sunday that we were caught napping; we had been napping for years. To speak of a surprise attack is to admit one's own weakness and unpreparedness. I hope that the National Security Council and the military services are prepared to defend us during an election campaign.

It is inexpedient and unwise when elections to the House and Senate are regulated by laws intrusted to the states. Congress is occupied, or should be (it is so authorized in the Constitution), with the nation's welfare; it should not be the sport of special and local interests which abuse national legislation and injure its efficiency by local chicanery (a moderate word for the abuses I have in mind).

Let the nation be given some majesty and firmness in its constituent elements. Every aspect of the laws and administration of elections to Congress should be withdrawn from the states and vested in Congress and in Congress alone.

Among the laws to be enacted to regulate campaign practices — on a par in intention with those of expenditures — is one concerning the use of television in presidential elections. The matter has been discussed; it is once again emphasized. For the two great national parties television time must be made equal and plentiful. No appearance by any candidate should be permitted without the accompanying appearance of his duly nominated opponent. The candidates should be required to speak to the same theme in national policy for the same length of time, with equal time for rebuttal, and at all times without a brief or a teleprompter.

Congressional Eligibility for the Cabinet

To be eligible for membership in the cabinet as President or as one of the Vice-Presidents, the candidate must be presently a member of the House of Representatives or the Senate or must have served at least four years in either house. This is a most drastic break with the arrangements made by the founders of the Republic for election via the electoral college and with subsequent alterations of the original plan. I do not grudge the electorate the right to decide who shall govern them, but I take my stand with the founders of the Republic, and feel myself even more justified than they by the complexity, ramification, and intensity of the social and political forces of our time, in insisting that it be a discriminating selection. At no time was it suggested that the presidential election should resemble a floating crap game or that the present gamble was a reliable way of choosing a President or preserving and steering the course of the Republic.

It was the intent of the founders of the Republic that candidates be sifted by a forum having personal knowledge of their skill in government in the mingled domestic and international problems of the entire nation. Governorships, military command, local celebrity, all these experiences may add luster to a man's career, but they do not necessarily qualify him for the highest office in the nation. The surer way to sift the wheat from the chaff is to rely on the forum of Congress. No one should be permitted to become a candidate for the Presidency or the cabinet unless he is or has been a member of Congress. This is to be the only route to the Presidency.

At this suggestion there is certain to be a bitter outcry. Congress! Talented men, "men of light and leading," do not serve in Congress! Many worthy men have despised the petty art of courting public office, the maneuvering that accompanies the enacting or avoidance of legislation, the indulgence of malice, selfishness, cupidity, subservience to special interests and to powerful individuals, the wilful display of ignorance, the sly tactics to avoid commitment of opinion or vote. (Think of the number of members of Congress who have been voluntary witness to their own sins.) But intemperate abuse and worse invective brand the whole when the guilt is individual and not inherent in the nature of the body itself. There are ways to insure a properly qualified legislature, some of which I shall suggest in an appendix. The character and operation of Congress will improve as its members gain in stature and repute; and this will be so if Congress becomes the one arena in which a man's demonstrated prowess in the tasks of legislation and executive devices and control (in everyday rivalry with fellow members) is the sole access to highest office.

Would not this recommendation mean that if at some critical time the nation was in need of an exceptional person the necessity of selecting men solely from among members of the legislature would exclude the choice of a superior person who had not served in Congress? I do not think so. For when the word exceptional is used in such a context, one is led to the belief that he is utterly exceptional, indeed, superhuman; but there would be no great need for a superman if we were governed by a President and an eleven-man cabinet. Talent and character are amply provided by twelve men, and collective responsibility assures the presence of these qualities. All the same, suppose a truly extraordinary man is required in a time of emergency? Rather reluctantly I have provided an opening in suggesting that candidates must be members of Congress. They may have been elected *very* recently. I am acting on the experience of Britain; when an unusual situation requires an exceptional man, exceptional means are available. For example, in 1940, when Ernest Bevin was needed as Minister of Labour and National Service. Hitler's descent on Norway and the Low Countries had toppled Neville Chamberlain; Churchill became prime minister. Bevin was given a post as minister and a seat in Parliament was vacated for him. Such vacancies can be contrived; a member of the prime minister's party will resign and allow for the election of the wanted man. It has been accomplished in English politics with a full sense of national responsibility. The man who gives up his seat in Parliament can be rewarded by some appropriate office of commensurate dignity.

The knowledge that the only way to the Presidency is through membership in Congress should have a powerful influence on improving the quality of Congress. Men who have ambition to serve their country may enter the legislature and there display their ability. Salary and other emoluments are more than ample for comfortable living. What apprenticeship in Congress might do as a selective process is to be gleaned from what has been said of the road by which British politicians reach cabinet office.

The party nominating conventions remain masters of the choice among the hundreds who have served or are serving in Congress. The party conventions are likely to require of the prospective candidate more than the four years' service I have postulated, since it will wish to have a broader picture of the political merit exhibited by the aspirant. It will say of some, "He is too young!" and of others, "He will never do, however long he lives!" and of still others, "No length of service will fit him for higher office!"

Some provision must be made by the sudden loss to Congress of as many as twenty-four members, the winning group, the President and eleven Vice-Presidents, and the losing group, the unsuccessful presidential candidate and candidates for his eleven-man cabinet. The losers will have missed the opportunity to resume service in House and Senate. Of course it is entirely unlikely that all participants in the presidential election will have been acting members of Congress; probably only a score or more will be lost. It would be advisable to replace the winning group by special elections in their own states, the candidates to be elected to either of the two houses. That this would affect the balance of voting in Congress is a hazard; but it could be arranged that the organization of both houses be committed, as now, to the majority party, not counting these newly elected members at large. As for the replacement in Congress of those candidates who failed to win election to the presidential cabinet, this would not be necessary; they could be regarded as elected to Congress by the fact of their appearance on the presidential ticket; and they too could choose in which house they wished to serve. This device would achieve one most important benefit: The losing presidential candidate would be preserved in Congress as a steady leader of the opposition between elections.

In this way, or something like it, the fear that Congress would be depleted of its leading figures, who, with their colleagues, form a counterweight of critics to the executive, would be met; while the disappointment of the losing team at having missed high office would have its compensation.

With adjustment of electoral representation to overcome the historic lag of misrepresentation in favor of rural areas, I would not fear for the representative character of the nominating conventions and their choices of a presidential-cabinet ticket from among eligible candidates, though the process of selection would be better served if the voting delegates were reduced to about 500. Under existing conditions intra-party factions come to agreement on choice of candidates. It is accomplished by a fearful wrenching and contriving and bargaining. It could not be worse if applied to twelve men in place of one; indeed, it might be easier and more satisfactory because it would allow for factional accommodation in policy and offices not possible when the throw of the dice is for one man alone. Assumption of responsibility by twelve men would involve some difficult adjustments of conscience as well as accommodation for varying policies, temperaments, and regional interests, but then the President himself is not immune to the slings and arrows of such pressures.

One can expect within the cabinet, when so selected and qualified and nominated and elected, the growth of a collective and cohesive loyalty to national and party interests. There is no reason to believe that dissent would split the cabinet. Extremists of whatever sort would resign or would be dismissed by the President. The appearance of the cabinet, acting as a team to lead the business of Congress, would help to weld the members together as a single organism. Even in smooth-running collectives (like the British cabinet) there are times of serious friction and contention, and even as they are overcome for the benefit of the nation, so would I expect human nature in the United States to comfort and control itself.

The President Names the First Vice-President

The President may designate the order of succession among his cabinet members and name his first Vice-President at a time suitable to him. This power gives the President clear precedence over his cabinet members and a certain disciplinary power; he would have a decided influence over the careers of his colleagues. It would provide for the transfer of office in a more suitable way than under the present presidential system. Assuming that the President and his cabinet have served together for some time, cabinet members would be fully involved in the work of Congress, their political party, and in the cabinet itself, and better prepared to assume greater responsibility by succession.

In the British system, the official second to the prime minister is almost certainly well-known to his political party. The prime minister can remove all doubt by designating a trusted colleague as deputy prime minister or as leader of the House of Commons, and this member would also continue to hold the leadership of a government department.

In the West German Republic, the chancellor (equivalent to prime minister) designates the vice chancellor. The chancellor will choose an able man who stands high in the party and has shown exceptional ability in inspiring the electorate during election campaigns. The choice does not prevent the party and the electorate from changing the order of preference when the chancellor leaves office or appeals to the electorate again.

In regenerating the American Presidency, it might be well to prescribe that the Vice-President succeeds to the Presidency in case of the President's disability, removal, resignation, or death; for the remainder of the term the first Vice-President assumes the full prerogatives and responsibilities of the President.

Executive Power Belongs to the Presidential-Cabinet

As the greatest need of the Presidency is relief from intolerable burdens of responsibility imposed on one man without the right of delegation, the remedy is that the powers of the Chief Executive are to be put into commission. The arrangement might follow the custom of the British cabinet system, to which we have referred; or perhaps it might follow fairly closely the disposition of executive power in West Germany. In the latter case, the "Chief Executive" would consist of the President himself and his eleven-man cabinet. The President is to determine and assume responsibility for general policy; within the bounds of general policy each cabinet member (a Vice-President) will conduct the business of his department independently and on his own responsibility. The procedure for this sharing of responsibility is to be adopted by the government as a whole.

In West Germany, economic policy is largely the policy of the chancellor and his minister of finance and economic affairs, but it is open for debate and argument and subject to acceptance by the other ministers. When disagreement occurs there are resignations, voluntary or otherwise, but no explosion or breakdown. Similarly, German foreign policy is the creation of the chancellor himself; some ministers may resign in protest, but the government does not collapse; it proves to have the suppleness and strength it needs, not only in relation to other nations but to a powerful and extreme opposition party in the legislature.

The rules of procedure call for the timely introduction into common counsel of all affairs that concern other departments.[1] When the German constitutional and democratic mind sets itself to a task, it is done with powerful intelligence and thoroughness.

It is not my intention to call for the slavish adoption of the governmental practices of other nations. I do not believe it to be possible to adopt any single system *in toto*. But current practices in other nations may be studied with profit to see the advantages and the disadvantages of a distribution of responsibility in a system of collective cabinet operation. Within such an administration there is collective counsel, enforced by vote, if necessary; and within the main lines, to which all contribute, the individual members, the Vice-Presidents, run their departments in accordance with general policy. The cabinet stands or falls with the President. If the legislature displays its want of confidence in the President, the cabinet will be included in the censure and both President and cabinet will be replaced. (But the ejection of the presidential-cabinet is *not* recommended as a part of the American system.)

The President Empowered to Dismiss Vice-Presidents

The President must be granted the power to dismiss any or all of his cabinet and to appoint others to take their place. (Both the British prime minister and the German chancellor have been granted similar powers.) This will preserve the President's strength and act as a safety valve for conflict among cabinet members, enabling him to bring them to heel and to induce cohesion. The President, of course, will take no action, still less drastic action, without preliminary soundings in his party and in Congress. He may replace cabinet members who have been ousted by appointing members of the House or Senate, in accordance with the stipulation regarding the qualifications for election to the Presidency and cabinet.

The President and his cabinet will assume the leadership of Congress, sitting in the House of Representatives, which is to be the primary assembly of the legislature, the Senate having been reduced in power and status by loss of its special power over treaties and appointments. The cabinet with the President will participate in congressional business — through messages, through debates, through the answering of questions. To allow for the press of business or special emergencies, leadership of the House may be deputed to the first Vice-President at the discretion of the President. But normally the President will attend sessions of the House two or three times, or more, each week. If it is feared that the duty of attendance would take precious time from the cabinet, then it is an exchange of a more precious good for a less precious one; the President and his cabinet will serve the nation by spending time in the legislature as well as in their offices and committee rooms. They may make fewer speeches to a miscellany of groups, but they will be better able to explain themselves in a responsible forum. To be in immediate touch with Congress will alert cabinet members to local problems and nationwide necessities, teach them the interdependence of all departments, and emphasize the need for a coherent general policy.

There are two very important reasons why the presidential-cabinet should sit in the House and lead its deliberations. When I use the word "reasons" I am not using it in the sense of an exercise in logical ratiocination or the pleasurable exercises of speculation, but in the sense of "the grinding necessities of a reluctant nation." Those grinding necessities are at least two.

First, in order to make effective the wishes of Congress and the people, in order to make effective the responsibility of the President and his cabinet, Congress ought to be a force with an independent base of authority and power. It is all very well to have the President surrounded by assistants, but they remain *his* assistants. If he does not like their advice, he need not take it, and they are in no position to insist, still less to use any kind of sanction or intimidation to compel a rehearing or demand an explanation of why he has refused to follow their counsel in whole or in part. The President's assistants know that the responsibility is his alone, and he may dismiss them, deprive them of their jobs, or ignore them, as President Eisenhower came to ignore Charles Wilson, his Secretary of Defense. The power of asking questions and of giving advice should be the independent power to get answers and to secure action or acceptable explanations. At the present time the President can do what he likes, and there is no one to step in and command him to look, listen, and beware.

Second, there will be better working relations between the executive and legislative branches. A connection exists, but it is faulty and intermittent, without weight or stability; it is that between the party leaders and the President. The fate of Alben Barkley and Senator Joseph Robinson under the scourge of Franklin Roosevelt's ardent and impatient policies may be remembered. (Who would care if another Barkley were to burst into tears if the liaison is efficient and helps to give America a helpful and protective government? No one, I think.) It is necessary to overcome the chasm that separates the branches. They may retain an independence, surely and desirably, without permitting the present ramshackle and immensely wasteful process.

The President Retains Veto Power

It would be wise for the President, after consultation with his cabinet, to retain the present veto power as it is. It could be overruled by 55 per cent of the votes in the House — the President and cabinet having a right to vote in this case. No item veto will be instituted.

I wish to maintain the strength of the presidential-cabinet, yet I wish to raise the influence, dignity, and attractiveness of the House. It is necessary to increase the power of the simple majority of Congress. The Senate is not to participate in the overriding of the veto; this will leave greater power in the House. I hope that the simple majority will enable party organization to be more powerful, less subject to the flight of factions. It is necessary to talk in exact percentages because American constitutionalism, like American football, compels one to bring out a yardstick to measure whether or not a down has been won.

The President May Resign with His Cabinet

At the President's discretion, but only when supported by a majority of his cabinet, the presidential-cabinet may resign. Following this, elections for the House, the Senate, and the presidential-cabinet would take place, the term of office being four years.

It may happen that the President and his cabinet are unable to obtain from Congress the laws, appropriations, and assent to foreign policy they request. They may feel their dignity and authority lost to a point insufferable and the welfare and safety of the nation in jeopardy. They cannot be forced to resign by a vote of no confidence from Congress, but, manifestly, a series of defeats of their measures, after all attempts to arrive at acceptable compromises, allowing for the cabinet's convictions, its sense of responsibility to Congress, the nation, and the party, will make resignation the only course. They then make known their intention to resign. Certainly they will not do so early and often, having spent a lifetime to reach high office. And Congress will not be capricious, destructive, or malicious in refusing to support the President and his cabinet. The opposition party may be zealous and vituperative; let them be so — sweet are the uses of vituperation! It blesses him that gives and him that receives; the attacker lets off steam, the attacked learns something and may find a way to turn the tables on those who censure him. With cabinet members available to respond in full assembly, the party in opposition will not dare to be irresponsible, since, being in full view of public gaze, it must fear that cavilling and caprice will be punished at the next election.

No Patronage, No Spoils — A Senior Civil Service

One day, in a memorable November, the newly elected President of the United States will call in his party managers and address them in these words:

"Let every government worker, regardless of his party, remain on the payroll. I need them; the nation needs them. I intend to trust each and every one to be active in enforcing my policies and enterprising and forceful in advising me faithfully. Only those will be discharged who are proved to be clearly unfaithful or clearly incompetent. My own party's incompetents will be fired, the opposition party's competents will remain at work, and all who remain will be honored for their service."

On that day the United States will have reached maturity, and the President who sees it through, and he will have courage, will be America's greatest President.

The President and the corps of Vice-Presidents will have thereby the assistance of some 4,000 career administrators at the top of the departmental pyramids to advise them on the scientific, technical, and administrative alternatives in the fulfilment of the policies on which their convictions, consciousness, and consciences are set. And hundreds of thousands of subordinate civil servants will carry out the decisions of the nation's statesmen with efficiency, economy, expedition, and continuing regard for the welfare and security of these United States.

Postscript on Political Parties

This postscript is pertinent, but not vital, to the argument of the preceding chapters. For there are people who will ask, "Just what is the relevance of the American system of political parties to a discussion of the regeneration of the Presidency?"

Such a question is likely to be raised by a number of eminent political scientists who believe that if the United States were served by a more coherent, responsible, firmly purposed two-party system the basic deficiencies of government institutions, including the Presidency, would be cured quite simply by the natural operation of the improved political parties.[1]

Their thesis demands consideration, but my general conclusions may be stated briefly at once: The President — to a small but still useful degree — would be assisted in bearing the responsibilities of his office by the more sustained and predictable assistance of reliable colleagues he would find among leaders of the House and Senate, national committees and party councils, if the parties were more thoughtful of and loyal to a national policy and if their organizations were re-formed, the more firmly to express and capture the national pattern of the measures and men the nation, not the diverse localities, needs. Nevertheless, the President's responsibility and burden of office keep him separated from Congress. He is untethered to Congress as an intermediate body standing between him and the nation; insistent upon personal policies which differ from party programs as conceived and manipulated by congressional leaders; he is without equal colleagues deriving their authority from election and formally sharing both his power and his responsibility. The reforms I have proposed remain essential.

Representative and responsible government is party government. When political scientists think to make American political parties more serviceable, they sometimes use a British model. They base their discussion on six characteristics:

First, British political parties are organized nationally. They begin at the grass roots, in cities and counties, and much of their original life is there, but they have freely associated themselves as a part of a nationwide federation. Their purpose is the better definition of national aims, the mobilization of voters for the national solution of national problems, the acquisition of the authority of the electorate for the task of statesmanship at the highest level; and a continuous rendering of an account of their trust to those who elected them. They look upon the nation as a unity, they represent the nation's interest, and they have established permanent national headquarters which, nourished by local units, give identity to their aims, character, and functions. American scholars would like such nation-building party institutions in operation in the United States.

Second, British political parties make themselves responsible for conceiving a pattern of a good society, that is, a general picture of what the nation ought to be and how the party must proceed to effectuate this society. Each party, of course, has its own picture. Emphatically, this does *not* imply the ideology of fanatics, but it does urge a kind of civil fellowship among all the separate interests, groups, and individuals that abound in the nation, holding particular views about what is morally and economically worthwhile in guiding one's life in that sphere where law can be helpful. Each party has a national vision, but the national vision of each is not exclusive or separatist, and it does not lead to violence, national disruption, or uncivic rancor, except among a handful of extremists who will be found in the best regulated societies. The parties fit regional differences and the differences of special interest groups into a coherent Conservative, Labour, or Liberal view of what is good and bad.[2] This is what many American political scientists wish to emulate.

Third, British political parties are in continuous operation. Their educational function never relaxes, their flow of literature never ceases, their pressure on members of Parliament and the cabinet continues from day to day; their readiness for by-elections is always evident. The national executives of each party, drawn from members of Parliament, members of the party outside Parliament, and party career officials and research workers, are in being and in vigorous operation from campaign to campaign. At a time of election they are at a peak of excited activity, but when the campaign is over they continue their operations and maintain a high level of animation among the electorate and elected officials.

Fourth, British political parties have party conferences annually. The conferences last for several days and are composed of delegates sent by local party committees. They come together to create the party program, to debate the work of party head-quarters and representatives in Parliament, to vote the platform, and to elect officers. There is an annual review of men and policy, an annual establishment of authority at the top at the direction of the grass roots, an annual necessity to develop an accommodation among all the prophets in the bosom of the party, and a clear promise to the nation of the party's plan for the nation.

Fifth, each member of Parliament has accepted the bylaws and program of the party, established by the annual conference; has expressed loyalty to national policy; and is expected to be loyal to the decisions of his party caucus which implement national policy from day to day. Parliamentary caucuses meet frequently, and their decisions, taken after long and hot debate, are binding. He considers himself first a member of a party, not the representative of a sovereign district, as members of Congress tend to do. He has his chance to dissent, his opportunity to find among other members enough support to amend, divert, or quash party policy, if he has the arguments to do so, is persuasive, and wishes to do so on the grounds of national policy. And he is allowed a certain latitude on conscientious grounds. If he becomes an habitual abstainer from party policy in Parliament, or if he shows an inclination to break away from the caucus, he will not be indorsed by national headquarters as a candidate at the next election, and lacking this party designation it is almost certain that he will lose his seat.

Sixth, the party is a link between the electorate, the members of Parliament, and the prime minister and cabinet. The party is a conveyor of political authority to Parliament and the cabinet; and it conveys, from cabinet and Parliament to the people, a degree of political responsibility.

These are the characteristics of British political parties that American scholars admire and believe will cure many of the awkwardnesses of national leadership. I have not thought it relevant to set forth a full and intricate account of party realities in Britain and all the nuances to be observed.

American scholars would have the Democratic and Republican parties embrace within their organizations all representatives, senators, and the President as permanent active members of a nationwide fellowship of principle and policy. *If* this should materialize, the gap between congressional and presidential leadership, which leads to grave flaws in policy and execution irritating to both branches and confusing to the electorate, would be bridged.[3] The constititutional separation of powers would be served by the political parties only where it was judged to be good. In this new dispensation the President would be encouraged, guided, by a party platform that was a true, if general, commitment to the electorate. This program would be a definite, activating, co-ordinating, impulse-giving element in his administration, to assist him, to be molded by him, and to prevail.

In structure, the party would have identity; its policy would be a national promise; the election of legislators and executives from its midst, a commitment; and political office would be a common and accountable trust. The fellowship of party thus envisioned would permit, require, and support an easy and continuous connection between the President and the top leaders in the party. The President has always been helped by party leaders, especially by those who belong to the majority bloc, and by the chairmen of congressional committees, in the enactment and financing of the policies he has espoused.

Scholars who argue so believe that the strengthening of political parties, their endowment with a national vision, would overcome the specific weaknesses of the Presidency, namely, his being one and alone, his lack of equal colleagues, his burden of office. He would be supported and comforted by party policy and by party colleagues.

Let us examine this thesis. If the Presidency remains as it is, untouched by reform, the improvement, as the result of the improvement of the quality of the parties, would be limited, though there would be some positive help. But as long as the President retains sole responsibility he is as little likely to call on the services of his party as at present he utilizes his cabinet members or shares his responsibility and authority with them. Furthermore, as long as Congress is invested with powers under the Constitution it requires its own apparatus of leadership. Therefore, party fellowship (as in Britain) is not possible, except at times like the Hundred Days of Franklin Roosevelt's first administration in 1933 and not lasting much beyond a crisis of fear. The British system, unlike the American, does not make a basic distinction between an ordinary member of Parliament and one who, after long years of distinguished service in Parliament, has been chosen a member of the prime minister's cabinet.

The President could be helped considerably to bear his constitutional load if he were acknowledged to be the leader of his party, if his party were a party, but for party reforms to be genuine and of utility would require that the President make a career of politics and advance to leadership while sharing with members of his party common experience in Congress. In other words, something very like the proposals I have outlined. Otherwise, the President remains a stranger to Congress and his party.

If American political parties were well developed, the President might well appoint the leaders of his party as cabinet members; but this would require them to vacate their seats in Congress, and much of the advantage of their appointment would be lost — unless the Constitution were amended to allow these men, and only these, to continue as members of Congress. If party cohesion were more firmly developed, the President might use his party colleagues in Congress as an unofficial but effective cabinet, much as he now makes use of his conferences with the "Big Four" or the "Big Six," the Speaker and majority leader of the House, the majority leader of the Senate, the Vice-President, and one or two congressional leaders close to these men. The number could be increased at will, and for his benefit, until we have established the Joint Council of Executive and Congress often proposed.[4]

Yet, the President's sole responsibility would remain — and this is the crux of the problem today. The President needs a collective council of colleagues having equal elective support and elective authority to assist and debate with him. There is everything to be said for devices to secure more sustaining help from the party for the President, but those proposed, I'm afraid, will not substitute for the pressing remedies that are needed.

It is difficult for a single leader, standing outside such a legislative body as Congress, to obtain the confidence, support, and affection he requires. One man, even a man of one's own party, is an open invitation to members of a numerous body with diverse local ties to take sides, quite sharply, for him or against him. If the executive were collective (or plural, or multiple, its synonyms), the chances of accommodation by Congress would be greater. Cabinet proposals would have a greater chance of a fair hearing and would not, from the outset, be doomed *in toto*.

The President might avail himself of such corporate party connections in seeking information and discovering and benefiting from the terms of co-operation. The President and Congress are more likely to inspire trust in each other, and unify their policies, if there is a composite nucleus around the President, drawn from a single party but with all its nuances taken into account, than through the confrontation of one man by 531, or 531 by one man.

Nothing could be more fissiparous than the fragmentation of American policy among the several committees of Congress, yet past and present evidence shows that the committee chairmen of a party in opposition to the incumbent President are often more ready to go along with his proposals than with certain elements in their own party.

I am inclined to believe that the melding of the agencies of political leadership — Congress and the President — would be assisted by the flanking of the President with elected colleagues who presented no obdurate phalanx to Congress except when first proposing policy and again at the moment of decision and action, in between deploying and exploring representative alternatives.

Some improvement of the President's instruments would follow the solidification of parties; but all that can be said is that *if* leaders of Congress agreed with presidential policy party incoherence and defection would be reduced and the program of the President and the high command of his party would prevail. *If* the other party were strengthened, the nation and the President would reap the benefits of an organized opposition — truly a help to the President because it presents a coherent alternative to his own proposals, truly a help to the nation because it assists in clarifying the issues and compels an explanatory response from the administration.

The crucial question is: Are we likely to get such parties? In the course of the next twenty years, another five presidential campaigns, there is a possibility that we might. Ever since 1865 two stubborn and grim factors have obstructed the formation of nationwide parties informed by a coherent pattern of values and cohesion in party action in Congress. They are the sectionalism of the so-called Solid South and the isolationism of the Midwest, the one militating against integration of the Democratic party, the other, of the Republican party.[5]

Racial sectionalism, with which is joined economic backwardness, is gradually (too gradually for me), but nevertheless perceptibly, being modified by the increase in voting rights, educational and economic opportunity, and the migration of Negroes from the South; and perhaps even more by a revolt of indignation on the part of Negroes and sympathetic whites, which ultimately will make impossible the more disgusting forms of political reaction. Voteless acquiescence and subservient votes will not be tolerated. Already there are promising links with Democratic fortunes outside the South, or, according to preference, with Republican party embryos in the South. Either will produce a healthier national party alignment than that which now exists.

Further, the developing industrialization of the South implies an assimilation of a hitherto sectional economy to that of the rest of the nation. It stimulates political concern in the national economy, the differentiation of upper, middle, and working-class interests and ways of life, and nourishes affinities with class interests in other parts of the nation. Thus Democratic and Republican parties grow more nationalized and lose the blight of "white supremacy." National concern in the fields of education, the social services, social security, and defense have a unifying effect, and the taking of sides about these matters tends to cut across the rancors of race and even of class.

With the growing impact of the conscience of the world, the United States, in open competition with the Soviet Union and the world of Pacific and Asian peoples (newspaper accounts and debates in the United Nations make it impossible to ignore tales of suffering and reproach and the many pleas for help), will find it expedient to take decisive action and put an end to filibustering, thus to reaffirm the Bill of Rights and insure civil rights for all.

Nor is this the only way for the Democratic party to become one party instead of two. Its leaders could follow the courage of President Truman and conceive and carry out its policy on the basis of justice, human rights, and prudence for all, and risk the defection of the Dixiecrats. The Democratic party can function without begging the vote of the South.

As for the Republican party, its sectionalism is caused by the contest between the industrial-commercial faction and the farm vote, the antagonism between Midwestern isolationists and the "internationalists" of the East and the Far West. Neither rivalry carries the force that it once did. Economic evolution has done away with the first, and the second is vanishing as ethnic minorities from Europe are assimilated beyond the rancors and remembered romanticism of early settlers, immigrant Germans, Poles, Russians, Scandinavians, who wanted no truck with Europe on the terms proposed by this American political party or that, and because the facts of modern warfare and economic internationalism and political education tend, too visibly, to erode the possibility of isolationism. Communications, the mass media, television sets in every home, destroy the geographic isolation of the Midwest, if such isolation, especially in rural areas, is accounted the cause of spiritual isolationism in world affairs.

Yet we may expect nationwide Democratic and Republican political parties to be of looser structure than the parties in Britain by reason of the enormous size and variation of this country, the rough egoism of interest groups, assisted by the constitutional provision that each state have two senators regardless of its population or economic importance.

There are political scientists who have argued that firmly based and intentioned political parties are impossible in the United States; and if they were possible they would not be desirable.[6] They point to the traditional disputes which divide the parties as well as the factions we have mentioned. They emphasize the great area, and its diversities, as contributing factors, making impossible the integration of a single national view. I believe they exaggerate. Some argue that Americans are inclined to fanaticism and that if two sides formed and were firm in structure the hostility aroused would be enough to split the nation. For illustration they point to the outbreak of the Civil War. This argument I find much too far-fetched. Others make a rather sordid forecast, and it is fortunate that only an occasional voice is heard in its support: If political parties were organizations with a pattern of a good society to guide them, it would be impossible for individuals to ask favors, for such requests would be rejected as not being in the public interest espoused by the party.

I side with those many scholars who believe that a party system, with the general characteristics (not identical!) of the British, springing from American needs and molded by American experience, is both possible and desirable. For example, as described by S. K. Bailey:

> Contrary to the view of many writers, the parties do not need to be strongly ideological or even strongly programmatic — that is, beholden to comprehensive and distinct sets of policies — in order to accomplish the kind of re-alignment of the party system that would stabilize the national power and help to make it responsible. There are vast areas of overlap in the rather vague programmatic shadows that our two great parties cast over the nation — and this is as it should be if consensus is to continue in the making of public policy and in the administration of foreign policy.
>
> But the centers of gravity of the two parties are quite distinct. The Democratic party is basically a party of innovation, with a "pro-government" bias. The Republican party is an essentially "consolidating" party with a limited government bias. . . .[7]

But if such parties do not become better developed, all the more need for the regeneration of the Presidency along the lines I have drawn. Indeed, the tendency toward improved political parties will be encouraged and made the more feasible if these suggestions are carried out. They will conduce to the formulation of nationwide policies, on alternative bases of values and interests, carried into effect by rival nationwide organizations. If every four years the nation proceeded to the nomination and election of a President and eleven Vice-Presidents, with a collective responsibility for the supreme statesmanship in the nation, such a process would be astringent, concentrating, focusing. The twelve-man presidential team would include leaders of the various main tendencies within each party brought together in the nominating process after experience in Congress. Some will answer this argument with the fear that diverse minds and characters will spring the executive apart. I believe this fear to be unfounded, given the nominating process, the fact of collective appearance on the presidential ticket of a single party, and, further, the fact that American politicians have long been immersed in the practice of Anglo-Saxon political institutions and behavior. Nor can we ignore the increasingly strong tendencies that make the nation a single unit in its economic, social, and moral problems and the responses of the federal government everywhere and equally thereto. Party extremists, as in all democratic systems that have attained routine stability, would be maneuvered to the outside; the moderates would govern and agree, with the usual conflicts and resolution of conflicts that are experienced everywhere among men of character, conviction, and responsibility. Moderation in this sense is contrasted with extremism; it does not connote a lack of conviction, creativity, cleverness, or courage, or any of those other qualities we have seen to be essential to American political leadership in this turbulent century. Such qualities are not reliably found in any one man; they are qualities much more surely possessed by a condominium of collectively elected executive colleagues.

Diverse Proposals for Presidential Reform

In recent years many scholars have devoted their attention to an examination of the strengths and deficiencies of the Presidency, and some interesting and symptomatic proposals have been formulated. I would like to give a brief account of some of the most typical.

Questions in Congress

It is proposed by certain scholars that the heads of departments, especially the cabinet members, be subject to questions by Congress in joint session at regular and frequent intervals (twice a week is suggested) as in the House of Commons and the lower houses of the British Dominions (where, however, questions are asked four days a week during sessions).

It may be objected that the time spent by cabinet members in Congress would decrease the amount of time they have for their regular duties. It would certainly force them to reorder their work load, which might be all to the good. It would mean curtailment of many public speeches, many of which could as well be given by their assistants. The highest government officials are

329

entitled to limit their public appearances or confine them to appearances on television where the largest possible audience can be reached.

Doubtless, in appearing before Congress cabinet members would have to rely on a few advisers to assemble the material on which they are to be questioned; but this would bring to bear on the advisers some of the determination of Congress, some of the perplexities concerning the conduct of the departments. Publicity of this kind is as good for the questioner as for the person who is questioned. It is possible that each department head would rely on one or two career men with an alert, informed, and comprehensive view, and this in turn might lead to the appointment of a permanent civil service career official to head the department and have authority over the various branches of the department.

I must, in frankness, express some doubt whether questions asked cabinet members can be as significant a means of control as it is in the British system. Questions in Congress could not commit the President to the course of action proposed or implied in the answers given by cabinet members. One can easily imagine the quarrel at the next cabinet meeting if one member of the cabinet had made such a commitment to Congress before clearing it with the rest. Of course if the answering of congressional questions led to the desired clearance so that collective counsel came to prevail, it would be a welcome improvement of the present system.

One of the most important instruments for securing co-ordination among the many departments and an acceptable momentum in the British government is precisely the asking of questions day after day. When several hundred legislators are stimulated to put their minds upon a single problem, the question is bound to arise if they are working to help each other, considering the implied criticism offered by those who question.

In seeking for a means of administrative co-ordination, the President's Committee on Administrative Management (1936) thought of every possible device except the tremendous and fundamental efficacy of an external legislative controlling body. The committee did not think of it because it was concentrated on the executive branch alone, and it was so concentrated because the committee members believed that the salvation of the nation, insofar as it depends upon action of government, lay in the executive branch and not in Congress. Administrative co-ordination cannot be left to instruments and procedures within the executive branch alone, still less to one man.

Cabinet Members to Appear before Congress

The government of the United States has benefited since Woodrow Wilson resumed the pre-Jeffersonian practice of appearing before Congress to present presidential policy at his will and with the Speaker's permission. Who could have predicted its inestimable value? At the very least it enables the President to use Congress as a sounding board for the nation. Department chiefs have the opportunity (some would say too much opportunity) to appear before congressional committees in order to advocate bills and appropriations emanating from their departments. But the public at large does not hear the discussions and cannot take the measure of congressmen, department heads, or the policies advocated. It is no answer to say that whosoever wishes may obtain a transcript of the hearings or that some newspapers summarize the hearings. A full report is generally some days or weeks away; and the press does not report discussion with any great comprehension. Only if congressional hearings were televised would there be an opportunity of gauging proposed policy.

Let departmental chiefs, in the matter of the most important bills and policies, say to Congress in full session what they say to its committees. Let them present their bills before the two assemblies, together or apart. If, as a result of this procedure, the President must make a preliminary commitment, let it be made publicly. Let the Secretary of Labor present to Congress the bill he tells the press is so much better than the bills already proposed. Let the implications of a presidential veto of a housing bill be explained in Congress by the proper department head, in a properly reasoned speech, followed by the observations of the majority and minority leaders of Congress.

Article One, section 6, of the Constitution says: "No person holding any office under the United States shall be a member of either House during his continuance in office." The executive branch cannot limit the freedom of congressmen in the exercise of their independent judgment, as George III, through his ministers, exercised an influence over the House of Commons and the House of Lords. But that influence was dependent on patronage and prestige; the prestige waned, and the patronage was abolished. The President deploys much patronage, the prime minister and British cabinet none. The President has found ways and means to exercise such power without being a member of Congress.

The President, faced with the prospect of having his department heads speak in Congress, will choose them with a view to their ability to do so as well as for other abilities. If a cabinet member had to defend a proposal, had to take a part in a public debate in Congress and make a speech of rebuttal in conclusion, the experience would prove a powerful benefit to the relationship between the President and Congress. The public would be alerted to the advantages and disadvantages of the proposals. Cabinet members would be encouraged in a common concern, and each would see when he was wrongly understood and would be careful not to intrude upon the affairs of another department.

Joint Executive-Legislative Council

Edward S. Corwin has observed the dreadful problems that imperil the nation and has reflected on the development and present competence of the institutions of top leadership in America in much the same way as I have evaluated them. But his attention is focused chiefly on the tortured leadership resulting from the separation of legislature and President, not on the sole responsibility of the President. Corwin is not a man of complacent disposition. He proposes a "new type of cabinet," to

> consist of legislative leaders plus department heads and even the head of independent commissions, as the business at hand may require. The legislative member of the Congress would derive from a joint legislative Council drawn from the two Houses and would be subject to change by them without notice.[1]

Corwin presumes that the presence of legislative leaders would end the practice of reducing the cabinet to an organ that meets infrequently and is thus rendered ineffective as a collective body for cogent thought and decision. He points out that "Presidents have been able to treat their Cabinets casually because the political strength of the Chief Executive is normally vastly superior to that of the department heads." [2] He does not mention the chief reason why the President fails to consult the cabinet — that the Constitution gives to the President alone the responsibility and the authority to act. Corwin believes that congressional leaders should have "enough independent power to make the President value their support." They could help him by promoting his measures in Congress; and they would control the President's whims. Such an alteration, Corwin says, would "provide the sort of consensus that is now lacking, though popular government inherently needs it, especially in an era of stress and uncertainty." [3]

Corwin would have the President choose a cabinet and consult with it concerning all important problems of state before making a decision; Congress, in turn, would pledge itself to consider and act on all the proposals of the President, whether or not they had been approved by the Joint Legislative Council.

What benefits does Corwin expect of his proposals? They are three. In the first place, the President would no longer have so many occasions for "autocratic courses and irresponsible pronouncements," since the lawmaking power would have been made available to him. Second, the processes of compromise, vital in a democratic government, would be enhanced, and the antagonisms between the branches of government would be reduced, since the relationship between them would be clearly understood. Third, representatives of local and national interests would be united in accord with the democratic system. [4]

One critic of Corwin's proposals offers some penetrating comments. The President would be forced to take the advice of a group not entirely chosen by himself, and the "flexibility of the present arrangement" would be lost (what irony to speak of "flexibility"). [5] Because the President has sole responsibility for the executive branch, the arguments of the founders of the Republic remain valid: If the President has the responsibility, he must have the right to appoint as he wishes. But Corwin does not deny the President the right to appoint cabinet members and department heads. The President is constrained only to meet with them more regularly, in the company of congressional leaders; he is not forced to do as they wish but only to consult them before coming to a decision. If we allow the President to maintain a kitchen cabinet, no objection can be made to Corwin's proposal that congressional legislators take part in cabinet meetings.

Difficulties — to the point of collapse — would arise when congressional leaders were of a party opposed to the President. If the simultaneous election of the two branches were instituted, Corwin's proposal would be more likely to succeed; we would expect Congress and the President to be of the same party. The proposal would have to remain in abeyance for those periods when the two branches were occupied by different parties.

However, though Corwin is surely aware that the deficiencies of statesmanship he wishes to remedy stem from the solitary responsibility imputed by the Constitution to the President, he does not bring this to the fore. Yet this factor is the root of both the aggrandizement of the President's power that Corwin deplores and the national perils that follow inevitably from putting the weight of Mount Everest on a mortal man. Atlas himself could not bear it.

A Central Council

Corwin's approach to the regeneration of American leadership is paralleled by Charles S. Hyneman, a percipient, well-informed student of the American tradition. It is after much mental travail that Hyneman concludes:

> I think there is evidence throughout this book that we have not achieved the consistency in instructions from the two political branches that the nation has a right to demand. It seems to me that the American people are confronted by a compelling need to make the political and governmental changes which promise to reduce conflict between Congress and President and give us decisions which are the result of agreement between the two political branches of our government.[6]

Hyneman observes that the founders of the Republic wrought their institutions when government had few and petty duties and treachery and oppression were much to be feared; and that there was no way of holding one branch of government within limits except by having the other two act as checks and balances. But, as I have pointed out elsewhere, the political parties which the founders of the Republic abhorred as potential and even certain dividers of the nation have become instruments for choosing the men who govern as well as for governing the men they choose — with some help from nagging pressure groups, the press, and others.[7]

Anxious to be helpful, but unwilling to offer remedies the people might not be able to utilize because unusual to their habitual ways of acting politically, Hyneman presents an argument and practical suggestions of an ameliorative nature. He insists that the President must continue to "supply vigorous leadership in legislation" because as a candidate he has made promises and supported them by argument during his election campaign, and Congress "can rarely if ever provide a leadership that the nation will listen to as the authoritative voice concerning the plans of the party that has been elevated to power."

Congress is needed to exercise its counterinfluence with integrity, courage, and independence, to prevent the President from forcing Congress to do his bidding. Yet we have shown that the veto power and the advent of moments of crisis give the President just this power. After all, nothing for nothing is the supreme rule of politics, and it implies force versus force. Hyneman looks on Congress as "the brake on the President and the administrative branch" rather than as itself a source of initiatory leadership, but he does not wish it to be a strong and truly independent brake; instead, he proposes a central council, "to improve working relationship at the top of our government that seems to me badly in need of improvement."

What is this central council and what are its objectives? It would consist of the leaders of the President's party, a small group chosen by him from Congress. Under leadership of the President they would choose others, some holding congressional positions, some heads of departments, some party leaders outside public office. This body would have responsibility to formulate and direct the execution of the program of the government-of-the-day.[8] The benefits of the arrangements would be to reduce greatly the likelihood that the President would personally and publicly commit his party to programs he could not induce his party to carry out. The council would make it more difficult for individual congressmen and others to seem to commit the party to policies they cannot get the party as a whole to accept.

The men on the council who are in Congress would hold important strategic posts in Congress, committee chairmanships and so on, as decided by the council. Of course, if Congress itself balked at this, the council would be of little use; the same would be true if the President was unable to gather men for the council simultaneously acceptable to him and influential with the party in Congress.

Hyneman realizes that a government divided between a President belonging to one party and a Congress controlled in one or both of its houses by a majority from the opposition party would be little helped by this device. But he argues that it would be no worse than the present situation. He is concerned, as I have been, with the incompetence of the cabinet "as an advisory body for the President or as a co-ordinating device for administration." He believes that its incompetence may stem from the fact that many cabinet posts go to men who are not influential members of the President's party. This may be true — but we have shown that "party" is a loose term, and that the President's solitariness as a candidate and as Chief Executive makes it virtually impossible for him to trust any cabinet. This is the major weakness needing cure, far more important than the separation of Congress and President, to which Hyneman, rightly, gives so much constructive care. His proposal would be of some considerable assistance, of course, in what we regard as the major problem.

The proposals for improvement of the executive branch and, with it, of its relationship with Congress, made by Corwin and Hyneman, are a more advanced variant of the proposal made by the Joint Committee on the Reorganization of Congress in its 1946 report. It is advocated by others who have studied the Constitution as it is interpreted today.

> That the majority policy committees of the Senate and the House serve as a formal council to meet regularly with the Executive, to facilitate the formulation and carrying out of national policy, and to improve relationships between the executive and legislative branches of government. . . .

The committee stated that its purpose was "to narrow the widening gap between the executive and legislative branches."

Appreciation of the intolerable weight of the Presidency was well expressed in 1936 by William Y. Elliott.[9] He proposed that the President be assisted by a large secretariat, and that this new body report daily to the President and the cabinet members. Their reports were not to come to the political chiefs in the form of departmental detail but in terms of groups of related activities which make up the total affairs of the federal government. Accordingly, the secretariat was to be organized into five divisions — fiscal, defense, social security, business conditions, and national planning. Each section was to form a board, with political appointees at the head of each; and each board was to integrate the activities and policies of the several departments individually responsible for the specific field. Presidential assistants were to be secretaries of various advisory councils to the boards, and their chairmen were to be selected from the best qualified congressional committee chairmen and cabinet members.

The service that the secretariat would render to the President would be, first, to indicate lines of policy and the probable effects and difficulties that might result. The secretariat would give the President the benefit of independent research and advise him of the congressional acceptability and the feasibility of policies under consideration.

Yet, with his experience in the practical operation of goverment, Elliott uttered this warning:

> If cabinet members continue to be chosen for the combination of political "availability" and fair-grade administrative talent — the President must turn elsewhere for that discussion and informal presentation of administrative policy which he so much needs.

In the twenty-three years since this warning was given, the fear it expresses has been borne out and the prospects of substantial improvement are no better than they were. For the trouble, as we have seen, is that the President alone is responsible for final decisions and cannot rely on his auxiliaries, the White House executive staff. The conditions of his election do not permit him to do a much better job of surrounding himself with cabinet members and others of like position with the qualities asked by Elliott. The problem is grave. It is the lack of a multiheaded mind and conscience vested with responsibility that makes the exercise of responsibility barely possible and renders the decisions of government of dubious efficacy.

A Presidential-Cabinet System

Charles Hardin, more deeply and expertly steeped in farm politics than any other political scientist in the United States, has found it necessary to go further than any of the proposals so far appraised.[10] He is distressed by the lack of government equipment necessary to meet and overcome the pernicious domestic and international dangers. Hardin is convinced of the nation's mortal danger, as expressed in the Rockefeller report. To meet that danger he is ready to propose something like a cabinet system of government. But Hardin does not call it a cabinet system. First, he would wish to discard the practice of electing the President for a fixed term — not so much because the man may be physically unable to fulfil the responsibilities of office but because he may not be qualified by intellect and character to meet these responsibilities. Hence, Hardin would have the President elected for a five-year term, with the proviso that, if necessary, he may be called upon to resign from office.

Second, the President, to be elected by the nation, would be required upon nomination to fill out a slate of ten candidates to run with him on his ticket. To decide the names to be included he would consult his party leaders; this he would do in order to insure their support during the election campaign. These ten would be the nucleus of his future cabinet. The President would retain his present powers, but the veto power would be amended. He would acquire an added power — the right to ask that Congress be dissolved and a new Congress elected. This is a most drastic addition to the President's powers.

Third, the President and his cabinet would sit in the House of Representatives, lead, have a vote in it, and be prepared to defend their policies before it. The losing presidential candidate would be the minority leader, and his ten colleagues on the rival ticket would form with him a kind of shadow cabinet.

Hardin's system meets certain requisites of American political leadership appropriate to the needs of this threatening age. It provides for a collegiate body closely integrated with the President. It provides for a national spotlight to be focused on them at election and during their tenure in office. It provides for a far more integrated leadership of Congress than we have at present. It provides for a concerted opposition composed of a team which commended itself to public attention at the last election and will again at the next.

Fourth, the veto power of the President would need modification within the devices proposed. When the President's own party is in control of the House, the veto would not be used except to block a congressional demand for the resignation of the President and his cabinet. A simple majority of the House could overrule this veto in order to avoid dissolution and give Congress the opportunity for reconsideration of its action. But if the opposition party was in control of Congress, as occurred in 1848, 1876, 1956, and 1958, the President would use the veto as he does now, and Congress could override it with a two-thirds majority.

Fifth, the term in office for the President and members of House and Senate would be five years, and there would be simultaneous elections. The President would have the right to dissolve Congress at his own discretion. On the other hand, Congress could rid itself of an unwanted President by enacting a bill to that effect.

Sixth, the Senate would be much reduced in power. Like the House, it, too, could be dissolved.

Seventh, by these measures the House would be raised to the major forum of government. It might have a neutral Speaker, since leadership would be provided by the President. The unequal districts would be corrected, and national law would regulate the elections of all national officers.

Hardin believes that with the foregoing proposals, though he does not provide expressly for the replacement of a President disabled physically, he has established the conditions under which his replacement would be possible and accepted. The President would be tested in an exacting forum for his qualities of leadership. Candidates for the Presidency might be drawn from the House itself. The system would encourage a stronger consolidation of the two major political parties.

Hardin would add to these proposals extraconstitutional arrangements designed to refuse party indorsement to members who persistently fail to follow the party's collective decisions. He considers various ancillary and consequential factors. Primaries for the selection of congressional candidates would be jettisoned; national party organizations would indorse candidates. The electorate would choose parties rather than individuals. Prospective congressmen would be expected to make commitments to the policy of their party or lose the chance of nomination.

A Responsible Opposition Leader

Paul T. David, director of governmental studies at Brookings Institution, notes that in the last fifteen presidential contests the party out of power won only five; as a result the United States has had a change of administration only once every twelve years. It is rare that a defeated candidate is renominated by his own party. The feat was accomplished for the first time by Grover Cleveland in 1892 and was repeated by Bryan in 1900. Dewey was the first unsuccessful Republican to be renominated (1948). Adlai Stevenson was given a second try by the Democrats. It may be that the parties are no longer anxious to discard their erstwhile leaders.

David believes it is most important for the healthy maintenance of a steady critique of the administration's forces to support the leader of the opposition party, though the leader has no official status once he is defeated.[11] David proposes to do this by asking Congress to provide the opposition leader with an annual salary of $50,000 (and expenses) and to allow him full access to government information, confidential as well as routine. This would make it possible for the leader to continue to function " in a position of dignity and recognized responsibility," as a leader of public opinion, making pronouncements on all necessary occasions, acting as the focus of party strategy for members of his party in Congress, guiding the organization of congressional campaigns, and preparing for the next presidential elections.

Very soon after the inauguration of the new President, the opposition leader could take charge of national headquarters and co-operate with and guide the work of the national and congressional campaign committees. There would be weekly meetings with congressional leaders, press conferences, and equal time on television and radio whenever the President's party is allowed it.

If his conduct of opposition leadership is found unsatisfactory by the party, he can be replaced at midterm. Whatever is decided, whether the party leader is retained or replaced, the party will have time to reorganize or otherwise strengthen its platform before the next campaign, by then only two years off.

This suggestion has great merits. Even if it were not feasible in the form proposed, some similar system, as I have suggested earlier, is needed to answer one of the most important lacks — an organized opposition — in the American political system.

Proposals for Congressional Reform

Deficiencies of Congress

1. The cohesive force of party sentiment and loyalty is lacking in Congress to a degree dangerous for the efficient organization and statement of national interest, vision, and policy. Party identification plays a considerable part in arriving at effective majorities to create and control top leadership policy in the conduct of domestic and foreign affairs; it provides, as well, an effective minority to find, pronounce, and prosecute alternate views. Even so, at critical junctures party identification is an uncertain guide, not to be depended upon, and offering an unpredictable, faltering, often jittery response to national need. Too many in the nucleus of each party are without agreed platforms, without regular fellowship of interest and ideals, and unable to escape the influence of pressure groups; and some members of each party are certain to be stubborn dissenters to any proposal.

2. There is far too little nationwide concern for the competence of the men who issue from the district to compose the nation's Congress; there is no established standard of ability, character, and political astuteness which must be met, and those who

are elected show undue concern for the welfare of their loudest constituents and too little for the welfare of the nation and the state of the world.

3. Congress is elected according to state election laws and state administration, and this deprives the election process of the national character it sorely needs. State-administered elections interfere with the solidification of party policy and organization for national objectives.

4. The residence rule as a qualification for Congress excludes talent, excludes from national politics men of brains and character who are ruled unqualified, and maintains the monopoly of local men who may be inferior to their potential competitors and are unable to benefit from the stimulation of rivalry.

5. The assumption of national statesmanship by Congress is frustrated by the widespread misapprehension that a member of Congress is no more than an agent of his district or state and is not expected to make important decisions regarding the nation as a whole. The fastidiousness of members of Congress, and their independence of mind when confronted by pressure groups, is enfeebled by the same confusion of primary responsibility.

6. The two-year tenure of Congress is too short to sustain the political detachment of legislators and militates against their educating themselves in national affairs.

7. The precious time of congressmen is wasted by constituents and lobbying groups asking special favors. The congressman is used as an errand boy when he might be developing his understanding of national policy.

8. Off-year elections certainly interfere with and sometimes destroy the unification of government and the articulation of national programs.

9. The several electoral periods for the offices of Congress and the Senate further disrupt the national vision; there is not a single American electorate but (including the Presidency) three — one for two years, in 435 districts; one for six years, broken every two years, for the Senate; and the President's own four-year term.

10. Legislative procedure in Congress is not directed in the service of the nation by the unifying influence of coherent party platforms, for:

a) Congress lacks a steady and responsible collective mind to propose, announce, and conduct its agenda;

b) departmental appropriations are not weighed against each other with sufficient deliberation, nor are specific appropriations adequately assessed;

c) appropriations are not weighed against the policy of taxation and what is economically sound;

d) legislation is concocted in the obscurity of committee rooms, with too little debate in open forum at the stage of substantive decision;

e) the Rules Committee of twelve members has excessive power, especially so when the custom of seniority misrepresents the mind of Congress as a whole. Seniority is not a reward of political merit; it simply gives status and power to men who have managed to retain a seat in Congress; these men are elected from "backward" areas, areas unprogressive socially and politically; as a result the Rules Committee is in no way representative of the United States as a whole;

f) rural over-representation in Congress, especially in decisive positions, is a blemish, a subordination of the nation to a minority of less-progressive citizens; and

g) the system of investigation by congressional committee has serious weaknesses.

11. Congress is without a concerted and responsible opposition to the President and to government departments.

12. The control by Congress of administrative policy is close and fairly continuous, but it loses effect by its tardiness, its personal irresponsibility, its want of persistence in enforcement, and its failure to provide enough opportunities for members of Congress to appear in open assembly before the people and the nation's press.

13. Congress, in the enactment of laws, the provision of appropriations, the levy of taxes, and the control of government policy, is inefficient; and an inefficient Congress brands itself as irresponsible.

Proposed Remedies

In apologetic brevity I list recommendations which will serve to enhance the political leadership of Congress.

1. Every aspect of elections to the House of Representatives and the Senate should be ruled by laws passed by Congress and not by the states, since Congress is the nation's legislature.

2. No state or local elections should take place on the day designated for elections of the House, the Senate, or the President.

3. Elections for the House, the Senate, and the President should be for the same term, four or five years; not staggered; and should be held on the same day. Off-year elections are thereby obviated.

4. The number of representatives should be increased to 600, to make the House rather more representative than is possible with only 435 members.

5. The residence rule should be expunged from the statutes and weakened as a custom.

6. The representation of districts should be reformed to arrive as closely as possible at equal representation for equal population.

7. Party caucuses should have authority over policy and voting loyalty.

8. The parties should resolve that merit as judged by party policy be the criterion for service on congressional committees, not seniority *per se*.

9. Majority rule should be established in the Senate by the abolition of the right to filibuster.

10. Committee investigations should be more firmly ruled for cogency of questioning and relevance to moderate the punitive impulses of some members.

11. A period for questions to be put to members of the President's cabinet should be instituted on two or three days every week, in full session of Congress, possibly in joint session.

12. Room should be made on the calendar for adequate periods of debate on resolutions concerning the administration's measures in all aspects of domestic and foreign policy, and these debates should be conducted in full assembly of House and Senate without extraneous business allowed to interrupt, as now occurs.

Notes

INTRODUCTION. "A More Perfect Union"

1. Eisenhower press conference, July 25, 1957. The actual words were, "I was very hard put to it when [Zhukov, in Berlin, shortly after 1945] insisted that [the communist] system appealed to the idealistic, and we completely to the materialistic, and I had a very tough time trying to defend our position."

2. The comparative number of science and engineering graduates in 1959 is, according to Mikoyan, 106,000 (Russia) and 35,000 (United States). In 1956 it was 60,000 and 30,000 respectively.

3. George V. Allen, director of the U.S. Information Agency, before the House Science and Astronautics Committee (January 22, 1960): "The achievement of placing in orbit the first earth satellite, without great advance fanfare, increased the prestige of the Soviet Union tremendously and produced a corresponding loss of United States prestige. . . . The Soviets were greatly exceeding world expectation of their scientific and technological capacities; we, on the other hand, were falling short of world expectation of us. . . . One interesting — and perhaps dangerous — effect of Soviet success in space has been the new credibility it has lent to Soviet claims in these other fields."

4. The figures are taken from the first two volumes of *Papers for the Subcommittee on Economic Statistics of the Joint Economic Committee of the U.S. Congress*, 1959.

5. Herbert Levine, in *New Leader*, June 1, 1959.

6. Editorial, *Life*, November 23, 1959. A more alarming note is sounded in the same journal, February 15, 1960. It supports the calculation that the Soviet superiority in ICBMs is most dangerous to the United States.

7. *Congressional Record*, February 19, 1960, pp. 2757 ff.

8. *New York Times*, December 1, 1959.

9. House Report No. 48 (86th Cong., 1st sess., May 28, 1959), pp. 13 ff.

10. See Anthony Eden, *Full Circle: The Memoirs of Anthony Eden* (Boston: Houghton Mifflin Co., 1960).

11. See Rockefeller Fund Reports, I (1958) *International Security, The Military Aspect* and II (1959) *The Mid-Century Challenge to U.S. Foreign Policy* (New York : Doubleday & Co., 1959), and "Biological and Environmental Effects of Nuclear War," *Hearings, Special Subcommittee on Radiation, Joint Committee on Atomic Energy* (86th Cong., 1st sess., June 22–26, 1959).

12. See S. K. Bailey, *The Condition of Our National Political Parties* (New York: Fund for the Republic, 1959).

13. Harold D. Lasswell, *Politics: Who Gets What, When and How* (New York: McGraw-Hill Book Co., 1936).

CHAPTER I. The Solitary Master Builder

1. July 26, 1789, *The Writings of George Washington*, ed. J. C. Fitzpatrick (39 vols.; Washington, D.C.: Government Printing Office, 1931–44), XXX, 361.

2. *Ibid.*, XXXI, 55.

3. March 9, 1797, *Letters of John Adams, Addressed to His Wife*, ed. Charles Francis Adams (2 vols.; Boston: Charles C. Little & James Brown, 1841), II, 246–47.

4. *Writings of Thomas Jefferson*, ed. P. L. Ford (10 vols.; New York, 1892–99), IX, 244.

5. Madison Papers, W. C. Rives Collection, Library of Congress.

6. From Leonard D. White, *The Jeffersonians: A Study in Administrative History, 1801–1829* (New York: Macmillan Co., 1951), p. 72.

7. House Report No. 79 (18th Cong., 2d sess., January 18, 1825), pp. 23–25.

8. December 29, 1948, *The Diary of James K. Polk during His Presidency, 1845–1849*, ed. Milo M. Quaife (4 vols.; Chicago: A. C. McClurg & Co., 1910), IV, 261.

9. *Ibid.*, September 23, 1848, pp. 130–31.

10. From Leonard D. White, *The Republican Era, 1869–1901: A Study in Administrative History* (New York: Macmillan Co., 1959), p. 105.

11. June 6, 1879, *Diary and Letters of Rutherford B. Hayes*, ed. C. R. Williams (5 vols.; Columbus, Ohio: Ohio State Archaeological and Historical Society, 1922–26), III, 557.

12. April 13, 1889, *Letters of Grover Cleveland, 1850–1908*, ed. Allan Nevins (Boston: Houghton Mifflin Co., 1933), p. 203.

13. William Walworth, *Woodrow Wilson* (New York: Longmans, Green & Co., Inc., 1958).

14. Harry S. Truman, *Memoirs* (2 vols.; New York: Doubleday & Co., 1955–56), I, 67, II, 508.

15. Madison voiced an almost universal concern: "Experience had proved a tendency in our government to throw all power into the legis-

lative vortex. The executives of the states are in general little more than ciphers; the legislatures omnipotent. If no effectual check can be devised for restraining the instability and encroachments of the latter, a revolution of some kind or other would be inevitable." *Debates in the Several State Conventions on the Adoption of the Federal Constitution . . .* , ed. Jonathan Elliot (2d ed., 5 vols.; Philadelphia, 1861), V, 327. Elsewhere, Jefferson (1783) inveighed against the possibility of legislators acting as despots, since despotism is not only a function of the numbers holding power but the temper in its exercise by one, or two, or 179.

16. *Records of the Federal Convention of 1787*, ed. Max Farrand (4 vols.; New Haven: Yale University Press, 1911–37), III, 301.

17. See the Attorney General's memorandum to the Senate Committee in the McCarthy Hearings, where a full statement of precedents appears.

18. President's Committee on Administrative Management, *Administrative Management* (Washington, D.C.: Government Printing Office, 1937), p. 2.

CHAPTER II. Power and Responsibility

1. See, for sumary, C. H. Prichett, *The American Constitution* (New York: McGraw-Hill Book Co., 1959), pp. 308–16, and cases cited. See also Edward S. Corwin, *The President: Office and Powers* (4th ed.; New York: New York University Press, 1957). This superb standard work has been my guide since its first edition, as well as the same author's *The Doctrine of Judicial Review and Other Essays* (Princeton: Princeton University Press, 1914), with which I first began the study of the American system of government.

2. The number of agencies under Jefferson's supervision was 9; under Theodore Roosevelt, 20; under Wilson, 39; under Hoover, 46; under Franklin Roosevelt, 63.

3. Lucius Wilmerding, Jr., *The Spending Power: A History of the Efforts of Congress to Control Expenditures* (New Haven: Yale University Press, 1943).

4. *Humphrey's Executor* v. *United States* (1935) and *Wiener* v. *United States* (1958).

5. See P. T. David and Ross Pollock, *Executives for Government: Central Issues of Federal Personnel Administration* (Washington, D.C.: Brookings Institution, 1957), pp. 8, 91.

6. *General Management*, pp. 35–36.

7. *Myers* v. *Postmaster General* (1926) and the *Humphrey* case (1935) previously referred to.

8. "Developments in Military Technology and Their Impact on U.S. Strategy and Foreign Policy," Senate Committee on Foreign Relations, Print No. 8, December 6, 1959.

9. *Debates and Proceedings in the Congress of the United States, 1789–1824 [Annals of Congress]* (42 vols.; Washington, D.C., 1834–56), I, 492.

10. It might be suggested that the powers do *not* belong to the people

themselves but to a legal fiction, that is, those people designated to wield power subject to the limitations and permissions and procedures given in the Constitution.

11. The classic justification appears, of course, in the writings of John Locke, a fundamental authority in the governmental conceptions of the Founders of the Republic, even as for the Declaration of Independence. Locke wrote:

"For the legislators not being able to foresee and provide by laws for all that may be useful to the community, the executor of the laws, having the power in his hands, has by the common law of Nature a right to make use of it for the good of the society, in many cases where the muncipal law has given no direction, till the legislative can conveniently be assembled to provide for it. Many things there are which the law can by no means provide for, and those must necessarily be left to the discretion of him that has the executive power in his hands, to be ordered by him as the public good and advantage shall require; nay, it is fit that the laws themselves should in some cases give way to the executive power, or that as much as may be, all the members of the society are to be preserved."

And the Founders of the Republic had confidence in "Nature and Nature's God."

12. *Youngstown Sheet and Tube Company* v. *Sawyer*, June 2, 1952.

13. *Political Science Quarterly*, September, 1952, p. 332.

14. James Burnham, *Congress and the American Tradition* (Chicago: Henry Regnery Co., 1959).

15. The constant use of "Chief" as applied to the President forces me to wonder if the term may originate in the western romances of Red Indians, e.g., "Him, heap big Chief!"

16. In 1841, Tyler was able by use of the veto to thwart the program of the Whigs who had won an overwhelming victory with Harrison. See Herman Kahn, *The Nature and Feasibility of War and Deterrence* (Santa Monica: Rand Corp., 1960), reprinted in *Hearings, Subcommittee on National Policy Machinery, Committee on Government Operations*, Part I (86th Cong., 2d sess., 1960).

17. See David Potter, *People of Plenty: Economic Abundance and the American Character* (Chicago: University of Chicago Press, 1954), for a historical and sociological appraisal of this judgment.

18. See *Economic Report of the President, 1953* (Washington, D.C.: Government Printing Office, 1953):

"The demands of modern life and the unsettled status of the world require a more important role for government than it played in earlier and quieter times. . . .

"Government must use its vast power to help maintain employment and purchasing power as well as to maintain reasonably stable prices.

"Government must be alert and sensitive to economic developments, including its own myriad activities. It must be prepared to take preventive as well as remedial action; and it must be ready to cope with new situations that may arise. This is not a start-and-stop responsibility, but a continuous one.

"The arsenal of weapons at the disposal of Government for maintaining economic stability is formidable. It includes credit controls administered by the Federal Reserve System; the debt-management policies of the Treasury; authority of the President to vary the terms of mortgages carrying Federal insurance; flexibility in administration of the budget; agricultural supports; modification of the tax structure; and public works. We shall not hesitate to use any or all of these weapons as the situation may require."

19. Indeed, no sooner was this page scanned on return from the typist than the steel strike became so onerous as to force a most reluctant President to evoke the "national interest" in getting the men to work again.

20. A. F. Bentley, *The Process of Government* (Evanston: Principia Press of Illinois, 1949).

21. David B. Truman, *The Governmental Process: Political Interests and Public Opinion* (New York: Alfred A. Knopf, Inc., 1951).

22. I follow the excellently contrived reports in the *Congressional Quarterly*. Among the many tables prepared by this journal is one on Eisenhower's legislative proposals and their fate.

Year	Proposals	Passed by Congress	Approval
1954	232	150	64.7%
1955	207	96	46.3
1956	225	103	45.7
1957	206	76	36.9

23. Lawrence H. Chamberlain, *The President, Congress and Legislation* (New York: Columbia University Press, 1946), especially pp. 450 ff.

24. The veto message of July 8, 1959, contains such justification as "a bill so excessive in the spending it proposes, and so defective in other respects that it would do far more damage than good"; "extravagant"; "inflationary"; "discrimination against our smaller cities"; and so on.

25. The figures are extracted, gratefully, from an unpublished thesis by Grace Swigart, written at the University of Chicago. The gross figures of vetoes applicable in the observations above are: Theodore Roosevelt, 23; Taft, 23; Wilson, 24; Coolidge, 23; Harding, 2; Hoover, 94; Franklin Roosevelt, 234; Truman, in eight years, 250; Eisenhower, in seven years, to September, 1959, vetoed 157 laws, whether of "public significance" or not.

26. Eisenhower's third veto of the Rivers and Harbors Bill in August, 1959, was overridden, for even Republican congressmen insist upon their annual share of "pork."

27. Truman, *Memoirs*, II, 479–80.

28. *Ibid.*, p. 24.

29. Louise Stitt, "Legislative History of the Fair Labor Standards Act," *Law and Contemporary Problems,* Duke University, Summer, 1939.

30. Richard E. Neustadt, "The Growth of Central Clearance," *American Political Science Review*, September, 1954.

31. See James F. Byrnes, *All in One Lifetime* (New York: Harper & Bros., 1958), pp. 22–130, for many intimate illustrations of the President's difficult relationship with Congress.

32. Richard E. Neustadt, "Presidency and Legislation: Planning the President's Program," *American Political Science Review*, December, 1955, pp. 980 ff.

33. These include cabinet and department heads, assistant secretaries, federal judges, members of regulatory commissions and the heads of other important boards and commissions like the TVA and AEC, diplomatic officers, the heads of federal field offices, district attorneys, marshals, collectors of customs and internal revenue, civilian heads of special career services like the Public Health Services, and so on.

34. See the brilliant and authoritative study by Joseph P. Harris, *The Advise and Consent of the Senate* (Berkeley and Los Angeles: University of California Press, 1953).

35. I paraphrase Paul P. Van Riper's *History of the United States Civil Service* (Evanston, Ill.: Row, Peterson & Co., 1958), pp. 442–43, 490. I lament the virtual impossibility of being more positive about the exactness of the figures, for I have searched, as well as he, and arithmetized much to clear up the mystery, and am as much baffled. The general dimensions seem to be sound.

36. "Inquiry into Satellite and Missile Programs," *Hearings, Preparedness Subcommittee on the Armed Services*, Part II (85th Cong., 1st sess., January 6, 1958), p. 1409.

37. By 1959, ambassadorships were held by 51 career men, and 23 posts were filled by men and women who had had no training for them. Of the 15 most important posts in western Europe, only 6 were held by career officials.

38. B. M. Rich, *The Presidents and Civil Disorder* (Washington, D.C.: Brookings Institution, 1941).

39. The editor of the *Reporter* (March 7, 1957) commented on the appeal of the administration to Congress to pass its resolution on the "doctrine" as "asking to be recognized as the Executive Branch of the government."

40. See *Hirabayashi* v. *United States* (1943) and *Korematsu* v. *United States* (1944).

41. Woodrow Wilson, *Constitutional Government* (New York: Columbia University Press, 1908), p. 60.

42. *Ibid.*, pp. 67–73.

43. See Malcolm Moos, *Politics, Presidents and Coattails* (Baltimore: Johns Hopkins Press, 1952).

44. Resolution of the House of Commons, December 17, 1783: "that to report any opinion of his Majesty, upon any bill, or other proceeding, depending in either House of Parliament, with a view to influence the votes of the members, is a high crime and misdemeanour, derogatory to the honour of the crown, a breach of the fundamental privileges of parliament, and subversive of the constitution." *Commons Journal*, XXXIX, 842.

45. James M. Burns, *Roosevelt: The Lion and the Fox* (New York: Harcourt, Brace & Co., 1956), p. 360.

46. Domestic status seems to determine political success, e.g., the contest

between bachelor Buchanan and his opponent; between bachelor and father Cleveland and his rival; Al Smith's dowdy wife; the brave, devoted, intelligent, and often embarrassing Eleanor Roosevelt.

47. Henry J. Ford, *The Rise and Growth of American Politics* (New York: Macmillan Co., 1900), p. 293.

48. See Angus Campbell, G. Gurin, and W. E. Miller, *The Voter Decides* (Evanston, Ill.: Row, Peterson & Co., 1954), p. 177.

49. *Foreign Affairs*, April, 1960, p. 362.

50. Cited in Leonard D. White, *The Federalists: A Study in Administrative History* (New York: Macmillan Co., 1948), p. 92.

51. William Ewart Gladstone, *Gleanings of Past Years* (7 vols.; New York: Charles Scribner's Sons, 1879), I, 242–43.

CHAPTER III. Qualities of Political Leadership

1. The consequences were economic misery for millions of workers, farmers, and white-collar workers. Yet Taft had need to be especially circumspect in this instance. His pledge was that the tariff must be reduced substantially, yet the Senate raised some 600 items, among them woolens, tobacco, steel, sugar, and cotton, to the advantage of the trusts, which, as it were, with his other hand Taft prosecuted. This blind action cost him the support of the Progressives for a second term.

I cannot forbear to quote Mr. Dooley on the free list allowed by the Senate to offset its increases: "Th' Republican party has been thru to its promises. Look at th' free list if ye don't believe it. Practically ivry thing nicissary to existence come in free. Here it is. Curling stones, teeth, sea moss, newspapers, nux vomica, Pulu, canary bird seed, divy-divvy, spunk, hog bristles, marshmallows, silk worm eggs, stilts, skeletons, an' leeches. Th' new tariff bill puts these familyar commodyties within th' reach iv all." Finley Peter Dunne, *Mr. Dooley Says* (New York: Charles Scribner's Sons, 1910), p. 148.

2. Arthur M. Schlesinger, Sr., *Paths to the Present* (New York: Macmillan Co., 1949), especially chapter v, "A Yardstick for Presidents." Schlesinger lists the *Near Great*: Theodore Roosevelt, Cleveland, John Adams, Polk; the *Average*: John Quincy Adams, Monroe, Hayes, Madison, Van Buren, Taft, Arthur, McKinley, Johnson, Hoover, Harrison; the *Below Average*: Tyler, Coolidge, Filmore, Taylor, Buchanan, Pierce; and the *Failures*: Grant, Harding. W. H. Harrison and Garfield are not included because they died soon after taking office. It will be noted that only one soldier is ranked among the great Presidents. Jackson's military service was sporadic, his career as a businessman and lawyer and in political office of greater importance. All the other military men are below average; Grant was a crass failure as President.

3. Truman, *Memoirs*, I, 36.

4. See Woodrow Wilson, re the Vera Cruz landing (1913): "I cannot get it off my heart. It was right. Nothing else was possible but I cannot forget that it was I who had to order those young men to their deaths!"

5. See the case described in the well-informed novel by Allen Drury, *Advise and Consent* (New York: Doubleday & Co., Inc., 1959).

6. For example, Eisenhower's decision to stand firm against Communist China's threat to Quemoy and Matsu and his refusal to order an air strike on Dien Bien Phu in 1954, as advocated by Admiral Radford, chairman of the Joint Chiefs of Staff, and (rather more guardedly) by Vice-President Nixon.

7. Otto von Bismarck, *Reminiscences,* Tauchnitz edition, III, 90–92.

8. Douglass Cater, *The Fourth Branch of Government* (Boston: Houghton Mifflin Co., 1959), p. 341.

9. No one has ever accused the *New York Herald-Tribune* of hostility toward President Eisenhower, yet in November, 1959, when the steel strike had lasted nearly four months, the editorial from which I quote appeared: "The whole point is to prevent the threat ['a grave threat to the national economy . . . as there is now'] from arising, not to deal with it desperately *in extremis*; the damage of the steel strike has already been done, and there is no cure but prevention. We must be prepared, therefore, to swallow a number of the objections against interfering with free bargaining, choosing the least of the visible evils to secure the national interest. For the one overriding lesson of the present steel strike is that it must not be permitted to happen again."

10. Walter Lippmann sketches the public mood: "Prepare for war in time of peace? No, it is bad to raise taxes, to unbalance the budget, to take men away from their schools or their jobs, to provoke the enemy. Intervene in a developing conflict? No, avoid the risk of war. Withdraw from the area of conflict? No, the adversary must not be appeased. Reduce your claims to the area? No, righteousness cannot be compromised. Negotiate a compromise peace as soon as the opportunity presents itself? No, the aggressor must be punished. Remain armed to enforce the dictated settlement? No, the war is over." *The Public Philosophy* (Boston: Little, Brown & Co., 1955), pp. 19–20.

11. Wolworth, *Wilson,* I, 337.

12. Truman, *Memoirs,* II, 305.

13. Press releases by Senator H. M. Jackson, October 14, 1957; correspondence with White House, June 30 and July 7, 1955.

14. Some problems are not tractable by charm alone. Arthur Krock, in the *New York Times* (November 29, 1959), apropos of Eisenhower's world trip for peace: "If the President makes his usual impression on peoples with whom he comes in contact, the public relations objective of his errand abroad will be successfully attained. . . . So while there is little doubt that his mission to the Pope, Asia, North Africa and the Mediterranean will be a personal triumph and will dispel many doubts of United States' policy in those areas, similar results of his second task [accomplishment at the Western summit . . . as a unifying negotiator among allies] are not anticipated with the same degree of assurance." Nor is it possible to forget the evaporation of the effect of the tour, in spite of what Joseph Alsop in the *New York Herald-Tribune* (December 8, 1959) called "the President's glowing presence."

CHAPTER IV. Surrender of Efficiency

1. Rhode Island and North Carolina were not yet a part of the union.

2. Alexander Hamilton, John Jay, and James Madison, *The Federalist or The New Constitution* (1787–88). I use the Everyman edition I bought in London in 1917. The passages treated in this chapter are in essays LXVII–LXXVII, pp. 342–77, especially essay LXX, pp. 357–64, and essay LXXI, pp. 365–73. All are by Alexander Hamilton.

3. Edmund Burke, *Thoughts on the Cause of the Present Discontents* (Oxford: Oxford University Press, World's Classics, n.d.), II, 13.

4. *U. S. News and World Report*, March 14, 1958.

5. This may have happened in the course of a press conference in August, 1959, when President Eisenhower uttered a tirade against criticism of his projected visit to the Soviet Union that left him at times almost inarticulate. He fulminated against the idea that the journey would reduce America's "prestige," though this was far from the charge contained in an article by Truman published the day before. Eisenhower's rebuttal that "prestige" was unimportant compared to "the future of the human race" was certainly a newspaperman's good debating point.

6. For the best discussion of the problem see Schuyler C. Wallace, *Federal Departmentalization* (New York: Columbia University Press, 1941).

7. See Ernest Kretschmer, *Psychology of Men of Genius* (London: Kegan Paul, 1931).

8. See D. M. De-Witt, *Impeachment and Trial of Andrew Johnson* (New York: Macmillan Co., 1903).

9. *The Federalist*, LXVIII.

10. *Ibid.*

11. *Chicago Daily Tribune*, July 13, 1959. Professional Republican politicians were appalled at the size of the budget, did not like the "program and progress committee" set up by the President to find out what goals the party should aim at, and did not find satisfactory the too few judicial appointments from among Republicans.

12. Clinton Rossiter, *The American Presidency* (New York: Harcourt, Brace & Co., 1956), p. 52.

13. Grover Cleveland had an operation on his jaw performed in utmost secrecy to avoid rumors of illness that would have affected the stability of the nation's market.

14. Witness the anguish to which Chancellor Adenauer was subjected by his own party on his policy for alliance with the West and his attempt to settle the successors to his leadership in his own way, and his notion that he could make the German figurehead Presidency into a rulership.

15. Thus, "A real responsibility in high politics can only be undertaken by one single directing minister, never by a numerous board with majority decisions. The decision as to paths and by-paths often depends on slight but decisive changes, sometimes even on the tone and choice of expressions in an international document. Even the slightest departure from the right line often causes the distance from it to increase so rapidly that the abandoned line cannot be recovered, and the return to the bifurcation,

whence it was left behind, becomes impossible." Bismarck, *Reminiscences*, II, 69.

16. Theodore Roosevelt, *Autobiography* (New York: Macmillan Co., 1913), pp. 388–89.

17. Truman, *Memoirs*, II, 473.

18. See James E. King, Jr., *World Politics* (Princeton: Princeton University Press, 1959), pp 418 ff., for a narrative of events in August, 1958. The President sent Congress a message via his press secretary, saying: "Even if he [the President] were given the money for this investigation . . . to study how or when the United States might surrender . . . it would not be spent. The whole matter is too ridiculous for any further comment." This may have been what the ostrich twittered. See also Paul Kecskemeti, *Strategic Surrender: Politics of Victory and Defeat* (Stanford: Stanford University Press, 1958).

19. Truman, *Memoirs*, II, 478.

20. Grover Cleveland, *Presidential Problems* (New York: Century Co., 1904).

21. Wilson, *Constitutional Government*, p. 60

22. *Ibid.*, pp. 67–73.

23. William Howard Taft, *Our Chief Magistrate and His Powers* (New York: Columbia University Press, 1916), pp. 139–40. Neagle was a marshal appointed by the Attorney General to guard Supreme Court Justice Stephen J. Field who had been threatened by a litigant in California. The litigant was shot dead by Neagle. State authorities arrested Neagle, and the federal government asked for habeas corpus for his release. Congress had not enacted a law to allow for such a case, but the Supreme Court argued that a power must be presumed to exist for a sovereign government, the United States, to protect judges in the course of their duties. It existed in the President, who has all the instrumentalities to do the job well, since they "aid him in the performance of the great duties of his office, and represent him in a thousand acts." *In re Neagle*, 135 U.S. 1, 311–12 (1890).

24. *Works of Abraham Lincoln*, ed. J. G. Nicolay and John Hay (New York: Century Co., 1894), X, 65–68.

25. Quoted in J. G. Randall, *Constitutional Problems under Lincoln* (New York: D. Appleton & Co., 1926), p. 18.

26. Truman, *Memoirs*, I, ix.

27. *Ibid.*, II, 2.

28. Quoted in *New York Times*, November 13, 1932.

29. *New York Times*, December 21, 1940.

30. Eisenhower press conference, May 4, 1956. R. J. Donovan adds an inadvertent postscript to this blithe view of the President's responsibilities. The President would sign documents only if they were initialed "O.K. S.A." [Sherman Adams].

31. Donovan, referring to President Eisenhower's address to the nation on the state of his health, writes, "He discussed the problem of his health very frankly." The President said, "It is, however, true that the opinions and conclusions of the doctors that I can continue to carry the burdens of

the Presidency contemplate for me a regime of ordered work activity, interspersed with regular amounts of exercise, recreation and rest. . . . But let me make one thing clear. As of this moment, there is not the slightest doubt that I can now perform as well as I ever have all of the important duties of the Presidency. . . ." What is meant by "as well as ever"? Did the public know? Did the physicians know? Did either know the awful burden of the Presidency when the office is *immersively* considered?

32. Arthur M. Schlesinger, Jr., *The Age of Jackson* (Boston: Little, Brown & Co., 1946), pp. 67 ff., 72–73.

33. Robert Sherwood, *Roosevelt and Hopkins: An Intimate History* (New York: Harper & Bros., 1950).

34. Robert J. Donovan, *Eisenhower: The Inside Story* (New York: Harper & Bros., 1956), p. 71.

35. Eisenhower press statement, June 18, 1958.

36. *Time Magazine* (February 16, 1959), not for the first time, gave a sketch of Eisenhower's personal friends. Thus: George Humphrey, successful industrialist and plantation owner; Barry Leithead, president of Arrow Shirt Corporation; William E. Robinson, chairman of Coca-Cola, former advertising and newspaper executive; Clifford J. Roberts, stockbroker; W. Alton Jones, of Cities Service; George Allen, Washington businessman; and General Alfred Gruenther, former commander of SHAPE.

37. *Time Magazine,* January 27, 1958.

38. Cater, *Fourth Branch of Government,* p. 164.

39. Louis W. Koenig, *The Invisible Presidency* (New York: Rinehart & Co., 1960).

40. *The Public Papers of Woodrow Wilson,* ed. R. S. Baker and W. E. Dodd (6 vols.; New York: Doubleday & Co., 1925–27), I, 220–22.

41. Wilson, *Constitutional Government,* p. 76.

42. *Polk: The Diary of a President, 1845–1849,* ed. Allan Nevins (New York: Longmans, Green & Co., Inc., 1952), pp. 360–61.

43. Walworth, *Wilson,* I, 283.

44. Roosevelt's message to Congress, with recommendations of the President's Committee on Administrative Management, 1938.

45. Truman, *Memoirs,* I, 228.

46. *Ibid.,* p. 330.

47. Herman Finer, *America's Destiny* (New York: Macmillan & Co., 1947), on Wallace's views then.

48. Truman, *Memoirs,* I, 420.

49. *Ibid.,* II, 60.

50. *Ibid.,* p. 355.

51. *Ibid.,* p. 460.

52. Harold L. Ickes, *The Secret Diary of Harold L. Ickes* (3 vols.; New York: Simon & Schuster, Inc., 1953–54), I, 147–57.

53. Walworth, *Wilson,* I, 310.

54. Truman, *Memoirs,* II, 260.

55. H. B. Westerfield, *Foreign Policy and Party Politics: Pearl Harbor to*

Korea (New Haven: Yale University Press, 1955), p. 15. Westerfield's prescription of extrapartisanship in foreign affairs is distinctly worth pondering for its suggestions of what troubles might be produced by presidential publicizing of a personal or party attitude:

"The very real dangers of general partisanship in the control of American foreign relations do not require any such drastic cure. The essential requirement is to keep the most important foreign policy issues out of presidential election campaigns. Given the localistic American party system — especially as it is reflected in the choice of congressmen — only in a presidential election can it be easily argued that a national mandate has been given, producing the special evils of partisanship which have already been mentioned: *(a)* threatening to bring about abrupt shifts in policy, *(b)* severely limiting flexibility by partisan commitments, *(c)* running the risk of stalemate, *(d)* tempting the President to use shock techniques to coerce support, or else *(e)* in an emergency forcing him to upset the consistency of his general foreign policy by sudden drastic concession to the opposition — all with no assurance, given the makeup of the parties and the mixture of foreign and domestic issues, that a truly popular mandate is possible. These dangers can be kept within manageable limits if the presidential candidates do not contend sharply over major foreign policies in the quadrennial campaigns."

CHAPTER V. The President Needs Rescue

1. See the statement by Louis Brownlow, *Hearings, Committee on Government Operations* (84th Cong., 2d sess., January 16–25, 1956), pp. 45 ff. See also Louis Brownlow, *The President and the Presidency* (Chicago: Publication Administration Service, 1949); also *Report, President's Committee on Administrative Management, 1936* (Washington, D. C.: Government Printing Office, 1936).

2. Quoted in *New York Times,* February 1, 1958, IV, 6.

3. *General Management,* pp. 5, 11–28.

4. Quoted by Douglass Cater, *Reporter,* June 25, 1959, p. 16.

5. Quoted in *Life,* March 16, 1959.

6. Editorial, "Great Step Toward Linking Policies and Acts," *New York Times,* January 19, 1960.

How sound, unfortunately, was my judgment (December, 1959) upon the inefficacy of "institutionalization," echoed by Arthur Krock's dismal admission of its failure in the U–2 airplane spy furore and administrative and policy botch. Under the heading "The Enigmas in the Pilot Powers Case," he writes *(New York Times,* May 10, 1960), "The final corollary conclusions sufficiently supported by this record are that co-ordination of policy and action has not yet been attained by the National Security Council and the Operations Co-ordinating Board, even in connection with procedures involving the peril of initiating nuclear war; and there are vital missing links between the President and his authorized agents." What use, in this case, was the "institutionalization" of the Executive Office and the National Security Council? It was worse than useless.

7. See *Hearings, Subcommittee on Reorganization of the Committee on Government Operations* (84th Cong., 2d sess., January 16–25, 1956), *passim*.

8. This and succeeding passages are taken from the account of the President's work given in *U.S. News and World Report*, November 22, 1957.

9. White, *The Federalists*, especially chapter iv.

10. *Ibid.*, p. 44.

11. It appears that Secretary of State Byrnes was appointed by President Truman, just arrived in office himself, as consolation for having lost the nomination as Vice President in 1944. Truman writes *(Memoirs,* I, 23): ". . . Byrnes undoubtedly was deeply disappointed and hurt. I thought that my calling on him at this time [to be Secretary of State] might help balance things up." That it might unbalance the United States apparently was not in the President's mind.

The same event may appear to others in a quite different light. Byrnes believed that the President was in need of help. Thus (and the text is useful for other phases of this essay): "The task of the President at that time was unusually heavy. President Roosevelt had found it unbearably hard to conduct foreign affairs in time of war and at the same time keep pace with events on the domestic front. He had had years of experience in office and had learned to live with his problems as they accumulated; in contrast, President Truman was facing without warning unfamiliar hazards both at home and abroad, with his Secretary of State necessarily absent from the capitol. While I remained in Washington, I saw him daily, giving him what help I could." J. F. Byrnes, *All in One Lifetime,* p. 280.

A calculation by J. A. Schlesinger (of Michigan State University), quoted in P. T. David, R. M. Goodman, and R. C. Bain, *The Politics of National Party Conventions* (Washington, D. C.: Brookings Institution, 1960), note 25, p. 62, shows that of the 159 cabinet members appointed since 1900 few had had no previous experience in public office, though some was of very brief duration. Expressed in percentages: *Elective office:* Vice-President, 0.6; members of Congress, 20.1; governors of states, 7.5; other state executives, 1.9; state legislators, 15.7; local officers, 11.9; defeated candidates for President, Vice-President, or state governor, 7.6; *Appointive office:* other cabinet posts, subcabinet officers, state and federal administrative officers, 55.3; *Judicial office:* federal, state, or local, 10.7; district attorney or other public legal office, 25.1. (Some cabinet members had held more than one public office.)

12. A mock cabinet meeting was presented on television in October, 1954, when Dulles was called upon to report on his latest tour of Europe. Ezra Taft Benson, Secretary of Agriculture, forgot his lines; Oveta Culp Hobby made a *gaffe* about the Saar; the President maintained a charming, if uncomfortable, reticence. See *Report to the President and the Cabinet by the Secretary of State,* published by the State Department in 1954.

13. See Jonathan Daniels, *The Man of Independence* (Philadelphia: J. B. Lippincott Co., 1950), p. 257. Truman said of Roosevelt's cabinet meetings: "Roosevelt never discussed anything important at his cabinet meet-

ings. Cabinet members, if they had anything to discuss, tried to see him privately after the meetings."

14. David and Pollock, *Executives for Government,* p. 10.

15. Sherwood, *Roosevelt and Hopkins,* p. 361.

16. Samuel P. Huntingdon, *The Soldier and the State* (Cambridge, Mass.: Harvard University Press, 1957), speaks with some appreciation of the British solution of the problem. There a Minister of Defense is a member of a collectively responsible cabinet; his policies and budget are the principal object of intracabinet deliberation; he has as his own direct assistants fifty military officers as well as top level civil servants headed by a chief staff officer and the permanent (career) secretary of the department. Moreover, the chief staff officer is his link with the Chiefs of Staff committee. In the U.S. Department of Defense, there is no equivalent to the permanent secretary, though such a position was recommended by the Hoover Commission of 1955.

17. *Ibid.,* p. 455.

18. Press release, Senator H. W. Jackson.

19. Senator Jackson's anxiety about the operation of National Security Council-cum-presidential strategic thinking is echoed in Walter Millis *et al., Arms and the State* (New York: Twentieth Century Fund, 1958).

20. See *Hearings, Subcommittee on National Policy Machinery* (86th Cong, 2d sess., February 23, 1960).

Perhaps the most incisive comment on the operation of the "institutions" around the President was made by George Kennan. See his remarks on the nexus of the State Department, National Security Council, and the Presidency reproduced in "Organizing for National Security," *Selected Materials on the National Security Council, Subcommittee on National Policy Machinery* (86th Cong., 2d sess., March 10, 1960):

"Such a diplomacy [which he defines in its characteristics] cannot emanate from the workings of a great bureaucratic apparatus. It requires, necessarily and properly, too much of the personal, too much of the private, too much — if you will — of the conspiratorial to be conceived and implemented in this way. The Chief Executive is faced today with the choice of by-passing the regular apparatus both as a source of information and inspiration and as a channel of execution, or of foregoing effective diplomacy altogether and contenting himself with the monumental inflexibility, the philosophical shallowness, the ideological obscurity, and the unimaginative execution which the great organization ensures."

21. Dean Acheson, "Thoughts about Thought in High Places," *New York Times Magazine,* October 11, 1959.

22. It is a pleasure to draw attention to an article by Arnold Zurcher, "The Presidency, Congress and the Separation of Powers," *Western Political Quarterly,* March, 1950. Looking at the Presidency from the standpoint of his leadership in the program of legislation Zurcher wonders whether the existing liaison is adequate for the future. Presidential leadership depends on the possession by the President "of consummate skill in political management." Yet that leadership is what he calls "fundamentally

ad hoc," that is to say, it has its up and downs according to the character of the individual who occupies the White House. He observes that since the President must bring to bear on Congress the pressure of public opinion, it may lead to his leaning on one or another of the pressure groups, the special interests. This is a serious risk in an age when the Presidency has become "plebiscitical," and threatens to upset the constitutional balance between Congress and the President. In my opinion the balance has swung heavily to the side of the President.

23. See F. Morstein-Marx, "The Bureau of the Budget," *American Political Science Review* (1945) pp. 653, 869 ff., and Harold D. Smith, *The Management of Your Government* (New York: McGraw-Hill Book Co., Inc., 1945). The anxieties of the job undoubtedly killed Smith.

24. Full Employment Act (February 20, 1946), Sec. 2.

25. See the very interesting article by E. G. Nourse and B. M. Gross, "The President's Council of Economic Advisers," *American Political Science Review,* April, 1948.

26. *Economic Reports of the President* (New York: Reynal & Co., Inc., 1959), p. ix.

27. *Ibid.,* p. 14. See E. G. Nourse, "Economics in the Public Service," *American Economic Review,* XXXVII (1947), and Gerhard Colm, "The Executive Office and Fiscal and Economic Policy," *Law and Contemporary Problems,* Duke University (Winter, 1956), pp. 710 ff.

28. Nourse and Gross, *op. cit.,* p. 290.

29. Herman Finer, *Theory and Practice of Modern Government* (New York: Henry Holt & Co., Inc., 1949), Part VI. See Brian Chapman, *The Profession of Government* (London: Allen & Unwin, 1959).

30. See Van Riper, *Civil Service,* chapter xii.

31. Leonard D. White, *Government Career Service* (Chicago: University of Chicago Press, 1935). See David and Pollock, *Executives for Government,* chapters v–vi.

32. Calculated by the Hoover Commission Task Force on Personnel, 1954. Some 100 positions have been created since then.

Heads of agencies and their deputies		230
Assistant agency heads		125
General managers of boards and commissions		10
Non-civil service bureau chiefs		250
Subordinate executives, including:		
Heads of staff offices	40	
Heads department information offices	50	
Political aides and assistants	300	390
	Total	1,005

33. The West German government has about six "political" career officials per government department, most with civil service qualifications. They may be transferred if the political chief demands it, but they can be dismissed only for incompetence, etc.

34. There are several reasons why the establishment of a government career service has not received support. Congress, it is said, prefers to

have each department fragmented, the bureaus only loosely co-ordinated. Congress prefers to divide and rule — and not for the sake of the nation. There is strong opposition to an *élite* corps of civil servants on the grounds that members would be alienated from the public. Further, it is argued that a corps of senior civil servants would have to be recruited, could not be appointed or promoted, and would be selected only on the basis of competitive examination.

The Hoover Commission proposes that senior civil servants be selected from those already in civil service and promoted on the basis of merit. I would sooner have this than nothing, but I feel certain that, in the long run, a "closed" service is needed. There are indications that this solution is unavoidable if the nation is to recruit competent leaders.

There is a complaint that the government cannot attract and keep sufficient executives, both political appointees and civil officers. Quite true, as long as the career is not made attractive. If young men were offered promising careers they would enter government ranks and remain. (See M. H. Bernstein, *The Job of the Federal Executive* [Washington, D.C.: Brookings Institution, 1958], pp. 138–39. "Every recent administration has experienced difficulty in filling its political executive positions on a satisfactory basis and in keeping them filled on such a basis.")

The second Hoover Commission Task Force on Personnel traced the difficulties to four factors:

1. Shortage of persons possessing both well-developed executive ability and well-developed qualities of leadership;

2. Failure to develop systematically the capacities which are essential in political executives;

3. Difficulties and disadvantages suffered by executives who shuttle back and forth between public office and private life; and

4. Psychological and financial barriers to a ready interchange between a career in politics and a career in business.

The shortage has become more serious in recent years. Increasingly, the government relies on men of executive ability to make financial sacrifices for the purpose of serving. But clearly, "the business of Government is not a part-time affair, nor a simple undertaking to be trusted to a parade of 'promising young executives.' " The public, especially the business community, complacently allows the supply of executive talent in government to erode; the result is a crippling loss of trained personnel.

It is necessary to say to ambitious young men and women in our universities: "If you join the career service, you will be assured a planned and secure line of advancement, with a steady increase in responsibilities, authority, and emoluments. If you learn what we think you should and show your competence, you will arrive at one of the top positions; there you will be of immediate assistance to the cabinet and the President. It will be interesting and important work, and you will have a hand in the formulation of policy as determined by the President and a chance to use the skills you have acquired."

Donald K. Price, dean of the Littauer School of Government at Harvard University, long-experienced in government, including service in the Defense Department, has urged that an administrative career service of the kind sketched here be established. (See Donald K. Price, *Government and Science: Their Dynamic Relation in American Democracy* [New York: New York University Press, 1954], and Herman Finer, "Government and the Expert," *Bulletin of the Atomic Scientists,* April, 1956.) Price's reasoning turns on how best to secure the contributions of the national sciences to government — all the potentialities of exact knowledge of nature to insure survival. Price would have the scientists' understanding integrated with the decisions made by the politicians. For this purpose, a corps of career administrators, not themselves scientists but understanding the significance of recent advances, would be the conduit between science and politics. The quest leads him to suggest much the same arrangements found in England, though he does not point out the similarity.

I have read the discussions of my colleagues on the difficulties of establishing a senior civil service, and it is as if their hearts were set on finding reasons for inaction. Instead of considering the problem as statesmen should, the issue has been obfuscated by trivialities; such a cocoon of fantasy and imagined difficulties has been spun that no action is deemed possible. But there is room for a small proportion of career appointments from outside the service, and for promotions from within, to guarantee competent administration. One post in five might be allocated in this way as the need arises. But if the ablest leaders in each generation are to be attracted into government, they must be offered a worthy life career.

For further discussion see Paul P. Van Riper, *Public Administration Review,* XVIII, No. 3 (1958), 189 ff., and W. Pincus, *ibid.,* No. 4, 324–31, Bernstein, *op. cit.,* chapters iii, iv, viii, and *Newsweek,* December 14, 1959.

35. Rossiter, *The American Presidency,* p. 26.

36. Quoted in White, *The Federalists,* p. 54.

37. Quoted in Rossiter, *op. cit.,* p. x.

CHAPTER VI. Gamble on a Solitary President

1. Finer, *Theory and Practice of Modern Government,* pp. 243–394.

2. P. T. David, M. Moos, and R. M. Goldman, *Presidential Nominating Politics in 1952* (5 vols.; Baltimore: Johns Hopkins Press, 1954), especially Vol. I.

3. Rossiter, *op. cit.,* pp. 230–32.

4. *Ibid.,* pp. 12 ff.

5. David, Moos, and Goldman, *op. cit.,* Vol. I.

6. Quoted in W. E. Binkley, *The Man in the White House* (Baltimore: Johns Hopkins Press, 1959), p. 86.

7. *Reporter,* March 3, 1960.

8. The reader may wish to refer to B. R. Berelson *et al., Voting: A Study of Opinion Formation in a Presidential Campaign* (Chicago: University of Chicago Press, 1954) ; Campbell, Gurin, and Miller, *The Voter Decides*;

Eugene Burdick and Arthur Brodbeck, *American Voting Behavior* (Glencoe, Ill.: Free Press, 1956); V. O. Key, *Politics, Parties, and Pressure Groups* (4th ed.; New York: Appleton-Century-Crofts, Inc., 1958); and, for more on nominating methods, see David, Goldman, and Bain, *The Politics of National Party Conventions.*

9. S. Keller, Jr., *Professional Public Relations and Political Power* (Baltimore: Johns Hopkins Press, 1956), p. 190.

10. Quoted in *New York Times,* November 6, 1958, p. 18.

11. *Economist* (London), August 2, 1952, p. 266.

12. Criticisms of the primaries may be noted in passing. They are not established by federal law, though they regulate the election of the highest federal authority, the President. Some state laws make them binding, some do not, and some are binding only in part. The campaigns require the candidates to be on the road from January in the year of the election, to make hundreds of speeches, travel thousands of exhausting miles, to find and expend large sums of money. Primary campaigns are not helpful in clarifying national issues because local problems (Florida oranges, Wisconsin cranberries) are the chief concern of the electorate, and there is no rival candidate of the opposing party present to debate national issues. Primary campaigns weary and bore the candidates by the endless repetition that seems to be necessary; they become less and less able to state problems and solutions incisively. And even so the messages reach only the smallest audiences, mainly party workers and not the electors.

13. *The Federalist,* essay LXVIII.

14. See Edgar W. Waugh, *The Second Consul: The Vice Presidency* (Indianapolis: Bobbs-Merrill Co., Inc., 1956): Irving G. Williams, *The American Vice-Presidency* (New York: Doubleday & Co., 1954) and *The Rise of the Vice-Presidency* (Washington, D.C.: Public Affairs Press, 1956); Ruth C. Silva, *Presidential Succession* (Ann Arbor: University of Michigan Press, 1951); and J. E. Kallenach, "The New Presidential Succession Act," *American Political Science Review* (October, 1947), pp. 931–41.

15. On December 3, 1957, James Reston in the *New York Times* wrote: "Eisenhower . . . has been out of Washington or convalescing in Washington 723 of the 1,777 days he has been President. Of these 723 days, 140 have been spent away on official business, 101 recovering from his three illnesses in Denver, Gettysburg or the White House, and 482 resting or vacationing at resorts or at his farm." The President's vacations have continued, and a protracted period each day is found for rest and recreation.

16. Henry Wallace, lecture at Harvard Law School Forum, April 6, 1956; and Eisenhower press conference, May 31, 1955. At a press conference in March, 1956, Eisenhower said: "Anyone who tries to drive a wedge of any kind between Dick Nixon and me is — has just as much chance as if he tried to drive it between my brother and me. We are very close, as I have told you before. . . . I am very happy that Dick Nixon is my friend, I am very happy to have him as an associate in government. I would be happy to be on any political ticket on which I was a candidate with him."

(Nixon had sided with Eisenhower against Taft on the "Texas steal" in 1952.)

17. See Samuel I. Roseman (ed.), *Working with Roosevelt* (New York: Harper & Bros., 1952). Apparently Roosevelt chose Truman as running mate because Truman had been loyal to the President's policies, was an industrious chairman of the Senate Committee on Government Operations, and, "coming from the central part of the country, he was geographically very acceptable. . . . He was from a border state . . . politically doubtful in 1944, and he could be expected to win . . . its votes."

18. The difficulty of discovering the sources of policy are clearly demonstrated by Eisenhower's remarks about Nixon over a number of years. If the reader is interested in discovering the potentialities of a candidate for the office of President, it is suggested that a study be made of the answers given by the President to questions at his press conference of March 16, 1960, as reported in the *New York Times:*

"Now, so far as I know, there has never been between Mr. Nixon and myself, and that's who you are talking about — [laughter] — so far as I know there has never been a specific difference in our points of view on any important problem in seven years.

"Now, there has been free discussion in every meeting that I have ever held, and he has certainly been always, not only free but even requested to give his honest opinions on these things, and in certain details or points there naturally have been, there are differences with everybody, that I have with everybody because I seem to have a genius for that.

"But I do say this, there has been never an important division of opinion or conviction. . . ."

19. Finer, *Theory and Practice of Modern Government,* pp. 579 ff. Finer, *Governments of Greater European Powers* (New York: Henry Holt & Co., Inc., 1956), pp. 139 ff.

20. The law of succession to the Presidency in case of the incumbent's resignation, death, disability, or removal is established in the Act of July 18, 1947, as amended. After the Vice-President, the succession is: the Speaker of the House of Representatives, the President pro tempore of the Senate, and the members of the cabinet, excepting the Secretary of Health etc., in this order: State, Treasury, Defense, Attorney General, Postmaster General, Interior, Agriculture, Commerce, Labor.

21. On March 3, 1958, President Eisenhower published a "clear understanding" he had with the Vice-President, holding good only between these two persons, that in the event of presidential disability the Vice-President would become the acting President, exercising the powers and duties of the office until the disability had ended. The President alone would determine his disability "if possible"; otherwise, it would be the responsibility of the Vice-President, "after such consultation as seems to him appropriate."

22. Speech by C. C. Pinckney in the South Carolina House of Representatives, January 18, 1788, quoted in Farrand (ed.), *Records of the Federal Convention of 1787,* III, 255–56:

". . . the time for which the President should hold his office, and whether he should be reeligible, had been fully discussed in the Convention. It had once been agreed to by a majority, that he should hold his office for the term of 7 years, but should not be reelected a second time. But upon reconsidering that article, it was thought that to cut off all hopes from a man of serving again in that elevated station, might render him dangerous, or perhaps indifferent to the faithful discharge of his duty. His term of service might expire during the raging of war, when he might, perhaps, be the most capable man in America to conduct it; and would it be wise and prudent to declare in our Constitution that such a man should not again direct our military operations, though our success might be owing to his abilities? The mode of electing the President rendered undue influence almost impossible; and it would have been imprudent of us to have put it out of our power to reelect a man whose talents, abilities, and integrity, were such as to render him the object of the general choice of his country."

CHAPTER VII. The Indispensable Solution

1. See Herman Finer, *Major Governments of Modern Europe* (Evanston, Ill.: Row, Peterson & Co., 1960), chapter 8.

POSTSCRIPT ON POLITICAL PARTIES

1. Report of the Committee on Political Parties, *Toward a More Responsible Two-Party System* (Washington, D.C.: American Political Science Association, September, 1960); and S. K. Bailey, *The Condition of Our National Political Parties.*

2. S. E. Finer, *Anonymous Empire* (London: Pall Mall Press, 1958); Samuel H. Beer, "The Representation of Interests in British Government: Historical Background," *American Political Science Review*, LI (1957), 613–50, and "Pressure Groups and Parties in Britain," *American Political Science Review*, LI (1957), 1–23.

3. See Holbert Carroll, *The House of Representatives and Foreign Policy* (Pittsburgh: University of Pittsburgh Press, 1958), especially pp. 232 ff., 261 ff. Carroll, after a well-informed and thoughtful weighing of the role of the House in making foreign policy, states (p. 238): "The evidence presented in the preceding chapters — the picture of unco-ordinated and slipshod control — supports the conclusion that . . . the House has been propelled into a new era of swift change but has stuck to traditions and habits which were barely adequate even in the 1880's when Woodrow Wilson surveyed the legislative body." Carroll observes that chaos is prevented, from time to time, by a few able representatives, the intrusion of party leaders, a strong plea from the President, or a conference agreement; only these repair or prevent rash action that threatens the integrity of foreign policy. And yet . . .

4. See my treatment of the subject in appendix A. Also see *Toward a More Responsible Two-Party System,* pp. 57 ff.

5. See Samuel Lubell, *The Revolt of the Moderates* (New York: Harper & Bros., 1956), and *The Future of American Political Parties* (New York: Harper & Bros., 1951); Key, *Politics, Parties, and Pressure Groups;* D. W. Brogan, *Politics in America* (New York: Harper & Bros., 1955), pp. 74 ff.; Paul T. David, "The Changing Party Pattern," *Antioch Review* (Fall, 1956); E. E. Schattschneider, "The Functional Approach to Party Government," *Modern Political Parties,* ed. Sigmund Neumann (Chicago: University of Chicago Press, 1956); V. O. Key, *Southern Politics in State and Nation* (New York: Alfred A. Knopf, Inc., 1949); Alexander Heard, *A Two Party South?* (Chapel Hill, N.C.: University of North Carolina Press, 1952).

6. See T. W. Goodman, "How Much Political Party Centralization Do We Want?", *Journal of Politics* (November, 1951), pp. 536–61; Julius Turner, "Responsible Parties: A Dissent from the Floor," *American Political Science Review* (March, 1951), pp. 143–52.

7. Bailey, *op. cit.,* p. 4.

APPENDIX A. Proposals for Presidential Reform

1. E. S. Corwin and L. W. Koenig, *The Presidency Today* (New York: New York University Press, 1956), pp. 94 ff.

2. *Ibid.,* p. 95

3. *Ibid.*

4. Corwin develops his proposal and the reasons for it, and the benefits to be obtained, in a further discussion in "The Problems of the Presidency," *A Constitution of Powers in a Secular State* (Charlottesville, Va.: University of Virginia Press, 1951), pp. 58 ff.

5. Richard F. Fenno, Jr., *The President's Cabinet* (Cambridge, Mass.: Harvard University Press, 1959), pp. 256 ff.

6. Charles S. Hyneman, *Bureaucracy in a Democracy* (New York: Harper & Bros., 1950), pp. 557–58.

7. Finer, *Theory and Practice of Modern Government,* especially chapter x, "The Separation of Powers."

8. Hyneman, *op cit.,* p. 572.

APPENDIX B. Proposals for Congressional Reform

1. For further discussion see David B. Truman, *The Congressional Party* (New York: John Wiley & Sons, Inc., 1960); Roland Young, *The American Congress* (New York: Harper & Bros., 1957); J. M. Burns, *Congress on Trial* (New York: Harper & Bros., 1949); Ernest Griffith, *Congress: Its Contemporary Role* (New York: New York University Press, 1951); and James Burnham, *Congress and the American Tradition* (Chicago: Henry Regnery Co., 1959).

Index

369